A Journey of Ideas

The Annotated Writings
of Francis Mading Deng

The publisher wishes to acknowledge and thank Dr. Douglas H. Johnson for his invaluable help and support for Africa World Books and its mission of preserving and promoting African cultural and literary traditions and history. Dr. Johnson and fellow historians have been instrumental in ensuring that African people remain connected to their past and their identity. Africa World Books is proud to carry on this mission.

ISBN (Paperback): 9780645719161
ISBN (Harcover): 9780645719154

Cover design, typesetting and layout: Africa World Books
Unit 3, 57 Frobisher St, Osborne Park, WA 6017
P.O. Box 1106 Osborne Park, WA 6916

Table of Contents

Acronyms

AACC: All African Council of Churches

ABC: Abyei Boundaries Commission

ACCORD: Africa Center for the Constructive Resolution of
Disputes

ALF: Africa Leadership Forum

ANCAUS: Abyei Ngok Community Association in the United
States

ANC: African National Conference

ARCSS: Agreement for the Resolution for the Conflict in South
Sudan

AVSS: Abyei Voice for Security and Stability

AWR: Abyei Women's Revolution

CEAWC: Committee for the Eradication of Abduction of Women
and Children

CPA: Comprehensive Peace Agreement

CSIS: Center for Security and International Studies

CSSDCA: Conference on Security, Stability, Development, and
Cooperation in Africa

CSCE: Conference for Security and Cooperation in Europe
DOP: Declaration of Principles
JCI: Jacob Blaustein Institute
JMEC: Joint Evaluation and Monitoring Committee
ICC: International Criminal Court
IDP: Internally Displaced Persons
HIID: Harvard Institute for International Development
IGAD: Inter-Governmental Authority for Development
KIC: Keep It Confidential
NCP: National Congress Party
OAU: Organization of African Unity
PCA: Permanent Court of Arbitration
R-ARCSS: Revitalized Agreement for the Resolution of the Conflict
         in South Sudan
R-JMEC: Revitalized Joint Monitoring and Evaluation Committee
RtP/R2P: Responsibility to Protect
RPA: Revitalized Peace Agreement
SAIS: School of Advanced International Studies
SPLM: Sudanese People's Liberation Movement
SPLA: Sudanese People's Liberation Army
SaR: Sovereignty as Responsibility
SAF: Sudan Armed Forces
SSPDF: South Sudan People's Defence Force
UNDP: United Nations Development Fund Programme
UNHCR: United Nations High Commission on Refugees
UNISFA: United Nations Interim Security Force for Abyei
UNMISS: United Nations Mission in South Sudan.
USAID: United States Agency for International Development
USIP: United States Institute of Peace
USIPP: United States Institute of Peace Press

Acknowledgement

In most acknowledgments for my books, I have always noted that every book is the product of collaboration involving individuals who are too numerous to be named. Only a few usually get specified. I have also often acknowledged members of my family for their contribution in a variety of ways. This is particularly true of this annotated collection of my writings.

One person should however feature in all acknowledgments and that is my beloved wife, Dorothy Anne Ludwig Deng. On February 19, 2022, we celebrated our 50th wedding anniversary. One of my greatest pleasures was once overhearing Dorothy respond to a question by a visitor when we were living in Ottawa, Canada, where I was serving as Ambassador. The visitor asked Dorothy what was the best thing that had happened to her in her life. "My marriage," she said. I have also heard her say on several occasions that she has had a happy life, most of which has been in our marriage.

For me, nearly all the things I have done since our marriage have been the products of the partnership with Dorothy. Although she holds graduate degrees and had an academic profession in a prestigious

American university, she devoted her life to supporting my national and international service and raising our four sons, Donald Deng, Daniel Jok, David Kuol and Dennis Biong, and the eight delightful grandchildren with whom the marriages of our sons have been blessed.

The works included in this volume are predominantly the products of collaboration in various ways with Dorothy and other members of our family.

I have chosen to include our wedding photo in this acknowledgment as a testimony to the personal, family, social, and professional partnership, and as a symbol of my love and profound gratitude to Dorothy.

Francis Mading Deng
Woodstock, N.Y.
November 2022

Foreword

This book is an annotated collection of the many works of Dr. Francis Mading Deng, South Sudan's most esteemed elder statesman, diplomat, academic, and writer.

Dr. Deng's first publication appeared while he was still a student in 1963. The sheer quantity of material that he produced since then makes him one of Africa's most prolific writers. There are one hundred and seventy-six titles included in this volume (some are co-authored), so many that an Appendix by Subject has been added. The collection however is not entirely comprehensive—some writings have been lost to time—and there are more titles to come. In 2022, three of Dr. Deng's classic works from the 1970s were reissued by Africa World Books, who will reissue another four books in 2023, while Dr Deng works toward three new titles.

In many ways this collection is a reference book; the rich pickings can be dipped into at random; it can be read cover to cover, or a specific reference can be located in the Appendix. Some of the annotations, particularly in Part Two, are brief and others very long. Titles that were not formally published, or were published by the national think tank, the Sudd Institute, have been reproduced in full. The titles analytically substantiate the central, conceptual principles of identity, dignity, diversity, and equality. These principles, within four interconnected levels: local, national, regional, and global, have fundamentally guided Dr. Deng's normative and professional outlook, and his cross-cultural transition. His exploration of these principles, especially identity, is compelling and very much ahead of its time, but there is more here than just these principles. Dr. Deng is a master of the craft of writing. He addresses his subjects with great clarity, intellectual rigor, wisdom, and insight. From his career in the diplomatic service and United Nations, he name-checks some of the most esteemed (and infamous) leaders of the 20th century: Wole Soyinka, Professor Mahmoud Mamdani, Edward Heath, Thabo Mbeki, Mengistu Haile Mariam, Isaias Aferworke, Yoweri Museveni, and Archbishop Desmond Tutu, while including personal anecdotes of Nelson Mandela, Jaafar Mohamed Niemiri, John Garang de Mabior, Olusegun Obasanjo, Boutros Boutros–Ghali, Ban ki-Moon, Sadig Al-Mahdi, Sergio de Mello and Omar Al-Bashir. The story of visiting Al-Bashir in prison poignantly humanises the fallen dictator in a most unexpected way. These stories lift this volume far above the usual expectations of an annotated collection.

This book is more than a marker of Dr. Deng's achievement, it urges us to understand who we are and why that matters and reminds us that people, "… need to read about themselves as much as others need to read about them."

Dr. Sara Maher
Consulting Editor, Africa World Books
Melbourne, Australia
November 2022

Preface

The motivation for collecting and annotating my writings is vague in my recollection. The explanation that comes to mind is that it is an indirect response to readers who have stated; "I have read all your books." I believe these were people who wanted to show me their appreciation and perhaps encouragement, but consciously resisted posing the questions that immediately came to mind; "Which ones?" or "How many?" as inappropriate. I know that none of those who claimed to have read "all" my books had any idea about the number of books I had written. And yet, I secretly felt that the reader should know the facts about which he or she was making an assertion.

Another possible source of motivation for collecting my writings was the uncertainty about the number of books often referred to by publishers when citing other works of mine in the books they had published. For years, the reference remained that I had published more than twenty, then thirty books, even when I knew that the number had significantly increased. I refrained from correcting the understatement. But I also privately entertained the thought that the misinformation was worth correcting.

It then occurred to me that I should let potentially interested readers know the facts about the number of books I had written and what I had written about, including some indication about the volume of articles I had published. Such information is of course important for the credentials of those fully in the academic career, to which I have also been at times engaged. I also felt that just listing the books and articles without a substantive presentation of what they are about would be too sterile, especially for those outside the academic circles who would not have easy access to the original sources. That was when I thought that annotating the writings would add significant value to the collection, especially for the more general readership. Not surprisingly, I could not recall all the titles of some booklets and many articles. Nor could I recall in the same depth what all the books or articles contained, most of which were no longer available or accessible to me. I decided that aiming at the whole truth should not obstruct telling a well-intended partial truth.

I also concluded that listing the writings without an organizing substantive framework would be too barren and that it would be both informative and more interesting to place the writings into a conceptual framework that would add some insight and depth to the publications. One aspect of a potential framework easily came to mind, and that is the ascending levels of my personal experiences to which my writings relate. These include the local level of my origin in my Dinka ethnic and cultural background in the rural context, through the national Sudanese level, to the level of the African continent, and culminating at the international level, specifically in my United Nations service. An earlier working title of the collection was 'Biographical Journey of Ideas.' My intention was to strike a balance between 'autobiography,' and the notion of ideas having a life of their own. But then I thought that the title was too ambiguous and decided to replace 'Biographical' with 'Experience.' This changed the title to, 'Experience and the Journey of Ideas,' which would make the correlation with my intellectual journey more explicit. But I was advised by one of my sons that the title was redundant since a journey implies experience. So, I settled for the present title.

Correlating the writings to the titles does not mean following a chronological connection of my physical activities with the works. The writings crisscross the various levels, for I could be active at the national level and write about local, regional, and international issues. Or I could be in a think tank in Washington DC in the United States and write about continental, national, and local issues pertaining to Africa, my country, or my ethnic community at the local level. Even when I was Ambassador abroad, I continued to be actively engaged in local affairs and write about them. And as Minister of State for Foreign Affairs, my colleagues in the Central Government used to teasingly question me whether I was Minister of Foreign Affairs or for Tribal Affairs. And my global UN mandates on internal displacement or genocide prevention thematically connected all levels, from local to global.

Alongside my organizing the writings based on levels, I thought of building on substantive themes of normative principles that would relate to the contents of the works. Although these are not explicitly stated or identified in the writings, they constitute fundamental values or norms that underlie the quest for the desired social or public order that is the overriding goal of all my writings. I also believe that these have been my guiding principles as I waded through the turbulent waters of the crosscultural currents that my life has gone through. These principles are identity, dignity, diversity, and equality. I have tried to elaborate on the principles in the introduction to the volume and other relevant parts of the collection.

Unfortunately, most of the books were published abroad and have not been easily accessible to readers in my homeland. In any case, most of them are now out of print. Certainly, the articles are mostly not accessible. Fortunately, Africa World Books (AWB) has decided to reprint some of those books that are of particular interest to the readership in our country and region. I am particularly grateful to Peter Lual Reech Deng, the founding publisher of AWB, who has made documenting, producing, and preserving the cultures and history of our people, especially the writings of South Sudanese, a patriotic mission to which he is remarkably devoted. Editing this vast collection of what must be described as raw materials, to make a readable, reasonably integrated whole, was a major challenge. I am deeply indebted to Dr. Sara Maher for undertaking this challenge. Her editorial meticulousness has added immense value to this and my other books which she has also edited. I remain profoundly grateful for that contribution.

Introduction

As the 2019 Guest of Honor for the El-Tayeb Salih Prize for Excellence in Writing, I was asked to say a few words at the opening ceremony on the theme of 'Identity in the Context of Globalization.' I was very happy with the choice of the theme as it was in line with concepts that had been at the center of my concerns and writings. It was a theme I believed also characterized the writings of El-Tayeb Salih, which is why it was chosen for the celebration of the Prize in his name.

I decided to identify four principles that I considered representative of the implicit cultural and moral values involved and relate them to the four levels of transition from local, national, and regional, to global. These principles are identity, dignity, diversity, and equality with the correlative levels of local, national, regional, and global. Although these principles are not explicitly stated in the organizational structure of the volume, they provided the inspiration and guidance in much of the writings included in this collection of annotated writings.

Identity is a fundamental attribute of every individual and group. It is the core of our shared humanity. Dignity, both subjective and objective, is a universal value of humanity, which is why universal human rights are grounded in human dignity. Subjectively viewed in relative isolation, every person, both as an individual and as a member of a group, sees his or her identity and that of the group, and the correlative cultural values, as the ideal model of God's creation. If it is not superior to all others, it is at least second to none. Diversity is the central feature of contact and interaction with other individuals and groups of varying identities. This raises the issue of comparison and possible differentiation or stratification into social and economic classes. Since each group subjectively views its identity and related value system as superior, there is an inherent potential for competition and conflict. From a conflict management perspective, this calls for equality as a foundation for mutual recognition and peaceful co-existence, and even cooperation. Where there are differences, there is a need to respect diversity and promote equality. There is also the prospect of pursuing a mutually enriching complementarity of diverse cultural values toward a unifying identity and value system.

Every social order is based or built on overriding values that determine its organizational structures, guidelines for desirable or acceptable behavior, and distribution of functional roles among its members. This section presents the Dinka as a model of cultural values that, though particular to one ethnic group, may be applicable to other groups in South Sudan and are perhaps universally shared.

Fundamental to the Dinka value system is a concept known as *kooc e nhom* (or *nom*), which literally means 'standing the head (of a dead person) upright,' a principle of genetic, moral, social, and cultural continuity after death. This principle is the core of the traditional belief in immortality. It is what Professor Harold Lasswell, the Chairman of my doctoral dissertation at Yale University Law School, called 'the myth of permanent identity and influence.' But this concept is more real than the word myth normally implies. *Kooc e nhom* involves active representation and participation of the dead in the affairs of the living. They are allotted property in the form of cattle and are honored through rituals periodically performed as the need for their engagement may require. They appear in dreams and are constantly called upon to intercede with God and the clan spirits to intercede on behalf of their living relatives. They even get married and have children by proxy. The Western Christian marriage vow the couple makes that they commit themselves to be together "until death does us part," does not apply to traditional Dinka values. This conception of immortality is central to the Dinka religious belief system in which the spiritual world is imminently connected with the welfare of the living.

Another overriding principle of the Dinka value system is *cieng* a concept of idealized human relations that is usually specified as *cieng baai,* the word *baai* applies to family, home, village, community, tribe, and country. *Cieng* is both a prescriptive and descriptive behavioral concept, what ought to be done and what in fact is normally done. It is used to mean culture, custom, law, behavior, conduct, mannerism, generosity, hospitality, nobility, and way of life. *Cieng* stipulates peaceful resolution of differences and is against violence. It signifies both what "ought to be,"and what in fact "is."

Cieng can be judged as good or bad *cieng,* but as a concept, it is generally considered as inherently good. I once asked a Dinka scholar whether there was nothing bad in *cieng.* After reflecting for a moment, his answer was a reverse question: "How can there be anything bad in *cieng*? If there was anything bad in *cieng* would it not have been abandoned a long time ago?" *Cieng* is ordained by God and the Ancestors who are closely watching to ensure compliance or impose severe punishment for gross violation. Contrary to those proselytizers who assume a spiritual vacuum to be filled by imported belief systems, the Dinka and their kindred Nilotic peoples are documented to be the most religious in Sudan, now divided into two countries in the Nile Valley. The Dinka call on God and Ancestors to guide and bless them in every move they make in their everyday life. Their unwavering faith that God will reward wrong and punish evil amounts to a level of dependency on Divine Intervention that borders on the abrogation of independent human responsibility.

A third moral and social concept among the Dinka is *dheeng*, which connotes dignity and *atheek*, meaning respect. It is a concept of both aesthetic beauty and proper conduct. One's physical appearance, how one dresses, walks, eats, talks, and behaves are all factors relevant to *dheeng*. *Dheeng* can be a status into which one is born and raised or can be acquired through personal accomplishments. The values of *dheeng* are closely related to those of *cieng*. A wealthy man is an *adheng*, endowed with *dheeng*, but only if he is generous, hospitable, and benevolent. If he is miserly, greedy, and selfish, he becomes *ayur*, the opposite of *adheng*. In a sense, *cieng* prescribes how people should behave, while *dheeng* classifies them according to their behavior and the degree to which they adhere to the ideals of the social order.

There are also values that are associated with leadership. Assuming the responsibility of leadership is called *dom baai*, controlling the land; taking reforms to address any inherited problems and improve the situation is *guier baai*; stabilizing the situation to ensure sustainability is *muk baai*. These principles are interconnected and mutually reinforcing. When a leader has seized control, introduced reforms (*guier*), and stabilized the situation (*muk*), he is said to have *dom*, the country or the unit in question.

This is the social order that instilled in the Dinka fundamental values of identity and dignity in their indigenous society. Like most isolated peoples, until diversity recently set in and began to challenge their old chauvinistic self-perceptions, the Dinka considered themselves and their social order the ideal model of God's creation. They are documented as exceedingly proud and conservatively resistant to change. This is now changing as they have come to recognize that there are new criteria for pursuing human dignity and are demonstrating a surprising desire to change and improve themselves through the new means to dignity. But their indigenous value system and correlative values continue to guide them in the context of diversity in which they contact and interact with outsiders and generate the quest for recognition and equality. There is no way they can accept a lower status in comparison to those with whom they interact. It can indeed be argued that they are using new tools to pursue old moral values.

Although I have focussed on the Dinka as a model, their social order and value system are by no means unique and can be said to have much in common with other ethnic groups in South Sudan or the wider region. I recall a South Sudanese scholar from Equatoria telling me that in reading my book. *The Dinka of the Sudan,*[1] he found striking similarities with his own ethnic group. In Ethiopia at a regional meeting, I was approached by a young Somali scholar who said that he had read the book and that if one replaced Dinka with Somali, the book would apply fully to Somali culture. This means that studying these societies not only facilitates learning about each other but also reveals our commonalities.

As noted at the outset, the biographical journey envisaged in this collection of publications begins with the local level as the starting point in the transition across cultures. This is the level at which identity is shaped and the sense of personal and collective dignity in the context of cultural values is developed. The national level is the second ascending context of interaction with other identity groups. This is the level

---

1. Reissued as *The Dinka, A Nilotic Lifecycle*, Africa World Books, 2022.

at which diversity emerges and with it the dynamics of comparative differentiation, classification, and stratification. These dynamics generate the demand for equality at the national level, which then extends to the regional level, where identities and, a sense of dignity broaden to embrace aspirational continental solidarity on equal footing. The global level, the zenith of the ascending order, entails both personal and institutional contacts and participation. As this level increases the distance from the regional and national levels, it commensurately strengthens awareness about regional and even national belonging with dignity and the demand for equality.

Applying these factors to the Sudan, now partitioned into two Sudans, the context is one in which an acute crisis of national identity resulted in an acute mismanagement of diversity, leading to gross inequality and violent confrontation that escalated to genocidal. This made partitioning the country into two independent states unavoidable. Even with the partition, the crisis of identity persists and, with it the ongoing demand for constructive management of diversity aimed at inclusivity and equality. Internal conflicts also continue across international boundaries with neighbors supporting each other's rebels. This renders separated states to remain *Bound by Conflict*,[2] the book I wrote after Sudan broke up into two independent states. The challenge is to transform the situation into one of being *Bonded by Solutions to Bonded by Solutions*, the title of a book I have written as a sequel to *Bound by Conflicts*, which awaits publication.

El-Tayeb Salih, in his literary works, implicitly promoted the four principles at the four levels which I have formulated as a framework for this collection. For him, as for me, the principles and institutional practices reflected individual and communal identity at the village

2. Francis M. Deng in collaboration with Daniel J. Deng, *Bound by Conflict: Dilemmas of the Two Sudans*, Fordham University Press, 2016 – see p. 103.

level and were pursued at the various levels at which he studied and worked up to the global level where he distinguished himself in the service of the BBC. His novels demonstrate the process of engaging interlocutors at these levels interconnected levels in a give-and-take process which facilitated for him cross-cultural mutual influences and enrichment with his international interlocutors.

It is in this conceptual framework that I understand and appreciate the literary contributions of the author El-Tayeb Saleh. I see these contributions at all the four levels as a process of cross-cultural inter-action and mutual influence. This requires constructive management of diversity to ensure respect for the identity and dignity of the inter-active entities to promote inclusivity and equality. While the levels are conceptually obvious, identifying the principles is a more discreet process that is often implicit rather than verbalized. These principles are however more easily recognizable as essential elements of interna-tional norms of universal human rights that all cultures should and mostly do share.

There are two additional principles which guide me in addressing the challenges of promoting the four principles at the four levels. They are the principles of optimism and opportunities during crises. Pessimism leads to a dead end while optimism generates constructive action. And in crises, there are always opportunities that need to be explored and utilized to find some positive in an otherwise negative context. I have tried to use this conceptual framework in classifying the annotated works I have included in this compilation.

Part One: Books

———————◆———————

Chief Arol Kachwol, an elder in his seventies, one of the people with whom I conducted extensive interviews about the history of our people, summarized in the following words, the cultural values of lineage continuity and the challenge of social change. Chief Arol addressed me in my Dinka name, "Mading":

> *... The world has been lived in for a long time. It is God who changes the world by giving successive generations their turns. Our forefathers, who have now disappeared, the way their world began, and the way they lived, they managed the affairs of their world. Then God changed things: things changed until they reached us, and they will continue to change.*
>
> *When God comes to change your world, it will be through you and your wife. You will sleep together and bear a child. When that*

happens, you should know that God has passed on to your children, borne by your wife, the things with which you had lived your life.

Your father, Deng Majok, if he had lived without a child until his death, his would have been the kind of life that continues only as a tale. But if he left behind a big son who can be spoken of, 'This is Mading, son of Deng,' then, even if a person had never met your father, but he hears that you are the son of Deng Majok in the same way he had heard of your father, he will meet through you your father whom he never met...

So, the world goes on by the will of God; God, the person who created people and who changes things. You, our children, your fame began when you were chosen to go to school and learn. Here you are, you have gone far. You have left behind the country in which your mother was married. But you were chosen by your father to go and learn the words of other people. And in your search for knowledge, things happened.

For instance, is this girl, your wife, not from America? And you have brought her back to your country. It is as though God has given her to Deng Majok, your Father. If you bear a child together now, in that child will combine the words of her country and the words of your country.

Man is one single word with God.[3]

As noted above, with those few words, Chief Arol Kachuol not only described the traditional Dinka cultural values and social patterns but also revealed the changes the Dinka have been going through since the intervention of colonial rule that introduced new concepts of change as a forward-looking development. Much of the writings

---

3. Francis M. Deng, *Dinka Cosmology*, Ithaca Press, 1980. Reissued as *Dinka World View: Elders Reflect on the Past, Present and Future of their People*, Africa World Books, 2023 – see p. 34.

in this collection document both tradition and modernizing change. It is therefore a documentation of a journey of both change and continuity through various phases that traverse the world of my experiences, through education and professional service.

The list of publications included here comprises books classified into the four levels on which my journey through cultures and related subject matter of ideas are focused, from local, through national, and regional, to global. I have also published numerous articles and chapters in books that are difficult to trace but are equally classifiable into the four levels. These levels do not only reflect the subject matter of the studies, but also the interconnected levels of my occupational activities.

United Nations Secretary-General Boutros Boutros–Ghali incidentally elucidated the linkage of the four levels in both concerns and remedial action when he offered me the position of Special Representative of the Secretary-General on Internally Displaced Persons in 1992. Boutros–Ghali had been Minister of State for Foreign Affairs of Egypt when I was Minister of State for Foreign Affairs of the Sudan. We had therefore worked very closely together. Boutros surprised me one day with a phone call to tell me that I had been nominated for the position and that he would be very happy to offer me the position.

I had not known anything about the position and therefore told Boutros–Ghali that while I was honored by the offer, I would appreciate receiving from his staff details on what the position entailed before giving him my response. Boutros said in response, "Francis, I know you well and I know how much you are concerned about these issues. Internal displacement is not only a global crisis; it is one that affects our continent of Africa the most; and in Africa, it is your country of the Sudan that is the most affected; and in the Sudan, it is your people of South Sudan that are the worst hit. I cannot see how you can turn down the offer. I will tell them that you have accepted. If you still have reservations, we can have more discussion later." Of course, I had no choice but to accept.

What should be underscored about the levels, as is well illustrated by the issue of internal displacement, is that the subjects covered have implications or relevancies that cut across the levels. To give a broader example, the study of various aspects of Dinka value systems, institutions, and patterns of behavior is both specific and relevant to virtually all the other levels. Herein lies a dilemma. On the one hand, writing about the Dinka runs the risk of allegations that my focus is tribalistic or chauvinistic. And yet, it is by knowing the specific cultures of our pluralistic society that we can develop a comprehensive understanding of our shared heritage and a unity that is enriched by our diversity.

The challenge is to reach out to the other groups in the pluralistic context to understand the particulars of each other's culture, the extent to which they share the essential elements and the prospects of integrating the variety of cultural elements into a collective or composite whole.

While the levels reflect the focus of the subjects involved that may have application and implications for the other elements, an important dimension is the fact that we are now interconnected by our mobility and participation at various levels. Through education, investigation, occupation, or search for opportunities, most people move to and fro between their base at the local level and the areas of their extended participation. In their extension to other levels, they take with them the essentials of the value systems and behavioral patterns of their original social order. This is more pronounced at the local and national levels, and more subtle at the regional and international levels. But to be valued as cross-culturally enriching at all levels, the transcendent or universal validity of indigenous values must be made evident, or they risk being dismissed as parochial and irrelevant beyond the local confine.

The imperatives of continuity in change are implicit in the fact that most people remain concerned with issues that are important for their areas and communities at the local level. Even when a person occupies a national or international position, the affairs of the local areas of origin remain of immediate interest. As one Dinka said in defense against criticism for continuing to serve the interest of his local community while in a national position, "We do not come from nowhere."

In my case, starting with the study of customary law, which, with the encouragement of my expatriate professors, I introduced to the Faculty of Law at the University of Khartoum. Later on, in my positions as Ambassador and State Minister of Foreign Affairs, I continued to be actively engaged in the affairs of my people, in particular the Ngok Dinka of Abyei, their relations with their neighbors, the Missiriya Arabs, and the role of the provincial and national governments in managing those relations. Some of my colleagues in the national government viewed my approach with both criticism and admiration, as they considered it laudable, but risky for a national figure to continue to be engaged in serving the interests of his or her local community while holding a constitutional post of national responsibility. Some people jokingly asked me whether I was Minister of State for Foreign Affairs or for Tribal Affairs. Rather than be embarrassed, I felt honored by the question.

It is important to note that a person elected by his or her community to a representative position in the national legislature of course has the obligation to serve the interest of his or her constituency. But that was not the case for me. I was never elected, nor did I ever seek to be elected, to any position by my people. In fact, I was once approached by Ngok Dinka and Missiriya elders jointly to ask me to run for Parliament in their shared constituency, which promised to be unopposed, but I turned their offer down. I wanted to continue serving their interest without being elected because I felt a responsibility that was inherent in my position as a member of the community and as an inherited leadership obligation.

I recall an incident that dramatized this point. In 1983, prominent members of my Ngok Dinka community, including the Paramount Chief and other members of our family, were arrested and detained with allegations of supporting a local rebellion that threatened to return the country to a civil war between the North and the South. The threat of a return to war indeed materialized that year. At the time, the government declared that the detainees would be charged and tried for treason, a crime punishable by death. I was then Ambassador in Canada and was back in Khartoum to attend the meeting of the Central Committee of the ruling Sudan Socialist Union. I took the initiative to mediate a resolution of the crisis between the Security Agency of the government and the detainees. After months of intensive efforts, I succeeded in having them released, followed by spectacular media coverage of that event.

The initiative, and indeed the outcome, generated controversy because it had political significance to the case of Abyei as a contested area between the North and the South. Some Southerners, including individuals in my own family, saw the arrest and detention as part of the struggle and that even if they were executed, they would be martyrs for the cause of liberation. One of the Southern Sudanese political personalities, who later became Governor of Bahr el-Ghazal Province, questioned the legitimacy of my action, asking by what authority I had mediated the release of the detainees. Was I elected and mandated by the Ngok Dinka community or did I arrogate to myself that role because of my position as the son of the Paramount Chief? I responded to him with indignation, arguing that if he was one of those who needed a paid job to serve the interest of his people, I was not. Whether he saw that as an assertion of leadership based on my being the son of a Chief or not was his own concern, not mine. He came to see me the next day and apologized for his conduct, but the difference in our approach had been revealed.

What is particularly important about understanding our local societies and their value systems is that they constitute vital elements of the pluralism of most, if not all, modern states. We must recognize and respect them as pivotal to the inclusivity of our unity in diversity. Besides, an important dimension of European colonial intervention in Africa, and the Northern Sudanese Arab domination of the African South, is that Black African communities were assumed to have a void of cultural, spiritual, and moral values. Perhaps because of my early transition across the cultural diversities of our country in the North and South, I became progressively aware of this denigrating attitude, which contrasted with the proud self-perception of our people that I was a part of and was therefore ingrained in my psyche. By the same token, I became increasingly aware of the advantages of cross-cultural interaction and mutual influence.

In Khartoum's Faculty of Law, we studied Western Law and Islamic Sharia, even Roman Law, but not African customary law. This is despite the fact that customary law governed over eighty percent of our country, North and South. From childhood, I had witnessed customary law being applied in my grandfather's and my father's courts. Largely stimulated by this background, including the broader leadership position of my family, and with the encouragement and support of some of my expatriate lecturers, it was my initiative that made the Faculty of Law develop an interest in studying the customary laws of tribal communities in rural Sudan. Even then, prejudice against customary law persisted. It was seen by some as too primitive to be worthy of modern recognition, by others as encouraging divisions and divisiveness, and by yet others as a counterforce to Islam, which they chauvinistically saw as providing the legitimate legal framework for the country.

A story is told of a Northern Sudanese judge in the South who saw a case of adultery against a Dinka woman. When he asked for the husband, he was told that he was dead. Surprised, he did not see why a widow would be accused of adultery. He was told that the woman was still married to the dead man and that in accordance with Dinka custom, she was living with his relative to beget children in the name of her dead husband. That, of course, is the customary legal concept known as 'levirate,' which the judge did not know; he, therefore, dismissed the case as nonsensical. The case went for an appeal to a Dinka judge who knew the custom and reversed the decision of the lower court. He wrote a note to the judge of the first instance who had decided the case, "For your information, a Dinka husband never dies."

I recall a conversation with a Northern Sudanese judge who had served in the South and we were both doing graduate studies at Yale Law School in the United States of America. He was a very decent respectful person who could not be accused of racial prejudice. And yet, obviously out of ignorance, he commented on the people of South Sudan, with a tone of sincere, but naïve, sympathy, "Poor people, they have no religion; they do not even know God." Although we had become friends, I felt indignant and compelled to educate him about the religious beliefs of the Nilotics. I told him that according to anthropologists who had studied the Nilotics, they were among the most religious people in Sudan. Again, with an impressive tone of sincerity and naïveté, he responded, *"Billahi al-Azeem!?"* By God Almighty!?

Another instance involved a Northern Sudanese scholar who challenged my commitment to national unity when reacting negatively to my writing a biography of my father. Rather than write about a tribal leader, he said that I should have written about one of the national leaders, of course, all Northerners. This was again a function of marginalization of the rural communities about whom the intellectual elites at the center were completely ignorant and which was acutely antithetical to the pride I felt about my father as an outstanding leader whose authority and dignity not only went beyond his tribe but transcended the prevailing North-South divide.

I have often recalled that in the Northern Secondary school, Khor Taqqat, which my brother, Zachariah Bol, and I attended, all the dormitories were named after prominent tribal chiefs, all Northerners, without a single Chief from the South. With a father who was widely recognized as a leading bridge builder between the North and the South, that gross inequity was very striking to me. In the same school, all the classes were named after prominent scholars and intellectuals from the Arab world, without a single name of an African. I became aware of that discrepancy in due course. It also became increasingly evident to me that these discrepancies needed to be corrected.

Documenting traditional value systems was for me part of correcting those inequities and a means of approaching development as an evolutionary process of self-enhancement from within, as well as an eclectic process of cross-cultural enrichment, which I eventually propounded in my doctoral dissertation at Yale Law School as the 'strategy of transitional integration.'

The same issues that are reflected at the local and national levels are relevant to the regional African level, where the need to study African cultures and their relevancy to the processes of statecraft, nation-building and the sociology of economic development has been increasingly acknowledged. As was the case with the national context, the assumption of the Eurocentric processes of statecraft and nation-building in Africa was that there was no culture or value system to build upon. Concessions were made by using native administration to ensure law and order in rural areas, but only as part of an inexpensive way of controlling and governing the natives. Europeans, therefore, offered their models for Africa to emulate. While Africans have struggled to correct this assumption since independence, there is still a great deal to be done to develop culturally oriented African systems of constitutionalism and governance.

The same objectives for documenting African cultures at the local, national, and regional levels are pertinent to the international level. For me personally, whether in my studies abroad, interpersonal relations, diplomatic representation, or implementation of United Nations mandates, I found the continued link to my cultural background and related value system very pertinent and useful. But the value of this link is inherent and not self-evident; it must be explored, analyzed, interpreted, expounded, advocated, and effectively shared.

Ironically, one of the reasons for my initially extending my interest to various aspects of Dinka society was my realization that Dinka customary law was intertwined with virtually all aspects of the Dinka worldview and social processes. But the conceptual and strategic value of this holistic view of the social order has to be cross-culturally revealed, explained, and promoted.

It is also ironic that it was in England and later in the United States that I found African customary law a recognized and respected subject of formal academic study. At Yale, I learned that law was the product of a constitutive power process in which people, individuals, or groups, guided by overriding goals, seek value-objectives, through institutions, using resources, with varying outcomes and effects. This gave me deeper insights into what I had learned from my study of Dinka customary law, the interconnectedness of all aspects of the social system, and correlative public order. Before I went to Yale, I would have been reticent to talk about "values" as metaphysical and antithetical to the positivist view of the law that was central to English jurisprudence, through which I had been introduced to the study of law.

Moral judgement in appraising the application of the law would also have been outside this positivist orientation. And yet, I greatly admired Lord Denning's dissenting opinions that were in my view morally based. I recall a decision in which he said something along the lines that a legal system that would not provide a remedy in that particular case would not be worthy of the label "civilized." I took that to be an invocation of a moral code and it resonated with my indigenous normative cultural values of what is morally right. Perhaps for the same reason, I was enamored with the English system of the Court of the Chancery whose main objective was equity, unencumbered by the strict rules of procedure of the regular courts.

My interest in Dinka culture began to grow and expand beyond its indigenous confines as I addressed questions rooted in the philosophy and the universality of law, building on a flexible interpretation of the Yale concept of law, science, and policy. What are the fundamental goals on which the system is based? What are the specific values whose pursuit law regulates? What are the sources for identifying those values? How are the values transmitted to the next generation? What is the Dinka worldview in which the value system is embedded? And how has that worldview been historically impacted by the changes the society has undergone? Most of my books on the Dinka have been the result of addressing these and related questions. It has also been a source of great satisfaction for me to experience the extent to which some of the Dinka cultural values I transmitted have been well received and much appreciated by many internationally, as universally valid, and cross-culturally enriching.

The interconnection of levels and the linkages I developed in the processes of change that I underwent can be said to be grounded in several fundamental truisms. One is that there are fundamental cultural values that are either evident and obviously worth retaining or are too deeply ingrained to be shed. The second is that in cross-cultural contexts, there is a give-and-take reality that is inherently mutually enriching but should be strategically and transparently promoted. A third is that the concept of globalization that is being increasingly upheld and advocated must be understood as implying localization in a way that spotlights the challenges of shared humanity and how to address them in an all-inclusive partnership and synthesis.

All this is embodied in what I have called the 'invisible bridge,'[4] a phenomenon that allows one to move to and fro between the context of origin and targeted destinations within the country and abroad. While there is a risk that my interest in my indigenous culture may be misconstrued as chauvinistic or ethnocentric, or as conservatively backward-looking and adverse to progressive change, a closer understanding and appreciation of its linkages of levels with national and regional levels, and on to the global level, should reveal that it is a dynamic, mutually enriching process of universal validity.

I have tried to annotate the books listed here with the objective of elucidating elements of the interconnection of levels which I have tried to explain in the foregoing commentary. I conclude this introductory comment by restating several principles by way of emphasis.

---

4. Also the title of my autobiography: *Invisible Bridge, An African Journey Through Cultures*, Africa World Books, 2021 – see p. 49.

First, there are fundamental values and principles in every society that are instilled in a person from early childhood as part of a process of acculturation that grows widens, and deepens throughout life. The widely acknowledged wisdom of the elders derives from the expansion, deepening, and application of the cultural moral code through experience.

Second, in the process of change, in particular, in the context of cross-cultural interaction, these indigenous values and principles continue to operate, whether through a conscious and calculated application or as an inherent deeply ingrained cultural orientation.

Third, through the process of modern education, whatever the discipline involved, the value system of traditional society can be interpreted and made relevant as an aspect of cross-fertilization of transitional integration. For me, the study of law lent itself to this integrative approach. Intuitively, I believe that this principle should also apply to other disciplines. In discussing the issue with my late brother, Dr. Zachariah Bol, who was then studying medicine in Europe, he initially argued that medicine is based on scientific facts that are universal and not culturally specific or relative. Years later, he changed his mind and agreed with me that the same principles indeed applied to medicine. He even aspired to study traditional Dinka medicine which he unfortunately never found the opportunity to undertake.

Fourth, this process of reinterpretation and application of traditional cultural principles to transitional integration and cross-cultural mutual assimilation can be consciously and strategically applied to harmonize between globalism and localism in a process that makes constructive use of diversity as a source of mutual enrichment.

This in essence has been my guide in all that I have done or tried to do, whether in my studies, in my professional work at home and abroad, or in interpersonal relations associated with individual social situations or in diplomatic interaction. And unlike my brother Bol, who did not get the opportunity to study Dinka medicine and apply his indigenous values in his medical profession, I was fortunate enough to receive institutional and personal support through the various phases of my academic and occupational endeavors. The core of this strategy is that there is a thread that links the various levels of my experience: local, national, regional, and global.

Presenting the Books in Context

The books in this collection are classified and contextualized into four levels: local, national, regional, and global, according to the subject matter, and dated and listed in ascending, chronological order of the publication date. It should be noted that the annotations on the books are not uniform; some are elaborate, while others are very brief.

A: Local Level

'Tradition and Modernization:
A Challenge for Law Among the Dinka of the Sudan'
Yale University Press, 1971

At Yale, the jurisprudential theory of *Law, Science, and Policy*, spear-headed by Professors Myers McDougall and Harold Lasswell, who supervised my doctoral work, saw law not as an objective concept whose normative force is given and imperative, but as a reflection of the outcome of the realities of community processes in a contested constitutive order. These realities are elements of a power process in pursuit of material, moral and other values by individuals and groups using resources, through institutions, with specific outcomes and effects. Human dignity, defined as the greatest shaping and sharing of values, was stipulated as the overriding goal guiding the system. Eight value categories were identified. They included four deference values: power, affection, respect, and rectitude; and four welfare values: wealth, well-being, enlightenment, and skills. Law is therefore the outcome of an authoritative exercise of power, an instrument that regulates an all-embracing political, economic, social, and cultural sector of public order. The current debate in the United States over the extent to which the Supreme Court, the majority of the judges being Republican appointees, has heavily leaned to the conservative ideological right, underscores the dynamics of power and related value judgments behind the law.

In applying this theoretical framework to the Dinka context, I identified the three concepts which I outlined in the Introduction, as constituting overriding norms of Dinka social order. The first is *kooc e nhom,* a concept of genetic and social immortality through the memory of the dead among the living, which Harold Lasswell, the chairman of my doctoral committee, recast as a concept of permanent identity and influence. The second is *cieng* (or *cieng baai*), a notion of ideal human relations reflected in unity and harmony and persuasive discourse in personal and communal relations at all levels of the social order: family, village, community, and country, all designated by the generic word *baai.* And the third is *dheeng,* a concept of aesthetic and behavioral dignity.

I saw law as a point of entry into the realities of the social order viewed holistically as an integral whole. In other words, law is the outcome of an authoritative decision-making in the exercise of power as the determining regulatory mechanism. As noted earlier, the word *baai* in *cieng baai* applies to family, community, village, tribe, or country. This means that the normative principles enshrined in the concept apply to all those levels. Law or custom is also one of the multiple meanings of *cieng.*

A major thematic finding of the study is the correlation between status in the stratified hierarchy of participants as determined by these fundamental societal norms and the degree of conformity to the norms. The more advantaged by the normative code of conduct people are, the greater the level of their conformity to the normative principles. Accordingly, adherence to the norms is greatest among the chiefs and elders and lowest among the youth and women, who seek alternative avenues to dignity. For male youth, they find this in their role as warriors, which they exaggerate by resorting to violence at the slightest provocation. For women, their source of dignity lies in their role as wives and mothers (or potential wives and mothers), with behind-the-scene influence on husbands and sons, which, in the context of polygamous jealousies and rivalries, is circumspect and viewed with suspicion by men, as dubious and divisive.

The policy implication of this normative finding is to promote inclusivity and equality among the participants. This would be in line with the overriding goal of human dignity as the broadest shaping and sharing of all values.

I postulated an approach that presented law as an instrument for shaping and guiding political, social, and economic development in a balanced process enriched by the integration of the values of tradition and modernity. My doctoral dissertation, titled *Tradition and Modernization: A Challenge for Law among the Dinka of the Sudan,* was strongly recommended by my committee members for publication by the Yale University Press. The book came out in 1971. A year later, it won the 1972 Herskovits Prize given by the African Studies Association to ;the author of an outstanding work on Africa published the year before." The Prize Committee described the book as "scholarly, well written, and theoretically stimulating." One reviewer described it as "an inside view with Western-educated eyes, followed by an evaluation and recommendations... which deserve the widest attention." That summarized what I hope the notion of the 'invisible bridge' signifies.

'The Dinka of the Sudan'

Holt, Rinehart and Winston, 1972 [5]

In England on the first leg of my post-graduate studies, I met Dr. Godfrey Lienhardt, a leading anthropologist and scholar of Nilotic studies in Oxford, who had studied the Dinka for his doctorate. We met by sheer chance, became good friends, and he asked me to

---

5. Reissued by Waveland Press in 1984, updated and reissued in 1986. Updated and reissued as *The Dinka, A Nilotic Lifecycle,* Africa World Books, 2022.

co-author a book on the Dinka in the Stanford University series of case studies in social anthropology that George and Louise Spindler, the editors of the series, had asked him to write. For various reasons, although we agreed on the methodology we would follow, a life-cycle approach, we were not able to co-author the book as planned.

Shortly after the publication of my dissertation *Tradition and Modernization,* another British anthropologist, Professor John Middleton, recommended me to the editors of the series and they asked me to write the case study on the Dinka. Having gone through the rigor of writing the doctoral dissertation that was to be published as a book, I felt free enough to write a book that would reflect my own style, using the life-cycle methodology that Dr. Lienhardt and I had agreed upon. *The Dinka of the Sudan* was in essence a brief restatement of the themes of my dissertation, but written in a simple, more accessible style, building, where appropriate, on my personal experiences.

In their "About the Book" introduction, the editors wrote: "This case study is written by Francis Mading Deng, the son of the late Paramount Chief of the Ngok Dinka. This fact in itself suggests that the reader is in for an unusual experience as he or she reads this case study. There are many passages in this book where we are privileged to enter the cultural system with the insider's view and his interpretation." They noted, however, that "This, by itself is not a guarantee of a good ethnography, for the perspective of the outsider is essential as well." They then proceeded to highlight the success of the book in bridging the internal and external perspectives: "But Dr. Deng also provides this other perspective... While reading this book, we experience the rich qualities of Dinka life and at the same time the intellectual gratification of conceptual analysis." It is particularly noteworthy that the Dinka value system is appreciated by external observers: "Dinka life has a quality that beguiles the reader. The gentlemanly qualities subsumed in the term *dheeng*, apparent in pride and manners, are of high importance. For instance, men must eat fastidiously, talk elegantly, and stand and walk with pride."

The Dinka of the Sudan was very well received, used in colleges throughout the United States and reprinted for decades, and it may still be in use as a reference in social anthropology courses.

'The Dinka and Their Songs'
Oxford: The Clarendon Press, 1973

The story behind the book of Dinka songs [6] is for me a very moving one. In August 1962, a Northern Sudanese colleague and friend, Tigani Omar El-Karib, and I paid a surprise visit to my brother, Zackariah Bol, and our young uncle, Bona Bulabek, Father's half-brother, by a different mother, who were studying medicine in Padova, Italy. They had planned to travel to Prague, Czechoslovakia, to visit Toby Maduot, who was studying there. They were all active in promoting the cause of Southern Sudan in Europe. Bol canceled out and remained with us, while Bulabek and Justo Muludiang, a Southern Sudanese colleague and friend of theirs, went on the trip. I had just graduated and was returning to Khartoum to take up my new position as a member of the teaching staff in the Faculty of Law, before proceeding to England on a post-graduate course. At their departure, early in the morning, before we woke up, Bona left me a note urging me to go home and see my loved ones before returning to Europe. This was despite the prohibiting conditions of the rainy season when travel by lorries, the main means of transport, was impossible.

During my first working day, as I proudly sat in my new office

---

6. Reissued by Africa World Books, 2022.

elevated from student to 'tutor,' I received a cable from Bol informing me that Bulabek had died in a car accident. I was devastated and could not stop myself from sobbing. Bulabek was a well-known genius, who was always top of his class, even when he jumped grades. He had the International Certificate worldwide and although he entered Khartoum University to study medicine, he was offered a scholarship to continue his studies there. Complications over the issuance of the visa made him accept another offer to study medicine in Italy. There, he continued to excel and while in his last year of medical studies, the year we visited them, he had already been offered a teaching position in the university. But Bona was not just a scholar; he was also a great leader. Whether in politics, scientific accomplishments, or academia, he was destined to be a great man. I could not help but wonder why God would give a person such exceptional attributes with great expectations and then take him away in such a senseless manner. Bona's death severely shook my faith in God, although unwavering believers maintain that even in such tragic situations, God always has a plan with a purpose that only He knows.

The government declined to have the body flown home, which outraged the South Sudanese when they got to know what had happened. Bulabek was buried in Italy, but we wanted the body to be eventually exhumed and repatriated back to the Sudan. I had to go home to raise the necessary funds for that objective. I traveled on horseback for five days from the Missiriya Arab town of Muglad to Abyei. Although the objective of my return home was different, I felt that I was fulfilling the advice, and now sacred will, of my late Uncle Bona Bulabek.

Despite the fact that the family was in mourning, I thought I should take advantage of the first and only tape recorder in Abyei which belonged to an Italian priest, to record Dinka songs both for my own enjoyment and as part of my documentation of Dinka culture. But I wondered whether that would be proper under the circumstances. I consulted my father, explaining that the songs would both keep me connected to my people and promote our culture abroad. Father immediately saw the value of my project and undertook to call renowned singers and attend the recordings himself. We conducted the recording in the only office which had electricity on which the recorder could be charged. The recording was a spectacular success. I recorded virtually all the different types of songs: war songs, individual men's ox songs, women's songs, initiation songs, cathartic songs, and religious hymns. The collection was a rare treasure. As my father and I were leaving the recording venue, walking with an accompanying crowd, I heard one person say, "What an intelligent machine. It listens and then immediately repeats the song exactly as it was sung." I often think back to that remark and marvel at the way technology has so radically changed the world of the Dinka.

In England, Dr. Godfrey Lienhardt, asked me to join him in the BBC Third Program on 'Man in Society,' in which he was to speak on the Nilotic ethnic groups of the Sudan. I suggested using excerpts from the songs I had recorded to back what I was to say. That proved very successful. Dr. Lienhardt later suggested that since he had texts of songs he had collected in his fieldwork among the Rek Dinka, perhaps we could cooperate in preparing a volume for the Oxford University Series on African Literature for which he, together with Professor E.E. Evans Pritchard and Professor W.H. Whitely, were editors. Later, Dr. Lienhardt suggested that since I had enough collection for a volume, and since he himself had already published, he thought it would be good to have the book carry my name alone.

The transcription, translation, and editing of the songs proved to be a significant cathartic exercise at a time when I was going through some political and health challenges. Wrongly accused by the Government of masterminding Southern rebel activities in Europe, I turned down a recall back to the Sudan which would have meant certain persecution. I was also threatened with blindness by an acute case of glaucoma that had remained undetected through my high school, and Khartoum University years. These crises were forcing me into exile and isolation from my people. I worried that I might lose my sight and never see my people again. Even if political changes eventually allowed my return, it would probably be at a time when I would be blind. Ironically, the songs did play the role I had expressed to my father; that they would keep me connected with my people and make our culture known abroad.

At Yale, as I had made considerable progress in preparing the volume of songs, I suggested to my doctoral committee that I use Dinka songs to substantiate the themes I was developing in my thesis. First, as the songs invoked the moral and social code of the Dinka, they would be a useful way of ascertaining the Dinka value system. Second, since songs often concern factual situations and represent complaints or lamentations related to the alleged violations of societal norms, they reflect conflict situations that are close to actual cases. In fact, songs are often composed and presented as a competition between individuals or groups, each stating its grievances or complaints. Although a song represents one side of a conflict, it is possible to glean the other side from the singer's complaint.

At first, the idea of using songs in a legal study seemed to be an anathema, almost laughable. But then my professors saw the point of my argument and found in the songs valuable material for the normative framework of Law, Science, and Policy, which provided the theoretical framework for my thesis. In his Foreword to *Tradition and Modernization,*[7] Professor Harold Lasswell wrote, "When Dr. Deng examines the rich efflorescence of Dinka songs, he is able to consider the manifest content of the text by the use of an analytical frame of reference that remains stable and provides comparable results when other data, such as the legal prescriptions of Dinka society or of any other society, are examined." He also noted, "The songs provide a remarkable means of enlarging the outsider's empathy with the Dinka people... We begin to sense how the legal component of the power process permeates the experience of a human being who has been socialized in Dinka society and to sense the opportunities and constraints that affect an 'agent' of deliberate change."

When Godfrey Lienhardt visited me at Yale, he read the manuscript of Dinka songs and wrote me a complimentary note, even though we were often together and he could have spoken to me directly. In the note, he wrote something along the lines of, "I have read the manuscript of Dinka songs and it is now clear to me that you will be the one to make Dinka culture known to the outside world." It was obvious that he wanted to put that point on record and I was deeply moved.

The editors of *The Dinka and Their Songs,* among whom was Godfrey Lienhardt, quoting from the Spindlers' Foreword to *the Dinka of the Sudan,* wrote, "From these songs, we sense the real qualitative differences between Western and Dinka patterns of thought and expression; and the common human quality of the emotions and motivations involved."

The book was very well received and got a rave review in the London Times *Literary Review of Books* as one of the best volumes in the Oxford Series of African Literature. The reviewer posed the question of whether that reflected the literary merit of Dinka poetry or the quality of the translation and editing. My brother Bol was

---

7. Francis Mading Deng, *Tradition and Modernization: A Challenge for Law among the Dinka of the Sudan,* Yale University Press, 1971 - see p. 15.

later to ask me teasingly, "Mading, are these really our Dinka songs, or have you made them up?" Obviously, either of the two options posed by his question would be most gratifying. Again, I felt that I had fulfilled the objective of promoting Dinka culture abroad, which I had used to elicit my father's support and which Godfrey Lienhardt had so generously predicted.

'Dinka Folktales: African Stories from the Sudan'
Africana Publishing Company, 1974 [8]

Dinka Folktales offered me the opportunity to substantiate the Dinka value system in the cross-cultural context which is central to this annotated collection. In my doctoral work, I had used some stories I remembered from my childhood not only to contribute to ascertaining Dinka values as required by the theoretical framework of Law, Science, and Policy, but also as a means of inculcating the value system into children as an informal method of educational socialization and acculturation. Several years after joining the United Nations Secretariat, I went to the Sudan; on my way to a mission to Gabon and on my return journey, I requested members of my family to record Dinka folktales. After the mission, I returned to Yale on a post-doctoral fellowship in the Law and Modernization Program and began to listen to the recordings of the folktales. The moment I started listening to the stories, I began to see even more their value as a lens into the Dinka value system. I was so captivated and excited by the stories that preparing the volume of *Dinka Folktales* became my top priority in the program.

What intrigued me the most about the stories was not only the way

---

8 Africana Publishing Company is a branch of Holmes and Meier. This book was later reissued by Africa World Books, 2022.

they reflected the essential elements of the overriding goals and the detailed elements of the value system I had explored and built upon in my doctoral dissertation but the way the tales dichotomized the world of the Dinka and those of the animals, represented by lions, to identify and ostracize those who grossly violated the Dinka moral code. As I grew up, of all the animals of the wild in the world of the Dinka, lions were the animals the Dinka feared the most. The voice of a roaring lion in the night sent chills to those sleeping, especially children, the primary audience of bedtime fairy tales. The Dinka word for bedtime tales is *koor,* the same word for lion.

Lions in the folktales alternate from animals to humans. Under certain circumstances, lions disguise themselves by becoming humans. Humans too alternate as animal qualities emerge in people, who though human, often very handsome men or beautiful women, transform themselves into lions and commit animal deeds, including killing and eating human beings. But humans who turn into lions are sometimes severely punished through beating and being forced back into becoming human again.

A striking contrast between the world of the Dinka and that of lions is that the so-called human lions are sometimes, though rarely, depicted as white or on horseback and possessing commodities normally associated with foreign traders. This led me to the assumption that these foreigners, otherwise identified as lions, are probably slave raiders and traders.

When I spoke in a conference on the North-South conflict in the Sudan, the publisher of Africana Publishing Company (a branch of Holmes and Meier Publishers) who attended the meeting, asked me to share the stories with him, which I did. He was so attracted by the stories that he immediately asked me to prepare a book of Dinka folktales which his company would publish. I shared the manuscript with some colleagues at Yale Law School. One of them, Professor

Michael Riesman, was so taken by the tales that he readily accepted my request for him to write an introduction.

Professor Riesman wrote an in-depth substantive comparative analysis of the stories, relating them to classic Western psychological and social theories that gave them universal value as literature and a mirror of society. The Introduction analyzed the stories with reference to Freudian and other Western interpretations relating to incest and other sexual prohibitions far beyond my Dinka perception of the moral framework of the tales. Riesman wrote, "Because the tales of the Dinka which Dr. Deng has here collected are so beautiful, their value as world art may overshadow their significance as devices of socialization and civic acculturation in traditional society... Viewed from this respective Dr. Deng provides us with stunning insights into aspects of Dinka life and social regulation which are at once different and exotic and yet easily recognizable as strains in the universal repertory of human experience." To crown their substantive and esthetic artistic contribution to the volume of *Dinka Folktales*, Martha Riesman, Michael Riesman's wife, added value through beautiful artistic drawings on the cover of the book and of each of the tales.

Shortly after the publication of the book, I went to Scandinavia as an Ambassador. The Executive Director of the Dog Hammarskjold Foundation decided to publish one of the tales, *Aluel and Her Loving Father*, in their magazine, *Development Dialogue*. The story involved an excessively loving father who jealously monopolized raising his baby daughter whose mother had died. When she grew up and was sought after for marriage, he possessively resisted all suitors. He eventually surrendered to pressure and consented to her marrying. But even then, he again resisted her leaving him for her husband. Eventually, he again gave in to pressure and agreed to let her go with her husband.

His daughter was married by a man who had resisted marriage in search for the perfect wife. When that man's father saw his son's bride, he becme so attracted to her that he wanted to take her for himself. In the ensuing feud between father and son, the son's mother took her son's side and persuaded him to kill his father. She also told her son that since their cattle were owned and controlled by his father, which meant that her son had no animal to slaughter to make a shield to use in fighting his father, he should kill her, his mother, use half of the skin to make a shield, and make from the other half a sleeping skin for him and his wife. I told the Director of the Dog Hammarskjold Foundation that the story might be too shocking for his Swedish readers, to which he responded, "It is good to shock people with good stuff."

Interestingly enough, I was later surprised to receive a beautifully illustrated book in French, (with a check for 500 euros which I never cashed through neglect). The book was a translated version of one of the stories from *Dinka Folktales. Atong and her Lion-Husband* had been translated by Mohammed Omar Bushara, and published by Grandir, Nimes, France, in 2013. Years later, I received a message from Csenge Zalka, a storyteller and author from Hungary, representing an organization called Vilags Foundation for Children in State Care. They had decided to publish folktales from around the world and requested permission to reproduce and publish one of the stories, *Diirawic and Her Incestuous Brother,* to use in their educational program. Zalka wrote, "Our organization supports children who are in the Hungarian foster and state care system. One of our main projects is training volunteer storytellers that visit children's homes and tell bedtime stories. We are especially interested in folktales that represent the various family situations that our children come from, and ways they can overcome family trauma." I did not understand what was meant by stories that 'represented the family situations their children came from,' as I did not think there would be any Dinka children in Hungry, as it was before Dinka migrants began to spread all over the world. I thought that they must have been thinking of some universally shared family values. In any case, I granted my permission.

Once again, I felt that *Dinka Folktales* provided valuable bricks in the 'invisible bridge,' I set myself to build which I substantiated in my autobiography.[9]

'Africans of Two Worlds: The Dinka in Afro-Arab Sudan'
Yale University Press, 1978 [10]

My initial approach to law as a mirror into the comprehensive and interrelated realities of the Dinka social order in which myths and historical accounts were infused into current developments and also shaping the direction of the future. This led me into becoming increasingly interested in painting a holistic portrait of a Dinka worldview.

I seized the opportunity of the first anniversary of the 1972 Addis Ababa Peace Agreement which was held in Juba in 1973 and was attended by regional and international dignitaries and Chiefs from all over the South. I was then Ambassador to the Scandinavian countries and was attending the anniversary and assisting with the diplomatic arrangements and activities. Although I was busy with official functions, I decided to interview the Dinka Chiefs who were attending. These included famous names I had heard about from my childhood. With the assistance of a young Dinka government official, Arthur

---

9. Francis Mading Deng, *Invisible Bridge: An African Journey Through Cultures*, Africa World Books, 2021 - see p. 49.

10. Reissued as *The Changing World of the Dinka*, Africa World Books, 2022.

Akuien, who introduced me and helped build confidence between the Chiefs and me, I was able to interview most of them.

I had a warm personal relationship with Abel Alier, the President of the Regional Government of Southern Sudan, having been a senior colleague in the Faculty of Law at Khartoum University and who preceded me as a graduate student at Yale Law School. Abel tried to persuade me to include on my list non-Dinka Chiefs. While I understood his motive as a noble one; he wanted an inclusive collection of South Sudanese heritage but also wanted to protect me from being viewed as narrowly focused on my tribe, instead of playing the role of a national leader, I told him that interviewing the Chiefs of other Southern tribes would lose my focus and make the project too defuse and broad to the point of becoming unmanageable.

Dorothy Ann Deng, my American wife, assisted me with the recording, which added an interracial and cross-cultural dimension to the conversation. Since we were newly married, the Chiefs reflected their cultural values and perception of marriage as primarily an institution for begetting children to continue the ancestral line. As my father had died two years earlier, their focus was that she would beget "Deng Majok," my father, for her first borne. They carried out physical rituals on her and prayed for that purpose.

When my wife conceived and bore a son, naming him posed a challenge. The Chiefs had prayed for a son who would be in a sense a rebirth of my father. Our son should therefore be called Deng. But since we had already chosen Deng as our family name, that name would make him Deng Deng, which is not a practice among the Ngok Dinka. We looked into a book of names and found that the name Donald was a Celtic word that meant Tribal Chief. We, therefore, named our son Donald. With his mother's initials, D.D. (Dorothy Deng), and our first son is also D.D. (Donald Deng), we decided to use the D name for our next three sons, Daniel Deng, David Deng, and Dennis Deng, which made their names a tongue twister in the family.

While the scope of the interview was widely comprehensive, I streamlined it to comprise the origin of things, including myths of creation and leadership, contact with the outside world, historical developments leading to the present, and future prospects for nation-building in the context of racial, ethnic, religious and cultural diversity. When I returned to my post and began to listen to the tapes, I became so engrossed in interpreting them that I did what I still find remarkable. I used two tape recorders, used earphones to listen to the recordings from one tape recorder while operating the other recorder to dictate my interpretations simultaneously into English. I tried to authentically reflect even the intonation of how the Chiefs spoke, raising and lowering my voice in tune with the tone I heard. It was an extraordinary performance.

I immediately began to work on the book while in Scandinavia and continued when I was transferred to Washington. When I finished, I presented the manuscript to Yale University Press, which published it in 1978. Professor A.H.M. Kirk-Greene of Oxford University and Professor Robert O. Collins of the University of California, Santa Barbara, both renowned scholars of African history, whom Yale Press asked to review the book, strongly recommended its publication. Kirk-Greene emphasized the rarity of African oral history and literature, while Collins stressed the originality of the methodology used.

A remarkable feature of the material was the similarity of some of the myths of creation and leadership with those of the Biblical and Koranic Scriptures. Some of the reviews saw this as evidence of Christian Missionary work among the Dinka. But the elders I interviewed who ranged in age from their sixties to their late eighties, were too old to have been influenced by the missionaries whose work among the Dinka began with our generation in the 1940s. Most of the Chiefs said that they had heard the accounts they recalled from their fathers and grandfathers, which made the origins of their mythical accounts even farther into their origins.

As I reflected on the materials and bearing in mind the interaction of peoples and cultures in the Middle East and North Africa, it should not have been surprising that the outcome would be cross-cultural and inter-religious influences, the remnants of which have been well documented by anthropologists. Unfortunately, conflicts and animosity, especially in more recent times, have tended to generate denials of any contacts or relationships between the parties to the point that seeing mutual influences is seen as tantamount to betrayal. That was indeed my experience when I presented the findings of my study to a conference organized by the South Sudanese Minister of Culture and Information, Bona Malual, a Dinka and a friend, who was in fact promoting the pluralism of the country in his Ministry. Some Dinkas who had attended the conference complained to their fellow tribesmen, "Francis is now saying that we are related to the Arabs."

It is interesting that Dr. John Garang de Mabior, the founding leader of the rebel Sudan People's Liberation Movement (SPLM) and Sudanese People's Liberation Army (SPLA), who was a friend, pursued the link of the South with the ancient kingdom of Kush (or Cush) to the North with greater political and intellectual rigor, backing his assertions with Biblical sources.

Another theme that emerged in the interview on which the Chiefs focused, and I can even say were overly preoccupied with, was the prioritization of a self-reliant development that contrasted sharply with the popular view of the Nilotics as conservative and resistant to change. They called for robust development projects in the areas of education, health, and infrastructure. What was more intriguing to me was that they proudly maintained that they were not begging for material support. All they were asking for was technology, for which they were ready to pay. They even bragged about their cattle wealth, which they said they were prepared to sell to secure the financial resources they needed for development. Although this was clearly an exaggeration, I saw their positive self-perception as an important asset that could be built upon and tested for pursuing the strategy of transitional integration approach to development as a self-enhancement process from within.

Politically, while appreciating the Addis Ababa Peace Agreement and lavishly praising President Nimeiri for his courageous leadership in making that possible, they saw separation in the long run as unavoidable because they did not think that the identity cleavage between the North and the South could be bridged. They clearly saw their culture in a more favorable light in comparison to that of the Arabs, despite the fact that they realized with great indignation that the Arabs considered their culture and Islamic faith as superior. They asserted that even within a framework of unity, these two identities must be kept separate. In that respect, their generally pessimistic, but in retrospect correct, view of the future differed from my own more optimistic, but eventually mistaken, prediction that the Addis Ababa Agreement would create a framework of peaceful interaction that would ultimately result in a unified, integrated, and equitable national identity.

Among the most touching were the words of Chief Arol Kachwol of the Gok Dinka, from which I quoted in the Introduction. Chief Arol summarized important aspects of the Dinka worldview, including the fundamental values of tradition and change among the Dinka. He emphasized the value of the family, including the enrichment of mixed marriages, with reference to my own marriage:

The way we see it, God has brought peace and reconciliation into your hearts. None of you is to hate the race of the other. Even if a man was a slave or descended from a slave, and he marries into a family, he becomes a relative; he becomes a member of the family. Even our brothers, who were taken away as slaves, by now they have probably found their circles and have combined with other peoples to create their own kinships. So, if a man has secured a wife, as you have married, it is for him to bear his own blood and to bear the blood of his wife's kin.

Chief Arol continued with the theme of the positives of intermarriage:

That's the way it goes. Tomorrow, the people of that tribe or the people of that race, God will take them and mix them with the people of that race. They too will bear their own races through their children. When that happens, whatever hostility might have been between people, should no longer be allowed to continue. Relationship kills those troubles and begins the new way of kinship.

This is quite remarkable for a people whose reputation in anthropological literature is one of being insular, isolated, chauvinistic, conservative, and resistant to change. All this might indeed be true. But true also is the dynamic aspect by which people are ready to enhance their status by new norms, once they appreciate that there are new criteria for enhancing their overriding value of dignity - *dheeng.*

'Dinka Cosmology'

Ithaca Press, 1980 [11]

Although this book was published after *Africans of Two Worlds,* it comprises the transcriptions of the interviews with the same methodological and analytical introduction. This version is more of source material than an analytical work. Its value lies in the fact that it reproduces the words of the Chiefs, unfettered by interpretation. The publisher wrote this about the volume: "This extraordinary record contains materials from intensive interviews conducted by Francis Mading Deng with chiefs and elders representing virtually all major sections of the Dinka. As the scion of a prominent line of Dinka Chiefs, as well as a national leader and scholar, Dr. Deng occupies a unique position as a participant observer, which disposed his informants to address him with rare sincerity, candor, and depth of feeling."

One of the chiefs asked me whether I was talking to them in my capacity as a government official or as the son of Deng Majok. He explained that he was asking because if I was speaking as a government official, then they would not tell the whole truth; "some things would remain unsaid." But if I was talking to them as the son of Deng Majok! "Nothing would be left out." Of course, I told them that I was speaking in my personal capacity and that they had nothing to fear.

Referring to the potential risks of punitive measures against what they said, they emphatically asserted that they were speaking their minds without fear of the consequences. Invoking the Dinka values of procreational immortality, they all stated that even if what they said should lead to their death, they had children to leave behind.

---

11. Reissued as *Dinka Worldview: Elders Reflect on the Past, Present and Future of their People,* Africa World Books, 2023.

The publisher's comment also highlighted an important aspect of the interviews: "While confiding in him (Dr. Deng), they also requested him to publish their accounts and make them known not only to national leaders but also to the general public at home and abroad." Virtually all of them said that they would sleep soundly, having gotten everything off their chests.

Finally, the publishers commented on my participant-observer standpoint: "As he has demonstrated in his several publications on the Dinka, Dr. Deng has a remarkable way of combining deep insight with strict adherence to the principles of scholarly objectivity." Again, this points to my objective of transmitting Dinka culture in my efforts at bridge-building nationally and internationally.

'The Man Called Deng Majok: A Biography of Power, Polygyny and Change'
Yale University Press, 1986 [12]

My interest in writing a book about my father was the indirect product of wanting to write a book about my grandfather, Kwol Arob, whom Father succeeded as Paramount Chief. When I was in England in 1962-64, I got to know K.D.D. Henderson, who had been Governor of Darfur Province, and Senior Aide to the Civil Secretary toward the end of the Anglo-Egyptian rule. Earlier, he had served as District Commissioner of Western Kordofan under which Abyei fell at the time.

As a scholar, Henderson wrote extensively on the Sudan, including on the Ngok Dinka-Missiriya Arab relations. He was a great admirer

---

12. Reissued by The Red Sea Press, 2009.

of my grandfather, Kwol Arob, whom he often described in detail, including the movement of his long fingers when in court. Henderson told me that he had wanted to write a book about my grandfather. I had grown up with great admiration for my grandfather as well, who was very much praised by the Dinka as an ideal leader, including in songs. Henderson's praise for him reinvigorated my interest in my grandfather and my desire to write a book about him.

My interest was also reinforced by a book about Seretse Khama of Botswana, which Bridget Astor, the wife of David Astor of *The Observer Newspaper*, gave me. I had been introduced to the Astors by German friends from the family of the well-known martyred diplomat, Adam von Trott zu Solz, executed by Adolf Hitler as part of the failed 20 July 1944 assassination attempt against him. The von Trott family were also friends with the Khamas. What impressed me the most about the Khama book was the similarity between our families and cultures, including the cattle social economy of our respective peoples, the role of chieftaincy, the power struggle within the ruling family, and the intervention of the British colonial administrators to determine the outcome.

In the end, I decided that I had more access to information about my father, whom I knew more intimately than I did my grandfather. Many individual leaders with firsthand knowledge of my father and his leadership were still alive and could provide me with adequate information for his biography. Besides, through the story of my father, I could also cover much about my grandfather.

When I returned to the Sudan as Minister of State for Foreign Affairs, I gave tape recorders to young members of my family, most of them students in the universities, and asked them to conduct interviews with a wide range of people, including Father's wives, children, relatives, Ngok leaders and elders, Chiefs and elders from the neighboring Dinka and Arab tribes, and Sudan government officials. I myself conducted some of the interviews with the Ngok Dinka and Arab Chiefs and elders, as well as with British administrators who had worked with my father and grandfather.

I began to process the tapes and focus on writing the biography of my father after I left the government service. Shortly after returning to the United States, I was surprised by a call from Prosser Gifford, the then Deputy Director of the Woodrow Wilson International Center for Scholars, who later became the Director, inviting me to join the Center and work on a research or writing project of my choice. It was perfect timing for completing the book.

My initial objective was to publish it as a trade book because of what I thought would be a popular appeal to a wide readership. I sent the manuscript to my Yale Press editor, Marian Ash, for advice. She said she would consult some colleagues and get back to me. Within a surprisingly short time, I received a message from her congratulating me that the manuscript had been enthusiastically accepted by the publication committee who had also chosen the title.

The renowned Oxford University historian Professor Kirk-Greene was one of the reviewers of the manuscript, and in recommending it for publication, noted that it was "An important and all too rare contribution to African biography." Professor Crawford Young, the noted scholar of African studies, and one of the peer reviewers who recommended its publication wrote, "This is a historical and cultural document of prime importance. Francis Deng combines the analytical skills of a professional scholar with insights of one familiar with this kinship world and illuminates many aspects of both Dinka and Sudanese society."

Yale Press submitted the book for the Herskovits Award, an annual award given the by the African Studies Association to the best scholarly work published in the United States. The Association's chairman wrote to inform me that the book had been strongly recommended for the prize, but narrowly ended in second place. I thought that with *Tradition and Modernization*[13] having won the award earlier, it was perhaps unlikely that a book by the same author would win the award again.

A number of themes about my father and the book are worth emphasizing in this review:

The first was his outstanding political, social and diplomatic skill, which he used in outwitting his father and half-brother in the contest for power that won him the succession to the position of Paramount Chief when his father favored his half-brother, Deng Makuei (Deng Abot).

The second is the strong support he received from his resourceful maternal relatives from childhood and throughout his challenging competition for leadership within his paternal circles. In this regard, Father's experience mirrors my own, which later prompted me to write the book: *Blood of Two Streams: Gender Balance in Parental Legacy.*[14]

The third was the exceptionally large family, with wives numbering around 200 by the time he died in 1969. From all sections of his Ngok Dinka tribe and the neighboring communities, his polygynous family was the largest in the known record of the Dinka, in the Sudan, and arguably in Africa. This unprecedentedly large family was very close-knit and striking in unity and harmony.

Fourth, he was an effective administrator who, from the time he and his half-brother assisted their father, demonstrated commitment

---

13. Francis Mading Deng, *Tradition and Modernization: A Challenge for Law among the Dinka of the Sudan,* Yale University Press, 1971 - see p. 15.

14. Francis Mading Deng, *Blood of Two Streams: Gender Balance in Parental Legacy,* IIHS-Fordham University Press, 2021 – see p. 45.

to law and order and brought an end to tribal warfare that was an endemic feature of Nilotic societies; one of the reasons he was favored by the British administrators for the position of Paramount Chief.

The fifth was that despite his traditional status, he was an innovator who modernized his administrative structures and introduced to his area modern services in the fields of education, health and market economy.

The sixth and last theme was the paradox of his unique accomplishments that made him both a legendary and yet tragic figure in the history of his people. This critically important point needs elaboration.

To overcome his father's prejudice against him and preference for the half-brother as the heir to the throne, Father had to prove beyond any doubt that he was by far the most qualified. He was unique in his unmatched, excessive, and some would say assertive generosity and hospitality. He had a remarkable combination of courage and persuasive skills with words and peacemaking within and beyond his tribe. And he very successfully reached out to the neighboring tribes to the South and North, especially the Missiriya Arabs, whose Paramount Chief was Babo Nimir. For these and more reasons, he towered far above his people and among his peers in neighboring tribes. One Northern Sudanese provincial Governor described Father in these poetic words: "In his clean white *Jibba*[15] and turban, he looked like a pyramid."

The core of the paradox of Father's life was that he struggled throughout it with the deep insecurity that drove him to prove himself by excelling and outpacing all within his scope of power and influence. An aspect of the paradox was he took his people to heights that only he could sustain. With his disappearance from the scene by the inevitable

---

15. Full-length garment worn by men.

destiny of mortality, his people fell tragically from the heights to which he had taken them. That is the legacy his family and his people painfully inherited from him and from which they are still suffering.

A Northern Sudanese educator, Ibrahim Mohamed Zein, in the interview for Father's biography, said this about him "For a very long time, I have wondered why social researchers or scholars who write books do not write about the personality of Deng Majok. I think he offered a tremendous opportunity for study... I personally think Deng Majok was a most extraordinary character."

Douglas Johnson, the renowned scholar of Sudanese history, wrote in his review of *The Man Called Deng Majok:* "This must be classed among the best books written on any aspect of the Sudan." He also wrote elsewhere that of my many publications, the biography of my father was the book closest to my heart and in many ways, my most important work. My father was the model I always aspired to emulate, obviously an impossible aspiration.

Toward the end of his life in a health care facility in Khartoum, with death only weeks away, (eventually occurring in Cairo), he told my brother Zachariah Bol and me that should he die, he must be taken to be buried in his home area of Abyei despite the prohibiting conditions of the rainy season that would make that virtually impossible. With self-esteem that matched his unique profile, which made us both laugh after we left him, he said that he was not someone to be buried wherever he happened to die, that he was widely known throughout the country, North and South, and that he should be buried in his tribe and should indeed have a tomb over his grave.

Remarkably, with the cooperation of the President of the Republic and the powers above, a short break in the rains made it possible for us to fulfill Father's near-impossible wish, and we took him to Abyei where he received all the elaborate rituals of burial appropriate for the exceptional leader that he was. And there is no doubt that a tomb will one day be erected on his grave. Meanwhile, one of the reviewers of *The Man Called Deng Majok* wrote that the book was perhaps the tomb our father had requested of us.

'Customary Law in the Modern World: The Crossfire in Sudan's War of Identities'

Routledge, 2009

Customary Law in the Modern World was a contribution to a research project for the United States Institute of Peace, (USIP). From its inception in the late 1980s, I have been closely associated with the Institute. I was one of the Jennings Randolph Distinguished Fellows with whom the Institute began its agenda. Amongst very highly accomplished senior personalities, I was the 'baby' in the group.

Customary Law in the Modern World comprises selections from *Tradition and Modernization,*[16] with updates based on interviews with lawyers in the Two Sudans, reflecting post-war developments in the country before the independence of South Sudan. The views of the lawyers who were interviewed underscored the strongly-felt sentiments of the people about the crisis of national identity represented by the pluralistic legal system in the crossfires of Sudan's war of identities. Customary law emerges in the interviews as the symbol of the identity the Southerners had fought so hard and so long to defend until they achieved their independence. While acknowledging that certain aspects of customary law, especially those that discriminated against women and children, needed radical reform, South Sudanese lawyers and judges I

---

16. Francis Mading Deng, *Tradition and Modernization: A Challenge for Law among the Dinka of the Sudan,* Yale University Press, 1971 — see p. 15.

interviewed saw it as the normative foundation of the legal system of an independent South Sudan. How reform was to be accomplished was never made clear and remains an unfulfilled aspiration.

Another book that began as a research project during my time with USIP was *War of Visions: Conflict of Identities in the Sudan*.[17] It was completed while at the Brookings Institution and was published first by the Brookings Institution Press. During my twelve years at the Brookings Institution, I established and directed the African Studies Program as a Senior Fellow. A second Fellowship at USIP resulted in two other books; *Identity, Diversity, and Constitutionalism in Africa*,[18] and *Self-determination and National Unity: A Challenge for Africa*.[19]

'Frontiers of Unity:
An Experiment in Afro-Arab Cooperation'
Routledge, 2010

In my various recordings with the elders from the Ngok Dinka and neighboring communities, the contested status of the Ngok Dinka of Abyei was featured. In the consultations in Khartoum preceding the 1972 Addis Ababa negotiations and in the preparations for the talks in London, which Bona Malual and I had been asked by Abel Alier to participate in. I managed to put the case of Abyei on the list of issues for negotiation. The Addis Ababa Agreement had a provision that gave the people of Abyei the right to decide whether to remain under the administration of the North, to which the area was annexed

17. Francis M. Deng, *War of Visions, Conflict of Indentities in the Sudan*, The Brookings Institution Press, 1995. Reissued by the United States Insitute of Peace Press, (USIPP), 2008 – see p. 84.

18. Francis Mading Deng, *Identity, Diversity, and Constitutionalism in Africa*, USIPP, 2008 – see p. 119.

19. Francis Mading Deng, *Self-determination and National Unity: A Challenge for Africa*, Red Sea Press, 2009 – see p. 122.

by the British in 1905 or return to the South. That provision was not implemented.

As a compromise, I proposed remedying the situation by granting Abyei an autonomous administrative status under the Presidency, delivering social services to the people, and generating a program of social, and economic integrated development under the direct responsibility of the President. I succeeded in securing the support of the President for the proposal, got funding from the United States Agency for International Development (USAID), and invited the Harvard Institute for International Development (HIID) to assist in implementing the project.

I decided to write a book about the special status of Abyei, the bridging role its leaders had historically played at the North-South borders, and our efforts in finding a solution. But with the continuing tension in the area, characterized by periodic violent clashes between the Missiriya and the Ngok Dinka, I decided to defer the publication of the book. The ongoing crisis in Abyei eventually triggered the local rebellion that fueled the return to full-fledged civil war in 1983. I eventually decided to publish *Frontiers of Unity: An Experiment in Afro-Arab Cooperation* in 2010, after the 2005 Comprehensive Peace Agreement (CPA), that ended the war.

The Abyei Protocol of the CPA gave the Ngok Dinka the same right that the 1972 Addis Ababa Agreement had given them to decide whether to remain in the North or return to the South. The Abyei Boundaries Commission, (ABC), was created to determine the borders of the Ngok Dinka and their decision was to be final and binding. The Abyei Protocol, including the decision of the ABC, was also never implemented. Khartoum claimed that the ABC had exceeded its mandate. Following the 2008 invasion of Abyei by the joint Missiriya Arab militia and Sudan Armed Forces (SAF), the ABC boundary demarcation was submitted, in 2009, to the Permanent Court of Arbitration (PCA), whose decision was again to be final and binding. Although the PCA revised the decision of the ABC and gave more territory to the Missiriya, their award, though initially accepted by both sides, was also not implemented. I updated *Frontiers of Unity* to include these latest developments before its publication in 2010.

'Abyei between the Two Sudans'

Co-editor with Luka B. Deng Kuol, and Daniel J. Deng,

Red Sea Press, 2020.

This book resulted from the resolution of a personal conflict between my friend Bona Malual Madut and close members of my family who are leaders among the Ngok Dinka and prominent members of the ruling Sudanese People's Liberation Movement (SPLM) in South Sudan. Bona Malual wrote a book, *Abyei of the Ngok Dinka: Not Yet South Sudan.*[20] For a people who had been part of the struggle of South Sudan from the beginning, this was a very painful denial of the birthright of the Ngok Dinka. The conflict was therefore not only personal but had also become inter-communal. As Bona was close to the top leadership of both countries, the conflict stood to harm the cause of the Ngok Dinka between Sudan and South Sudan. Although the book came out at the critical time of the reconciliation talks, I managed to intervene and mediate between Bona and my relatives. But the book remained a very offensive historical document that needed a response.

After extensive consultations, it was agreed that instead of responding to Bona's book specifically, it would be more constructive to

---

20. Bona Malual, *Abyei of the Ngok Dinka: Not Yet South Sudan,* CPI, Anthony Rowe, 2017.

document the experiences of individuals in the armed struggle of South Sudan which demonstrated beyond doubt their identity as Southerners. Apart from my chapters that discuss the conflict and reconciliation, and a detailed commentary on Bona's book, the chapters are mostly documentation of the cause of the Ngok Dinka's role in the liberation of the South as South Sudanese.

'Blood of Two Streams: Gender Balance in Parental Legacy'

IIHS-Fordham University Press, 2021

This book is a combination of some of the materials from my earlier interviews, recast in a conceptual framework that streamlines themes that are quite familiar, but viewed in a new light and with a new focus. It is well known that in patriarchal societies like that of the Dinka, the emphasis tends to be placed on the paternal kin and ancestral genealogy. And yet, it is also well known that relations with the mother are normally closer than those with the father. Because of this ambivalence between the special love and affection with the mother and the stipulated proximity to the father, the Dinka seem to recognize the close relationship with the mother as a function of the heart and that of the father as a function of the mind. These two forces interplay in the life of every person in varying degrees.

In my own case, the contribution of my maternal lineage in shaping and supporting my position in my paternal circles and even in society was very pronounced. And from what I learned about my father, my case was a replica of my father's own experience. The fact that society tends to place one-sided emphasis on parental identity is a gross distortion of the glaring truism that every person is a product of father and mother and their respective kin groups.

This is the simple theme which *Blood of Two Streams* substantiates from the perspective of the individual to the family, on to the community and the country, and ultimately to the inter-racial and cross-cultural identity of our mixed family. In that respect, the issues involved are local and global, personal and universal.

'Tribute to Dr. Zachariah Bol Deng: Brother and Friend'
Detcro Research and Advisory, Nairobi, 2021

My phone rang at 4.40 am on January 18, 2021. It was from Santina, Bol's wife, in Birmingham, England, where their family resided. I was aware that Bol's long sickness had entered a critical stage and that the end was in sight, indeed imminent. I had left my phone open and close to me in case she called. When she did, I knew what she was going to tell me: Bol had just passed away. All I could say was the obvious: "We must be strong. That is the inevitable destiny. The end might come sooner or later, but whenever it comes, it is unavoidable." She had done a heroic job in taking care of Bol. Bol himself had done a great deal in life for his people and his country. He had led a good life and raised a wonderful family. He was leaving behind a good number of children and grandchildren to continue his name, in the belief of 'kooc e nhom,' immortality by continuing to live through the living. The reality however had a much deeper effect on me than I was revealing or fully realizing. I could not conceive of Bol as dead. What did death really mean anyway!?

My tribute for my brother, Dr. Zachariah Bol, was a brief account of our life together, our family background, our education, our cross-cultural transitions, and our personal and professional service to our people and our country. Bol and I were very close and were often referred to in our family as twins. And although we had our differences, we mostly agreed on matters relating to our family, community, and country. We consulted each other on both personal and public issues. We agreed to divide roles so that I would protect the interest of our Abyei area in the National Government in the North, where I served as Ambassador to important posts abroad, and as Minister of State for Foreign Affairs. Bol meanwhile promoted our cause in the Regional Government in the South, where he served as a physician and later joined politics to become Deputy Speaker of Parliament and then Minister of Health.

Given the predicament facing our people of Abyei, as they agonize over the impasse between Sudan and South Sudan in determining the future status of the area, I cannot help but wonder what Bol would say about the situation today. In a way, it is not a new question, for we were always preoccupied with discussing the situation in our area of Abyei. Sadly, like most citizens of Abyei, we painfully saw our area left out of the value of peace at the end of the two civil wars with the North, in which the sons and daughters of Abyei had fought gallantly and made the ultimate sacrifice with their lives. Over the years, I proposed and advocated an interim arrangement that would make Abyei, a self-governing area between Sudan and South Sudan. This would ensure security and stability, and encourage and support the return of refugees and internally displaced people to their areas of origin from which they have been forced to flee by persistent attacks by the Missiriya Arabs. The returnees, with the support of successive governments, and provided with essential services and development opportunities, could promote their peaceful coexistence and cooperation with their neighbors to the North and South. Such an arrangement would not only restore peace and harmony to that border region, but would also reinforce closer bilateral relations between Sudan and South Sudan, and create conditions of confidence for them to amicably agree on the future status of Abyei as a border area that should remain connected to both countries, whatever the status is ultimately agreed upon. Toward the end of his life, Bol became an unwavering supporter of the proposal.

Stabilizing Abyei as a border area has the prospect of turning the area into a hub for regional, inter-communal, and inter-state trade and development cooperation. I see Abyei as an area that can rise from the ashes of prolonged attacks by the North to become a beacon of development opportunities and prosperity for the Ngok Dinka and their neighbors to the North and the South. This is a vision that is now modest, but with creative thinking and action can continue to grow into unforeseeable potentials that will pave a common ground and transcend destructive divisions in the mutual interest of all the concerned communities.

'Remembering Chief Deng Majok:
A Leadership of Glory and Tragedy'
Detcro Research and Advisory, Nairobi, 2021

This book began as a tribute for which the family requested me to write for the occasion of remembering the fiftieth anniversary of our father's death. In a way, it was an abbreviated and updated version of my book, *The Man Called Deng Majok: A Biography of Power, Polygyny, and Change.* As the title shows, the thesis of the book is that Father's life was one of glory and tragedy. With this thematic yardstick in mind, I focus my analysis on two related issues in our father's life. One is his ambivalent relations with his father, Chief Kwol Arob, and his half-brother, Deng Makuei Deng Abot, with whom he competed for leadership. The other is Father's unprecedented achievements as a leader, which was a central feature of his struggle for power.

The two areas were therefore closely interconnected and mutually augmenting throughout Father's life. Father's glory was in his spectacular achievements as a leader. The tragedy was that this came with a heavy price not only because he spent his entire life painstakingly striving to prove himself as unquestionably the best qualified for leadership, but also once he was gone, he left a vacuum that could not be filled and his people fell from the great heights to which he had taken them, into the devastating crisis which they are now tragically experiencing.

'Invisible Bridge: An African Journey Through Cultures'
Africa World Books, 2021

This book chronicles the earlier phase of my life in our traditional Dinka village of Noong, then through various phases of education. Beginning with the first elementary school in Abyei, then to primary and intermediate schools in Southern Sudan, to a secondary school in Northern Sudan, and on to the University of Khartoum. While in Khartoum, I first gained exposure to Europe through a program of summer vacation exchange visits with German universities. In 1961, as the only Southern Sudanese in a group of twelve students, and again in 1962 as the leader of the group, and still the only Southern Sudanese. After graduating from Khartoum University, I went abroad for postgraduate studies in the United Kingdom and then on to the United States, where I obtained a doctorate at Yale Law School, after which I joined the United Nations as a Human Rights Officer in 1967.

The book ends on my return to the Sudan in August 1969, with my brother Zachariah Bol, who was practicing medicine in the United Kingdom. Tragically it was to attend to our father who was terminally ill and died in Cairo shortly after. We miraculously flew his body back home during the forbidding conditions of the rainy season to find the area devastated by the civil war between North and South Sudan. Security forces were terrorising people with arrests, torture, and summary executions. After a month in the area endeavouring to ameliorate the security situation in tortuous cooperation with the commander of the security forces, with minimum success at best, Bol returned with me to New York. There we agonised over the tragedy that had befallen our people. We pondered our own role in discharging the responsibility of leadership that had descended upon us as Father's senior sons. That would indeed become the subject of a second volume in the series I planned to eventually comprise the comprehensive story of my journey between cultures.

The 'invisible bridge' I envisaged in this book, (the first volume), is a conceptual phenomenon that enables us to move to and from between the interactive and interdependent cultural contexts of the world in which we now live. Because it is conceptual, intangible, and invisible, it is not easy to perceive and therefor cross. The reality and the vision of it are within each one of us and require deep introspection into ourselves, our origins, our surroundings, and our motivations in undertaking what is often a hazardous journey. This internal phenomenon must be externally projected to form a suspended bridge on which to cross back and forth between these contexts, metaphorically and physically.

The 'invisible bridge' is both a philosophy of life and a moral framework of response to specific situations. But, in addition to being difficult to conceive, this bridge is delicate and fragile; it is easy to miss or ignore; many may not even be aware of its existence. When not properly perceived and constructively utilized, the result may range from a messy journey of culture shock on arrival, or worse, to a tragic fall into the turbulent waters of the racial, ethnic, and cultural crosscurrents. The punitive consequences result both from violating the code of conduct of one's upbringing and failing to live up to the values and moral code of the new social order.

'Warriors From Abyei in the Liberation of South Sudan'
Africa World Books, 2022

Warriors From Abyei is about four sets of individual experiences in the liberation struggle of the people of South Sudan. Although united by the common cause of the struggle, the individuals involved were provoked into rebelling by different triggers within that common cause, demonstrating the various ways in which the grievances manifest themselves under the rubric of the shared sense of indignation and determination to right the causal wrongs.

The stories also point to the paradoxes of armed struggle and whether two wrongs make a right. Does winning the war of liberation unequivocally translate into an overall correction of the situation and a progressive march forward or does it leave the goal of liberation an unfinished business? And in a cost-benefit assessment of what is achieved, does it mean that the massive loss of lives and destruction was a sacrifice worth making, or could somewhat similar results have been achieved with fewer sacrifices?

The individuals whose stories are narrated in this volume include a child who was only nine years old at the time of his war experience during the first war (1955-1972), and a man, and three women who are speaking of the second war (1983-2005).

The man, Pieng Deng Kuol, was a brilliant student of engineering at the University of Khartoum, where he was first in the class.

Awuor Deng, who tells the story of her rebellion jointly with one of her half-sisters from a different mother, was a shining star in her class in secondary school in Khartoum when she chose to leave the school because of what she saw as a racist insult by one of the teachers, and she persuaded her half-sister, also called Awuor, to join her in rebelling. The two are half-sisters to Pieng, from the same father and different mothers.

Nyenagwek Kuol, whose story is the third in the narratives, moved to Khartoum with her family both to escape from the insecurity of the war and to seek opportunities for a better life. She diligently sought education and was a highly motivated student of information technology in college. She was fortunate enough to find good employment alongside her studies and she received recognition and successive promotions. When she became increasingly exposed to the indignities of racism in her work, she chose to join the rebellion.

The fourth is the extraordinary story of Raphael Tikley Abiem, a cousin of Pieng and the sisters. As a nine-year-old child, he was driven by anger to leave his education in a prestigious Catholic school in the North to join the rebellion. Tikley Abiem's first task was to carry a large sum of money in a plastic bag tightly tied, indeed 'plastered,' to his back, to take to the rebels in Congo to buy guns for the rebel army. Fortunately, after suffering the horrors of war too early in life, he returned to the Sudan and resumed his studies to the highest levels of the academic ladder.

The proximate triggers for joining the rebellion differed significantly in three of the cases. For Tikley, despite his age at the time of his rebellion, his account presents a context already ablaze in the war of resistance in the South. The reasons he gave for rebelling were the same ones that had triggered the Torit mutiny by Southern soldiers in 1955, which escalated into the full-fledged civil war that had been raging for a decade when he joined.

Pieng witnessed a succession of horrific brutalities of his people by the security forces in his area which cumulatively developed an intense hatred of the Arab regime that was brutalizing his people. Awuor experienced demeaning treatment in her class by her teacher, aggravated by the racist attitude of another teacher, which not only infuriated her but reflected the broader racial discrimination against the Blacks by the Arabs that had provoked the war of liberation which she decided to join. The case of Nyenagwek was the most surprising because she was rising in her employment, which got her involved, by the Arabs, in the work of the Committee for the Eradication of Abduction of Women and Children, (CEAWC). She was driven into rebellion by what she witnessed in the effect of enslavement among the children, some of whom had been brainwashed into denying their identity as Dinka, instead identifying themselves as Arabs, and despising their own people. This contrasted sharply with the sense of pride and dignity among the rebels whom she encountered in the course of the work of the committee which made her decide to join the rebellion.

The declared objective of the rebellion by the Sudanese People's Liberation Movement/Army (SPLM/A) was not separation, but the creation of a New Sudan of full equality without any discrimination on the ground of race, ethnicity, religion, or culture. That war, fought for over twenty years, was ended by the 2005 Comprehensive Peace Agreement, (CPA). On 9 July 2011, the South won independence from the North and declared itself the Republic of South Sudan which was warmly received by the international community as the 193rd Member of the United Nations.

The goal of the Ngok Dinka in the struggle was both a demonstration of solidarity with their people of South Sudan and the related demand of disaffiliating themselves from the North and returning to the administration of the South. Although the 1972 Addis Ababa Agreement gave them the option to decide by a plebiscite whether to remain in the North or revert to the South, that provision of the Agreement was never implemented. The CPA also granted them that same option through the Abyei Protocol. In the interim, the people of Abyei are to maintain dual citizenship of both Sudan and South Sudan. In effect, Abyei is constitutionally recognized by the government of South Sudan as part of South Sudan, a status that the government in Khartoum does not recognize. They still consider Abyei a part of Sudan and continue to block the implementation of the Abyei Protocol.

As a result of all this, the status of Abyei remains in limbo, precariously poised between the two Sudans. It is interesting that in their devoted commitment to the struggle, the people of Abyei fought as Southerners and rarely referred to the cause of their area as the reason for their joining the war. Only once, when Abyei was excluded as part of the South by the Machakos Protocol in 2002, that stipulated the principles for a resolution, did Pieng voice his indignation and affirmed the cause of Abyei as the primary reason for his joining the liberation struggle. Pieng's protest was registered and catered for in the Abyei Protocol.

Despite the monumental achievement of South Sudan's independence, in less than three years, specifically in December 2013, South Sudan tragically exploded into an ethnically based civil war that has continued to devastate the country ever since. Although it was halted by a precarious peace agreement in 2015, it erupted again only a year later in an even more devastating violence. Regional and international efforts resulted in a Revitalized Peace Agreement (RPA) that was signed in September 2018, but whose implementation has only been piecemeal and very tenuous.

The question that can legitimately be posed is whether the massive loss of lives, the devastating destruction of the country, and the chronic instability that has retarded development and aborted the process of nation-building could not have been avoided. The racist character and religious chauvinism of the North, though persistently denied, were overtly manifest. Farsightedness and enlightened self-interest should have guided the parties to enter into constructive dialogue in an earnest commitment and endeavor to address the genuine grievances of the people of South Sudan and the marginalized non-Arab regions of the North. The options which were eventually adopted or became inevitable included autonomy for the South, federalism, and even the concept of the 'One Country Two Systems' mechanism proposed by the Washington Center for Security and International Studies, (CSIS), which I was honored to co-chair. These options were all in sight but were rejected, leaving partition the unavoidable last resort.

Decades of mass atrocities, physical destruction, and grave suffering of the people have led to a situation of continued violence, lack of services, economic stagnation, and little progress in building the nation. This has left the many people who had contributed to the liberation struggle to wonder whether that was what they fought and sacrificed decades for – going back to 1955 – several months before the independence of Sudan in 1956.

On the other hand, South Sudan as an independent country now exists and will continue to exist, which is a monumental accomplishment. The vast natural resources of the country are also there and will remain a potential, waiting to be realized. Even the area of Abyei, often described as oil-rich, can look forward to the time when the people will reap the fruits of their God-given wealth. All these will need continued struggle of a different form, hopefully, peaceful and determined, for ensuring peace, security, stability, development, and nation-building. This requires blind faith that the sacrifices made by the heroes, many of whom have fallen as martyrs, and others of whom are still struggling through very hard times, have not been in vain and that the reward for the precious blood they have shed, and the grave suffering they have endured, will materialize in due course.

'Abyei Rising From the Ashes'

Detcro Research and Advisory, Nairobi, June, 2022

When I was working on this book in June 2022, Abyei was burning, literally and metaphorically. The theme of 'Abyei Rising from the Ashes' invokes the mythical image of the phoenix, a magical creature that rose from the ashes and, represents "a magical and gentle soul" that "brings good luck, peace, balance, harmony and prosperity," and also "symbolizes fire and passion – the flames of true inspiration."[21] Spiritually, Abyei also represents the concept of 'Primal Vision' which is closely associated with the indigenous African religious belief system that is reflected in the profound religiosity of the Dinka. Their strong and unwavering belief in God permeates their views on the conflict situation they are currently experiencing, their overwhelming faith in the ultimate power of God as the Dispenser of Divine Justice, and their conviction that right will eventually prevail over wrong.

Abyei has also become a link between the local and global dimensions of justice and the universality of human dignity. The late Deng Abot (Deng Makuei) Kuol Arob, Deputy Paramount Chief of the Ngok Dinka, told me in an interview on the biography of his brother, the late Paramount Chief Deng Majok Kuol Arob, that Abyei is like the eye which is so small but sees so much. I now reverse that to say

---

21. https://worldbirds.com/phoenix-symbolism.

that although Abyei is so small, the eyes of the world are focused on that small spot. Located at the turbulent border of the Arab Muslim North and the African secular South of what was Sudan, and bordering communities from both countries, Abyei is potentially both a gulf and a bridge between Sub-Saharan Africa and North Africa and by extension the Middle East. The late Paramount Chief of the Ngok Dinka, Deng Majok, used to present himself and by implication the Abyei area, as the needle and thread that stitched North and South into a unified Sudan. The bridge that Abyei metaphorically built between North and South Sudan is now crumbling and urgently needs salvaging. With the recent violent contests over the area, the United Nations now has the United Nations Interim Security Force for Abyei (UNISFA), which symbolizes the link between the local and global spectrums of international peace and security. The presence of the United Nations in Abyei signifies the outer reach of the global responsibility to protect.

This book tries to address the multifaceted crises afflicting the nine Sub-tribes or Chiefdoms of the Ngok Dinka of Abyei. The context is the unresolved issue of the status of Abyei between Sudan and South Sudan, which leaves this area of strategic geopolitical importance in a vulnerable status of virtual statelessness, without the protection normally associated with statehood and the rights of citizenship. Related to this is the genocidal threat posed by neighbors in the Sudan, the Missiriya Arab, and more recently the Twic Dinka neighbors in South Sudan. This conflictual situation contrasts sharply with the historical role Abyei used to play as a peaceful and conciliatory link between the Arab Muslim North and the African secular South of what was Sudan.

This situation presents the Ngok Dinka with formidable challenges. The first is to develop strategies for defending themselves against the genocidal assaults from their neighbors on both the northern and southern fronts. Related to that is the need to adopt a self-reliant approach to development as a process of self-enhancement from within, building on indigenous cultural values and institutions, and using local human and natural resources and resourcefulness.

The overriding cultural values to build upon include: Connection to the mythical world of God, Clan Deities, and the Ancestral Spirits; the worldly principles of continued identity and influence of the dead among the living; unity, harmony, and peaceful resolution of conflicts; dialogue and the power of persuasion over violence and coercion; and a strong sense of collective and individual identity, integrity and dignity, which reinforce the esthetics of beauty and adherence to the ideals of the moral code of conduct.

These values determine the division of responsibilities and functions in the society, including the involvement of God, Clan Deities, and Ancestral Spirits in the affairs of the living; the role of the chiefs and elders in promoting peace, unity, and harmony; the military function of male warrior age-sets and their female counterparts in defending the area and enforcing the moral code of conduct among their members; and the overall complementary role of women as partners in the management of the affairs of the family and the community.

These cultural values and the roles of different categories of participants need to be revived, revitalized, reinterpreted, reformed were needed and applied in pursuing the strategy of transitional integration in a culturally oriented approach to development. This would aim at promoting competitive and cooperative individual and collective activities in agricultural production, livestock development, construction of roads, and building of schools, health centers, and other public utilities, as well as programs for youth employment and women empowerment. Organizing sports and social and cultural activities would encourage bonding and reinforce a value-oriented sense of identity, integrity, and dignity. Given the recurrent attacks against the Ngok Dinka, building the defense capacity of the area by modernizing the warrior age-set system, unifying it to include all the nine chiefdoms, and providing training and equipment for the warrior youth, should be a high priority. This self-reliant approach however requires complementary support and partnership from regional and international friends and sympathizers.

But first and foremost, the genocidal threat facing the Ngok Dinka must be addressed and resolved as a matter of utmost urgency. The African Union, the United Nations, and the Troika countries - the United States, the United Kingdom, and Norway - which have been at the forefront of mediating for peace in the region, should expedite the resolution of the issue of the final status of Abyei. The situation demands a program of action from the Ngok Dinka themselves. With the support of friends and concerned partners, they must exert pressure on the key decision makers at the national, regional, and international levels to bring a speedy end to this crisis. Consolidating peace, security, and stability in Abyei would enable the area to play the bridging role it used to play and forge a culture of peaceful coexistence and cooperation between and among the border communities that would reinforce cordial bilateral relations between their respective states of Sudan and South Sudan and their wider affiliations in Africa and the Middle East.

'Abyei at a Critical Juncture'

Detcro Research and Advisory, Nairobi, July, 2022

One of the most remarkable experiences I have ever had was meeting with two Ngok Dinka Diaspora communities in the United States of

America in October 2021, to discuss my proposal for the resolution of the conflict over the issue of Abyei's status between Sudan and South Sudan. The first was with the Abyei Ngok Community Association in the United States (ANCAUS), which took place on the 16th of October. The second was with the Abyei Women's Revolution (AWR) group, which took place over four days from October 22 to 25. For several years, both groups had been urging me to talk to them to discuss the proposal I first made in 2014, including in a submission to the UN Security Council, when I was Permanent Representative of South Sudan to the United Nations. Different groups kept telling me that while they supported the proposal, they needed more clarification.

I had already shared the proposal with various Ngok Dinka constituencies at home and abroad, including with the Chiefs, elders, youth, students, and varying formations of curious individuals. The proposal had already proved to be very controversial, apparently supported by the vast majority of our people, but strongly opposed by a vocal minority. I came to the conclusion that the circles asking for clarification were endless and that public discussions only generated more controversy. I, therefore, decided not to give more talks to explain the proposal, as that was becoming too divisive. After several visits to the United States during which the communities kept asking me to address them and I declined, I eventually succumbed to their request and agreed. This publication embodies the minutes of the meeting with the ANCAUS, which was much shorter than the meeting with the AWR, whose minutes are voluminous and more difficult and time-consuming to prepare for publication, which I hope to do in due course.

The proposal continued to be debated among the Ngok Dinka, supported by the majority of the people, but opposed by a vocal and influential minority in Juba. With recent attacks from the Southern border by the Twic Dinka, the Ngok Dinka of Abyei, faced an existential threat from both the North and the South, with no reliable protection nationally or internationally. Although the Government of South Sudan has made Abyei a Special Administrative Area within South Sudan, that arrangement has not been officially recognized by the Sudan or the international community. With the final status of the area still undecided, the people of Abyei are now in a state of virtual statelessness, without the protection and material assistance that a state is normally expected to grant its citizens.

With the persistent and worsening crises in the Abyei area, the initiative had been reactivated by various Ngok Dinka groups, among them the Abyei community in the United States. Following discussions held with Diaspora groups in which the proposal gained considerable support, the community formed Abyei Voice for Security and Stability (AVSS) and Keep It Confidential (KIC) to formally adopt the proposal. The two entities jointly organized a workshop to debate, endorse and promote the proposal. Representatives of the Ngok Dinka communities, at home, and members of the Diaspora from literally all regions of the world participated in the workshop. The workshop lasted for over a month and ended with the unanimous adoption of a revised version of the proposal. It was also decided that since the proposal represented the legitimate aspirations, demands, and expectations of the Ngok Dinka, it should be 'owned' by the people and be promoted as amended and not continue to be viewed as my proposal.

This report of the month-long consultation of AVSS/KIC, which is still being prepared as I write in July 2022, will capsulate the main themes of the workshop deliberations, the justification for the proposal, and the core principles of the proposed self-governance for the area to ensure security and stability as prerequisites for the development and prosperity, not only for the Ngok Dinka but also for their neighbors to the North and the South. The goal is to turn Abyei from being a contested area to become a conciliatory link between the neighboring communities and the two governments of the Sudan and South Sudan.

B. National Level

'Dynamics of Identification: A Basis for National Integration'
Khartoum University Press, 1973 [22]

The issue of identity as a factor in the conflicts that have devastated Sudan in its modern history and the potential of addressing it to promote the cause of peace and unity has been a major subject in my writings. *Dynamics of Identification: A Basis for National Integration in Sudan* is one of my shortest books that has been most influential. I undertook the study as a project for a post-doctoral Fellowship I received under the Yale Law School Program of Law and Modernization. In a way, the Yale Law Schools' theory of Law, Science, and Policy provided a framework for approaching the issue of identity formation and transformation. Law is the outcome of a powerful process in which the controlling authority regulates competition by individuals and groups for material, moral and spiritual values within the normative framework of overriding values. The Yale Jurisprudential School stipulates human dignity, defined as the broadest possible shaping and sharing of values. This means maximizing the production of values with full equality in distribution.

In *Dynamics of Identification*, I argued that identity as a concept evolves over a period of time and is therefore deep-rooted and sensitive. It is proudly acknowledged, jealously guarded, and reluctantly

---

22. Also published in *Africa Today*, 20, no. 3, Summer 1973, p. 19.

surrendered. Yet, though alterable only at a slow pace, it is a dynamic process that is capable of adaptation and even transformation under favorable conditions.

The premise of the book was that identity in the Sudan, rooted as it is in deep-seated traditional values, and yet dynamically adaptable, is the outcome of a power process through which certain elements of identity, Islam and Arabism, were favored, rewarded, and promoted as assimilating models of self-enhancement, while Africanism of race, culture and belief system were looked down upon and denigrated as synonymous with slavery connotations. The South on the other hand morally looked down on Arabism and Islam as models of domination that had to be resisted. *Dynamics of Identification* documents the historical process by which the myths of identity shaped the self-perception of the various groups in the North as Arabs, with Islam as an integral component of that identity and a means of enhancing their status above the denigrated identity of being a Black African and a 'heathen.' Ultimately, these forces dichotomized the country into Arab-Muslim North and the rebellious African secular South.

Dynamics of Identification discussed the restructuring of identification that was taking place, culminating in the Addis Ababa Agreement, which recognized the racial, ethnic, cultural, and religious diversities in the country. The Agreement granted the South the right to autonomously govern itself within the framework of national unity. I argued that the dynamism of the process also offered the prospects of reshaping the currently divisive identities to promote a common ground of a shared Sudanese identity based on full inclusivity, equality and dignity for all groups as citizens without discrimination based on race, ethnicity, religion, gender and culture. This envisaged a strategy by which the various identity claims could be accommodated and balanced in a system that recognized diversities equitably while leaving open channels of communication and interaction to evolve an integrated identity for the country as a whole.

Published in 1973, the book proved to be a forerunner of the New Sudan Vision that the Sudanese People's Liberation Movement and Army (SPLM/A), specifically its leader Dr. John Garang de Mabior, later postulated and propounded. At the time of its publication, the book generated considerable debate and controversy. It was construed by some as advocating assimilation, for others as a calling for the Africanization of the country, and correctly, by a relative few, as a basis for promoting a framework of unity with respect for diversity as a transitional process toward a unifying national identity of full equality. As that conceptual vision merged with that of a New Sudan, it met with the fate of short-term rejection and a long-term challenge for the country, even after its partition into two independent states of Sudan and South Sudan.

What is particularly striking is that *Dynamics of Identification* introduced me to the pivotal importance of identity as a factor in conflicts and provided me with a lens for approaching the myriad of issues that became my preoccupation in most of the issues I later addressed. One word, identity, became the thread that conceptually tied the essential themes of the various works on the conflicts in the Sudan and Africa, as well as in my UN mandates on internally displaced persons and the prevention of genocide.

'Peace and Unity in the Sudan: An African Achievement'
Co-author, Khartoum University Press, 1973

I wrote *Peace and Unity in the Sudan: An African Achievement* and submitted it to Khartoum University Press for publication, shortly after I had completed *Dynamics of Identification*. I had only recently been appointed Ambassador to the Scandinavian countries following the 1972 Addis Ababa Peace Agreement and I wrote the book at the request of the Foreign Minister who had been instrumental in my appointment.

The objective of the book was to present the achievement of peace as the result of African mediation which was primarily through the All African Council of Churches (AACC), and Emperor Haile Selassie of Ethiopia, who hosted the negotiations. I believe it was also a strategic move by the Sudan to co-opt the Organization of African Unity (OAU) to be identified with, and supportive of, the peace agreement. In fact, the book was to be presented by the President to the Heads of State and Government of the OAU in celebrating its anniversary on May 25, which happened to coincide with the anniversary of the revolution of the Sudan. I believe we were given the assignment in February or March 1973, which meant that we had only about three months to write and produce the book.

Two young diplomats, Isaac La, a South Sudanese, and Yousif Said, from the North, were assigned to me to assist in preparing the book. Together with my Deputy Head of Mission, Mohammed Ibrahim El-Mekki, also from the North, and my wife, we all worked so hard that one of the team almost rebelled. However, we were able to finish the book in an exceptionally short time. Apart from chapters on the history of the conflict and the proceedings and terms of the agreement, which were drafted by my staff, most of the substantive part of the book was written by me. My perspective focused on the process of identity reconstruction that led to the Agreement, the framework of unity in diversity that the Agreement established, and the prospects of evolution toward an integrated unitary national identity devoid of the divisive factors of race, ethnicity, and religion. *Peace and Unity,* was in essence a revised and updated version of *Dynamics of Identification* recast as an authentic statement of government policy.

I knew that the Foreign Minister and I were on the same page about the policy orientation of the book. To make sure that the book authentically represented government policy, we agreed that the manuscript should be read by a veteran scholar and diplomat who was a special advisor to the Minister. Ironically, he was one of the peer reviewers whom Khartoum University Press had asked to review the manuscript of *Dynamics of Identification.* He had recommended its publication, describing it as well researched. When he read the manuscript of *Peace and Unity in the Sudan,* he fully endorsed the book.

The Director of Khartoum Press and I then worked feverishly, day and night, and got the book out in a record two weeks, just in time for presentation to the Heads of State and Government on the 25th of May. The book was well-designed and beautifully produced. It is well received within the country and abroad, in both policy and scholarly circles.

Years later, as the political climate changed away from the framework of the Addis Ababa Agreement, eventually leading to the erosion of the principles articulated in the book. This erosion demonstrated that identity is both fluid and rigid, and flexibly malleable, but also rigid and jealously guarded and preserved.

Two personal experiences strikingly brought this home to me. One was at a dinner that a diplomatic colleague hosted for me with several of our colleagues. The discussion focussed on *Dynamics of Identification,* which had just come out. Toward the end of the discussion, one of the diplomats who were very frail with a terminal illness from which he died shortly after, said in a feeble voice, "Dr. Deng, the roots of Arab-Islamic identity in the Sudan go very deep. They cannot be easily transformed into something else." Years later, three months after the Islamist Revolution of National Salvation of Omar Hassan Al-Bashir seized power, I went to the Sudan and held extensive discussions with the leaders of the coup. One of the people I met was an officer who was said to be the intellectual of the Revolution. I told him about the radical shift that had taken place in the Southern liberation struggle from secession to the transformation of the country toward a New Sudan of full equality without any discrimination on the ground of race, ethnicity, religion, or culture. He listened very attentively and although I had been told that he had only fifteen minutes, we spoke for over an hour. At the end of patiently listening to me, he said, "Dr. Deng, I have very much enjoyed listening to all that you have said. But I just want you to remember one thing, there is another point of view." That other point of view was their Arab-Islamic agenda that would rule the country for thirty years and is still tenaciously resisting any attempts to democratize and secularize the system of governance in the country.

'Diplomacy and Development in the Sudan'
Editor, Ministry of Foreign Affairs, Sudan, 1974

It was in the conducive climate of the 1972 Addis Ababa Agreement that the Ministry of Foreign Affairs organized a symposium on international development cooperation to which representatives of major aid agencies and international experts were invited. The Minister of Foreign Affairs, Dr. Mansour Khalid, asked me to assist in organizing the symposium. I also presented a paper that became a chapter in the book and in which I reflected on the themes of both *Dynamics of Identification* and *Peace and Unity in the Sudan*, relating them to the creation of a climate conducive to development and gaining international partnership. He also asked me to edit and prepare the proceedings and papers of the symposium into a book. The outcome was *Diplomacy and Development*.

'AfroArab Relations: A Contextual Perspective on History'

Ministry of Information and Culture, 1976 [23]

This booklet was in fact the paper I had presented at the conference organized by the Ministry of Culture and Information which published the booklet. The Minister was Bona Malual, a friend with whom I had worked closely for the cause of peace. Bona and I joined the government at the same time following the Addis Ababa Agreement that ended the first civil war in 1972. As Minister, after the Agreement, Bona was endeavoring to promote the principles of unity in diversity and relations between the North and the South were much improved. This also had a positive impact on African-Arab Relations generally. The climate was indeed conducive to Arab investment in the Sudan. The conference was indeed a reflection of that climate.

The paper was a summary of the core findings of the interviews with Dinka Chiefs and elders that resulted in *Dinka Cosmology* and *Africans of Two Worlds: The Dinka in Afro-Arab Sudan*.[24] The fact that I was invited to present a paper with those findings indicated that the Ministry and perhaps the government itself were receptive to my ideas. Although the Minister was a Dinka and a friend who was quite familiar with my views, that did not mean that Southerners generally were equally amenable. In fact, most of them were not. This was demonstrated by the fact that I learned later that a Southerner who had attended the meeting went and complained to a group of Southerners, "Francis is now saying that we are related to the Arabs."

---

23. Paper presented to the symposium on Afro-Arab Liberation and Development.

24. *Dinka Cosmology* reissued as *Dinka Worldview: Elders Reflect on the Past, Present and Future of their People*, Africa World Books, 2023 and, *Africans of Two Worlds: The Dinka in Afro-Arab Sudan* reissued as *The Changing World of the Dinka*, Africa World Books, 2022.

'Recollections of Babo Nimir'

Ithaca Press, 1982

Although *Recollections of Babo Nimir*[25] is one of the shortest of my books, it is one of the most read and appreciated in Sudan. Apart from the merits of the book, I believe the reason is that people are pleasantly surprised that I, a member of the Ngok Dinka community, would write a book about the Paramount Chief of the Missiriya Arabs, who have been in conflict with my own Ngok Dinka tribe. In fact, members of my Dinka community, including from my family, opposed the initiative. From my perspective, there were several reasons why writing a book about Nazir (Chief) Babo Nimir was the right thing to do.

First, my father and Nazir Babo Nimir were very close friends and political allies, although the power struggle and the conflict between their respective tribes negatively impacted their relations later in their life. Second, I, in my small way, had become part of their close ties. I remained close to Chief Babo even when his relations with my father were strained. Thirdly, a major principle I had learned from both my father and Babo Nimir is that in a conflict situation, a leader can best bridge conflicting positions by reaching out to the person more removed from him rather than side with the person closest to him, of course without losing sight of fairness and justice.

When I met with Nazir Babo Nimir, to interview him on the biography of my father, he asked me, "You want to write a book about your father, who is going to write a book about me?" I was deeply touched by his question because I understood it to imply that he considered me his son also. Nazir Babo had well-educated

---

25. Reissued in 2018 by the Babo Nimir family, with an Introduction by former Prime Minister, Sadig Al-Mahdi, and a Foreword by Babo Nimir's son, Sadig Babo Nimir.

children, any one of whom could have written a book about their father. But not every person writes a book about his or her father. After all, my father had many children, and yet I was the only one who wrote a book about him. I was therefore shocked when at least one of the leading members of Babo Nimir's family misconstrued his question, as a complaint that his children were not rising to the task of writing his biography. Personally, I felt honored by his question and responded instantly that I would do both and would in fact begin with the book about him. That interview was one of the most gratifying I carried out.

By then, my father had been dead for fourteen years. There was no urgency in completing his biography. Babo Nimir on the other hand was an old man who presumably did not have many more years left in life. I had to fulfill my undertaking to him within the shortest time possible. But how could I do that? I had interviewed Babo Nimir for a book I was working on, and later published as *Bonds of Silk: The Human Factor in the British Administration in the Sudan.*[26]

I thought that if I combined the interview with Nazir Babo about his life, the interview with him about my father, and the one on the British administration in the Sudan, as chapters in that order, with a substantive introduction, and produced them in English and Arabic under one cover, I would have a decent size book within a short period of time. That was precisely what I did with remarkable success.

Babo was not only a very influential Paramount Chief of a major Arab tribe but was also a national political leader, who had played an important role in the national independence movement, which made him a member of the negotiating delegations that went to Cairo and London to engage the governments of the Anglo-Egyptian Condominium Government in Sudan.

---

26. Francis Mading Deng, *Bonds of Silk: The Human Factor in the British Administration in the Sudan,* Michigan State University Press, 1990 – see p. 80.

Recollections of Babo Nimir offers remarkable insights into the role of traditional authorities in maintaining law and order and ensuring peace and security throughout what was the vast million square miles territory of the Sudan at a minimum cost. Babo Nimir compared the function of the traditional leaders and central government agents to that of a fountain pen and a lead pencil, explaining that while there is a major difference in their costs, there was no difference in the quality of what they wrote. The book also offers insight into national politics and the dynamics of party rivalry in what eventually became the common front in favor of independence. I remain very pleased and proud that I had the opportunity to produce the book.

I finished the book in Canada in time for Babo to see the bound proofs which I sent to him before the book was formally produced. Fearful that his days were probably numbered, I asked that it be handed to him immediately. I was told that Nazir Babo carried the book with him wherever he went and proudly showed it around.

I am glad that *Recollections of Babo Nimir* was reissued by the family of the late Chief in 2018, with an Introduction by former Prime Minister, Imam Sadig Al-Mahdi, and a Foreword by Sadig Babo, one of the sons of Babo Nimir. I was deeply moved by what both said not only about the importance of the book and the leadership role Nazir Babo had played for his tribe and the country, but also made laudatory comments on the contribution I had made to the cause of peace, unity, and nationhood in the country.

Sadig Babo wrote something I discouraged him from including in his Foreword because it seemed exaggerated and potentially threatening to our own family unity and solidarity. He said that my father had shared with Babo Nimir his special feelings for me and his intention to take me out of secondary school to prepare me to succeed him as Paramount Chief, Babo allegedly persuaded my father against the idea urging him to have me complete my education. Babo went on to tell my father that with my education, I would eventually become a national leader above both of them: my father and Babo himself. Knowing how much Father valued education, I could not see how he could have wanted to take me out of school.

I recalled my father telling me that my brother Bol and I had become sons of the Sudan and had gone beyond tribal leadership. He, therefore, sought my opinion on which of our other brothers I thought he should appoint to assist him in the leadership and to be prepared for the leadership of the tribe. But then I also recalled that when we were in high school, Father asked me which of us; Bol and me, was older. I told him that it was for him to tell us not we to tell him. He then said he thought I was older and that he wanted me to leave school to run for parliament. I told him that I was underage to be a member of parliament. He thought that could be arranged, presumably because determining our dates of birth was a flexible estimate. Fortunately, the issue died there.

Identity became a major preoccupation for me in my writings over the years. It has obviously been a very controversial issue since it touched on the core of the identity crisis that was tearing the country apart. Fortunately, my views on the crisis of identity became increasingly accepted over time. Even former Prime Minister Sadig Al-Mahdi, who initially saw my views as anti-Arab and anti-Islam, became more appreciative with time. In his Introduction to the second edition of *Recollections of Babo Nimir,* he wrote: "The importance of this book lies in the decisive acknowledgment and recognition of Dr. Francis Deng. He is a complete one-off–an amazing mixture of intellect, academic, and politician with a rare vision that helped shape and reshapes the political and socio-cultural space in Sudan. In his thrilling corpus of memoirs, he cast valuable light on the biographies of the leading figures of our nation, notably Nazir Babo Nimir."

Although the former Prime Minister and I have maintained cordial ties for years and always engaged in an exchange of views over pressing national issues, this was unexpected praise from him. I was deeply touched and inspired to continue in the direction he so lavishly acknowledged and praised.

'The British in the Sudan 1989-1956'
Co-editor with Robert Collins. Macmillan, 1984

Co-edited with Robert O. Collins, our collaboration was to a significant extent inspired by *Bonds of Silk: The Human Factor in British Administration in the Sudan.*[27] In a chapter to this edited volume, to which a number of authors contributed, I summarized the gist of the themes we covered. In our preface, we cited Melville Herskovits, the founding father of Africanist studies in the Western world, who made a famous observation,

"Whenever peoples having different customs come together, they modify their ways by taking something from those with whom they newly meet. They may take over much or little, according to the nature or intensity of the contact, the degree to which the two cultures have elements in common or differ in basic orientation. But they never take over or ignore all; some change is inevitable."[28]

The book is an exploration of what happened when the colonial masters and their subjects met and interacted, as representatives of two different races, cultures, backgrounds, values, and outlooks. The answer

---

27. Francis Mading Deng, *Bonds of Silk: The Human Factor in the British Administration in the Sudan,* Michigan State University Press, 1990 – see p. 80.

28. M.J. Herskovits, *The Human Factor in Changing Africa,* 1962, p. 6.

must be that they give and take and therefore influence one another. This in a sense requires correcting the one-sided emphasis on the fundamental condemnation of colonialism to consider the by-product of mutual influences of cross-cultural interaction. As we move away from the trauma of colonial domination, this aspect is likely to be more appreciated. I recalled two stories that illustrate the point.

One was told to me by K.D.D. Henderson, the former Governor of Darfur province in Western Sudan. As he left his post in Darfur, an old man approached him and said, "Mr. Henderson, you are now leaving our country and going back to your country. I am an old man, and I don't think we will meet again in this world. As for the next, my religion tells me that there is no room in Heaven for those who are not Muslims. I suspect your religion says the same about people who are not Christians. I hope they are both wrong and we will meet again in Heaven." That reflected a level of religious tolerance that he had not entertained before getting to know Henderson.

The second story occurred when my brother Bol and I took the body of our father back home amidst the first North-South civil war in which the security forces in the area were terrorizing the local populations with arrests, torture, and summary executions. Mahdi Arob, our great uncle, the oldest member of our family alive, requested to talk to us a distance from the surrounding crowd. Bol was then studying medicine in England, and I had also attended London University for post-graduate studies. Our uncle asked whether we were in contact with the British administrators who had been in the Sudan. When we answered in the affirmative, he looked positively reassured and said, "Before they left for their country, the District Commissioner came here and met with our people. He told us that they were leaving, returning to their country, but that they would keep a close watch over the situation in our country. If we failed to get along, they would be back. Please go and tell them that we have failed to get along!?" That was sadly a negative comment on our independence and paradoxically a positive reflection on colonial rule.

Although my chapter in the edited volume focused on the perspective of 'the ruled,' my interviews, which were analytically presented in *Bonds of Silk,* were conducted with three sets of representative groups: Northern Sudanese, Southern Sudanese, and British administrators. All of them reflected ambivalence about the experience. Northern Sudanese objected to the British as foreign rulers, but otherwise admired their system and mannerism of governing. Southern Sudanese admired the British administration but objected to the discriminating manner they treated the South compared to the North. The British admired the Sudanese of both the North and the South but were unhappy about the manner in which they were ungratefully and prematurely chased out of the country before completing their mission as they had planned it; and they regretted the unfair way they had treated the South in handing it over to a Northern Government of an independent Sudan that would dominate and marginalize the South.

'Seed of Redemption: A Political Novel'

Lilian Barber Press, 1986

In 1983, I turned down the assignment as Ambassador to Ethiopia. President Nimeiri had assigned me to confront the South Sudanese leaders of the new rebellion that would culminate in the creation of the Sudanese People's Liberation Movement (SPLM) and the Sudanese People's Liberation Army (SPLA). As Ambassador I would have had to support and indeed promote the position of my government against the rebels, even though they were fighting for the cause of our people against the Arab-Islamic domination of the North. I was forthright with the President. I told him that our young people were rebelling for a cause. What would I say to them? Nimeiri's response was that I should tell them that although they had a cause, they should not betray their country. Needless to say, this was not a persuasive response.

There was also the ideological difference between Sudan under Nimeiri, and Ethiopia under the Marxist President Mengistu Haile Mariam. As the Presidents did not see eye to eye ideologically, I asked Nimeiri what I should say to Haile Mariam. His answer was that I should tell him that although we disagreed, we should not allow ourselves to be used by the superpowers. That was of course was another unconvincing response. I discussed the issue at length, but Nimeiri was persistent. I initially gave in, but the more I thought about it, the more I became convinced that I should not accept the assignment.

I wrote my letter of resignation without seeking an appointment with the President. In any case, he was leaving the country for the US. From what I was told, he was visibly moved when reading my resignation. He directed the Foreign Minister to give me any posting of my choice. I told the Minister that I did not want any alternative assignment and organised my return to the US.[29]

As I flew from Khartoum via Amsterdam, I asked myself whether I was turning my back on my country. The answer was of course an unequivocal "No." What then would I do? I had no plans or any idea what I would do next. Although my wife supported my decision to resign, with a family of four young children and a wife who had given up her academic career to raise those children and support my service

29. Later, I told Dr. John Garang de Mabior, the leader of the rebel movement, about my having turned down the appointment of Ambassador to Ethiopia to avoid being forced into a confrontation with him and his fellows. He responded humorously, "You should have accepted and been Ambassador to both of us." I responded in kind by humorously reminding him of a conversation we once had in which he said that the most dangerous agent is a double agent. "You would have been an exception," he said, which made us both laugh.

to my country, I would later conclude that while reckless, I had made the right decision. In any case, I decided the first thing I would do was to put in fiction form some of the ideas about the crisis of national identity in our country that I had written in scholarly works. I wanted the message to reach the hearts and minds of the Sudanese people at the popular level. I began to outline in my mind what such a fiction might entail.

As soon as I landed in Amsterdam, I bought two legal-size writing pads, and throughout most of my flight to New York, I began writing. From time to time, the Englishman sitting next to me would ask a question. I would briefly answer him and go back to my writing. About forty minutes before landing in New York he spoke in a very determined voice, "I really must interrupt you; who are you and what are you writing about?" That was when I stopped writing and we talked until we landed.

Although I had a broad outline in mind, it is still difficult to explain how I conceived what I was writing within such a short period. It must be that the ideas had developed and consolidated over time and that I was provoked and stimulated by the fact that the positive policy developments I had supported, had written about personally and officially, and had ostensibly been endorsed at the highest levels, were being undone by the same leadership that had championed the reform agenda. *Peace and Unity: An African Achievement*,[30] which the President had proudly presented to the Summit of the OAU Heads of State and Government, had virtually been turned into a fraud by some influential spoilers. It was as though the book had been some disingenuous ploy for deluding Africa that Sudan was, at last, coming back to its African roots.

---

30. *Peace and Unity in the Sudan: An African Achievement* – see p. 64

Getting the message across through a novel form that would no longer be a monopoly of a conniving elite but would be in the public domain must have intuitively occurred to me as the next weapon available. Once I started writing, I could not stop. I cannot explain how it happened. It was as though someone was dictating to me, and I was simply writing it down. The story unfolded seamlessly. For the weeks and months that followed, I continued to write. When we went for our annual camping on Long Lake in the Adirondacks in Upper New York State with members of my wife's extended family, and I was reluctant to interrupt my writing by going, she told me that people were always free to do what they wanted and that I could write, if I wanted. I continued to write at the lake. At one point, David, the third of our four sons entered our tent and found me doing just that. "Dad, you are working! I am going to tell on you!" he said. I laughed, stopped writing, and went with him to join the group.

The *Seed of Redemption* was my first novel. In it the hero is the descendent of a Dinka woman given into slavery while pregnant, to redeem her abducted brother who was to succeed their father as the Chief of their tribe. The spiritual leaders of his family and tribe had prayed over her and prayed that she would bear the fruit of her people's redemption. The story starts as a genuine fiction and then developed into a fictionalization of known historical events that invoked the memory of Ali Abdel Latif and his colleagues, the South Sudanese young military officers who were descendants of slave soldiers and who were in the Egyptian Army of the Anglo-Egyptian Condominium Government. They staged the 1924 rebellion against British rule and called for self-determination for the Sudan.

It is ironic that when Dr. John Garang, returned to Khartoum after the second war ended, to be sworn in as First Vice President of the Republic and President of the autonomous South Sudan, the photograph of Ali Abdel Latif was placed next to his on the front facing wall of the Khartoum Hilton Hotel, where he was staying, signifying the continuation of the struggle of the Black Sudanese. I thought that it was an unwise move as it might provoke a racist reaction from the Arabized Northern population. Surprisingly, a prominent Northern Sudanese politician and scholar disagreed with me, arguing that it was an appropriate historical connection.

'The Search for Peace and Unity in the Sudan'
Co-editor with Prosser Gifford, Woodrow Wilson Press, 1987

After resigning from the government, I was offered the position of an Associate Fellow at the Woodrow Wilson International Center for Scholars. There, I helped organize a conference on ending the conflict in the Sudan. All of the Sudanese political parties were invited. All of them attended, except for the Islamic Front, which transformed itself into the Islamic Charter Front. Although the Front did not attend the Conference, they sent a copy of their Charter as one of the background documents for consideration. I also invited Former President of Nigeria, General Olusegun Obasanjo, and former African American Ambassador to the UN, Andrew Young, as Senior Statesmen, to offer advice. That conference resulted in this book, co-edited with Prosser Gifford, the Director of the Center.

The papers presented at the conference, which became chapters in the book, ranged on a variety of aspects of the conflict, from historical background to the current situation, and onto a vision into the future. The theme of identity featured significantly. Surprisingly, there seemed to be a broad agreement on the issues, including the need to separate religion from politics, except for the position of the Muslim Brothers of the National Islamic Front as reflected in their Charter, which I made available at the conference.

That book provided the basis of the initiative I undertook with General Obasanjo to mediate a resolution of the conflict, shuttling between successive governments in Khartoum and the leadership of the Sudan People's Liberation Movement.

'Bonds of Silk: The Human Factor in the British Administration of the Sudan'

Co-authored with M. W. Daly, Michigan State University Press, 1989

This book was motivated by my desire to balance the one-sided focus on the political dimension of the colonial experience by exploring the human dimension involved. I wanted to understand the dynamics of interaction between the rulers and the ruled who represented different races, cultures, religions and worldviews. What preconceptions did they have of each other before their encounter? How did they interact to one another in their official and personal relations, as masters and subjects, or as partners? What influence did they have on each other's perspectives? To what extent did their preconceptions change over the period of their relationship? What is the legacy of the colonial experience from the human perspective? What memories do they hold of the experience?

I interviewed Sudanese individuals from both the North and South, civil servants and tribal leaders, who worked with the British, and former British colonial administrators who served in both regions. The picture that emerged is strikingly human and very ambivalent. Among the Sudanese, a strong objection to foreign domination combined with great admiration for the British as efficient, fair-minded and humane rulers. In fact, the title of the book came from a tribal leader in the North who said that if it were not because they were foreign rulers, which was unacceptable on principle, he would have nothing negative to say about the British. "When they had to chain you,"he said, "they do not use iron chains; they use silk," - hence the title. The main objection of the South Sudanese was the unequal treatment of the North and the South by the British and the way they abandoned the South to the domination of the North.

The British also admired the Sudanese very highly and remember their experience with great fondness and nostalgia. They however resented what they saw as ingratitude for their service and the unceremonious manner in which they were forced to leave. From a human relations perspective, they generally were closer to Northerners than Southerners, although they felt protective of the South and regretted the way they left without a fair deal for it. At a time when colonialism stands universally condemned from a political perspective, the experience of the Sudan reveals that from a human perspective, it was a cross-culturally enriching process. I witnessed first hand in my contacts with the former British administrators in the United Kingdom the impact that experience had in their lives and the memories of profound respect and affection they still hold for their Sudanese counterparts, colleagues and friends. The book fully accomplished what I had hoped to explore and prove.

'Cry of the Owl: A Novel'
Lilian Barber Press, 1989

Seed of Redemption, received mixed reactions, highly praised by some, and criticized by others as transparently more political than fictional. Shortly after it was published, I embarked on the second novel, *Cry*

of the Owl, intent on making it more genuinely fictional, but with the same theme of the national identity crisis in the country. The novel is about two individuals who represent the extreme polar points in the crisis of national identity that divides the country between the Arab Muslim North and the African secular South. Though acutely divided by this identity cleavage, they discover at the very end of the novel that they are indeed half-brothers. The one who represents the Arab-Islamic agenda is a full-blooded Dinka who was abducted into slavery as a baby and was never recovered or found. The one who represents the African secular agenda is the product of the Arab slave master who impregnated the abducted Dinka woman during the brief period of her enslavement before she was freed by a Dinka surprise rescue attack on the slavers' camp. The pregnancy was never revealed as the time was too short to raise any suspicion. It is only through the dramatic revelations toward the end of the story that the truth surfaces.

The book was translated into Arabic under the title *Taa'ir El Shoum,* which, literally retranslated, means *Bird of Doom,* by the renowned Islamic Scholar, Professor Abdullahi Ahmed An-An'im, then a Professor of Law at Emory University. Among the Dinka, when an owl cries or makes sounds sitting on a hut or a tree near the vicinity of a home, it is considered a warning that some disaster is about to strike the family or community. The source of the impending misfortune must then be spiritually diagnosed, and appropriate measures are taken to avert the crisis.

The powerful and direct Arabic title is therefore more pessimistic than the original title. To the Dinka, the owl only alerts to danger and is not itself a source of danger, although there is some evil spell associated with its being a bearer of bad news. That is why the image of the owl among the Dinka borders between being evil and wise. The West focuses on its wisdom. The Arabic translation of the English title is more awesome. It immediately conveys the magnitude of the crisis, which the English title does not. Actually, I got to like the Arabic title as much as the English.

The novel proved to be very popular and of course controversial. One journalist whom I believed had not read the book but knew the sensitivity of the issues it dramatized called it Sudans' *Satanic Verses* and I, the Salman Rushdi of the Sudan. The book was in fact banned by the ruling Islamic regime of Omar Hassan Al-Bashir. I am probably better known for that novel in the Sudan than for any other of my numerous books. And Abdullahi An-Na'im was to tell me years later that he was more known in the Sudan as the translator of that novel than he is for his own scholarly books. The question is: Why? Although I have no answer, I believe the book achieved its intended objective of touching the hearts and minds of the Northern Sudanese who are thereby compelled to recognize the truth about their distorted self-perception.

'The Challenges of Famine Relief: Emergency Operations in Sudan'

Co-authored with Larry Minear,

The Brookings Institution Press, 1992

One of the assignments I received shortly after leaving government service was a request from the United Nations to undertake a study of the emergency operations in the Sudan during the drought-induced famine in the late 1980s. A former Swedish Ambassador was asked to do the same over emergency operations in Ethiopia. At about the same time Larry Minear and Thomas Weiss also undertook a study of Operation Lifeline, a famine relief program that began operating in

Southern Sudan in 1989. At Brookings, we decided to combine the results of our investigations and co-author a book for the Brookings Institution. That was *The Challenges of Emergency Relief* which I co-authored with Larry Minear.

The challenges of famine relief were subsumed by several dilemmas, the externality of assistance, lack of connection to the internal structures and resources, failure to build internal resilience, and exiting at the end of the emergency with no continuity to strengthen internal coping capacity to meet future exigencies.

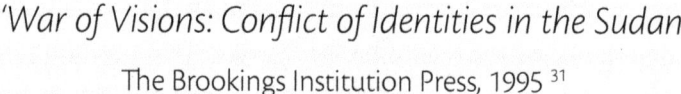

'War of Visions: Conflict of Identities in the Sudan'
The Brookings Institution Press, 1995 [31]

One of my major products at Brookings was *War of Visions: Conflict of Identities in the Sudan,* which was published by Brookings in 1995. I first conceived of the research project as one of the first Jennings Randolph Distinguished Fellows of the newly established United States Institute of Peace, (USIP), while I was still at the Woodrow Wilson Center. My working title for the book project was "Myth and Reality: The Crisis of Identity in the Sudan." The core of the thesis was the same as in my previous works on identity, although *War of Visions* is a more comprehensive account of the history of the conflict in its complex dimensions. The most critical factor is, of course, the history of slavery and the dehumanizing way it categorized people and relegated the Blacks to a sub-human status from which people could exit and be assimilated into the more respected Islamic-Arab identity. The legacy of this discriminating process of assimilation still lingers on in the Sudan to this day.

---

31. Reissued by the United States Institute of Peace Press, 2008.

A major source of information for the book was interviews with South Sudanese intellectuals, Northerners, and Southerners, unfortunately, all men. Except for a few who candidly acknowledged and articulated the crisis of identity in the country, the overwhelming response was a denial that paradoxically underscored the crisis. Northerners made the usual attempt to deny and diffuse racial differences and disguise their racism by arguing that Arabism was a cultural and not a racial concept and that the decisive factor was the Arabic language. The unwitting implication was that it was more acceptable to differentiate and discriminate on cultural than on racial grounds.

Ironically, Southerners also asserted that there was no crisis of identity, arguing that both sides knew exactly who or what they were racially or culturally. They claimed that they were Black Africans and Northerners were Arabs. They dismissed the argument that Northerners were not the Arabs they claimed to be. Their argument was that the issue was not the color of skin, but the state of mind, and that as long as Northerners considered themselves to be Arabs, they should be accepted and treated as such. The implication was that Northerners and Southerners were racially and culturally different and therefore could not form one nation. The essence of this argument was a demand for separation on the grounds that Southerners were entitled to their own nation based on their identity which was distinct from that of the North.

The position of the South was reflective of the widely held view among scholars that the determining factor in identity is what people subjectively claim to be, not what they objectively are. Of course, if subjective self-identification has no bearing on the shared space and does not impinge on the rights of others, then there might be no need to challenge the delusions of distorted self-perception. But if such distorted self-perception becomes the basis for the distribution of power and other resources as well as the enjoyment of all the rights accruing to citizens, which inevitably becomes discriminatory, then it should be challenged. People must then be made to stand in front of the mirror and ask themselves some serious questions about their appearance and recognize the discrepancy between what they claim to be and what they objectively are.

A few Northerners described the attitude of Northerners on race with a focus on the color of skin. One stated, "Black is depicted in Arabic literature as something not good. That is why people are described not as black but as brown or green. Green in the Sudan means that their *asl*, ancestral origin, is not Negroid." Another Sudanese wrote, "The first order in rank is *asfar*. This literally means "yellow" but is used interchangeably with *ahmar* to denote "whiteness." *Ahmar* literally means reddish, but it is used interchangeably to denote a range of color shades, from light to dark brown. The third-ranking is *akhdar*. This literally means green, but it is used as a polite alternative to "black." Last and least is the word *azreg* to mean "black," which is the color of *"abid,"* which means slave. In order to avoid describing themselves as *aswad,* "black," the collective Northern consciousness renamed their color *akhdar,* "green." Whereas a very dark Northerner is *akhdar,* an equally dark Southerner is bluntly *aswad,* black.

As I note in *War of Visions,* Sudanese passports never describe the holder as "black." The description used for the overwhelming number of holders is "green" the standard color of the nation in official Northern Sudanese eyes. Indeed, "green" is seen as the ideal color of skin because it reflects a brown that is not too dark, giving association with Black Africa and possibly a slave background, and not too light which would hint association with a Gypsy-type (*Halabi*) race, or connection with European Christian infidel race, *Khawaja,* which is also undesirable.

It is a paradox that people among whom the color of skin does not sharply separate racial categories, to the point that Sudanese consider themselves Arabs despite their dark color of skin, should be so conscious of shades of distinguishing colors of skin among themselves. An Egyptian diplomat, who had served in the Sudan, once told me that he had never met a people who were as conscious of skin colors as the Sudanese. And yet, the consciousness of skin colors in the Sudan carries with its ambiguities and ambivalences that make the concept fluid, flexible and tolerant, though also a discreetly distinguishing and discriminating factor, more explicit in jocular conversations than in serious designation.

War of Visions proposed three options for resolving the identity crisis in the Sudan: the creation of a national identity framework for a united New Sudan of full equality and non-discrimination on any ground; agreeing on an arrangement of unity in diversity in which the differences coexist in a loose form of differentiated unity; or outright partition. Sadly, the last option prevailed in the end.

'Preventive Diplomacy: The Case of Sudan'
African Center for Constructive Resolution of Conflicts, 1997

This book, one of the shortest of my books, was requested of me by the Africa Center for the Constructive Resolution of Disputes, (ACCORD), a South-Africa-based think tank with which I was closely associated. The book was to be the first in a series that ACCORD was planning to launch. It was also at a time when the conflict in the Sudan was drawing much attention from Africa and indeed the world.

ACCORD presented the series' authors with a conceptual framework that included the following issues: Background; Identity factors; Participants, Power, and Interests; Issue or Regime Change; Precipitants and Conditions; Analysis of the Course of Events; Hypothetical Analysis of the Course of Events; Process: Post-Conflict Peace-building; Leverage; and Lessons from the (Sudanese) Case. While I endeavored to follow the list in this framework, I tried to inject my thesis on the Sudan as reflected in my books: *Dynamics of Identification, Peace and Unity in the Sudan* and *War of Visions.*[32]

The book was launched in Cape Town at a function that was attended by President Nelson Mandela and his future wife Graca Machel and the Diplomatic Corps. The Executive Director, myself, and President Mandela made remarks in that order. What struck me the most about the event was Mandela's very gracious humility. In his remarks with his characteristic dignified modesty, he began with jokes about how Graca Machel had overshadowed him on their recent visit to China. At the end of the event, Mandela was asked to greet the cook and the serving staff. Their leader remarked how honored they were to serve him and Mandela responded with, "And I am very honored to be served by you." A prominent Egyptian lady came to him requesting to be photographed with him. "My grandchildren will not forgive me if I do not take a photo with you," the lady said. Mandela responded: "And my grandchildren too will not forgive me if I do not take a photo with you."

Mandela and I exchanged autographed copies of the book. In my copy to him, I wrote something to the effect that he was a model of leadership that exemplified the ideals of the responsibility of sovereignty. In his copy for me, he very generously referred to my attributes as a scholar, diplomat, and statesman. It was a flattering tribute far

32. See pages, 62, 64 and 84 respectively.

above what I expected or deserved. I was urged by colleagues to treasure the copy for posterity. One of the ironies of life is that treasure has disappeared. I either safeguarded the book in a safe spot where I cannot find it, gave it to someone by mistake, or the book was erroneously taken by someone.

'Their Brothers' Keepers: Report of the IGAD Resource Persons'
Inter-Africa Group, 1997

At the beginning of the IGAD initiative to mediate the conflict in the Sudan, the Addis Ababa-based Inter-Africa Group, a think tank that was engaged in activities aimed at promoting peace and security in the Sub-Region and Africa, put together a team of people they called Resource Persons to assist the process. I emerged as the Rapporteur for the team. We worked very closely with the Heads of State and Government, and Foreign Ministers of the IGAD countries. I believe we influenced the peace process and outcome in a significant way. I was asked to document our work in a book, which I called *Their Brothers' Keepers*.

At the beginning of the process, I had a crucial discussion of the situation with President Isaias Aferworke of Eritrea. I was informed that the President, who was in Washington, wanted to see me. When I went to the Ambassador's residence for the meeting, I was told that the President had only twenty minutes for the meeting, but it lasted for well over an hour and we established a solid relationship. The President would later refer to me in his meeting with the UN Secretary-General, Ban Ki-Moon, as "my good friend."

A major theme in my conversation with President Aferworke was why the SPLM/A, specifically its leader, Dr. John Garang, called for unity in a country that so blatantly discriminated against its people. The President told me that as refugees in the Sudan, they closely observed racial and ethnic stratification. The first-class citizens were the Arabs of central Sudan. Second, came the Muslim non-Arab Sudanese in the marginalized regions of the North. Then came the refugees from Ethiopia and Eritrea. Southerners came last as fourth-class citizens. How could that be a basis for national unity? I added that if one considered the *Falata*, the Muslims from Nigeria and other countries of West Africa, they would probably come fourth, placing Southerners in the fifth order of racial stratification.

I, however, explained to the President that the position of the SPLA, as represented by Garang, was more complicated than one of simple commitment to national unity. I explained the history of racial stratification in the Sudan and how it divided the country on the basis of myths of identity that made Arabized Africans, who are only partially Arab, and who constitute a minority, dominate the overwhelming majority of the country, who were Black Africans. The vision of the SPLM/A, and particularly Garang, was to explode the myths of identity and liberate all Sudanese from discrimination on the bases of race, ethnicity, religion, culture, and gender. That was the core of the New Sudan Vision. President Aferworke was fully persuaded.

President Aferworke reminded me that we had met in Khartoum when I was Minister of State for Foreign Affairs and he was a 'fugitive,' as he put it. I was then leading the Sudanese delegation in bilateral talks with Ethiopia in which the cause of Eritrea featured prominently. We supported Eritrea and were negotiating with Ethiopia on an appropriate solution to the Eritrean problem. I personally wanted to negotiate a solution that would give the Eritreans full rights of self-government within the framework of national unity, an arrangement comparable to that of the 1972 Addis Ababa Agreement, which

Ethiopia helped broker. Although President Nimeiri agreed with my approach, for the Eritreans and most of my colleagues in the government, that was unacceptable.

As he recalled, Aferworke and I first met when I was briefing the Eritrean leaders in Khartoum on my efforts on their behalf, which was not acceptable to them. As I recall, they thanked me for my efforts but told me that the future of Eritrea could only be determined by the Eritreans themselves. The Eritreans indeed eventually did that by gaining their independence from Ethiopia, through armed struggle, on May 24th, 1993.

An interesting aspect of IGAD mediation in the Sudan is that it was requested by the Sudanese leaders as a favor from Eritrean and Ethiopian allies whom they had supported in overthrowing President Mengistu Haile Mariam and whom they expected to support them in return. But the Eritrean and Ethiopian leaders were people who had fought for the ideals of liberty and equality in their country and who had witnessed closely the racial, religious, and cultural discrimination the people of South Sudan were experiencing in their own country. Their response to the request of their Sudanese allies was to accept to mediate, but only by seriously addressing the genuine grievances of the people of South Sudan.

In their Declaration of Principles, (DoP), to which our Resource Group contributed in shaping, the IGAD mediators stipulated that the unity of the Sudan must be a priority, but that the grievances of the people of South Sudan had to be addressed. They argued that Southerners had not been parties to the self-determination that achieved Sudan's independence. South Sudanese were therefore entitled to the right of self-determination. And while the unity of the Sudan should be the preferred option, a framework for equitable unity must first be agreed upon as a precondition. The separation of religion and state must be a central element in creating a unity framework. Otherwise, Southerners were entitled to opt for secession.

The Government of the Sudan initially opposed the DoP, but the prolonged mediation process that progressively involved key partners in Africa and the international community, including the Troika countries of Norway, the United Kingdom, and the United States, as well as the United Nations, culminated in the Comprehensive Peace Agreement, (CPA). The CPA granted the South the right of self-determination through a referendum. That right was to be exercised after a six-year interim period. The options would be to maintain unity within an interim framework of 'One Country, Two Systems,' proposed by the Task Force on US-Sudan Policy to End Sudan's War, which I co-chaired with Stephen J. Morrison of the Center for Strategic and International Studies in Washington. After the interim period, the people of the South would decide through a referendum whether to retain that arrangement or opt for independence as a sovereign State. That right was overwhelmingly exercised in favor of independence, declared on July 9, 2011.

'Partners for Peace:
An Initiative on the Sudan with General Obasanjo'
Inter-Africa Group, 1998

Shortly after the book, *The Search for Peace and Unity in the Sudan*[33] was published, I got a surprise phone call from General Obasanjo asking about a follow-up to the conference. When I told him that the book was out, he said we should not let it gather dust on the

---

33. Francis Mading Deng and Prosser Gifford, *The Search for Peace and Unity in the Sudan*, Wilson Center Press, 1987 - see p. 79.

shelves, but should use it as a basis for a peace initiative to end the war. That is how we began our peace-making diplomacy. *Partners for Peace* was the documentation of our efforts as we engaged the warring parties.

Obasanjo and I shuttled between successive Governments in Khartoum and the leadership of the SPLM/A in Addis Ababa and the IGAD region. Two specific experiences in the process are worth recalling. The first had to do with a meeting we were organizing between Prime Minister Sadiq Al-Mahdi and Dr. Garang. We arranged the meeting very diligently, but discreetly. The meeting was to be hosted by the Former President of Switzerland at some beautiful resort area. The President of Switzerland would make available his plane to take Garang from any location in the region. We worked on the agenda and developed a framework for the discussions and guidelines for a possible agreement. When the arrangements were all set, the Prime Minister announced that he was taking off a few days to rest. The Swiss plane was ready to pick up Garang. I kept in close contact with the Director of his office, Deng Alor, who happened to be my cousin, to make sure that there would be no last-minute surprise. But sadly there was.

The night before Garang was to be picked up, we received a message from him, through Deng Alor, that he would not be able to make the planned meeting. The reason he gave was that while he had agreed with the principle of the meeting, he had not agreed to a date or a venue. In any case, he was deep in the jungles of South Sudan and could not make it within the specified time and location for pick-up. To my pleasant surprise, Deng Alor courageously showed me copies of the messages he had exchanged with Garang to refute the claim that he had not agreed to the date and the venue. We were outraged. I drafted an angry letter that was tantamount to a break with a man whose leadership I had fully supported and whose vision for the country I shared. Garang was indeed my friend.

Obasanjo, after initially endorsing the letter, changed his mind and suggested that we should sleep over the letter before sending it. The following morning, his position had softened. He argued that we should appreciate Garang's position as Commander-in-Chief who was fighting a war. Obasanjo had fought and won the Biafra war in Nigeria (1967-1970). I, therefore, realized that he was speaking from an empathy rooted in experience and agreed to change the tone of the letter, though not the substance of our disappointment. Interestingly enough, the Prime Minister was more understanding of Garang's position than we were, but for a different reason. He thought that President Mengistu Haile Mariam of Ethiopia, who hosted and supported the rebel movement, obviously did not support the peace initiative and Garang could not afford to alienate his benefactors.

The other incident was with President Omar Hassan Al-Bashir, the leader of the Islamist Revolution that had overthrown the government of the elected Prime Minister. Three months after his take-over, and following a meeting with Garang in Addis Ababa, I decided to visit Khartoum on my way back to the United States. Garang and my friend Bona Malual, with whom I worked closely on the affairs of the Sudan, had been in the Addis meeting and advised me against going to Khartoum, as they were afraid for my security. But I insisted that talking to all sides was part of my principle in the search for peace. In Khartoum, and with the facilitation of Colonel Martin Machel, a member of the Revolution Command Council, I had a series of meetings with all the Council members and was even granted the request, albeit with considerable hesitation, to visit the former Prime Minister Sadig Al-Mahdi and senior members of his government in the infamous Kober Prison where they were detained. Colonel Bakri Hassan Saleh, who was in charge of security, escorted me to Kober. Colonel Bakri jokingly told me that being allowed to visit the political detainees was their investment into the future and that they hoped I would visit them in prison when their turn came. Their turn ironically did indeed come thirty years later and I visited Al-Bashir and Bakri in the same Kober prison.[34]

I was persuaded to address a conference that was discussing war and peace issues, which I did with surprising frankness that generated much controversy, with some appreciative and others critical of my being given the platform at all, arguing, "This is Garang himself." My diplomatic passport was withdrawn on the pretext that diplomatic passports be given only to active Sudanese diplomats, which I no longer was. It was however returned shortly after. Although my discussions with the leaders and talk at the conference were contentious, the visit was overall very successful.

Shortly after my Khartoum visit, President Al-Bashir sent two of the members of his Revolution Command Council, Colonel Martin Machueib and Colonel Bakri Hassan Saleh, to meet with me in London and extend to me an invitation to renew our peace initiative with General Obasanjo. After the meeting in London, I was to proceed to Khartoum to plan the details of our moves. We agreed to visit Bona Malual, who was then residing in Oxford. As a well-known critic of the regime we wanted to involve him in the discussion. Bona Malual had attended the Woodrow Wilson conference with the political parties, and he and I were working closely on the problems of the Sudan. Bona was even more hardline than me in our candid discussion with the colonels. I told them that while we would be ready to resume

---

34. More on this story on p. 433.

our peace initiative, there had to be some promising grounds for the initiative to have any promise of success. I said we would reflect and monitor the developments for an appropriate time for our intercession.

The London meeting was to be secret, but it was leaked in the media. On my way back to the United States, I happened to be on the same flight with the Assistant Secretary of State for African Affairs, with whom I was working closely in Washington. He had seen the leaked news of our meeting. He suggested that we meet at the State Department to discuss possible ways of seizing the opportunity to engage the new regime. In our discussions in Washington, the Assistant Secretary of State surprised me with a proposal. He said that if the regime was serious in its proposal of a federal system, and if the SPLM/A was sincere about its commitment to unity on a mutually acceptable basis, we should end the war by asking the government to withdraw its troops from the South and make the SPLM/A undertake not to exploit that to pursue a separatist agenda. At first, I dismissed the idea as outrageous and obviously unacceptable to either side of the conflict. But the more I thought about it, the more I found the idea intriguing and a potential ground for bringing an immediate end to the war. We agreed to pursue the proposal but to present it to the parties as my idea which I was confident the United States government would support.

I called Obasanjo and persuaded him to support the idea and that we should go to the parties together to transmit the proposal. I joined him in Lagos. He was able to obtain the Presidential plane and we flew to the region. Our first stop was Khartoum, where we were very well received. We adjusted the word from troops 'withdrawal' to 'disengagement.' Al-Bashir suspiciously asked what 'disengagement' meant. We gave an honest answer that amounted to withdrawal without the word. The proposal was not rejected outright; our senior statesman,

Abel Alier, and even some of the government leaders welcomed it in the hope that it would end the war.

In Addis Ababa, we presented the proposal to Dr. John Garang with three of his fellow commanders, Dr. Riek Machar, Dr. Lam Akol, and Deng Alor. After our presentation, Garang asked Machar who was next to him in seniority, what he thought. To our utter surprise, Machar said that since they were committed to the unity of the country, they should not support a proposal that might be construed as separatist. Garang then turned to Lam Akol, who said that his position was the same with that of Machar. It was the turn of Deng Alor, my cousin. Deng Alor's response was prudently, "No comment." Garang then concluded by saying that since they were fighting to free their land, why would they reject a proposal that would free the land peacefully and end the killing? He however objected to our being used as the messengers, as we were obviously identified with their cause. If the US really wanted to propose that solution, they should take it to the parties directly themselves. Ironically, the two commanders, who opposed the idea as separatist, would later rebel against Garang and call for the right of self-determination with the objective of South Sudan's independence. When I later had the opportunity to ask them separately about that contradiction, Riek bowed his head in silence while Lam said he was towing the party's line.

When we returned to Washington to report back, we found that the idea had become more controversial than had been originally envisaged. Some generals in the Pentagon opposed it. Even in the State Department, there were apparent differences. The US Charge' in Khartoum, who was in Washington at the time, came to see me at the Brookings Institution and said that if he were to follow up the proposal as US policy, he should be prepared to be kicked out of the country. He however said that if that was the policy, the US should be more transparent about it as their initiative.

The idea was killed, replaced by the US proposing instead a separation of forces by which the parties would withdraw their troops to specified distances out of Juba, an idea which both parties dismissed. I would later be blamed by Khartoum as having initiated the disengagement idea with a separatist objective in mind.

'Sudan: From Genocidal Wars to the Frontiers of Peace and Unity'

Institute of International Humanitarian Affairs, Fordham University,

Occasional Paper, No 3 September 2006

While this booklet provides an overview of the Sudanese conflict, I wrote it at a time when the international community was focused on the crisis situation in Darfur, where allegations of genocide were being rampantly made. The paper tried to argue several points. First that the crisis in Darfur should not be approached in isolation from what was happening in the country as a whole and any solutions to the myriad crises in the country had to be approached comprehensively. Second, genocide had to be seen as an extreme form of identity-related conflict, resulting not so much from mere differences, but from how those differences are managed. The conflicts in the Sudan were based on the mismanagement of diversity which accorded some racial, ethnic, religious, and cultural groups the dignity of being the in-groups, who enjoyed the rights of citizenship, while other groups were discriminated against, marginalized, excluded, and denigrated as out-groups. The solution therefore could only be found in constructive management of diversity to promote full equality of citizenship without discrimination on any ground. Third, the conflicting parties needed the mediating role of regional and international partners. Their humanitarian and mediation involvement should not be blocked by the negative use of sovereignty as a barricade against external involvement. Sovereignty must be perceived positively as a concept of state responsibility to protect and assist its citizens, if need be, with the assistance of the international community. In a sense, this was an advocacy for the New Sudan Vision.

The paper also argued for prioritizing sub-regional and regional responses to crises. Given its vast territory of nearly a million square miles, with ten neighbors, and separated from two additional neighbors, Saudi Arabia and Yemen, only by the Red Sea, Sudan needed regional cooperation in addressing internal problems that spill over these borders and affects the peace and security of the neighboring countries. Considering the reluctance of the major countries to put their young men and women in harm's way in third-world countries, the role of regional actors, reinforced by international support as needed, was becoming increasingly imperative.

'New Sudan in the Making?'
Editor, Red Sea Press, 2010

Despite my optimism about an evolving unifying national identity, I began to recognize that the situation in the Sudan was far more complex than I had realized and this was first brought home to me by a colleague in the Ministry of Foreign Affairs who told me in reaction to *Dynamics of Identification*,[35] that Arabism and Islam were too

---

35. Francis Mading Deng, *Dynamics of Identification: A Basis for National Integration*, Khartoum University Press, 1973 – see p. 62.

deeply rooted in the Sudan to be easily changed. And he was right, as Nimeiri's own political maneuvers and Al-Bashir's Islamic theological entrenchment would eventually demonstrate.

But my conviction persisted as I reflected in my two novels: *Seed of Redemption*[36] and *Cry of the Owl* [37] and later in the book: *War of Visions: Conflict of Identities in the Sudan.*[38] Nevertheless, I began to acknowledge that we were confronted with a situation where we had to choose from three options: creating a new identity framework of equality; coexisting in our diversity or an outright partitioning of the country. I titled the book *New Sudan in the Making* indicating that the Vision of a New Sudan was incrementally emerging. When I realized that this was not as certain as I had hoped and indeed anticipated, I caught up with the production process and changed the title by adding a question mark at the end. The book was then published under the title, *New Sudan in the Making?*

When I first conceived of the book as an edited volume to which many Sudanese thinkers, scholars and politicians would contribute chapters, I was quite optimistic about the prospect of building a new, restructured, progressive Sudan with which all Sudanese from all regions of the country would identify on equal footing. I assumed that the country was already on its way toward that destiny. The book was therefore a comprehensive review of where the country had started, where it was at the time the book was being written, and where it was clearly headed. The various chapters complemented each other to complete the picture of the past, present, and prospective future.

---

36. Francis Mading Deng, *Seed of Redemption: A Political Novel,* Lilian Bar- ber Press, 1986 – see p. 75.

37. Francis Mading Deng, *Cry of the Owl: A Novel,* Lilian Barber Press, 1989 – see p. 81.

38. Francis M. Deng, *War of Visions: Conflict of Identities in the Sudan,* The Brookings Institution Press, 1995 – see p. 84.

When I added the question mark to the title, I was becoming less certain about the distance from the destination, but the question itself indicated that I had not lost confidence in the merits of that destination. Far from it, the picture painted in the chapters of the book indicated that the country had made considerable progress toward its desired goal. The fact that we had not yet arrived at the destination was merely a failure in degree not in the value of the progress made and the certainty of the ultimate goal. Sudan would continue to be challenged by the Vision of the New Sudan.

Furthermore, the independence of South Sudan did not mean that the Vision of a New Sudan could not apply to the new nation. The principles of full equality within a national identity framework that allows all groups to enjoy the rights of citizenship without discrimination on any ground apply universally to all countries characterized by the diversity of race, ethnicity, religion, or culture. My extensive travels around the world in connection with my two UN mandates on internal displacement and genocide prevention revealed to me that there is hardly any country in the world that is monolithically free of some elements of diversity. The experience of South Sudan, since independence, demonstrates, that the Vision of New Sudan is still as valid as it was, and still is, in the Old Sudan.

'Sudan at the Brink: Self-determination and National Unity'
Fordham University Press, 2010

As the date for the referendum of South Sudan was approaching and international concern about the risks involved for regional and international communities should the South opt for secession was rising, the United Nations Mission in Sudan organized a symposium in Khartoum to discuss ways in which the unity option might be pursued. I was asked to give the keynote address. At first, I resisted because I thought that it was too late to make unity attractive. I was however urged to make the address and say precisely what I thought. I did. But while predicting a vote for secession, I argued that the only way to give unity a chance was to immediately implement a system of 'One Country, Multiple Systems,' that would expand the formula of 'One Country, Two Systems,' proposed by the Task Force on US Policy on Ending the War in Sudan, which the Center for Strategic and International Studies in Washington had formed and which I had co-chaired. I suggested that the formula which was initially intended for North-South conflict be applied to all the five regions of the country, North, South, East, West, and Center, each one governing itself autonomously with all equitably sharing the power at the center.

After the Symposium, I discussed the idea with Secretary-General Ban Ki-Moon who had reservations. He thought that 'One Country, Two Systems' was precarious enough and that 'One Country, Multiple Systems' would be worse. But he asked me to prepare a note for him on my proposal. I then put together a short book comprising my presentation to the Khartoum Symposium, my note to the Secretary-General, and the 1989 key-note address I made to the 1969 conference on peace issues by the Islamist Revolution of National Salvation in which I advocated the Vision of the New Secular Sudan or accept loose coexistence or expect the outright partition of the country.

Although I predicted separation as unavoidable, I argued that unity and secession were degrees of ongoing relations that could be strengthened or weakened according to the will of the leaders and the people. With the right systems in place in the Sudan and South Sudan, bilateral relations could be improved to the level of close association.

'Sudan's Genocidal Wars'

in 'Sudan's Killing Fields: Political Violence and Fragmentation'

By Laura N. Beny and Sandra Hale, The Red Sea Press, 2015

This is a wide-ranging discussion of the wars of identity that incrementally affected virtually all regions of the Sudan, with the crisis of identity as the root causes and the Vision of a New Sudan of inclusivity and equality as the long-term solution.

'Bound by Conflict: Dilemmas of the Two Sudans'

In collaboration with Daniel J. Deng,

Fordham University Press, 2016

The research for this book was undertaken with funding from USAID and the State Department to assess the process of implementation of the CPA. The research process entailed several field missions to the country and the region. It became quite apparent from the start that the process of implementation was facing serious challenges that not only made the interim period of shared national government quite dysfunctional but that unity was not being made attractive as stipulated in the agreement. Secession, therefore, seemed inevitable.

I also went to Abyei and the border regions of South Kordofan and the Blue Nile, which had joined the South in the liberation struggle for a New Sudan but had been left in their marginalized position in the North by the CPA, with a vague stipulation that their views would be sought on their administrative status within the unity of the Sudan. That was not done. During my visits to the two regions, I witnessed intense debate in the communities on how they identified themselves. It was clear that people strongly identified themselves as Africans with more in common with the South than had previously been the case. The South was seen as an older brother who could not abandon a younger brother in danger. They argued that they had fought together with the South, had died in the South, and continued to be in the leadership of the SPLM. How could the South become independent and abandon them in the North? They however hoped to get the support of an independent South Sudan in their continued struggle. But if that happened, Sudan would almost certainly undermine the independence of South Sudan by recruiting and deploying South Sudanese tribal militias against the government of South Sudan, which eventually did indeed happen.

After the independence of South Sudan, war broke out in less than two years, proving right those who had opposed the independence of the South. In the case of the Sudan, this was a self-fulfilling prophesy as it recruited, trained, armed, and deployed tribal militias to destabilize South Sudan to prove their earlier arguments against secession. I revised and updated my reports under the project into this book with a thesis that despite the secession of the South, the two countries were still bound together by conflicts that spill over their borders and involve them by proxy, with each accusing the other of supporting its armed opposition groups. The policy implication of the study was that the two needed to cooperate with each other to solve their internal problems in order to improve their bilateral relations. In the book, I reiterated the point I made in *Sudan at the Brink*,[39] that unity and separation are degrees of an ongoing relationship that could be strengthened or weakened according to the will of the people and their leaders. The challenge then was how to turn being "bound

---

39. Francis Mading Deng, *Sudan at the Brink: Self-determination and National Unity*, Fordham University Press, 2010 – see p. 101.

by conflict," to being "bonded by solutions," through cooperation in solving each other's internal conflicts.

When the book was published, I was the Permanent Representative of the newly independent Nation of South Sudan to the United Nations. I made many statements on the situation in South Sudan and relations between the Two Sudans, including the contested area of Abyei.

'Reflections on South Sudan's National Dialogue'
United Nations Development Programme (UNDP), 2018

This book was the outcome of developments in South Sudan that had taken the country to a crossroads, poised between the threat of a slide back to war and devastation, and a constructive march toward the consolidation of peace, security, reconstruction, and development. The challenge is primarily internal, but it is inextricably connected to relations with the Sudan, the sub-regional organization IGAD, the African Union, and the international community, acting bilaterally, multilaterally, and through the UN playing the key mediating role.

Internally, the two major processes taken in response to the developments were the Forum for the Revitalization of the 2015 Agreement for the Resolution of Conflict in South Sudan (ARCSS) that erupted in 2013, and the National Dialogue which the President of the Republic, Salva Kiir Mayardit, declared in December 2016, and formally launched in May 2017, with the formation of a Steering Committee. I was appointed Deputy Rapporteur and the spokesman of the National Dialogue and was also given the responsibility of ensuring the quality of the National Dialogue documents. I was also involved in the Revitalized Peace Process representing the category of Eminent Persons with Professor Moses Machar, former Vice President in the Sudan before partition.

The Steering Committee produced a series of documents that outlined the root causes of the crises afflicting the country; shared the experiences of other countries that had carried out national dialogues; compiled the views of the people in the reports of the 15 subcommittees that conducted grassroots and specialized consultations throughout the country; proposed guidelines for re-organizing the state; developed principles for comprehensively addressing the concerns of the people in a permanent constitution for South Sudan, and formulated a strategy document calling for national action in the implementation of the recommendations of the National Dialogue.

As I was involved in both processes, I consistently made the point that the South Sudan National Dialogue and the Revitalization of the 2015 Peace Agreement were complementary and mutually reinforcing. Both processes aimed at stopping the war that was resumed in 2016, but while the revitalized agreement, taken as a whole, shared the same long-term goals with the National Dialogue, its immediate priority was to end the violence through security arrangements and power-sharing as first steps toward more comprehensive aspects of statecraft and nation-building, with the leverage of regional and international support. National Dialogue, on the other hand, was a top-down and bottom-up process that aimed at consolidating peace, security, stability, and development throughout South Sudan. Although the Revitalized Peace Agreement (RPA) was comprehensive in its substantive chapters, the immediate focus of the peace process was largely centralized on the warring parties and their leaders. National Dialogue on the other hand was a comprehensive process in its coverage of both issues and levels of participation.

The basis for their complementarity was therefore quite obvious. And yet, both sides resisted complementarity, sometimes vehemently, as they suspected each other of undermining their work. It took me a long time and intense efforts to persuade both sides to see and accept the potential value of complementarity and cooperation. Even then, efforts to realize that potential never materialized.

Since the work of the National Dialogue went on for over four years, *Reflections on South Sudan National Dialogue* was an interim document.[40]

'Visitations: Conversations with the Ghost of the Chairman'

Red Sea Press, 2020

Although *Visitations: Conversations with the Ghost of the Chairman* is a merger of fact and fiction, popularly known as "faction." The Chairman is easily detectable as Dr. John Garang de Mabior, the late Chairman of the SPLM and Commander-in-Chief of its Army, the SPLA, and the narrator of the story is myself.

Dr. Garang and I developed a close friendship that was grounded in our intellectual pursuits and a determined passion to articulate and adopt a positive response to the challenges facing our people in modern Sudan. When the fictionalized narrator was under heavy medication during a post-operation recovery at home, the drugs triggered hallucinations in his mind that ushered in visitations from his old friend, who had earlier appeared to him in a dream and whom he obviously missed deeply and wished would come back again. The reconnection to the spirit of the Chairman paved the way for the extensive recollections of their shared or complementary experiences that make for the compelling story narrated in this book.

The ideas of Garang and those of the narrator initially ran parallel to each other, but in due course converged around their people's struggle

---

40. The five volumes of the National Dialogue report was published in 2022 with the support of the Office of the United Nations Development Program in South Sudan. The Foreword for the report, written by Francis Mading Deng and Bona Malwal Madut, is listed on p. 205.

in the framework of the Vision for a New Sudan. The reader also gains insight into the Sudanese politics of identity and how these men approached it from their differing standpoints of a liberation leader and a scholar diplomat. At some point, the two began to collaborate more closely to promote the struggle and the vision internationally. Lastly, the story leads into the developments since the tragic death of Garang in a helicopter crash and the theatre of South Sudanese post-independence crises, chronicled through the visitations of the Chairman and the conversations between the two friends.

 ## 'From Bound by Conflict to Bonded by Solutions, A Sequel'[41]

This book was in essence documentation of the process envisaged in *Bound by Conflict* [42] which advocated cooperation between the two governments of Sudan and South Sudan in helping resolve their internal conflicts and thereby become "bonded by solutions." Most conflicts in the subregion of the Inter-Governmental Authority for Development, (IGAD), are internally based; but they spill across the borders to generate conflicts between neighbors and threaten regional peace and security. The title of this book, *From Bound by Conflicts to Bonded by Solutions,* invokes a normative principle that horizontally and vertically applies to all social and political entities, including family, community, tribe, nation, and organizations, governmental and non-governmental, regional and international. A major challenge in all these contexts is whether to be divided and torn apart by conflicts that paradoxically keep the parties negatively bound together or be "bonded by solutions" to those conflicts by cooperating in the process.

---

41. Publication pending.

42. Francis M. Deng in collaboration with Daniel J. Deng, *Bound by Conflict: Dilemmas of the Two Sudans,* Fordham University Press, 2016 – see p. 103.

Ultimately, this poses a challenging choice between keeping those perceived as outsiders from interfering in the internal affairs of the entity concerned and cooperating with them to help in the search for mutually beneficial solutions.

At the most immediate level of a local social unit or community, it is a matter of mutual support among neighbors as the book *Their Brothers' Keepers*,[43] that wrote about the IGAD peace initiative that eventually achieved the 2005 CPA. In the broadest context of relations among nations, it is a choice between negatively asserting sovereignty as a barricade against foreign interference in the internal affairs of a country, or cooperating regionally and internationally by stipulating *sovereignty as responsibility*, a positive concept of shared responsibility involving partnership to resolve problems in the mutual interest of promoting peace and security comprehensively.

This book focuses on the experience of the Two Sudans to substantiate the thesis that resolving internal and interstate conflicts requires shifting from confrontation to cooperation in addressing the dilemma of being "bound by conflict," (as described in my 2016 book), to become positively "bonded by solutions," which this study sought to substantiate.

Both internal conflicts and the regional proxy wars they trigger are nearly always identity-related, whether the differences involved are racial, ethnic, 'tribal,' religious, cultural, or territorial. What generates conflict is not the mere differences based on these factors, but the fact that the differences are mismanaged. This mismanagement often dichotomizes populations into in-groups, who are presumed to enjoy the rights of citizenship, and out-groups, often victims of discrimination, marginalization, exclusion, and denial of the rights that should accrue from citizenship. The policy implication of this

---

43. Francis Mading Deng, *Their Brothers' Keepers: Report of the IGAD Resource Persons*, Inter-Africa Group, 1997 - see p. 89.

analysis is to adopt strategies for the constructive management of diversity to promote inclusivity, equality, non-discrimination, and enjoyment of the rights of citizenship.

This study aims at several interrelated objectives. The first and overarching objective is to reverse the current trend of internal and inter-state confrontation resulting from domestic conflicts that cross international borders to negatively bind neighboring countries in mutual animosity and acrimony and to foster instead constructive bonds of cooperation in addressing each other's internal conflicts and thereby promoting peace and security within, between, and among neighboring members of the sub-regional organization, the Inter-Governmental Authority for Development, (IGAD).

The second objective of the study is to understand the root causes of these internal conflicts, primarily from the perspective of forms of identity, including race, ethnicity, religion, and culture, and how they cross the borders to affect bilateral and regional relations, endangering regional and international peace and security.

The third objective of the study is to develop strategies for the prevention, management, and resolution of the conflicts involved and their negative impact on bilateral relations and regional, and ultimately international peace and security, primarily through cooperation in developing strategies for constructive management of diversity.

The study places these internal and regional dynamics into the wider international normative framework by examining some major areas of concern. Among these is the global quest for the protection of human rights and the related humanitarian issues pertaining to the plight of internally displaced populations. These concerns ultimately relate to the need to recast sovereignty from being perceived as a barricade against international interference in the internal affairs of a country to being stipulated positively as a concept of state responsibility for its national population, with the complementary support of the international community as needed.

These themes break the chapters of the book into five parts: Part One: Conceptual Framework, which covers the policy agenda for the region; Part Two: National Context, which deals with specific national issues of governance that pertain to conflicts; Part Three: Regional Dynamics, gives examples of inter-state conflicts emanating primarily from shared communities and the linkages created by internal conflicts spilling over the borders; Part Four: Global Issues, presents international phenomena and related norms that are connected with internal and regional conflicts; and Part Five: Two Sudans in Perspective, places in regional perspective the crises within and between the Two Sudans.

The book is based on two different methodological approaches. My own chapters build on policy studies and professional work-related experiences. The chapters by Abraham A. Awolich and the chapter co-authored by Daniel Jok M. Deng and myself are based on more standard scholarly research. I hope the reader finds these approaches complementary and mutually reinforcing.

C. Regional Level

'Human Rights in Africa: A Cross-Cultural Perspective'
Co-editor with Abdullahi Ahmed An-Na'im,

The Brookings Institution Press, 1990

While I was at the Wilson Center, I was joined by Abdullahi Ahmed An-An'im as a Fellow. An-Na'im is a renowned human rights schol-ar-activist and one of the leaders of the liberal Islamic Republic Brotherhood. It had always been my view that it was wrong to approach human rights as an imposition by the West and alien to non-Western societies and cultures. Motivated by my interest in Dinka culture and related religious values, and mindful of the prejudice against African traditional religions as 'primitive,' I proposed that we hold a conference on cross-cultural perspectives on human rights in Africa, where different cultures and religions coexist and interact. And indeed, the conference was attended by scholars with expertise on the human rights concepts of different cultures and religions. *Human Rights in Africa: A Cross-Cultural Perspective* demonstrates that there is a contextualized, universal legitimacy to the concept of human rights.

'Conflict Resolution in Africa'

Co-editor with I. William Zartman, Introduction

By Former President of Nigeria, General Olusegun Obasanjo.

The Brookings Institution Press, 1991

In developing and establishing the African Studies Program at The Brookings Institution as the Cold War was coming to an end, we addressed a set of questions: What are the priority areas of concern in Africa that need scholarly analysis, with policy implications, capable of practical application? What will be the likely implication of the end of the Cold War for the policy study of these issues for practical application in the field?

The answer to the first question was obvious. The African policy areas that ready came to mind were: prevention, management, and resolution of conflicts; democratic governance based on popular partic- ipation; respect for fundamental rights and civil liberties; and gender equality; and environmental integrity. Conflict prevention, manage- ment, and resolution topped the list.

It is widely recognized that domestic and regional conflicts in Africa pose challenging issues for scholars and policy analysts. Although they are of less strategic interest to the major powers compared to the security concerns of these powers, the destruction and humanitarian suffering they impose on the populations are matters of international concern. These conflicts inflict a heavy toll in terms of war damage to productivity, scarce resources diverted to armaments and the military, and the resulting insecurity, displacement internally and externally, and destruction to the environment.

Concerning the implications of the end of the Cold War, the starting point was to recall that in Africa, as was indeed the case everywhere, conflicts, both internal and regional, and response to their humanitarian consequences, were approached as part of the proxy wars of the superpowers. States depended on the superpowers for their prevention, management, and resolution and for responding to their humanitarian consequences.

The end of the Cold War would have the positive effect that the strategic interests of the superpowers in the conflicts around the world would cease and conflicts would then be seen in their proper national or regional contexts. But responsibility for managing and resolving conflicts and responding to their humanitarian consequences would have to be reapportioned accordingly to give priority to the countries and regions concerned. But as human rights and humanitarian concerns would still engage the international community, this shift would not mean that States were free to do whatever they wanted to do internally, and shield themselves from the scrutiny and intervention of the international community.

We began the program at The Brookings Institution with a research conference on conflict analysis in October 1989 that involved leading African, American, and U.S. scholars in the field to clarify the pertinent conceptual issues that should be considered by the program. The chapters of this book comprise the papers presented at the conference in which the experts reviewed the scholarship on conflict resolution in Africa in light of current changes on the international scene, assess the potential implications of these changes for regional conflicts, analyze the specific issues involved in African conflicts, evaluate the prospects for conflict prevention, management, and resolution, and recommend case studies and themes for further, long term research. I coedited the volume with Professor I. William Zartman, with an introduction by Former President of Nigeria, General Olusegun Obasanjo.

A series of regional and country-specific studies that included East Africa, West Africa, Southern Africa, and the Sudan were subsequently conducted by experts in the field and produced in books published by Brookings. The regional list included: *The New Is Not Yet Born: Conflict Resolution in Southern Africa* by Thomas Ohlsson and Stephen John Stedman, with Robert Davies,[44] *Governance as Conflict Management: Politics and Violence in West Africa*,[45] and an unpublished volume prepared on East Africa. Several published country-specific studies included: *South Africa: The Struggle for a New Order*,[46] *Somalia: State Collapse: Multilateral Intervention and Strategies for Political Reconstruction*,[47] *Democracy and Development in Africa*,[48] and *Managing Ethnic Conflicts in Africa*,[49] as well as my own work including *War of*

44. Thomas Ohlsson and Stephen John Stedman, with Robert Davies, *The New Is Not Yet Born: Conflict Resolution in Southern Africa*, Brooking Institute Press, 1994.

45. *Governance as Conflict Management: Politics and Violence in West Africa*, edited by I. William Zartman, Brookings Institute Press, 1997.

46. Marina Ottaway, *South Africa: The Struggle for a New Order*, Brookings Institute Press, 1993.

47. Terrence Lyons and Ahmed I. Samatar, *Somalia: State Collapse: Multilateral Intervention and Strategies for Political Reconstruction*, Brookings Institute Press, 1995.

48. Claude Ake, *Democracy and Development in Africa*, Brooking Institute Press, 1996.

49. Donald Rothschild, *Managing Ethnic Conflicts in Africa*, Brookings Insitute Press, 1997.

Visions: Conflict of Identities in the Sudan,[50] *Human Rights in Africa: A Cross-Cultural Perspective*[51] and *Challenges of Famine Relief.*[52]

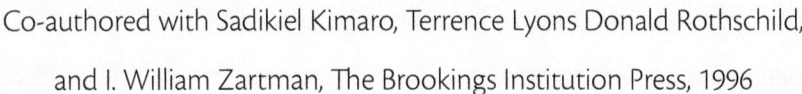

'Sovereignty as Responsibility: Conflict Management in Africa'

Co-authored with Sadikiel Kimaro, Terrence Lyons Donald Rothschild, and I. William Zartman, The Brookings Institution Press, 1996

One of the outstanding outcomes of the Brookings Africa Program was the development of the concept of Sovereignty as Responsibility (SaR) which has been widely acknowledged as a major accomplishment in international norm-setting. It has also been credited as having triggered the development of the normative principle of the Responsibility to Protect, popularly known by the acronyms RtP and R2P, which has proved to be more controversial than its mother concept because it is perceived as advocating overriding sovereignty with international intervention.

Our work in recasting Sovereignty as Responsibility was rooted in assessing the impact of the end of the Cold War on the required approach to internal and regional conflicts. The starting point was that the change would involve a shift from seeing national and regional conflicts as proxy wars between the superpowers to seeing them in their proper national and regional contexts. This would have the positive implication of having a better understanding of the root causes and finding appropriate contextualized solutions. It would also mean

---

50. Francis M. Deng, *War of Visions: Conflict of Identities in the Sudan,* The Brookings Institution Press, 1995 - see p. 84.

51. Abdullahi Ahmed An-naim and Francis M. Deng, *Human Rights in Africa: A Cross-Cultural Perspective,* The Brookings Institution Press, 1990 - see p. 111.

52. Francis Mading Deng and Larry Minear, *The Challenges of Famine Relief: Emergency Operations in Sudan* The Brookings Institution Press, 1992 - see p. 83.

reapportioning responsibility away from dependence on the superpowers for solving the problems, which, because of the ideological rivalry of the patrons, often aggravated the conflicts involved. Instead, it would give priority to the role of the countries, the sub-regions, and the regions directly involved.

However, given the increasing concerns of the international community with human rights and humanitarian issues, no country would engage in violation of international norms in these areas and seek to shelter itself by invoking national sovereignty as a shield against international scrutiny and intervention or involvement in one way or another. While both SaR and the affiliated concept of the responsibility to protect build on these three pillars, SaR is understood to emphasize the first two pillars while RtP/R2P is perceived as emphasizing the last pillar, international intervention.

We then developed conceptualizing our book title, *Sovereignty as Responsibility*, with the subtitle, *Conflict Management in Africa*. The book, which was co-authored by leading scholars in the field, began with charting the normative framework focusing on identity as a primary factor in internal conflicts, then analyzed the principles of governance as conflict management, which in turn required constructive management of diversity in the political and economic shaping and sharing of power and wealth, and the apportionment of responsibilities among the states concerned, in cooperation with regional organizations and the international community.

'African Reckoning: A Quest for Good Governance'
Co-editor with Terrence Lyons, The Brookings Institution, 1998

The challenge that followed from this conceptualization and analysis was to delve deeper into what precisely was the substantive content of the responsibility associated with sovereignty. Here again, we convened a conference of experts on the thematic title "Sovereignty, Responsibility, and Accountability: An African Challenge." The experts were to present papers on the evolution of the concept of sovereignty, which was originally conceived of as the absolute prerogative of the sovereign monarchy, to become increasingly the democratic will of the people. This has since been complemented by the emergence of international human rights and humanitarian norms which impose responsibilities on the states and limit the assertion of sovereignty against international oversight, scrutiny, and involvement in internal affairs.

African Reckoning, which I co-edited with my colleague, Terrence Lyons, was the product of that conference. The volume seeks to advance understanding how state sovereignty may be modified by reconceiving the concept in terms of a state responsibility and accountability. It also examines the records of states, regional organizations, and international governmental and non-governmental organizations in light of these standards. The conference sought to develop this approach to sovereignty further, spell out its contents, and develop strategies for institutionalizing it for governance and state performance.

African Reckoning is designed to lay a foundation for addressing in a more systematic and substantive way the responsibilities of sovereignty, the extent to which states are discharging them, and the system of regional and international accountability to which states are being subjected. The international community's stipulation of universal standards that states must observe in their treatment of their own people, notably in matters of human rights, means that governments must be held accountable internationally for their domestic performance.

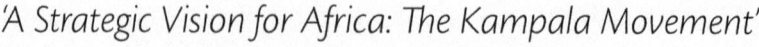

'A Strategic Vision for Africa: The Kampala Movement'

Co-authored with I. William Zartman,

The Brookings Institution Press, 2002

This volume, which I co-authored with Professor I. William Zartman, addressed security concerns in Africa. This was an elaborate commentary on the process leading to the Conference on Security, Stability, Development, and Cooperation in Africa, (CSSDCA), which Former President Olusegun Obasanjo had initiated in the late 1980s and which aimed at applying to Africa the Helsinki Initiative in Europe that resulted in the Conference for Security and Cooperation in Europe, (CSCE). The designation of the initiative as the Kampala Movement emanated from the fact that a gathering of some 500 people, including several Heads of State, met in Kampala, Uganda, to deliberate over the initiative, adopted it, and recommended its submission to the Organization of African Unity, (OAU), for consideration and adoption. As a member of the Board of the Africa Leadership Forum, (ALF), a think tank that I had helped President Obasanjo establish, I had been actively involved in the development of CSSDCA and was honored to chair the security working group at the Kampala conference.

The proposal for the adoption of the framework by the OAU was blocked primarily by Libya and the Sudan, as they felt threatened by the initiative. When Obasanjo was incarcerated by the Nigerian dictator, Sani Abacha, in 1995, he asked me to act for him as the interim Chairman of the ALF. In that capacity, my colleagues and I continued to expound on the principles of CSSDCA to promote the process intellectually and expand on its application in various indirect ways. When Obasanjo was eventually released from detention, he and President Thabo Mbeki jointly championed the campaign to have CSSDCA adopted by the OAU. They eventually succeeded and the principles of the initiative were incorporated in the organization's mechanism for conflict management. Some people saw this as a death sentence to the initiative, while others saw it as a victory. Whichever of these positions one takes, what is important is that the main principles of the CSSDCA now form an integral part of the African policy framework for conflict management.

In his Preface to the book, President Olusegun Obasanjo wrote, "Africa is a continent endowed with material and human resources. There is no justification whatsoever for the people of Africa to be the leading recipients of outside humanitarian assistance that can only sustain life at a minimum level of survival. Africans are fleeing by the millions within their countries as internally displaced persons or across international borders as refugees. Most of them are destitute, depending only on international charity. National sovereignty can only be meaningful if it discharges a certain level of responsibility in providing adequate protection and assistance to citizens and all those under state jurisdiction. Otherwise, failure to do so exposes a country to international scrutiny and maybe intervention on humanitarian grounds."

'Identity, Diversity, and Constitutionalism for Africa'
Foreword by General Olusegun Obasanjo, Former President of Nigeria,
United States Institute of Peace, 2008

The core argument of this book is that if an African nation's constitution and the attendant governance framework are to embody the *soul* of the nation, as indeed they are expected to do, then they must reflect the cultural values and norms of all the people of the nation and their respective world views as starting points in constitutionalism.

Constitutionalism is defined as a mechanism for controlling, regulating, and managing the exercise of power in a process by which people, individuals, and groups, pursue material and other values, through institutions using resources with outcomes and effects. Constitutionalism in Africa must be seen as a process that begins and ends with a mere elaboration of a constitutional document, but rather as a living process that is constantly evolving with the participation of its people to promote their ownership of their governing frameworks and make them reflect the political, economic, social, and cultural dynamics of the continent and its populations.

The main objective of constitutionalism is good governance. The achievement and consolidation of peace, security, stability, and development in Africa is in turn a function of good governance, the core of which is democracy, a concept that has generated a great deal of controversy, particularly in the African context. This book argues that the overarching universal principles of democracy and their contextualized application must go hand in hand. While the normative principles of democracy, particularly those related to elected governments, freedom of speech, and the rule of law, are universal, they need to be adjusted to specific contexts by putting into consideration local realities and making effective use of indigenous cultural values and institutions.

The Western concept of democracy has tended to focus on elections, which poses a serious dilemma for ethnically diverse societies where people tend to vote on the bases of their politicized ethnic or religious identities. The core of the dilemma is that on the one hand democracy requires that the will of the majority prevails and should be respected. On the other hand, that can become a dictatorship of numbers where the majority imposes its will on the minority. In countries where access to power means access to resources and services, the stakes can become very high and the elections highly charged. This can lead to violent, even genocidal conflicts.

This book makes the argument that the way forward is to marry the best of the Western system with the best of the African indigenous systems to retain those elements of Western concepts and practices of democracy that have universal value while refashioning African constitutive systems by drawing on the indigenous values and institutions. These should include various forms of consensus-based conflict prevention, management, and resolution; incorporating customary law and traditional authorities in the modern governance system; harmonizing the interest of the individual and the group in decision-making; respect for ancestral values by operationalizing the principles of permanent identity and influence in decision-making; devolving power to the communities as a basis for ensuring unity in diversity; promoting gender equality by translating traditional respect for women as wives and mothers at home to give them equal positions in public life at par with men; transforming traditional reverence for nature as a sacred aspect of God's creation into the modern respect for the environment; and developing an indigenized approach to development as a self-enhancement from within rather than an external commodity to be imported.

In his Foreword, General Olusegun Obasanjo wrote, "It was indeed the need for Africans to assume control over their destiny and develop an integrated, cross-cultural approach that I established the Africa Leadership Forum and initiated the Helsinki-like process that led to the Conference on Security, Stability, Development, and Cooperation in Africa (CSSDCA), an Africanized version of the Conference on Security and Cooperation in Europe (CSCE). The idea was to lay a foundation for Africa's sovereign responsibility. And promote international cooperation on the basis of constructive complementarity and mutual respect for one another's value system."

Obasanjo extended the argument by stating that the world might also have something to learn and adopt from Africa: "I share Dr. Deng's view of an Africa that builds on its time-tested cultural ideals, and institutionalized practices. But if Dr. Deng will forgive me for taking his argument a step further, I might also note that these values have much to offer not only Africa but the world as a whole. Just as Western democracy enshrines certain universal values, so does the African worldview. In a world where every community is increasingly obliged to acknowledge and interact with many other, often very different, communities the traditional African focus on building consensus instead of fostering competition has obvious relevance. Equally, the African concern to root the individual within the community is highly pertinent to societies in which migration and industrialization have generated atomic isolation and alienation."

Obasanjo was articulating the core of the principles of the 'invisible bridge,' and continuity in change that have been at the core of the Transitional Integration strategy which I have advocated in various works.

'Self-determination and National Unity: A Challenge for Africa'
Editor, Red Sea Press/Africa World Press, 2010

This book elaborates through case studies the themes presented in the *Identity, Diversity and Constitutionalism in Africa*.[53] In addition to my Introduction and a chapter by Mona Ndulu on ethnic diversity as a challenge to African democratic governance, expert contributors wrote on the cases of Ethiopia, Nigeria, Sudan, and South Africa. The

---

53. Francis M. Deng, *Identity, Diversity and Constitutionalism in Africa*, United States Institute of Peace Press, 2008 - see p. 119.

US Institute decided to have this complementary volume produced by a different publisher.[54]

The book addresses a concern that is becoming increasingly recognized, that African countries in varying degrees are striving to transcend the simplistic adherence to Eurocentric models of governance and constitutionalism. These models are premised on societies that are relatively homogenous. African contexts on the other hand are mostly characterized by racial, ethnic, and religious diversities, with correlative differences in cultural values and institutions. The case studies in this book were intended to provide insights into how elements or principles of individual constitutions and broader processes of constitutionalism and governance systems respond to these challenging issues.

An overriding normative principle of the study is a concept of self-determination that entitles individuals and groups to play a pivotal role in the management of their own affairs. It is ultimately a principle that respects the dignity of individuals and groups at all levels, from local to national. The assumption of the study is that a state that discharges its responsibility toward its citizens, individuals, and groups, and ensures the enjoyment of the full rights of citizenship, through constructive management of diversity, democratic participation, equitable sharing of wealth and development opportunities, and respect for the dignity of all reflected in the enjoyment of human rights and civil liberties, is not likely to be threatened by separatist demands for self-determination. On the other hand, a state that fails in these justified principles of good governance can expect the aggrieved groups to remedies that could lead to a demand for varying degrees of self-determination that could lead to secession.

This challenge is by no means limited to Africa, for there is hardly

---

54. The Red Sea Press and Africa World Press function as one publishing house.

any country in the world that is in some fashion and degree without diversity. The need for constructive management of diversity is therefore global. As most indigenous African societies are governed through autonomous structures and consensus building, they practice varying forms of constructive management that are still relevant in the modern context and might indeed be universally applicable.

D. Global Level

'Protecting the Dispossessed:
A Challenge for the International Community'
The Brookings Institution Press, 1993

In March 1992, the UN Commission on Human Rights requested the Secretary-General to appoint a Special Representative on Internally Displaced Persons, (IDP). As mentioned earlier in this volume,[55] Boutros Boutros–Ghali, the UN Secretary-General, with whom I had worked closely as Ministers of Foreign Affairs of our respective countries, surprised me by a phone call offering me the position. I had no idea about the issue or what the position would entail. I expressed my appreciation to Boutros but told him that while I was honored, I needed to know more about the position before taking a final decision. I asked him to have his staff give me details, but Boutros spoke to me in a way that meant I of course accepted the offer.

Like refugees, internally displaced persons are victims of civil wars, internal strife, communal violence, forced relocation, and gross violations of human rights. They are deprived of essential needs, such as

---

55. See p. 3 & 4.

food, shelter, clothing, physical security, basic health care, and education. Because they remain within the borders of their countries, they do not receive the protection and assistance that, under the UNHCR 1951 Refugee Convention, the international community provides for the refugees, as a displaced population seeking refuge across international borders.

My mandate signified the beginning of an international response to the crisis of internal displacement. My assignment was to study the problem, the international legal standards for protecting and assisting the internally displaced, the institutional mechanisms for the enforcement of the existing norms, and any additional measures the international community might take to address the crisis.

Protecting the Dispossessed was my first study under the mandate. I undertook missions to six countries during the first year: the former Yugoslavia, the Russian Federation, Somalia, the Sudan, El Salvador, and Cambodia. My first mission to the former Yugoslavia was at the peak of the conflict in Bosnia, where the human suffering I witnessed was indescribable. Somalia was at the worse phase of state collapse. The war in El Salvador was raging. The humanitarian conditions of the South Sudanese around Khartoum were dismal and in Cambodia, the killing fields and the museum of the victims brought back to life the horrors of the genocidal atrocities of the Khmer Rouge. Russia was the first to invite me and their concern was the alleged plight of the Russians in the now independent states of former Soviet Republics.

Over the years of my work on the mandate, I would witness the consequences of the horrors of atrocities generated mostly by various forms and degrees of identity conflicts.

Protecting the Dispossessed is a revised version of the report I submitted to the Commission on Human Rights in March 1993. It reviews the state of the law and enforcement mechanisms in the countries

I visited. It analyzes internal displacement as an aspect of the wider problems of nation-building. It also offers recommendations about what the international community could do to address not only the symptoms represented by internal displacement but also their root causes in the domestic conditions. But my work that year was only a first step in what would be 12 years of an intense program in promoting international responses to this global crisis. My own country and people would continue to be the most affected. And indeed, in my statements in the affected countries, I always said that I was not preaching from a moral high ground, but talking about a crisis of which my own country and people were among the worst hit.

'Masses in Flight: The Global Crisis of Internal Displacement'

Co-authored with Roberta Cohen,

The Brookings Institution Press, 1998

This book, which I co-authored with Roberta Cohen, my co-founder and co-director of the Brookings Project on Internal Displacement, resulted from a discussion I had with UN Secretary-General Boutros–Ghali on the mandate. The story with Boutros–Ghali on this matter was more colorful. I was reporting to him and discussing the next steps. My assignment was initially to be for one year. The mandate was considered very sensitive because certain States feared that it posed a potential threat to sovereignty. The position of Representative of the Secretary-General, rather than that of an independent Rapporteur of the Commission of Human Rights, was a compromise based on the assumption that the Secretary-General would be more respectful of sovereignty and would exert appropriate control over his Representative. The advocates of the mandate on the other hand expected me to recommend that the mandate be renewed but the mechanism be changed from Representative of the Secretary-General to Special Expert, Rapporteur, or a Working Group. I thought that the position of the Secretary-General carried more weight and potential influence. It would also be easier to request the renewal of the same mandate than recommend a new mandate that would almost certainly be controversial. I wanted to recommend the renewal of the mandate of the Secretary-General Boutros–Ghali agreed with me, so my mandate was renewed.

When I next met with the Secretary-General, he suggested that I conduct a comprehensive study of the problem in an independent research institution to address a number of critical questions: Who are the internally displaced? Where are they around the world? How many are they? What are their needs? To what extent are their needs being met and by whom? What are the gaps and how can they be met? What role can the international community, in particular the United Nations, play in meeting their needs? Boutros was clearly counting on my disposition for research and writing of which he was well aware. He asked me to prepare a concept note for the project which we could discuss.

I was quite enthusiastic about the project. I was able to persuade the leadership of the Brookings Institution to endorse the project. We also won the support of our funders. Roberta Cohen, who had already been working on the human rights of internally displaced persons for an NGO, was recruited as a Senior Fellow to work with me in establishing the Brookings IDP Project and assist me on the research agenda and other activities on the mandate. We prepared the outline Boutros–Ghali had requested. I proudly went to present it to him. A senior Indian staff member from the Office for Humanitarian Coordination, whom we knew to be resistant to the mandate, was called in to attend the meeting. He was not an exception in his negative attitude as many in the UN were. Agencies were somewhat apprehensive about the mandate which they saw as a potential encroachment on their turf. So, when Boutros–Ghali responded with ambivalence to the concept note, I could see the satisfaction on the face of the staff member.

Boutros–Ghali said that the research proposal was too ambitious. He said he had in mind a brief policy paper and not a full-size book. As a scholar, he said that, like me, he had a professional interest in writing books, but he did not want a book that would gather dust on a shelf. He wanted something brief that could be acted upon. I was furious. I told him that I had done exactly what he asked me to do. The anger behind my words must have been quite obvious. Boutros–Ghali kept assuring me that like me, he liked writing books, and that he was not opposed to the project in principle but wanted something that could be produced quickly and applied. He said that we could perhaps work on both.

I went back to Washington DC by train, fuming with anger all the way. As soon as I arrived at home, I gave Boutros–Ghali a phone call and was immediately connected to him. Before I could speak, he said he had in fact wanted to call me to ask me to be his representative on the Board of the University of Peace. Whether that was an independent initiative or an attempt to make up for the anger he had generated in me, I could not tell.

I, nonetheless, gave Boutros my mind about my surprise over his contradictory behavior. Boutros then went out of his way to reassure me that he welcomed the book project, but also wanted a policy brief. He even said that he would be happy to write an introduction for the book I was planning to write. When I later reported to my colleagues and the leadership at Brookings Institution the disagreement I had with Boutros over the proposed research project, it was as though their commitment to the project was strengthened by the challenge of the Secretary-General's ambivalence. John Steinbruner, the Director of the Foreign Policy Studies Program reaffirmed his support for the project, adding "Some things are worth fighting for." Clearly, this was one of them.

'Forsaken Peoples: Case Studies on Internal Displacement'
Co-editor with Roberta Cohen, The Brookings Press, 1998

My co-director of the Brookings IDP Project, Roberta Cohen, and I, decided to substantiate the themes of the conceptual, normative, institutional and operational framework we had developed in *Masses in Flight* with empirical material from the field. We therefore commissioned experts to carry out case studies of representative countries from the various regions of the globe. We produced *Forsaken People* as a co-edited volume. The ten countries covered in the book had suffered severe problems of internal displacement. They included: Burundi, Rwanda, Liberia, and the Sudan in Africa; the former Yugoslavia and the Caucasus in Europe; Tajikistan and Sri Lanka in Asia; and Colombia and Peru in the Americas.

'Guiding Principles on Internal Displacement'
Developed in collaboration with Roberta Cohen, Walter Kaelin, Robert Goldman and Manfred Novak, UN Office for Humanitarian Affairs, 1998

Our first assignment on the internal displacement mandate was to compile and analyze existing norms to determine the extent to which they were adequate for protecting and assisting IDPs. At first, building on my connections at Yale and Harvard Law Schools, we brought together a team of professors and students to help us put together relevant international norms. We then expanded the circle of experts with field experience to further develop the framework of analysis. There was strong resistance against developing a legal framework, the arguments being that there were applicable legal norms already in place and that introducing new norms would weaken existing ones.

A comprehensive compilation and thorough analysis concluded that while there was a reasonable amount of existing laws that were applicable to internal displacement, they were widely dispersed, not sufficiently focused on the needs of IDPs, and did not in any case comprehensively address those needs. We eventually put together an expert international legal team with the strategic support of my close co-director, Roberta Cohen. The core team included Robert Goldman from the American University in Washington, Manfred Novak from Vienna University in Austria, and Walter Kaelin, from Bern University in Switzerland, who chaired the legal team and later succeeded me as Representative of the Secretary-General. Many more legal experts from the relevant UN agencies and other institutions joined the process.

As there was strong resistance to developing a 'legal' or 'normative' framework, we requested to develop an "appropriate" framework, and, although the framework we developed was based on existing principles of human rights law, humanitarian law, and analogous refugee law, we decided to call it "Guiding Principles." And instead of asking for their formal adoption by the Commission on Human Rights, we had them merely take note of them.

The Principles comprehensively cover the areas of prevention of displacement, providing protection and assistance during displacement, and finding solutions that would lead to voluntary return in safety and dignity, reintegration into a pre-displacement community, or resettlement in alternative areas of their choice. The Guiding Principles were indeed intended to be a normative basis for promoting and guiding the application of the principles of Sovereignty as Responsibility, through cooperation between Governments and the United Nations.

Although we did not seek formal adoption, members of the Commission were quite supportive, and we had indeed lobbied hard to ensure consensus. Only one member expressed reservation that his government was committed to the established procedures in international norm setting and that the method we had followed was 'window legislation,' about which they wanted to register their reservation.

Remarkably, the Principles were soon adopted and applied, first by the Office of the High Commissioner for Refugees, even before they were formally endorsed by the Inter-Agency Standing Committee, which also requested its member organizations to use them in their field operations. Increasing numbers of Member States began to enshrine them in their national legislation and national courts began to invoke them in their decisions. Within a relatively short period of time, the Principles became recognized as having matured into international customary law. Africa then led the international community by using the Principles to develop the African Convention on the Protection and Assistance of Internally Displaced Persons in Africa. Adopted in October 2009, the Convention came into force on December 8, 2012.

Ironically, I later visited the country whose member had registered reservation on the method by which the Guiding Principles had been developed and adopted. At a luncheon given in my honor by the Ministry of Foreign Affairs, the same diplomat who had registered reservations on the Guiding Principles, now back at the Headquarters, was called upon to make welcoming remarks. I could not believe the very positive and indeed flattering comments he made on the conduct of the mandate and the value of the Principles.

Some countries however remained reserved, even resistant, to the Guiding Principles for the same reasons many states had been opposed to the mandate. Sudan, which had the largest number of internally displaced persons in the world, was among them. I was however determined from the start to win the support of the Sudan, both because of our people's need and also because it was my country, precisely one of the reasons Boutros–Ghali had used to persuade me to undertake the work. Sudan was in fact one of the countries I visited the first year of my appointment. In discussions with the Sudanese authorities I argued that because their people were the most affected, they not only needed to demonstrate to the world that they cared about their people and that they needed and supported United Nations action on the matter, but they should indeed play a leadership role on the issue. That way they would not only receive international assistance for their needy population, but also gain moral support and legitimacy internationally. I was eventually able to gain support for my position among key individuals, including the Minister of Foreign Affairs and the First Vice-President. But the official position remained at best ambivalent.

Then something quite remarkable happened. I wanted to organize a national conference in the Sudan on the Guiding Principles to promote their acceptance and application. Although the Foreign Minister was supportive, he knew that there was resistance within his government. Then he proposed an arrangement that would counter the opposition. He told me that our people were afraid of being singled out and targeted for scrutiny and criticism. If we made the conference regional and invite IGAD to champion it, no one country would feel targeted and all of them might even admit that they all shared the problem and had a vested interest in finding solutions. That was what we did. The IGAD member States responded very positively. Sudan, in partnership with IGAD, hosted a very successful conference that adopted one of the most progressive statements in support of the Guiding Principles. That was indeed a strong illustration of the value of the regional approach. We applied that approach to other regions in our program of action.

'Critical Choices'

Co-authored with Wolfgang H. Reinicke and in collaboration with

Jan Martin Witte, Thorstein Benner, Beth Whitaker,

and John Gershman, IDRC Books, 2000

The new global environment requires new approaches, new ideas, and innovative tools to address new challenges in areas as different as weapons control, climate change, genetic engineering, and labor standards. *Critical Choices* looks at one such tool: global public policy networks. In these networks, governments, international organizations, the corporate sector, and civil society join together to achieve what none can accomplish on its own. This book explored both the promises and the limitations of this new form of global cooperation and discusses how such networks might contribute to better managing the risks and making use of the opportunities that globalization presents. Finally, it offers provocative advice and solid recommendations on how the United Nations can foster such networks in the years ahead.

'Ten Principles in Negotiating Human Relations'
Fordham University Press, 2003

These principles were initially prepared for a seminar on negotiations at the School of Advanced International Studies (SAIS) of Johns Hopkins University in Washington, DC., which was conducted by Professor I. William Zartman. The principles were subsequently presented at the peace negotiations in Naivasha, Kenya, which eventually resulted in the 2005 CPA. They were also included in a chapter that appeared in two separate books: *Sudan at the Brink,*[56] and *Reflections on South Sudan National Dialogue.*[57]

I see negotiations and the closely related field of diplomacy as essentially management of human relations involving individuals, groups, or nations. Some people would argue that conflict is the normal state of human interaction and that it is futile to try to prevent or resolve conflicts; the most that can be done is managing conflicts. This can only be valid if it is understood to mean that grounds for conflict exist in normal human relations and that the occurrence of conflict is therefore normal. If it means that conflict is the normal pattern of life, then I would consider that position both empirically questionable and normatively ambiguous. Far from seeing conflicts as the normal state of human interaction, I believe that people are more apt to cooperate and harmonize their incompatible or potentially conflictual positions, and that conflict is in fact a crisis that signifies a breakdown in the normal patternof behavior. In this sense, conflict involves a collision of incompatible positions resulting from a failure to regulate, reconcile or harmonize the differences.

---

56. Francis Mading Deng and Kevin M. Cahill, *Sudan at the Brink: Self-determination and National Unity* Fordham University Press, 2010 - see p. 101.

57. *Reflections on South Sudan's National Dialogue,* UNDP, 2018 - see p. 105.

In the normal course of events, society is structured around fundamental values and norms that guide behavior and regulate relations so as to avoid destructive collision of interests or positions. If people observe the principles of the normative code, which they generally do, the normal pattern would be one of relative cooperation and mutual accommodation, even in a competitive framework. To call that state one of conflict would be to put a negative value judgment on positive motivations and endeavors, and on a relatively high degree of success is peaceful interaction, which is normally the pattern in human relations.

Even more important than strict empirical interpretation would be the normative implications of holding conflict the normal state of human existence, which would tend to foster a disposition that is fundamentally adversarial, suspicious, and conflictual. The extent to which members in a community or group reflect this disposition may depend in large measure on the culture and its normative code, and beliefs that characterizes national, ethnic, or other groups and orient their behavior.

It is important to emphasize that the objective is not merely to resolve a conflict, but to resolve it in a mutually satisfactory manner. The achievement of peace and reconciliation becomes a common objective, but one that is only possible if both sides feel that the solution proposed is indeed in the mutual interest. Since both were prepared to enter into conflict in the first place, it means that each must have a subjective view of right and wrong that gives them some degree of right and places some degree of wrong on the opposing party. These subjective perspectives cannot be ignored when negotiation takes place or when the proposals are made for resolving a conflict, even though they need not and should not be allowed to have too much influence on such processes. Ultimately, while there is indeed a hierarchy of rights and wrongs in resolving disputes through negotiations, there should be no absolute winner or loser.

The proposed principles on negotiation should be seen in the context of the normative framework outlined above. These principles derive from personal experiences and are rooted in values, norms, and mores that emanate from a specific African family and cultural background among the Dinka in South Sudan. They cover experiences in interpersonal relations, third-party mediation, and diplomatic negotiations, with overlaps. Although personal and rooted in the Dinka, South Sudanese, and African cultural contexts, they represent values that can claim universal validity, despite cross-cultural variations on the details and their applicability.

While I believe that these reflect shared human values, it would be presumptuous and even hazardous to assume that they are universal, scientifically proven negotiation techniques that are applicable to all situations and cross-cultural contexts. A case can of course be made for expert knowledge in negotiation and there is a particular role to be played by individuals with expertise. But to be effective, synergy between universal techniques and culturally specific methods need to be developed.

'Talking It Out: Stories in Negotiating Human Relations'
Routledge, 2006

In essence, *Talking It Out* represents an individual application of the princples stipulated in the preceding publication. More directly, it *was* the byproduct of a project that elicited stories on the cultural perspective on negotiations. Guy Olivier Faure and Jeffrey Z. Rubin had involved me in an edited book on the themes of *Culture and Negotiation: The Resolution of Water Disputes.* I contributed a chapter on Northern and South Sudan in a chapter titled: 'The Nile: A

River that Unites and Divides.'[58] Subsequent to that project, Faure and Rubin wrote requesting that I contribute to another project on the cultural approach to the study of negotiation. They wanted stories in negotiations broadly defined. They referred to my experience and expressed the opinion that they thought I could contribute interesting stories from my personal experience. That inspired me to contribute not only one story but a collection of stories from my experiences in several contexts and applying the cultural norms from my Dinka-African background. These included interpersonal relations in the family, tribal and national Sudanese context; interpersonal interactions and relations abroad; and experiences in my diplomatic practice. That collection, with my cross-cultural analysis, produced a volume that my colleagues considered to be a significant contribution meriting publication. The book was very well received. I placed it in the category of the global context precisely because it cuts across all levels, from local, through national and regional, to global.

'Idealism and Realism: Negotiating Sovereignty in Divided Nations'
Dag Hammarskjold Foundation, 2010

This booklet reproduces the text of my 2010 Dag Hammarskjold Lecture, jointly organized by the Dag Hammarskjold Foundation and Uppsala University. I shared the dilemmas of balancing the invocation of normative ideals with the pragmatic need to engage with governments and other responsible authorities to provide protection and assistance for the needy populations worldwide. This dilemma is not theoretical, but one with pressing existential consequences in

---

58. Francis M. Deng, 'The Nile: A River that Unites and Divides' in *Culture and Negotiations: The Resolution of Water Disputes,* Guy Olivier Faure and Jeffrey Z. Rubin, (eds), Sage Publications, 1993 - see p. 192.

the real world of complex challenges, in which the delicate balance between asserting the norms of international protection for vulnerable populations clash with the negative assertion of sovereignty as a shield by governments.

For me, the way out of this quagmire is constructive engagement with controlling authorities. As I stated in my lecture, "I know that this is not the approach favored by those who believe that on these matters we should cry out loud, stand on the mountaintop and preach what is right and condemn what is wrong. However, when we do that, we might satisfy our conscience, but how much can we help the people who need to be helped in a practical way?"

The theme of my lecture was inspired by my experience in negotiating with governments on my two mandates, first as Special Representative of the Secretary-General on Internally Displace Persons for twelve years, from 1992 to 2004, and then as Special Advisor of the Secretary-General on the Prevention of Genocide for five years, from 2007 to 2012. But my initial involvement with human rights protection goes back to my first appointment in the United Nations Secretariat as Human Rights Officer in 1967.

Both mandates are essentially related to human rights and humanitarian principles which are primarily issues of internal governance and the protection of fundamental rights and civil liberties. They are at the core of nationhood. Although statecraft and nation-building are primarily internal challenges to every country and the states involved in regional conflicts; the saying that no one is an island is increasingly true of nations. The time for using national sovereignty as a shield against the outside world is gone. Peace and security of every nation are intrinsically tied to the peace and security of the immediately concerned neighbors, the wider region, and ultimately the international community. Human rights and related humanitarian concerns are the normative bases for the shared responsibility to protect and assist populations in need within national borders.

Human rights are universal and are inherent in the dignity of all individuals and groups without discrimination on the bases of race, ethnicity, nationality, religion, culture, or gender. No reasonable person can therefore oppose human rights protection as a fundamental principle of human dignity. By the same token, and paradoxically because of its sanctity, the inherent dignity of the human being as God's most valued creature in our human perception, the normative core of human rights is often perceived in religious terms as reverence for God's creatures. The issue is therefore very sensitive and controversial when applied to specific situations of conflict. This is particularly the case when it involves allegations of violations by governments or individual leaders in societies that are sharply divided by an acute crisis of national identity based on race, ethnicity, religion, or culture.

This mostly entails a negative assertion of sovereignty as a barricade against international intervention to enforce the protection of human rights for all groups without discrimination on any of the identity factors. This is why in discharging my UN mandates on providing protection and assistance to internally displaced persons and strategizing for the prevention of genocide, I recast sovereignty positively as a concept of state responsibility and not negatively as a constraining principle.

Both mandates are extremely sensitive and are perceived as posing a threat to national sovereignty from international intervention. This threat is more perceived than real. More often than not the problem is international indifference rather than a credible threat of intervention. Coercive intervention is only likely under conditions where the state has collapsed, leaving a vacuum to be filled, or the government is so weak and the intervening force is so overwhelmingly strong that there is no credible resistance, or the interest of the intervening power is comparatively so great that it is worth putting their young people at risk.

Nevertheless, to overcome the constraints of sovereignty, I had to develop strategies for constructively engaging governments to cooperate with my mandate and improve the prospects of assisting and protecting the populations in need under state jurisdiction.

Sovereignty as Responsibility is the principle that guided my work on internal displacement. As I have often said, the first five minutes with the president or the minister concerned were critical in establishing the basis for constructive engagement. Basically, I explained that I recognized the problem as internal, that it fell under state sovereignty, that I respected national sovereignty, but that I did not see it negatively as a barricade against outside involvement, rather, I saw it as a positive concept of state responsibility for its people, with the support of the international community, if needed. My role was to act as a catalyst for promoting international cooperation in support of sovereignty. That settled well with governments.

I applied the same approach to the mandate on genocide prevention. Dealing with genocide is of course even more sensitive than internal displacement. The mere mention of the word evokes denial and an unwillingness to discuss. What I did was to demystify genocide by presenting it as an extreme form of identity-related conflicts emanating not from mere differences, but from the way we manage differences. In many countries torn apart by conflict, there is a sharp dichotomy between those who are perceived as first-class citizens, who enjoy all the rights of citizenship and those who are discriminated against, marginalized, excluded, denigrated, and denied the full rights of citizenship. The remedy, therefore, is to ensure inclusivity, full equality, and respect for the dignity of all individuals and groups without discrimination on any ground. This approach too appealed to most governments.

There is also the issue of accountability and punishment for gross violations of human rights. The debate over peace and justice tends to make the issue one of either or, which is misleading in most cases. The real question is one of prioritization and practicality. No one can argue against holding accountable those individuals who commit atrocity crimes. But it is also difficult to see how leaders threatened with punitive measures can cooperate in ending conflicts to which they are parties.

This requires giving priority to achieving peace and cooperating with the individuals whose role is pivotal to the process. The dilemma however is whether a leader who expects to be made accountable once peace is achieved would cooperate in promoting peace.

In principle, it can be persuasively argued that accountability through the International Criminal Court (ICC) is a positive development in international criminal law. If the expectation can be credibly established that those who commit atrocity crimes will be apprehended and punished, that might be an effective deterrence. But how credible is the threat of criminal accountability in most cases? An empty threat can be more dangerous than no threat. Barking without biting or shouting from the mountaintop without practical action only creates adversity that does not provide practical solutions.

My main argument is that while protecting human rights is a universally shared goal, allegations of violations are also sensitive and tend to evoke denial and defensiveness. Such denials often lead to preventing entry into the countries concerned and thereby concealing evidence and inhibiting dialogue on how best to address the problem to ensure protection and humanitarian assistance to the needy.

An alternative is to give prevention priority over punishment and to define human rights situations as entailing problems that need to be addressed by the state concerned, and, if need be, with international cooperation. This can best be pursued through the normative concept of Sovereignty as Responsibility with its three pillars: State responsibility, international assistance to enhance State capacity to discharge its national responsibility, and a more robust international action to fill the vacuum of responsibility in case of State failure to discharge its responsibility. All this calls for balancing idealism with realism to address the paradox of state responsibility.

Part Two

Other Writings

———◆———

Conceptual Overview

As with the books in Part One, the material in this collection are classified and contextualized into four levels, according to the subject matter, dated, and listed in descending order:

A. Local Level
B. National Level
C. Regional Level
D. Global Level

I must emphasize that this is not an exhaustive collection of the material I have written over the years as I have not kept a comprehensive record of my writings and could not recall many. The point, therefore, is merely to illustrate the issues with which I have been concerned at the four interconnected levels.

A. Local Level

'Learning in Context'

In *Learning and Development: A Global Perspective*

By Edward W. Ploman and Alan Thomas, (eds),

Toronto: Ontario Institute for Studies in Education, 1984 [59]

In this paper, I gave a brief account of the Dinka value system and of knowledge as a normative concept for the transmission of the value system. 'Knowing the words,' the Dinka notion of knowledge implies knowing and adhering to the code of conduct that embodies the prescribed principles of ideal human relations. A person who does not know the words is one who is obstreperous, reckless, and lacks prudence of judgement. A person who knows how to speak well does not mean knowing the words in the normative sense.

An incident I encountered during the civil war may illustrate the point. When I was Ambassador, I persuaded the Government to restore chieftainship after it had been capriciously abolished by the President in retaliation to the rude manner he felt he had been received by the people of Abyei who were demanding the implementation of the Addis Ababa Accord that gave them the option of joining the South. The brother who had succeeded our father as Paramount Chief had been assassinated by the security forces in the area. Some people, including another of our brothers who had contested the succession of the brother who had become Paramount Chief, were suspected of being accomplices to the assassination. As a result, our family and the

---

59. This paper was presented as a paper at the Global Learning Symposium sponsored by the United Nations University, Canadian International Development Agency, and Ontario Institute for Studies in Education, April 28 May 1, 1985.

tribe became acutely divided. Power was given to people who were informants of the security forces. The tribe urged me to restore chieftainship and to have one of our brothers appointed Paramount Chief.

The Government agreed to restore chieftainship and have one of my brothers appointed to the position. The condition for that was that I should resolve the conflicts in our family and the tribe and unify our family and the tribe. My brother Bol and I went to Abyei for that purpose. After days of intensive discussions within the family and the tribe, we succeeded. One of the critical meetings was with the security informants whose leader had maintained an ambivalent relationship with our father, alternating from being incarcerated to being a close associate. As we discussed the situation, he bragged about his oratory abilities, arguing that no one, except perhaps our father, was a better speaker than him. To that, our Uncle responded, "No one has ever questioned your ability to speak well; what people doubt is your heart." That was a clear moral distinction between ability with words and abiding by the moral principles of knowing the words of wisdom.

Foreword to 'Clean the Crocodile's Teeth: Nuer Song'

By Terese Svoboda, Greenfield Center,

New York: Greenfield Review, 1985

This book is a volume of Nuer songs collected and translated by Terese Svoboda. The songs were collected among the Nuer in Ethiopia. Before I became better informed by Ms. Svoboda, I assumed that the Nuer in Ethiopia were South Sudanese refugees. I got to know that there are indeed Nuer who have been Ethiopian citizens long before the civil war forced so many from South Sudan, including Nuer, to flee for refuge in Ethiopia.

Foreword to 'A *Nilotic World*:
The Atuot-Speaking Peoples of the Southern Sudan'
By John Burton, New York: Greenwood Press, 1987

This book was the doctoral thesis of John Burton, an anthropologist who essentially argued that the Atuot are a different ethnic group and not a section of the Dinka that they had always been assumed to be. Culturally, the Atuot represent a fusion of the Dinka and the Nuer, whose languages they fluently speak, including their own. In fact, I went to school with many students from the Atuot group and we always considered them Dinka. The study of John Burton was a remarkable instance of reconstruction of identity, not least through academic engineering.

Unfortunately, his study was viewed by the Dinka as a deliberate way of dividing a people who otherwise saw themselves as one. In fact, while he and his wife were staying with us in our house in Khartoum, John Burton one evening returned to the house after a social event, very shaken by a physical threat he had just experienced from a Dinka, Manoah Taban Pabek, an engineer, from the Agar Dinka who are closely associated with the Atuot. John Burton felt that his life was credibly in danger. I strongly objected to the hostile manner some Dinka reacted to his thesis, which to me indicated insecurity about the clarity of the identity of the Atuot as Dinka. Although John Burton had close contacts among the Atuot, who presumably welcomed his thesis, I doubt that his book had any impact on the general self-perception of the Atuot as Dinka.

'Response to Catholicism:
Pursuit of Well-Being in a Developing Society,'

In *Vernacular Christianity*, Wendy James
and Douglas H. Johnson, (eds), New York: Lilian Barber, 1988

This chapter documents both the process by which Catholicism was introduced to the Dinka, which adopted two contradictory but equally successful strategies. One was that proselytization was based on the assumption of a spiritual vacuum that had to be filled. On the other hand, the promotion of Christianity was carried out by the use of cultural practices, specifically the institution of songs that is very popular among the Dinka. Ironically, the devotion of traditional religious values and practices reinforced the fervor with which the Dinka accepted Christianity. Rather than fill the assumed vacuum of religious beliefs, Christianity was indeed strengthened by the Dinka belief system. In the end, it would seem difficult to determine which of the two belief systems, traditional or Christian, is superstitious.

One area that comes to mind was when we were discussing with our father his required consent for us "to have our heads sprinkled with holy water," in other words, to be baptized as Catholics. Father asked why we wanted to be baptized. We gave the reason we had been taught, that only those who were baptized would go to the "Home of God," (Heaven), while the others would burn in the "Home of Fire," (Hell). Of course, the Dinka did not believe that people would rise from death and be assigned to Heaven or Hell. Father responded by asking whether, assuming that those who were baptized would go to Heaven and the rest would burn in Hell, we, the children, would be happy in Heaven while the rest of the family burned in Hell. Again we told him what we had been taught, that on the "Day of Final

Judgement," people would be judged as individuals and not as families. It took me many years before I understood and appreciated Father's question. In retrospect, our people accepted the conversion of their children as part of the education that was connected with conversion rather than a step toward a higher level of religious belief.

'Behind the Name Mading'

The Journal of the Anthropological Society of Oxford

Volume XIX, no. 2, Trinity, 1988

I wrote this article in response to a request from Dr. Godfrey Lienhardt, the Oxford anthropologist expert on the Dinka whom I met very casually during my early days in London in 1962. He soon became a close friend and collaborator in various projects on the Dinka. I have no idea whether he was aware of the story behind my name or was driven by his knowledge that there is always some reason behind names among the Dinka. I know that Godfrey welcomed my story as a validation of his request to me.

The story goes back to the fact that my mother was betrothed before puberty in a fierce contest that was eventually won by my father with the strong support of her father, Mijok Duor. When a Dinka girl marries after being betrothed before puberty, a sacrifice is made to atone to God and the ancestral spirits because the idea of marriage before puberty, even in the form of betrothal, is a degree of ethical violation. This is called *agorot*. The bull that was sacrificed for my mother's *agorot* was of Mading color pattern, white with sprinkles of brown spots on both sides. Uncle Ngor, my mother's younger brother, was to give me more details many years later in a tape-recorded conversation that moved me profoundly with the depth of thought and feeling that my maternal grandfather Mijok Duor had invested in my being. According to Ngor, my grandfather said to a relative by the name of Dau Malek: "I have given the girl away. Give me the bull, Mading; your bull Mading will not be bartered for a cow-calf. Give him to me to be sacrificed for the spirit, *Agorot*. Give him to me while he is young, with horns still untouched (according to the custom of training horns to grow into shapes desired by the owner of the bull). That is what I want. That is the bull we should sacrifice for Achok."

He then called a number of elders from his clan to join him in invoking the bull and sacrificing it in the house of my father-to-be, Deng Majok. They went and stood their sacred spears in the ground and prayed as they invoked the bull for sacrifice. My grandfather said, "God, what I have to say is not much. We ask you to give Achok a son whom we shall name Mading after the bull we are about to sacrifice. That is all we ask of you." As Ngor put it, "They prayed and prayed and then sacrificed the bull. Then they left and said, 'It is now up to God to decide whether to accept our prayers or to reject our word.'"

I was born at Maker, the home of my maternal grandparents, several miles from Noong, my father's first home. No one knows the precise date of my birth, but historical coincidences, and my mother's recollections, suggest that I was born in the autumn of 1938. Despite my grandfather's wishes that I be named Mading after the sacrificial bull, my father's family named me Arob after my father's grandfather. On hearing that, my maternal grandfather Mijok was infuriated. He went to my father one early morning and said: "All I wanted from the marriage was that Head [of Deng Majok][60] that drove away the cattle from my daughter's engagement and imposed his will on me. And I appealed to God for divine justice. If God has responded by giving me

---

60. The 'Head [of Deng Majok]' is referring to characteristics that Mijok admired in the Deng Majok.

my Mading, how could you think of naming him Arob Biong? This Mading of mine, never ever call him by any other name." Father later spoke to his family and said, "I do not want to hear the child called Arob anymore. He will be Mading."

I did not know this background as I grew up. Indeed, I wondered why I was the only one among my brothers with a name that was not one of the names in our long line of ancestors. However, once I knew the story behind my name, I must say that it assumed a special moral, spiritual and social value that I deeply appreciated and still do.

'Eyes on Abyei:
Competing Perspectives on Rural Development,'

Afterword in *Between a Swamp and a Hard Place*
By David Cole and Richard Huntington, Harvard Institute for
International Development, Harvard University Press, 1997

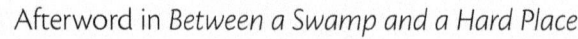

Uncle Deng Abot, Deputy to Father as Paramount Chief, in an interview with him for the biography of my father, told me that Abyei is like an eye, which is very small but sees so much. I later reversed that metaphor to argue that while Abyei is so small, the eyes of the world are now focused on it. While Abyei had been spotlighted by the international community, especially through the Abyei Protocol of the 2005 CPA that ended the second civil war in the Sudan (1983-2005), this book chapter applies more specifically to Abyei in the aftermath of the first civil war.

The 1972 Addis Ababa Agreement that ended the first North-South civil war (1955-1972), gave the Ngok Dinka of Abyei the right to decide in a plebiscite whether to remain under the administration of Kordofan

Province in the North to which they were annexed by the British in 1905. It soon became obvious that Khartoum was not willing to implement that provision and the autonomous regional government of South Sudan did not want to risk going back to war with the North over Abyei.

That was when I proposed an alternative solution that was premised on the fact that the Ngok Dinka wanted to join the South not so much because of racial or ethnic solidarity with the South, but because of the gross mistreatment they were receiving from the Arab-dominated government in Khartoum. If the Ngok Dinka were granted the right to manage their own affairs under the direct oversight of the President and provided with services and development opportunities, they would find it advantageous to play the bridging role they had historically played between the North and the South. That proposal was accepted by both the government in Khartoum and the regional government in the South. We were able to secure funding from USAID and invited the Harvard Institute for International Development, (HIID) to assist in the implementation of the project.

We soon encountered differences on the strategy for the development between my original approach and that of the HIID. I had requested the HIID to follow the development strategy proposed and expounded in my doctoral dissertation which was published in my award-winning book, *Tradition, and Modernization*,[61] the core of which was the strategy of transitional integration. The idea was to build on indigenous values and institutions to generate development as a process of self-enhancement from within. The HIDD on the other hand wanted to experiment with a concept of development, that was then quite popular, and wanted to apply appropriate technology that would minimize the need for external resources.

---

61. Francis Mading Deng, *Tradition and Modernization: A Challenge for Law among the Dinka of the Sudan,* Yale University Press, 1971. See p. 15.

While I agreed with the need for reducing external dependency and wanted to promote self-reliance, the HIID approach was not oriented to the cultural values of the people. An example of this culturally-disoriented approach was the insistence of the HIID's use of bulls for ploughing, which the Dinka objected to as antithetical to the dignity they associated with their cattle wealth. Although we eventually reconciled our contrasting approaches to development, the unresolved crisis in Abyei continued to escalate until it eventually exploded in a local rebellion that contributed to the full-scale resumption in 1983 of the North-South war. Unfortunately, history repeated itself over Abyei, as elaborated in my 2010 book, *Frontiers of Unity: An Experiment in African-Arab Cooperation in the Sudan.*[62]

'The Cow and the Thing Called 'What':
Dinka Cultural Perspectives on Wealth and Poverty'

Journal of International Affairs, (Columbia University),

Vol. 52, No. 1, Fall 1998

The Cow and the Thing Called What, is a myth of how the Dinka acquired the cattle wealth at creation. According to the myth, God asked the Dinka at creation: "Black Man, there is the thing called 'What' and the Cow, which one would you like?" The Dinka chose the Cow. God said to him that the thing called 'What' had hidden values that he should consider seriously before deciding. God suggested that the Dinka taste the milk of the Cow before making up his mind. The Dinka tasted the milk and said, "Let us have the Cow and never see the thing called 'What.'" According to the myth, clearly being reinterpreted

---

62. Francis Deng, *Frontiers of Unity: An Experiment in African-Arab Cooperation in the Sudan.* Routledge, 2010 – see p. 42.

in light of the current cross-cultural world, God then gave 'The Thing Called What' to the white and brown races. Nowadays, the Dinka go further in their diminishing self-esteem in the comparative modern world that has denigrated their cattle wealth. They admit that 'The Thing Called What' became the source of the inventiveness and modern wealth of the Europeans and the Arabs. One Dinka elder even said to me, "Our Founding Fathers chose the Cow and denied us The Book which was what God called 'The Thing Called What.'"

The implication of this myth that has been of concern to me is the tendency to see change as an externally induced process. This implies approaching development as an alien concept to be exported from the rich developed world to the backward, primitive, poor communities of the Third World. Implicit in that is a concept of wealth and poverty that is gauged by the criteria of the market economy with monetary value as the criterion for measurement where the poverty line is living on one US dollar a day.

This also contrasted with the Dinka perception of wealth which was largely based on cattle and by which they perceived themselves not only as wealthy but as the envy of the world. And indeed, the Dinka are among the wealthiest cattle-owning communities in Africa. The average bridewealth is about fifty cows and can rise to hundreds among wealthy families. Even if one adopted the monetary criterion, can a man be said to live on one dollar a day if he owns the Dinka average wealth of fifty cows with equal numbers of sheep and goats, heads a polygamous family of several wives, (with each wife owning a self-built hut), in a village with two, also self-built cattle byres, and all growing sufficient food crops for subsistence, with some surplus to barter for other commodities, while having a daily supply of liters of milk, and occasional meat from the herd?

Two sets of considerations flow from this baseline. One is to see these resources as assets for a decent living. The other is their potential use as resources for development, perceived as self-enhancement from within rather than a commodity to be imported from outside. And then there is the even more fundamental issue of positive self-perception as an asset that should be factored into the indicators of human development. What is also important is the implication of categorizing people as poor, shifting a positive self-perception to a demeaning status of negative comparison. This is compounded by the fact that the Dinka are now exposed to the outside world and all the amenities of the modern world that was outside their knowledge in their splendid isolation. The outcome is to accept the inferiority of the comparative status, which in turn generates resentment and animosity popularly known in Western political economy as class struggle.

'Scramble for Souls:
Religious Intervention Among the Dinka in Sudan'
In Proselytization and Communal Self-Determination in Africa
by Abdullahi An-Na'im, (ed), New York: Orbis Books, 1999

This chapter was a paper presented to a conference organized by Professor Abdullahi An-Na'im of Emory University[63] School of Law on the subject. An aspect of cross-cultural dynamics that has always been behind the domination of foreign rulers in Africa and the introduction of alien religions, specifically Christianity and Islam, has been the assumption of a spiritual vacuum among the traditional Africans. The irony is that the Dinka and the Nuer in Southern Sudan have been documented as the most religious peoples in the Sudan. Another

63. In Atlanta, Georgia, United States of America.

irony is that while there are cultural specificities that reflect differences, the long history of cross-cultural interaction in the Nile Valley led to religious diffusion that has injected traits of Christianity and Islam into the religious beliefs of the Nilotic peoples.

In my writings on this issue, I have been critical of condescending religious intervention by Christian and Muslim proselytization while expounding the principles of the traditional religious belief system. When I first wrote a series of articles about this issue in the early 60s, which were published by the Hibbert Journal of Comparative Religion, I mentioned to Dr. Godfrey Lienhardt that I expected to be excommunicated from the Catholic Church. With humor and wisdom he responded, "Francis, I think the Pope has far more important things to do to worry about excommunicating you."

'Abyei: A Bridge or a Gulf? The Ngok Dinka on Sudan's North-South Border,'

In *White Nile Black Blood* by Jay Spaulding and Stephanie Beswick, (eds), Lawrenceville: The Red Sea Press, 1999

This article documents my efforts to resolve the crisis situation in Abyei between the North and the South of Sudan which has been a matter of concern for me since childhood. During the lengthy peace process that eventually culminated in the 1972 Addis Ababa Agreement, which ended the seventeen-year long civil war (1955-1972), I was able to influence the negotiations that eventually included in the agreement a provision giving the Ngok Dinka the choice between remaining under Northern administration, to which it was annexed by the British colonial rule in 1905 for administrative convenience and to provide them with better protection from Arab slave raiders, or revert to the

South. President Nimeiri resisted the implementation of that provision, and the autonomous government of South Sudan, under the Addis Ababa Accord, did not want to risk going back to war with the North over Abyei.

There was however another reality about Abyei. Despite the hostilities in their border area, the traditional elders of Abyei succeeded diplomatically in forging cordial ties with their Missiriya Arab counterparts to the North which resulted in relatively peaceful coexistence and cooperation between their respective communities. Ngok leaders became the intermediaries between the Arab North and the African South at that turbulent border to the extent that they were able to redeem Southern slaves and return them to their areas during the pre-colonial nineteenth century hostilities of the slave raids in the South. That peaceful and cooperative coexistence between the Arabs and the Dinka was reinforced by the colonial administration through evenhandedness in regulating relations between the border communities.

That balance was disturbed following independence, especially with the war between the North and the South in which the central government treated Abyei as part of the enemy South. The government recruited, trained, armed, and deployed the Missiriya Arabs as a militia force against the South. Ngok Dinka youth on their part joined the Southern Sudanese rebel movement (SPLM/A), and fought alongside their fellow South Sudanese and distinguished themselves for their valor and unwavering commitment to the struggle. They were therefore intent on exercising the choice given them by the Addis Ababa Accord in favor of rejoining the South. The refusal of the Government to implement the provision generated a tense situation in Abyei; quite an explosive situation that posed a serious threat to the viability of the peace agreement.

That is when I came up with the proposal of building on the positive aspect of the history of inter-communal relations in the area to enable Abyei to be a bridge of peace and reconciliation between the North and the South. I made the case in a concept policy paper in which I argued that the Ngok Dinka wanted to rejoin the South not so much because of sentiments of racial and cultural affinity as was a protest against the mistreatment they were receiving in the North, dominated, subjugated and denigrated, a situation that sharply contrasted with the pride and dignity for which the Dinka were known. I proposed that if the Ngok Dinka were given the right to run their own affairs through a mini version of the autonomy granted to the South, and provided with social services and development projects, building on their cultural values and institutions based on the principle of development as self-enhancement from within, they could be positively inspired to revive their traditionally bridging role between the North and the South. The proposal appealed to the leadership of the central government, especially the President, and the Regional Government of the South, specifically the President, presumably because it got them off the hook of the Abyei predicament.

Starting from the time I was appointed Ambassador to the Scandinavian countries and then to the United States, from which I was appointed Minister of State for Foreign Affairs, funding for the project came from USAID and the Harvard Institute for International Development (HIID), assisted in its implementation.

The project however met with considerable controversy. While it was appreciated by most of the Ngok Dinka in the area, it was opposed by the political elite who saw it as surrendering the cause of joining the South, opposed by the Missiriya Arabs as favoring the Ngok Dinka over them, and resisted by the provincial authorities as interference by the central authorities in matters falling under their jurisdiction.

The oppressive administration of the Northern officials and harassment of the Missiriya Arabs generated tensions that triggered the local rebellion that contributed to the resumption of hostilities that lead to the fully-fledged return to the war in 1983. That war was eventually ended by the 2005 CPA, which culminated in the independence of South Sudan in 2011.

Tragically, history was to repeat itself. The Abyei Protocol, which was included in the CPA, gave the Ngok Dinka the same right that the Addis Ababa Agreement had given them–to decide by a referendum to choose between remaining in the North or joining South Sudan. As was the case with the Addis Ababa Agreement, the Sudan Government reneged on implementing the Abyei Protocol. Several agreements have been made since to resolve the impasse over Abyei but without any positive outcome. The crisis over Abyei, therefore, continues unresolved and remains a potential trigger for confrontation between the Two Sudans. The situation continues to challenge me with the search for a solution that can build on the positive aspects of the history of the area to revive a constructive basis for playing the bridging role it had historically played. That is a story for subsequent publications.

'The World of the Dinka:
A Portrait of a Threatened Culture,'

In *Traditions, Values, and Humanitarian Action*

By Kevin M. Cahill, a joint publication of Fordham University Press

and the Center for International Health and Cooperation, 2003

This chapter provides an overview of the Dinka value system and the degree to which it has been impacted by the forces of foreign domination and an externally oriented view of development. As a result of these external pressures, the Dinka, who have been well documented as traditionally proud, ethnocentric, and resistant to any change that implies assimilation into a foreign value systems, are beginning to recognize their comparative disadvantages in the modern context, leading to a negative self-image. This diminishing self-perception, which is a challenge to the people's sense of dignity, calls for correction through a better understanding of the positive aspects of the indigenous value system and the promotion of a cross-cultural, mutually enriching strategy of transitional integration.

Foreword to 'DINKA: *Legendary Cattle Keepers of Sudan*'
By Angela Fisher and Carol Beckwith, Rizzoli, New York, 2011

This is an artistically beautiful, large table book of photographs of the Dinka, focusing on their devotion to cattle. The photographs were taken at a time when young men and women mostly went naked. In asking me to write a foreword, the authors indicated that while they had taken photos of peoples and cultures from around the world for decades, the Dinka were by far their favorite people. While I was pleased to have been asked to write a foreword, I realized that some of our people might be disturbed by the nudity. But apart from the fact that this was a reflection of our reality, I thought that the beauty of the photos and the environment by far exceeded the sensitivities of externally rooted embarrassment about nudity. Indeed, I said that much in my foreword.

I had an experience over the book that confirms the interactive perspectives on nudity. Once, when I was Under-Secretary-General and Special Advisor of the Secretary-General on the Prevention of

Genocide, the Secretary-General of the United Nations, Ban Ki-moon visited my office in his rounds to the offices of his senior staff. I occupied a spacious office in a building on 47th Street between First Avenue and East River Drive overlooking the river. As the Secretary-General entered my office, his attention was immediately drawn by two things, the view of the river and the *DINKA* book, on the table. He began turning the pages and making complementary comments. I rather nervously commented on the nudity of the photos, adding that some of our people might be put off by that, to which he responded; "But this is beautiful art."

Later when I was the first Permanent Representative to the United Nations, of the newly independent country of South Sudan, I was visited in my office by the Minister in the Office of the President, a Dinka, and the Minister of Foreign Affairs, a Nuer. The *DINKA* book was on my desk. They became so engaged and admiring of the book that when the Dinka Minister asked how he could get a copy, I gave him my specially bound copy in a leather case with its warm inscription by the authors.

B. National Level

'Man and Society'
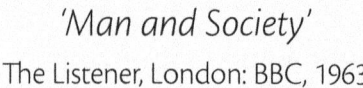
The Listener, London: BBC, 1963

This was a version of the presentation Dr. Godfrey Lienhardt and I made in the BBC program on the theme of Man in Society, which gave me the opportunity to use some of the songs I had collected in 1962 and which eventually led to the book, *The Dinka and Their Songs*.[64]

---

64. Francis Mading Deng, *The Dinka and their Songs*, published in 1973 by Oxford University in *The Series of African Literature*. Reissued by Africa World Books, 2022 – see p. 19.

'Property and Value Interplay Among the Nilotics,'

In *Traditional and Modern Economic Theories and*

Practices in the Developing Countries of Africa

Iowa Review, vol. 51, no. 1, Spring 1966 [65]

This article was initially prepared for a project with a Professor of African Law at London University. It was reproduced at the request of a colleague at Yale who was from Iowa.

'The Future of Customary Law in the Sudan'

In *A study of the Legal System and the Problems of Nationbuilding*

Malaya Law Review, 1969, pp. 26886

This is a version of an article that was first published in the *Sudan Law Review and Reports*, in 1965, reproduced at the request of a colleague at Yale from Singapore who was a lecturer in law in Singapore Faculty of Law.

'Pursuing Peace and Unity in the Sudan'

A report of a personal peace initiative with General Olusegun

Obasanjo, former Head of State of Nigeria, 1986

Following the All-Party Conference which I organized at the Woodrow Wilson International Center for Scholars, whose results were published in the book, *The Search for Peace and Unity in the Sudan*, General Olusegun Obasanjo, Former President of Nigeria, who had attended

---

65. This article was first published in *Sudan Law Review and Reports*, 1965.

the conference, and I, undertook a peace initiative that saw us shuttle for years between successive governments in Khartoum and the rebel SPLM/A. I later documented our initiative in the book, *Partners for Peace*.[66]

'The United Nations and the
Emergency Operations in the Sudan'

A study prepared for the United Nations Office of
Emergency Operations in Africa, 1986

This report was initially prepared for the United Nations Emergency Operations in Africa which was in response to the massive drought crisis in Sub-Sahara Africa in which a former Swedish Ambassador and I were commissioned to look into the UN response in the Sudan and Ethiopia. This report was subsequently incorporated in our co-authored book, *The Challenges of Famine Relief: Emergency Operations in the Sudan*.[67]

'Conflict in the Sudan'

Life and Peace Review, vol. 2, no. 3, 1988

This was one of the earliest writings about the crisis of identity in the Sudanese conflict.

---

66. Francis Mading Deng, *Partners for Peace: An Initiative on the Sudan with General Olusegun Obasanjo*, ALF Publications, 1998 – see p. 92.

67. Francis Mading Deng and Larry Minear, *The Challenges of Famine Relief: Emergency Operations in Sudan*, The Brookings Institution Press, 1992 – see p. 83.

'A Three Dimensional Approach to the Conflict in the Sudan'

In *Religion and National Integration in Africa*

By John Hunwick, (ed), Illinois: Northwestern University, 1989

I presented this paper when the African Program organized a meeting in which several experts on the Sudan, including Abdullahi Ahmed An-Na'im, participated. My contribution focused on my theme of identity in which three factors, race, culture, and religion were central interconnected factors.

'In Sudan, Masses Die as Rebels, Government Use Food as a Weapon'

Los Angeles Times, Part V, September 5, 1989

This article was written at the time the famine crisis in the Sudan was at the most critical level when the number of deaths had generated an intense international relief response, especially in the United States and the United Nations, eventually resulting in Operation Lifeline Sudan. Senator Edward Kennedy was to include in *Congressional Records* a passage from my article in which I wrote, 'It is not the dead who suffer; it is those who cause their death and those who watch them die.'

'Identity Factors in the Sudanese Conflict'
In *Conflict in Multi-Ethnic Societies*
Foreign Service Institute, 1989 [68]

This is typical of my analysis of identity as a factor in Sudan's proliferating conflict, a theme which I began to spell out in earlier publications; *Dynamics of Identification*,[69] and *Peace and Unity in the Sudan, An African Achievement*,[70] and my two novels: *Seed of Redemption*[71] and *Cry of the Owl*.[72]

'What Is Not Said is What Divides'
In *Management of the Crisis in the Sudan*
by Abdel Ghaffar Ahmed and Gunnar Sorbo,
(eds), University of Bergen, April 1989

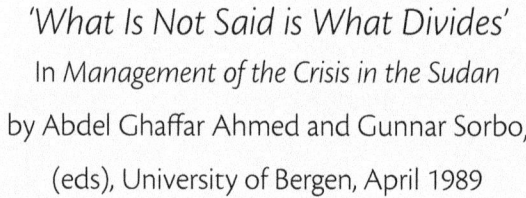

This article elaborates the thesis that the Sudanese tend to avoid discussing the sensitive issues that are the core of the conflicts in the Sudan, foremost of which is the crisis of identity in the country.

---

68. The article was published again as, *'The Identity Factor in the Sudanese Conflict,'* in *Conflict and Peacemaking in Multiethnic Societies*, by Joseph V. Montville, (ed), Washington: Heath and Company, 1991.

69. Francis Mading Deng, *Dynamics of Identification: A Basis for National Integration*, Khartoum University Press, 1973 – see p. 62.

70. Francis M. Deng co-author with the Ministry of Foreign Affairs, *Peace and Unity in the Sudan: An African Achievement*, Khartoum University Press, 1973 – see p. 64.

71. Francis Mading Deng, *Seed of Redemption: A Political Novel*, Lilian Barber Press, 1986 - see p. 75.

72. Francis Mading Deng, *Cry of the Owl: A Novel*, Lilian Barber Press, 1989 – see p. 81.

'War of Visions for the Nation'

In *Middle East Journal*, vol. 44, no. 4, Autumn 1990

This article was written while I was working on the book, *War of Visions in the Sudan: Conflict of Identities in the Sudan*.[73] It was in essence a summary and a precursor of that book which was published in 1995.

'Sudanese Conflict In Perspective: an Action Memorandum'

A report prepared for the Carter Center Consultation of the

International Negotiation Network. Atlanta, Georgia, January 15-17, 1992

A paper prepared to assist President Carter in his efforts to mediate in the Sudanese conflict.

'Islamic Fundamentalism in the Sudan:
A Symptom of an Identity Crisis,'

In *Perspectives of Global Responsibility*

by Hans d'Orville, (ed), New York: Inter-Action Council, 1993

The essence of this article was to distinguish between the role of religion as such as a factor in the national identity configuration and the emergent Islamic fundamentalism which was aggravating religious identity in the Sudanese conflict. The argument was that traditional Islam was eclectic and tolerant while Islamic fundamentalism was

---

73. Francis M. Deng, *War of Visions: Conflict of Identities in the Sudan*, The Brookings Institution Press, 1995 – see p. 84.

monolithic and intolerant of religious pluralism, thereby fueling religiously related conflict of identity.

'We Must End the War'

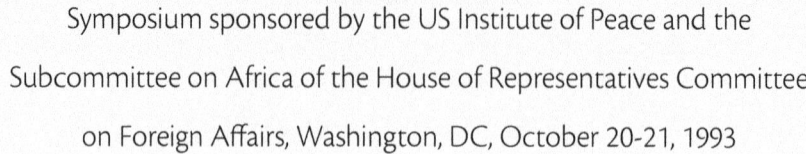

Symposium sponsored by the US Institute of Peace and the

Subcommittee on Africa of the House of Representatives Committee

on Foreign Affairs, Washington, DC, October 20-21, 1993

This was again one of the activities undertaken by the Resource Group in support of the IGAD Peace Process.

'The Nile: A River that Unites and Divides'

In *Culture and Negotiations*

By Guy Olivier Faure and Jeffrey Z. Rubin, Sage Publications, 1993

This chapter explores water conflicts surrounding the Nile River between North and South Sudan and contextualized these conflicts amidst religious, territorial, and cultural conflicts characterizing the history of the region and the historical and spiritual message attached to this body of water. The chapter relates the North-South conflict to the Jonglei Canal Project which has been severely contested and explores the problems associated with negotiating a consensual outcome to the conflicts due to differences in cultural values, ideologies, and identity.

'The Sudan: Stop the Carnage'

The Brookings Review, vol. 12, no. 1, Winter 1994

Toward the end of the 1990s, the tragedy of the war in the Sudan, specifically in the South, was compounded by massive famine triggered by prolonged drought that had devastated the region for years and frustrated agricultural activities. The delivery of humanitarian assistance was often blocked by the parties who were in effect using famine as a weapon of war.

'The Tragedy in Sudan Must End: A Personal Appeal to Compatriots and to Humanity'

Mediterranean Quarterly, vol. 5, no. 1, Winter, 1994

This article was another appeal to address the crisis of war compounded by famine in which the parties were using the denial of food as a weapon in war.

'The Prospects for Peace in Sudan'

A follow-up to the October 1993 symposium, organized by the US Institute of Peace and the Africa Subcommittee of the House Foreign Affairs Committee, April 12, 1994

This was one of the activities carried out by our Resource Persons' Group for the IGAD Peace Process.

'Negotiating a Hidden Agenda: Sudan's Conflict of Identities'

In *Elusive Peace: Negotiating an End to Civil Wars*

by William Zartman, (ed), The Brookings Institute, 1995

This article argued that in the discourse of the crises in the country there was a tendency to avoid the core of the problems because of their sensitivity and the difficulty of confronting them head-on. There was denial of the fact that the crisis was racial or religious, the disingenuous argument being that Arabism was cultural and not racial and that there were Muslims in the South and Christians in the North. In other words, the issue of identity was considered too sensitive to address and was therefore avoided. This was the core of my article that would become popular in the South, *'What is Not Said is What Divides.*[74]

'Sudan: Is There a Path to Peace?'

Humanitarian Monitor, no. 2,

InterAfrica Group Publication, February 1995

I wrote this article shortly after the IGAD leaders had undertaken their peace initiative and the Addis Ababa-based Inter-Africa Group invited several individuals, including myself, to be Resource Persons to the initiative. I became the Rapporteur of the Group and wrote several reports and eventually a book, *Their Brothers' Keepers,*[75] about the process.

---

74. Francis Mading Deng, *What is Not Said is What Divides,* in *Management of the Crisis in the Sudan,* Abdel Ghaffar Ahmed and Gunnar Sorbo, (eds), University of Bergen, April 1989 - see p. 164.

75. Francis Mading Deng, *Their Brothers' Keepers: Report of the IGAD Resource Persons,* Inter-Africa Group, 1997 – see p. 89.

'Mediating the Sudanese Conflict: A Challenge for the IGAD'

CSIS Africa Notes, no. 169, February 1995

This was one of the papers I wrote on behalf of the Resource Persons and which contributed significantly to the peace process.

'Auf der Suche nach einer sudanesischen Identität: Eine Antwort auf Khalid al-Mubarak'

(Dialogue with Khalid al-Mubarak)

Inamo, (Informationsprojeckt Naher und Mittlerer Osten)

No. 11, Spring 1997

Khalid Mubarak's response to my writings on the Dinka, and my novels on the crisis of identity in the Sudan, was to question my declared commitment to national unity based on equality, alleging that I was in fact a chauvinistic Dinka tribalist. He however targeted three of us in his attack, myself, Dr. Mansour Khalid, a liberal Northern Sudanese Minister of Foreign Affairs, who shared my views on Sudan's crisis of identity, and Dr. John Garang, of the SPLM/A who championed the Vision of New Sudan. Khalid Mubarak specifically questioned my writing a book about my father instead of writing about one of the national leaders, of course, all Northern Sudanese. My response to his attack was to note that it was indeed proof of the racism and chauvinism that I was striving to address.

'Sudan: The Challenge of Nationhood'

In *A Sourcebook on Self-Determination and Self-Administration*

by Wolfgang Danspeckgruber and Arthur Watts, (eds), Boulder:

Lynne Rienner Publishers, 1997

This article tried to reconcile the demand for self-determination aimed at independence and the principles of unity within existing borders. National governments, regional, and international organizations are caught up in that dilemma, sympathizing with the oppressed within the existing borders of countries, but wanting to preserve the territorial integrity of those countries otherwise torn apart. Building on the premise that secession was not an end in itself, but a yearning for freedom from administrative domination. Self-administration within national unity is proposed as a remedy to that dilemma. In the Sudan, that was initially applied through the 1972 Addis Ababa Agreement. The unilateral abrogation of that agreement led to the resumption of the civil war in 1983. Self-administration as internal self-determination was no longer credible and the secession of the South in 2011 became inevitable.

'Droht der Sudan zu Zerreiben?' (Sudan's Civil War: Escalation toward Peace or Disintegration of the Nation)

Der Uberblick, 4/97, December 1997

The core of the question this article addressed is an assessment of the challenges posed by the wars of identities in the Sudan and whether the country would reconstruct its national identity framework or break up. With the independence of South Sudan, the latter has been the answer, but the question still applies to the remaining country of the Sudan where identity conflicts persist, though less severe in terms of the challenge they pose to the unity of the country

'Debt to Godfrey Lienhardt'

In *Special Issue in Memory of Godfrey Lienhardt,*

by Ahmed Al-Shahi and Jeremy Coyote, (eds),

Journal of the Anthropological Society of Oxford, 88, 1, 1997

In this piece, I retell how Godfrey and I met in 1962 and how he significantly contributed to my self-education in anthropology and encouraged and assisted me in a number of my works on Dinka culture.

'Dilemmas of Foreign Assistance: Lessons from Sudan'

The Brown Journal of International Affairs, Vol. IV, Issue 2. 1997

This article summarizes the challenges of foreign humanitarian assistance discussed in the book, *The Challenges of Famine Relief: Emergency Operations in the Sudan.*[76] The challenges are essentially the dilemmas of foreign humanitarian assistance which comprised the externality of the assistance, lack of connection to the internal structures and institutions, failure to build internal capacities, and exiting without anything to leave behind to enhance coping capacity to deal with future emergencies.

---

76. Francis Mading Deng and Larry Minear, *The Challenges of Famine Relief: Emergency Operations in Sudan,* The Brookings Institution Press, 1992 – see p. 83.

'Africa's Dilemma in the Sudan'

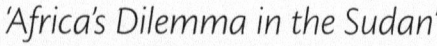

The World Today, March 1998, Volume 54, Number 3

The core of Africa's dilemma in the Sudan is that a country that is essentially African, racially and culturally, with elements of Arab influence, identifies itself as fundamentally Arab and only geographically African the same way the Arab countries on the continent of Africa perceive themselves. This is the core of the war of identities that have been tearing the country apart since independence from the Anglo-Egyptian colonial administration and that was the national problem the SPLM/A had rebelled against and tried to correct.

Foreword to *Day of Devastation, Day of Contentment: The History of the Sudanese Church Across 2000 Years*

By Roland Werner, William Anderson, and Andrew Wheeler,

Nairobi, Kenya Paulines Publications Africa, 2000, pp. 9-11

Day of Devastation is a comprehensive, positive review of the process of proselytization in the Sudan, the challenges confronted by the Christian Missionaries over the years amidst myriad internal crises, and the hostile policies of the Muslim Arab governments since independence. In the Foreword, I presented an appreciative evaluation of the contribution of the Christian Church in the South and a more nuanced critique of the attitude toward traditional belief systems.

'War and Genocide: Disappearing Christians of the Middle East'

Middle East Quarterly, winter, 2001, pp. 12-21

This article is about the identity wars in the Sudan pitting the Arab Muslim North against the African Christian in South Sudan.

'U.S. Policy to End Sudan's War:
Report of the CSIS Task Force on U.S-Sudan Police'

February, 2001 [77]

This report documents the work of the Task Force that held contentious discussions which began with an overwhelming view that Sudan was not of particular strategic interest to the United States, that the only interest of the US was Sudan's involvement in international terrorism, its destabilization of the neighboring countries, and the humanitarian tragedy caused by the war. The issue should be left to the concerned European countries with remote support from the United States. They also argued against the self-determination of the South with the risk of breaking up the country.

Almost singlehandedly, I argued for reversing the order of US concerns and made the point that Sudan was indeed of strategic interest to the US. As it is a meeting point of major religious and cultural regions of Christian Africa and the Arab Middle East. It could be a point of cooperation or conflict that could extend to the Middle East. Sudan's alleged involvement in international terrorism is due to the fact that they were reacting to the support of the Christian West for South Sudan and therefore join the Islamist anti-West terrorists on

---

77. Task Force co-chaired with J. Stephen Morrison.

the principle that the enemy of my enemy is my friend. I also argued that destabilizing the countries of the neighbors was also for the same reason that they are supporting the South in the war. As for humanitarian tragedy, it was also a consequence of war. End the war and Sudan would stop involvement in terrorism; it would stop destabilizing the region, and the humanitarian tragedy would end. I also argued that the United States could not afford to be indifferent to the crisis in a country of such regional and international strategic importance.

I also argued that if the unity of the Sudan was the preferred outcome, the way to ensure it is not to say that no one supports self-determination for the South, but to tell the government in the North that unless you address the genuine grievances of the South, the unity of your country is in danger. I argued that to save the unity of the country, we must make the impossible possible, and reconcile the irreconcilable visions of the North for unity, and of the South for secession. After a lengthy intensive exchange of views, the Task Force adopted the formula of 'One Sudan; Two Systems.' That formula became the guiding principle in the negotiations that ended in the CPA.

'Green is the Color of the Masters: The Legacy of Slavery and the Crisis of Identity in the Sudan'
Academia.edu, 2004

This article explores the connection between slavery and the humanitarian crisis in modern Sudan as an evolutionary process covering overlapping qualitative phases. The first phase witnessed the prevalence of slavery against the Sudanese Blacks alongside a process of Arabization and Islamization that allowed the races to mix and elevate the resulting hybrid into a category that was esteemed above the enslavable categories. During the second phase, the British ended the slave trade and the crude form of slavery but allowed the practice and the related attitude of racial stratification and discrimination to continue. The third phase ensured protection of the South through a separatist policy that isolated the South and kept it undeveloped, which relegated the South to an inferior status. The fourth was the dominance of the North over the South. The last phase was the liberation struggle that was initially separatist but eventually favored full unity in a New Sudan. The chapter ends by posing critical choices: unity in a restructured New Sudan, coexistence in a framework of unity in diversity, and outright partition.

Foreword to 'War and Faith in Sudan'

By Gabriel Meyer, William B. Eerdmans Publishing Company

Cambridge, U.K. 2005

This book documents the war in the Nuba where the suffering of the people is very much the same as in Darfur and South Sudan. Unlike the situation in Darfur where the people are Muslims, there are Christians among the Nuba although the Muslims are the majority. This makes the Nuba closer to the South than the Darfurians. Meyer's book in fact stresses the role of religion as a factor in the war of identities among the Nuba. This is in effect a new development since the Nuba used to be identified as part of the North and mostly saw themselves as Arabs. In fact, Meyer quotes Yusuf Kuwa, one of the leading commanders of the SPLA, saying that they were orientated in school to proudly identify themselves with Arab ancestry and that it was only recently that they discovered and acknowledged their

African identity. This was clearly the impact of the South on the Nuba. Ironically, in the first civil war, the Nuba were largely the foot soldiers the Arabs used in the war against the South.

Foreword to 'Civil Wars and Revolution in the Sudan'
By Robert O. Collins, Tsehai Publishers, Hollywood, CA, 2005

Robert O. Collins' book is a collection of essays written over the years. While documenting the challenges the country has suffered, the author provides a glowing praise of the Sudanese people known for their warmth, kindness, generosity and dignified mannerism. In my Foreword, I tried to address the sharp contrast between these positive attributes, especially in the interaction of the Sudanese with the outside world, and the brutality with which they relate to each other internally. I attribute this discrepancy to the crisis of identity, which makes the conflicting grounds view each other disparaging and denigrate 'the other' as less than human and therefore not meriting the respect and deferential treatment associated with human dignity. The solution is therefore the search for a new uniting national identity that accords dignity to all as citizens.

'Sudan's Turbulent Road to Nationhood,'
In Borders, Nationalism, and the African State
By Ricardo Rene Larémont, Boulder, Colorado,
Lynne Reiner Publishers, 2005

This chapter is again a history of the violent conflicts that have devastated the country since independence and the latest steps toward peace and the optimistic march toward a new dispensation within the stip-ulated framework of a New United Sudan in which citizenship and not divisive identities are the norm for nationhood.

'The Challenges of War and Peace in the Sudan'

A Report on Project Activities carried out between January 1ˢᵗ to

December 31ˢᵗ 2005, supported by the U.S. Department of State through

Worldwide Humanitarian Services Inc, and Kush Inc, January 2006

This report was commissioned by the State Department following the 2005 Comprehensive Peace Agreement (CPA), to assess the imple-mentation of the Agreement.

'UNDP Sudan – UN Contribution to

International Assistance Co-ordination Project'

A Report on project activities carried out

between January 1ˢᵗ to December 31ˢᵗ, 2004 [78]

This is a self-explanatory project sponsored by our Brookings-SAIS Project on Internal Displacement.

'Sudan: A Nation in Turbulent Search of Itself'

The Annals of the American Academy of Political Science, 2006

This article provides an overview of the crisis in the Sudan as reflected in its multiple wars of identity throughout the country and the need

---

78. As per the Memorandum of *"Understanding between UNDP Sudan and the John Hopkins University SAIS Center for Displacement Studies,"* January 2006.

to address them comprehensively in a short term framework of unity in diversity with a longer term goal of integration in a New Sudan of full equality without discrimination on any ground.

'African Renaissance: Toward A New Sudan'
In *Prospects for Peace, Oxford, Forced Migration Review*
By Marion Couldrey and Tom Morris, (eds), 2006

The thesis and theme of this paper is similar to the above, but with a more optimistic assessment that the CPA and its credible implementation represented a step in the direction of a New Sudan.

Foreword to *'Darfur Diaries: Stories of Survival'*
By Jen Marlowe, Aisha Bain and Adam Shapiro, Nation Books, 2006

This book is a powerful documentation of the tragedy which has been called genocide. In addition to the stories of individuals, it is also an account of how the Sudanese in the marginalized areas in the North began to scrutinize their misidentification as Arab and join the quest for a New Sudan. What impressed me the most was the courage the young investigators displayed in documenting the suffering of the people under very dangerous conditions, the similarity of what was happening in Darfur and what had been happening in South Sudan, and the increasing realization that the solution to the crisis throughout the country was a restructuring of the country toward a New Sudan of full equality without discrimination on racial, ethnic, religious or cultural grounds.

'Sudan at the Crossroads: Audit of the Conventional Wisdom'

MIT Center for International Studies, 2007

This publication was an 'audit' of the conventional understanding of the genocidal war in Darfur in isolation of the acute crisis of identity that had started in the Southern part of the country and spread to the marginalized regions of the North in the 1980s. The paper argues that the Darfur conflict was an integral aspect of a nationwide crisis that should be addressed comprehensively on the basis of the vision of New Sudan stipulated by the SPLM/A.

'Darfur: A Portrait of National Identity Crisis in Sudan: Audit of the Conventional Wisdom'

MIT, Center for International Studies, 2007

This article argues against the conventional wisdom in the West to see the alleged genocidal conflict in Darfur in isolation. The article explains that the conflict in Darfur is an extension of the wars of identity in the Sudan which began in Southern Sudan early in the 1950s, extended into the Nuba Mountains and Blue Nile in the 1980s and then into Darfur in the early 1990s. Only by seeing it as a manifestation of an inclusive national identity crisis can the problem in Darfur and the rest of the country be appropriately addressed and resolved at its roots.

'Sudan: Education, Culture, and Negotiation'

In *Even in Chaos: Education in Times of Emergency*

By Kevin M. Cahill, (ed), Fordham University Press

and the Center for Humanitarian Cooperation, 2010

Education normally connotes schools, formal institutions of learning, for children and youth. This formal education poses special challenges in emergency situations. Education in the broader sense of information gathering and knowledge generation about a given situation poses its own challenges in emergency situations. These challenges include: understanding the dilemmas that emergency situations present for those involved in humanitarian operations; developing knowledge and appreciation for the cultural context and the values of those who are being assisted; learning about the root causes of the conflict that has generated the emergency; searching for the models of constitutionalism and governance for resolving the conflict; establishing mechanisms for ensuring peace, security and stability; and identifying culturally-oriented principles for preventing, managing and resolving conflicts.

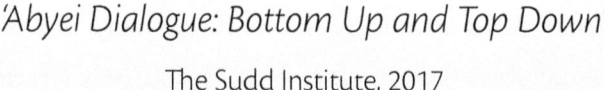

'Abyei Dialogue: Bottom Up and Top Down'

The Sudd Institute, 2017

The experience documented in this article is particularly remarkable in that it started as a personal problem between leading individuals, extended to regional relations between neighboring communities, became incrementally connected to the responsibility of the national government for addressing the Abyei crisis, and ended with the challenges facing Sudan and South Sudan over the case of Abyei.

The starting point is a conflict that persisted for years between Bona Malual and leading Ngok Dinka individuals in the SPLM/A and the Government of South Sudan. As is well known, Bona Malual's leadership extends from his base in the Twic Dinka community, to the Greater Bahr el-Ghazal region, on to the level of South Sudan, with connections to the leaders of the Sudan, and outreach extending to the international community. The Ngok leaders with whom Bona Malual was in conflict are individuals who contributed enormously to the South Sudanese struggle and continue to play crucial roles in the post-independence Government of South Sudan.

Considering Bona Malual's influence at the leadership levels of both South Sudan and Sudan, his adversity toward Ngok Dinka leaders inevitably impacted negatively on his approach to the case of Abyei. It not only deprived the area of the constructive role he could have played in the search for a solution to the Abyei crisis, but also reflected a negative attitude to the area by association. Reconciling Bona Malual with Ngok Leaders, therefore, became an urgent imperative.

Years of efforts by myself eventually achieved the reconciliation and the unification of cooperative efforts between Bona Malual and his Ngok Dinka adversaries, followed by the unification of efforts to address the Abyei problem. Throughout reconciliation talks, the leadership of South Sudan was kept informed and were in full support of the process.

Following the reconciliation, Bona Malual and the myself proceeded to Khartoum to dialogue with the leaders of the Sudan. On our return, we visited Abyei to brief the community and solicit local support for our efforts. That occasion demonstrated that the reconciliation had extended to the neighboring Twic community whose Chiefs and elders attended the Abyei gathering and discussions. The Governors of Twic and Gogrial States also attended. All demonstrated their solidarity with the Ngok Dinka people.

I argued that the ensuing challenge was how to sustain this spirit of reconciliation and the unified approach to the Abyei problem. That would entail addressing the crises at all levels, including the urgent need for the stabilization of the area which requires providing security, encouraging the return of the displaced populations to their areas of origin, delivering essential services, generating socio-economic development projects, fostering peaceful and cooperative relations with neighbors to the North and South, and intensifying the dialogue with the Sudan to expedite the search for a final solution to the Abyei problem. Included is a detailed menu of recommendations for pursuing this goal.

'National Dialogue: A Policy Framework'
The Sudd Institute, 2017

President Salva Kiir Mayardit initiated the South Sudan National Dialogue in December 2016 amidst the civil war that broke out in December 2013, barely two years after the independence from the Republic of the Sudan. The IGAD sub-regional organization brokered a peace agreement in 2015 which broke down only a year later. The Revitalization of the 2015 Agreement was undertaken by IGAD just before the National Dialogue was initiated, which raised questions about the relationship between the two processes. Some saw them as competitive, while others considered them as complementary. I share this latter view.

I wrote this article shortly after the President announced the National Dialogue in December 2016, with me as one of four Advisors to him as the Patron and a Steering Committee of 'eminent personalities and persons of consensus.' The President subsequently reconstituted the Steering Committee and relinquished his role as Patron to ensure the independence of the process. The Steering Committee comprised a leadership composed of two Co-Chairs, a Deputy Co-Chair, a Rapporteur, two Deputy Rapporteurs, three women members, and a Secretariat. The Plenary of the Steering Committee was expanded to be more comprehensively representative.

'Inter-Communal Cultural Dialogue: Identity and the Constructive Management of Diversity'

A project proposal by Francis M. Deng, 2020

1. The Premise of the Proposal

It has always been my view that South Sudan's National Dialogue should reinforce our indigenous culture of dialogue and extend it more broadly to generate discussions and exchange of views on a wide variety of issues that are pertinent to state and nation-building and broaden it to the regional and international contexts in which we now participate. One of the central issues that emerged in the grassroots and regional consultations of the National Dialogue is the intense hostility among communities, focused in particular on what is perceived as Dinka domination and the nation-wide devastation caused by the conflict between the two major ethnic groups, the Dinka and the Nuer, who are seen as dominating the government, the army and the security sector.

In particular, there was a near-universal condemnation of the role allegedly being played by the Jieng (Dinka) Council of Elders in shaping and guiding government policy. While the Council might have had significant, though limited, influence in some decisions, this wholesale allegation is a grossly exaggerated fiction that I know is irritating to the national leadership. But perceptions are sometimes as powerful as the reality they misrepresent and therefore need to be seriously considered and addressed.

The dominating role of these two Nilotic groups is often associated with cultural hegemony presented in some areas of the country as a conflict between Dinka cattle herders and Equatorian farmers. As one person from an Equatorian consultation put it: "People who try to dominate others don't know that all the tribes in South Sudan have their own cultures, and all these cultures are not the same. If I go with my own Kakwa culture to the Bari community and want to rule over them with our Kakwa culture, it will bring a very big conflict."Another person, referring to the Dinka and the Nuer, said, "It is as though the country belongs to two big tribes." Yet another said, "The Dinka claim that they are the majority; does it mean that we the minorities have no rights?"[79]

What motivated me to study different aspects of Dinka culture from the late 1950s, in the University of Khartoum, was precisely the kind of concern articulated by these individuals. Those who dominated us in the Sudan or invaded and colonized Africa assumed that there was a cultural vacuum that needed to be filled. While there were, of course, material motives behind colonialism, this assumption of a cultural void and the need to 'civilize the natives' provided a degree of moral justification. I felt very strongly that in my own modest way, and having grown up confident about my cultural identity, pride, and dignity, I must contribute to dispelling that misconception.

And yet, ever since I began studying Dinka customary law in Khartoum University, which I pursued in post-graduate studies in the United Kingdom and the United States, and later expanded into

---

79. *South Sudan's National Dialogue Reports, Volumes 1 to 5,* United Nations Development Programme (UNDP), 2021.

many other aspects of Dinka culture, I have been conscious of the dilemmas of studying a particular ethnic group in the context of a pluralistic nation. That was a field supposedly left for foreigners who would presumably not be accused of parochialism. An African studying his own people exposed himself to allegations of tribalism, chauvinism, and divisiveness. To me, to be intimidated by that negative assertion would be a denigrating denial of one's identity.

Identity, which begins from early life in the context of a family, community, and expanding social formations, and related cultural value-systems, is essential to the integrity and dignity of the individual and the community to which he or she belongs. It is from those roots that an individual or a particular group finds the moorings of inner security in the broader context of a pluralistic nation and beyond. Denying one's identity implies diminishing one's value-system and a sense of authenticity and integrity. It means risking one's center of gravity and inner security.

I recently read an inspiring book about reconciliation in South Africa and the leadership role of Nelson Mandela, by Professor Fanie du Toit, a white South African. The author states: "Importantly, Mandela seemed to be able to adopt ever-widening allegiances and causes, yet it is equally clear that he never renounced the traditional loyalties and deeply held beliefs that first promoted him to join the liberation struggle... By not abandoning his identity as a Xhosa and an African, and by valuing the universal dimensions reflected in his local identity, he was able to demonstrate how the universal should be anchored in, and justified in terms of, the local and the particular. In other words, it is possible to conclude that his embrace of the fight for the rights of all South Africans while drawing on his particular identity and heritage to do so, played some role in his decision to pursue reconciliation as political strategy."[80]

Professor du Toit explains that it was indeed the contrast between the identity and dignity he enjoyed in his local background and the indignities of discrimination under apartheid that provoked Mandela to rebel: "When he moved to Johannesburg as a young lawyer some years later, Mandela discovered that his boyhood freedom had in fact been limited to those idyllic childhood days, and that the freedom to be a professional adult simply did not exist for him as he set out to start a career in law. That began his fight for basic individual rights … In time, after he experienced firsthand, the recalcitrance and racism of the regime, he joined the ANC and eventually turned freedom fighter, beginning a new clandestine life in pursuit of rights for his people."[81]

When I first read Jomo Kenyatta's book, *Facing Mount Kenya*,[82] I was somewhat critical about a national leader who had inspired and led his people to liberate themselves from colonial domination to become so parochial as to write about his tribe. It was much later in my intellectual growth and political awareness that I realized that what Jomo Kenyatta did in studying his own society was a deeper level of the struggle than I had realized. Kenyatta indeed became a model I would eventually follow.

The saying that you can take a person out of the village but you cannot take a village out of a person can be adjusted to say that you may take a person out of his traditional social setting but you cannot take fundamental traditional social values out of a person. And this does not mean getting stuck in tradition, but realizing the deeper merits of those indigenous values as a vital resource that continues to inform and enrich one's enhanced role at various levels of one's transition across cultures, nationally, regionally, and globally.

---

80. Fanie du Toit, *When Political Transitions Work: Reconciliation as Interdependence,* OUP, 2018, pp. 11-12.
81. Ibid, p. 21.
82. Jomo Kenyatta, Facing Mount Kenya, East African Educational Publishers, 1938.

2. Conceptual Framework for the Dialogue

I believe it is correct to assume that every coherent and cohesive society has a social system based on fundamental values and institutional structures that determine the way it mobilizes and utilizes its human and material resources and allocation of responsibilities. Over a long period of experience, trial and error, this eventually results in a functional framework of optimum communal acceptance by broad consensus and establishes a stable system that is self-sustaining and resistant to disruptive change. Such shocks as violent conflicts may be so severe as to shatter the established order and challenge it with the emergence of a new system, necessitating the imperative of developing a new logic for determining and allocating functional rules. But change must be a process of reforming what exists, not the obliteration of what is existing, to be replaced by something totally new or novel to the society

Given the premise that every cohesive society has a culture that is part of the identity in which its members find their pride and dignity, it is my considered opinion that we need to understand the particulars of our different cultural identities to fully appreciate our shared identity and dignity not only as citizens of a proud unified nation but also as fellow human beings who share the dignity of our common humanity. This is the core of the idea behind this proposal. I believe that thoughtful individual representatives of various ethnic groups within a state should meet to discern the central elements of their own individual cultural values, their differences, and similarities, and how they can build on those particulars to promote a sense of national identity, enriched rather than divided by our diversity, and our transition across other cultures at all levels, national, regional and international.

Being a Dinka myself, and mindful of the potential allegations of tribalistic chauvinism, I have always presented my studies of Dinka culture with caution. My intention is to document Dinka culture not to claim special status over other traditional cultures in our country, but as a portrait of one system and a starting point into cross-cultural documentation of our cultures and a comparative analysis and exchange of views to discern our differences and commonalities on which to build our state and nation.

I begin my discussion of Dinka culture with an overriding concept which I believe is more widely shared by our indigenous South Sudanese peoples and which, according to the renown Oxford anthropologist, the late Dr. Godfrey Lienhardt, the leading expert on the Dinka, represents "the only notion of immortality they (Dinka) know."[83] Dinka religion promises no heaven after death, only continuity through the living, even though some form of continued existence after death is recognized as a projection of this world into the next. Genetic and social continuity in this world is ensured through a concept known as *kooc e nhom,* 'standing the head of a dead person upright,' a concept which Professor Harold Lasswell in his introduction to my *Tradition and Modernization; A Challenge for Law Among the Dinka of the Sudan*[84] termed 'The myth of permanent identity and influence.' But among the Dinka, this is more than the word myth usually connotes; it aims at ensuring the continued presence and participation of every individual after death through memory and representative participation of the relatives and all those the person had touched in this world.

This accounts for the practice of what anthropologists call *levirate,*

---

83. Godfrey Leinhardt, *Divinity and Experience: The Religion of the Dinka,* Oxford: The Clarendon Press, 1961, p. 26.

84. Francis Mading Deng, *Tradition and Modernization: A Challenge for Law among the Dinka of the Sudan,* Yale University Press, 1971 -- see p. 15.

which requires that a child-bearing widow lives with a relative of the dead man to continue bearing children to the name of her dead husband. The concept also obligates the relatives of a man who dies before marrying to marry a wife for his spirit or ghost to beget children in the name of the dead man. Anthropologists call this 'ghost marriage.' While *kooc e nhom* theoretically applies to every person, it is more related to men because of the dominance of the patriarchal lineage or clan system.

Chief Arol Kachwol, one of the Chiefs I interviewed for my books, *Dinka Cosmology*, and *Africans of Two World: The Dinka in Afro-Arab Sudan*[85] summarized the cultural values of lineage continuity and the challenge of social change in the following words:

"It is God who changes the world by giving successive generations their turns. When God comes to change your world, it will be through you and your wife. You will sleep together and bear a child. When that happens, you should know that God has passed on to your children, borne by your wife, the things with which you had lived your life.

"Your father, Deng Majok, if he had lived without a child until his death, his would have been the kind of life that continues only as a tale. But if he left behind a big son who can be spoken of, 'This is Mading, son of Deng,' then, even if a person had never met your father, but he hears that you are the son of Deng Majok in the same way he had heard of your father, he will meet through you your father whom he never met" [86]

85. Francis Mading Deng, *Dinka Cosmology*, Ithaca Press, 1980 – see p. 34. Re-issued as *Dinka World View: Elders Reflect on the Past, Present and Future of their People*, Africa World Books, 2023. *Africans of Two Worlds: The Dinka in Afro-Arab Sudan*, Yale University Press, 1978 – see p. 28 - reissued as *The Changing World of the Dinka*, Africa World Books, 2022.

86. Francis Mading Deng, *Africans of Two Worlds: The Dinka in Afro-Arab Sudan*, Yale University Press, 1978 – see p. 28. See also Chief Arol Kachuol's chapter in *Dinka Cosmology*, Ithaca Press, 1980. Reissued by Africa World Books, 2022 as *Dinka World View: Elders Reflect on the Past, Present and Future of their People*.

The value of the concept is not limited to the Dinka, but is inter-racially and cross-culturally expandable. Referring to my American wife, who was accompanying me on her first visit to South Sudan shortly after our wedding, and was assisting me with the recording, Chief Arol Kachuol introduced the important issue of mixed marriages and implications of relations across tribal or racial divisions:

"Where is this girl, your wife from? Is she not from America? And you have brought her back to your country. If you bear a child together now, in that child will combine the words of her country and the words of your country. It is as though God has given her to Deng Majok, your father."

"So, the way we see it, God has brought peace and reconciliation into your hearts. None of you is to hate the race of the other. That's the way it goes. Tomorrow, the people of that tribe or the people of that race, God will take them and mix them with the people of that race. They too will bear their own races through their children. When that happens, whatever hostility might have been between people, should no longer be allowed to continue. Relationship kills those troubles and begins the new way of kinship."

"Man is one single word with God." [87]

One positive by-product of the wars of liberation that have devastated and shattered the people of South Sudan for decades is that they have both divided communities and also brought different groups into greater contacts thereby increasing intermarriages that were previously frowned upon, enhancing the prospects of national integration. By the same token, it makes it even more compelling to know the individual

---

87. Ibid.

cultures that are coming together, mixing and forging a common national identity and shared values of unity and harmony.

And indeed another fundamental principle of the Dinka value system is *cieng*, a concept of ideal human relations aimed at unity, harmony and conciliatory management of differences. Godfrey Lienhardt and Father Arthur Nobel, the pioneering Catholic Missionary who extensively studied the Dinka, both elaborately discussed *cieng* as representing the Dinka notion of what ideally their society is and should be. The concept however has a wide range of interrelated meanings, including custom, law, behavior, conduct, treating a person, living together, and way of life. *Cieng* is both prescriptive, what ought to be, and descriptive, what in fact happens. It is supposed to be inherently good, unless qualified as bad. It is sometimes specified as *cieng e baai*, and *baai* means home, village, community, tribe or country. *Cieng* is therefore specific to a social unit and inclusive to expanding circles, ultimately embracing humanity.

Built into *cieng* are fundamental principles of what might qualify as human rights. But the Dinka believe that *cieng* should cover respect not only for humans as God's creatures, whatever their race, culture, or religion, but also non-human creatures of God. It requires being in harmony with humanity and nature. As one elder put it to me, one must respect even birds that fly in the sky, the fish in the river, the trees and all things that do not speak; they also have the dignity of being creatures of God. Despising them risks divine wrath that might be disastrous for the wrongdoer. "Even your precious things that you so carefully guard and protect will be destroyed."[88]

The paradox is that while *cieng* prescribes peaceful persuasive

---

88. Chief Thon Wai, in Francis Mading Deng, *Africans of Two Worlds: The Dinka in Afro-Arab Sudan,* Yale University Press, 1978, p. 65. Reissued as *The Changing World of the Dinka* by Africa World Books, 2022. See also Chief Thon Wai's chapter in *Dinka Cosmology,* Ithaca Press 1980. Reissued as *Dinka World View: Elders Reflect on the Past, Present and Future of their People* by Africa World Books, 2023.

means for resolving differences and is strongly against the use of force, violence was a frequent feature of what are often referred to as the warrior Nilotic tribes, including the Dinka and the Nuer. This was largely due to the division of roles that made chiefs and elders the peacemakers and organized young men into warrior age sets whose identity and dignity rested in being warriors, supported by their female counterpart age-sets, to defend society against external aggression, a role they exaggerated by going to war at the slightest provocation, often in defiance of the chiefs and elders.

Another fundamental concept among the Dinka is *dheeng,* which can best be translated as dignity. Closely associated with dheeng is *atheek,* respect, which is considered pervasively central in human relations. *Dheeng* and the related value of *atheek* are concepts which cover such elements as physical appearance, the esthetics of beauty, and artistic expression in song and dance. It also covers proper conduct in relationship to others, which includes observing the ideals of *cieng*. One can have *dheeng,* and be respected as *adheng,* which can best be translated as a gentleman (the concept also applies to women), either by virtue of the status one is born into or which one acquires by merit. One can be an *adheng* because of wealth, but that must be connected with generosity or benevolent attitude toward others. Otherwise, one may be rich, and an *adheng* by wealth, and yet be known as *ayur,* the opposite of *adheng,* if he is miserly or ungenerous.

These moral values apply to power and leadership. When a person assumes authoritative control of the community, the tribe or the country, he is said to *dom baai,* and *baai,* as I said, covers home and expands up to the tribe and the country. *Dom* also applies to physical seizing or holding of cattle. But *dom* is not merely physical control; it implies pacification and ensuring peace, security, and order. The next requirement is *guier* (putting in order) *baai,* which means improving the situation by solving any problems that existed before assuming control. Two concepts relate more directly to physical control and exercise of authority to ensure stability of the improved situation. One is *mac baai,* which internally means to tie or bind, a term normally used to mean tying a cow to a peg with a rope. *Mac* also refers to family or kin. The other word is *muk baai,* which means 'keeping,' a word that also applies to cattle and to nurturing a child, and implies stability.

These values are circular and mutually reinforcing. To have *mac* or *muk baai* is also to have *dom baai,* back to the normative meaning of authoritative control. To be a successful leader requires living up to these values. The word for a chief, *beny,* also means rich, generous, and benevolent. All these principles and the values associated with them tend to agglutinate and carry benefits with responsibilities.

There are other concepts expressed in words that are often recurrent in popular usage and which have a significant place in Dinka culture and practice, especially for leadership. One is *Yich,* which literally means 'truth', but also means 'right.' The expression, "*Ke yich*" simply means "It is the truth." But to say, "*Ke yich du*" means "It is your truth," which means "It is your right."

Another conceptual term is *luk,* which means resolving a dispute. But it also means to persuade to a point of view. The combination reflects the Dinka normative process of settling disputes which is not an adversarial determination of rights and wrongs, as is the case in Western judicial process, but a conciliatory process of resolving a dispute in an amicable way aimed at reaching a consensus and achieving reconciliation.

The Chief among the Dinka does not wield a coercive force by which to impose his will on his 'subjects,' but is primarily a moderator whose authority and effectiveness rest of his managing relations between and among his people through his ability to persuade. His only coercive function is social approbation for compliance with his decisions and condemnation or ostracism and in extreme cases divine intervention in the form of punishment for disobeying him. It is noteworthy that although the chief had no military or police force, the Dinka were highly praised by British colonial administration as exceptionally law-abiding and their society free of such crimes as murder as opposed to killing in inter-communal fights or theft as opposed to taking what is owed to one through forceful self-help.

Herman Bell who was District Commissioner of Western Kordofan under which the Ngok Dinka were administered together with Arab tribes from 1937 to 1939 wrote about the lack of crime in the Ngok Dinka area: "I can't remember that we ever had any serious crime in that part of the District. Among the Baggara of Missiriya, there were frequent quarrels and fights. The same applies to the Hamar in the North. But I seem to remember that the Ngok Dinka were a particularly law-abiding people... I cannot recollect that either within the tribe or as between them tribe and the Baggara they ever had any serious trouble when I was there."[89]

Godfrey Lienhardt wrote on the Dinka cultural method of resolving disputes: "I suppose everyone would agree that one of the most decisive marks of a society we should call in a spiritual sense 'civilized' is a highly developed sense of justice, and here, the Nilotics, with their intense respect for the personal independence and dignity for themselves and others, may be superior to societies more civilized in the material sense... The Dinka and the Nuer are warlike people and have never been slow to assert their rights as they see them by physical force. Yet, if one sees Dinka trying to resolve a dispute, according to their own customary law, there is often a reasonableness and a gentleness in their demeanor, a courtesy and a quietness in the speech of those

---

89. Francis Mading Deng, *The Man Called Deng Majok, A Biography of Power, Polgyny and Change*, Yale University Press, 1986 - see p. 35.

elder men, superior in status and wisdom, an attempt to get at the whole truth between them."[90]

The normative principles of *cieng* are also almost identical to the now world-famous Bantu concept of *ubuntu*, which Nelson Mandela, Archbishop Tutu, Thabo Mbeki, and other African leaders and scholars universalized. Essentially, *ubuntu* is a concept of shared humanity in which the interest of the individual are in harmony with the community or humanity. In the words of Professor Fanie du Toit, *ubuntu* "is a cultural ideal popular throughout Sub-Sahara Africa that emphasizes social interconnectedness as the most basic reality that shapes both individual and society."[91]

A similar concept prevails in Ethiopia. Prime Minister Abiy Ahmed Ali, in his acceptance speech for the Nobel Peace Prize, invoked the Amharic concept *of medemer*, which means togetherness for synergetic unity, peace, and reconciliation. Prime Minister Abiy Ahmed saw *medemer* as a concept of social compact of love, forgiveness and reconciliation. According to the Prime Minister, *medemer* stipulates that you are your brother's or sister's keeper. He called on the Ethiopians to use the best of their past to build a new culture.

Among the Akan people of Ghana, the concept of 'personhood,' which has also been well studied and documented, embodies similar moral principles. According to Kwasi Wiredu, the Akan view personhood as constituting an individual within a community that expands from the family to the lineage, clan, nation, country, and humanity. Members in these concentric circles are expected to share rights and privileges that match obligations based on the reciprocal golden rule of 'do unto others what you would have them do unto you.'

In Rwanda, the concept of *gacaca*, which has been used as a method

---

90. Francis Mading Deng, *The Dinka of the Nile Valley* in Man and Society, *The Listener,* 69, 1963.
91. Fanie du Toit, *When Political Transitions Work: Reconciliation as Interdependence,* Oxford University Press, 2018, p. 195.

of addressing the disputes associated with the 1994 genocide to lessen the burdens of the tribunals formally carrying out the trials of genocide is a traditional way of "discussing together on a grass patch." As a means of resolving conflicts and promoting unity and harmony in the community based on customary laws, codes, and institutions, *gacaca* has much in common with the concepts applied in other regions of Africa.

Beyond the specific example of *gacaca*, I see Rwanda as a success story in culturally contextualized development. I visited the country in the 70s, 80s, and only several months after the 1994 genocide, pursuant to my UN mandate on internal displacement. And I visited again ten years later. The transformation I found was unbelievable. Rwanda now looks like a modern European country in the heart of Africa. When I asked how they did that, the gist of what I was told was that they invoked their cultural values to stimulate their model of development. And the cultural values they mentioned to me were almost identical to those of the Dinka. And that should not be surprising since their culture has much in common with our traditional cattle-oriented economies and cultural values.

I was told that in their development strategy, they invoked, for instance, their notion of dignity, which was almost identical to the Dinka concept of *dheeng*, with its esthetic, physical, moral, social, and spiritual connotations. The argument they presented to their people was that you could not have dignity if you are not physically clean, if your house is not well built and kept neat, or if the areas surrounding your house are not clean and tidy. Not only are the houses in Kigali well built and well kept, but the city as a whole is meticulously clean, with flowers and trimmed hedges featuring prominently. While this is reminiscent of the clean manner in which our traditional villages are kept, it contrasts sharply with the filth one finds in many of our towns.

Another cultural value I was told they built upon was a concept of unity, harmony and solidarity, which closely corresponds to our people's concept of *cieng baai*. This concept was used to mobilize people to help each other in building their houses and public utilities, cultivating their fields to increase production, and constructing roads, all with modest state contribution as a stimulus. In a way, this collective work was applied by colonial administrators among the Dinka to use the age-set system to build roads and public structures, but was abandoned after independence as colonial exploitation of forced labor.

It is my belief that indigenous African value systems should be relevant to the development of a culturally oriented normative framework of good governance, conflict prevention, management, and resolution; good governance; respect for humanitarian rights; gender balance; socio-economic development; and protection of the environmental. Even the notion of permanent identity and influence which may be viewed as conservative and backward-looking, can be a powerful way of linking the past with the present to shape the future. It can inspire people to perform and achieve as a means of both honoring the continuation of the ancestral line and enhancing the prospects of being remembered in perpetuity. Toward that objective, we need to have a better appreciation of our own local cultures both for self-awareness and as a basis for building national unity by engaging in constructive dialogue with other groups in the country to promote mutual understanding, accommodation and cross-cultural process of give and take toward equitable integration. This process of internal dialogue between and among cultures can then be extended to more inclusive regional and international contexts.

In his Foreword to my book, *Identity, Diversity and Constitutionalism in Africa,* Former President of Nigeria, General Olusegun Obasanjo, wrote, "I share Dr. Deng's view of an Africa that builds on its time-tested cultural ideals, and institutionalized practices. But if Dr. Deng will forgive me for taking his argument a step further, I might also note that these values have much to offer not only Africa but the world as a whole. Just as Western democracy enshrines certain universal values, so does the African worldview. In a world where every community is increasingly obliged to acknowledge and interact with many other, often very different communities, the traditional African focus on building consensus instead of fostering competition has obvious relevance. Equally, the African concern to root the individual within the community is highly pertinent to societies in which migration, and industrialization have generated atomic isolation, and alienation."[92]

It must be borne in mind that cultures are not static and while a degree of stability and continuity is a central feature of cultures they also evolve and at times change radically under certain compelling circumstances, such as wars as noted earlier. The wars that have raged in South Sudan for decades are illustrative of such circumstances. And while it may be too soon to assess the impact of the Covid-19 crisis on culture, the role of culture, both in the spread of the disease and in how to fight the disease might be very pertinent.

3. Broadening the Scope of Dialogue

As the foregoing statements indicate, my view is not to see the need for for Inter-Communal Dialogue in South Sudan in isolation from the regional and the global contexts, but to approach it as a stepping stone to a broader incremental dialogue of cultures. I therefore decided to identify four interconnected principles, which I consider representative of the normative framework involved in cross-cultural relations, and relate them to the four equally interconnected levels of transition toward globalization. These principles are: identity, dignity, diversity, and equality. The correlative levels are: local, national, regional, and global.

---

92. Francis Mading Deng; *Identity, Diversity and Constitutionalism in Africa*, Foreword by Former President of Nigeria, General Olusegun Obasanjo, United States Institute of Peace, 2008, p. 144.

From a substantive point of view and as a point of comparative departure, these can be embodied in the conventional constitutional principles of the bill of rights, non-discrimination, the rule of law, and equality before the law. In this paper, I lean heavily on my own works on these principles, both academically and professionally, at the correlative levels of the state and regional and international organizations. The dynamics can be even more embracing to include non-governmental organizations, and a wide variety of interpersonal and inter-group relations, in which the four normative principles interplay at the four levels of interaction.

Identity is a fundamental characteristic attribute of every individual and group. It is the core of our shared universal humanity. Dignity, however, defined, both subjective and objective is a universal value of humanity, which is why human rights norms are grounded in human dignity. Viewed in relative isolation, every person as an individual and as a member of a group sees his or her identity and that of the group and their correlative cultural values as the ideal model of God's creation, presumptively superior to all others, certainly second to none. Diversity is the central feature of contact and interaction with other individuals and groups of varying identities. This raises the issue of comparison and possible stratification. Since each group subjectively views its identity and related value system as special, there is an inherent potential for competition and conflict and therefore a quest for equality as a foundation for mutual recognition and peaceful cooperative co-existence. More often than not, groups representing these principles at various points of the four levels tend to relate to one another in varying degrees of differentiation, adversity and conflict. The goal then is to reverse this toward mutual understanding, respect, unity, harmony and cooperation.

4. Format of the Proposed Dialogue

The format of the dialogue I envisage would be a two-prong process involving a broad-based survey and a focused group discussion forum in which representatives of major cultural cluster groups in South Sudan will participate with a select number of regional and international representatives as participating observers. This would create a layered process in which the internal South Sudanese process would be a first step to be followed at an appropriate time by an extended cross-cultural dialogue involving regional and international participants. It is my intention to involve the Ebony Center, United Nations Mission in South Sudan (UNMISS), and other partners as co-sponsors of the Dialogue Forum with funding from sources sympathetic to this cross-cultural approach.

5. Conclusion

I have no illusion that what is proposed here is a daunting task whose realization may be elusive. However, I am convinced that it is needed and even if all we can do now is simply debate the issue, that exercise would be a necessary step in awareness-raising and hopefully stimulate a creative exchange of views, whose fruits might incrementally ripen to be reaped in due course at all levels of our participation as a people and a nation.

'Inspiration for Education in South Sudan'

An opinion piece [93]

South Sudan is a country in desperate need for good news to inspire hope and motivate people to free themselves from the debilitation of pessimistic despair into an optimistic drive for positive action. With all

---

93. First published in parts by the Nation in Nairobi, Kenya, July, 2021, as *'Education is key to unlocking the potential of South Sudan.'* Reproduced in full by the Sudd Institute in its Weekly Review, 2021.

the daunting challenges facing the Government, President Salva Kiir Mayardit, with his Vice President for Service Delivery Cluster, Hussein Abdelbagi, and the Minister for General Education and Instruction, Honorable Awut Deng Acuil, and her staff, should be highly commended for the wonderful way they successfully championed progress in education amidst the foreboding challenges of Covid-19, the pervasive security threats, and the dire economic situation in the country.

This was dramatically reflected in the very successful way Primary Eight and Senior Four Exams were heroically conducted in 2020 in an era of pandemic devastation, tenuous security conditions, dire economic situation, and natural disasters. The Ministry was able to fly examination papers to areas that had been hardly reachable under the security conditions prevailing in the country. A report released by the Ministry effectively states what was done:

"Given the current status of road network, security concerns, and natural calamities, such as floods in South Sudan, one would hardly believe that all the candidates who participated in the recently conducted primary examinations would be reached. However, because of the courage, the zeal, and the determination of South Sudanese Teachers, Security, and the Police Service, our Invigilators were able to walk on bare feet through swamps of unsafe waters to catch canoes on shores of rivers so that a child's educational aspiration is ensured. In the same latitude, security officers risked their lives by accepting to go to places where their institutions have no presence so that a child's safety during the examination is guaranteed." [94]

94. Ministry of General Education and Instruction, South Sudan, 2020.

In a conversation with Honorable Minister Awut Deng, she told me of occasions when they would fly to an area, only to be forced to turn back because of forbidding weather conditions, and then fly back the next day, with the determination that they must deliver the materials for the exam. That was repeated in various areas until all the examination areas of the 64,138 candidates were reached. Equally touching was that not a single one of the children contracted the Covid-19 virus, or was prevented from taking the exam by intervening ill-health, an added blessing from the powers that be. Putting this in the broader context of education in South Sudan, I must say that one of the things I find most encouraging in Juba is to see children of various ages dressed in an impressive uniform and walking to, or from, school. I find the sight of these children uplifting. Even more than the long term promise of the future I see in them is the fact that their families or some bene-factors are investing in their education under conditions of severe hardship in the country. As I observe these children, I feel confident that our country has a bright future.

Going back to the history of education in South Sudan and how far our people have progressed, I recall our days of pioneering educa-tion under very constraining circumstances of cultural esistance to education. One of the reasons people resisted sending their children to school was because they feared that it would take them away from the ways of their traditional society. The popular saying among the Ngok Dinka was that children were fed with the hearts of vultures. For the Dinka, to whom the functions of the heart and the mind are closely connected, this implied that the children would lose the cultural values associated with a combined conscientious heart and mind: prudence, compassion, decency, and social responsibility.

Mothers were particularly opposed to their children going to school.

The following lines from a song we used to sing in our recruitment campaigns around the tribe are illustrative of the attitude at the time:

> *"Our mothers are crying all over the land;*
> *'Our children have all gone away*
> *No child is left in the land.'*
> *I do not blame you, mothers,*
> *There is nothing you know – nothing!*
> *The word of education is creeping on*
> *It is reaching communities all over the world;*
> *In Khartoum, a child is born and goes.*
> *Should I appease you only with a white cow?*
> *What about the White One in the Market?"*

A wife of a Chief whose only daughter was sent to school by her husband pleaded with a spiritual leader to intervene on her behalf to stop the girl from going to school. Unfortunately, she succeeded and sung about her success with a sense of euphoria:

> *"I went after the Great Cierdit in the area of Anyar,*
> *He said, 'I will see you in the mourning.'*
> *I am a tortured person,*
> *I am a destroyed person*
> *To beget a child, only to be taken away.*
> *O my people, where will I go?*
> *O Dinka people, what will I do?*
> *An only child like the stand of a drum*
> *How can I hear of her gone to town?*
> *I heard the name of Achol and could not sleep*
> *I could not sleep, but what could I do?*

O son of Rian, O son of Rian,
If you have given my daughter back to me
My relations with you will now be good.
Mawiir Ajingker, if you have left her to me,
Our relations will now flourish."

Initially, in some Dinka areas, Chiefs did not want to send their children to school and encouraged others to send their children instead. But some Paramount Chiefs not only sent their sons to school, but persuaded the chiefs under their authority to also send their sons to school. Unfortunately, at the beginning, in most areas, girls were not included, but later they were also sent to school. Those Chiefs foresaw that the future lay with education. And indeed the sons and daughters of those Chiefs who had the foresight have been among the modern leaders of South Sudan.

Eventually, most people incrementally recognized the superiority of modern education over their indigenous knowledge. They also saw the employment opportunities that accrued with education. Even elders began to say, "You educated youth have acquired knowledge that we, your elders, do not have and that you are now the leaders of the future." They argue, understandably, that the modern context requires modern education. The reason people are now keen to send their children to school is that they realize the value of education, not only for acquiring knowledge but only for accessing gainful employment and political leadership. They want to prepare their children for a fruitful future.

Everyone now wants to send children to whatever schools they can access, but only those who can afford it send their children to quality educational institutions. The irony is that when people were resisting sending their children to school, education was fully subsidized. Now that it is becoming too costly for the average person to afford it, education has become popular. This paradox calls on the state to step in and, as much as possible, make education a national priority.

It is with this national policy aspiration in mind that I once again applaud the heroic efforts of the Honorable Minister of Education and Instruction, Awut Deng Acuil, with her team and all those who assisted them, to successfully conduct the 2020 examinations amidst the formidable challenges of Covid-19, pervasive insecurity, economic hardships, and natural disasters. As the Minister and her staff attest, the support they received from President Salva Kiir Mayardit and his Vice President Hussein Abdelbagi was pivotal to their success. This success will hopefully continue to inspire and strengthen the determination of the leadership to endeavor as much as possible, despite the constraints of the current situation in the country, to make education a right to which every child should have access.

Foreword to 'The National Dialogue, with Bona Malual'
South Sudan's National Dialogue Reports, Volumes 1 to 5,
United Nations Development Programme (UNDP, 2021) [95]

South Sudan National Dialogue was initiated by President Salva Kiir Mayardit in December 2016 and formally launched in May 2017. The process was expected to last for only several months. Instead, it lasted for five years. The National Dialogue was undertaken at the same time the process of the revitalized process was initiated. As I was involved in both processes, I saw the similarities, differences, and complementarities between the two processes.

Both processes aimed at achieving peace, security, stability and

___

95. Bona Malual was Rapporteur for the National Dialogue and Francis Mading Deng was Deputy Rapporteur and Spokesperson.

development for the country. The differences were reflected in the fact that the National Dialogue was home grown, internally initiated, and primarily funded by the Government, while the Revitalized Peace Process was externally initiated by the Inter-Governmental Authority for Development, IGAD, in collaboration with the African Union, AU, United Nations, UN, and the Troika countries of United States, United Kingdom and Norway.

The complementarity of the two processes lay in their differences, with the National Dialogue enjoying the legitimacy of being domestically initiated and owned, while the Revitalized Peace Process was externally initiated with the leverage of the regional and international initiators and their partners. The National Dialogue was inclusive in its substantive and geographical coverage, with the exception of a few areas in which insecurity prevented access. Although the six chapters of the Revitalized Peace Process were also substantively inclusive, the focus in the negotiations was on chapters one and two on power sharing and the related security arrangements. The peace process has also tended to be centralized between the parties in conflict and their individual leaders.

Despite their obvious complementarity, which I consistently advocated, mutual suspicion and indeed animosity between the leaders of two processes blocked any collaboration between them. Some leaders on both sides in fact objected to the word complementarity which they mistakenly argued implied the dominance of one side over the other.

Another difference and potential basis of complementarity is that while the National Dialogue has no follow-up mechanism, although its leadership recommended one, the Peace Process has a Reconstituted Joint Monitoring and Evaluation Commission, (R-JMEC), comprising, regional and international guarantors and stakeholders, with national participants.

The National Dialogue Reports have been clustered into five volumes, beginning with the initial preparatory discussions and ending with the national conference.

Volume 1 comprises background information including a note on the concept of the National Dialogue initiative by the President; lessons learned from other national dialogues; procedural issues relating to the framework and guidelines for the National Dialogue consultations; and the formation of the 15 regional subcommittees and their reports. The subcommittees were formed on the basis of the 10 states clustered under the three greater regions of Bahr el-Ghazal, Equatoria and Upper Nile, the two administrative areas of Abyei and Pibor, and three thematic issues covering the national capital, security, and refugees.

Volume 2 comprises the grassroots consultations conducted in the former 10 states clustered under the three greater regions of Bahr el-Ghazal, Equatoria and Upper Nile; the two administrative areas of Abyei and Pibor; and three thematic issues covering the national capital, security and refugees.

Volume 3 includes reports from three regional conferences of the greater regions of Bahr el-Ghazal, Equatoria and Upper Nile.

Volume 4 comprises special studies and thematic issues: an appeal for action on Abyei; an appeal for international support for elections; building a shared vision for the new nation; a call for national action and establishing a permanent national constitution; recommendaions for national reconciliation; completing the implementation of the Comprehensive Peace Agreement; establishing a South Sudan land policy and administration; establishing a foreign policy for South Sudan; and developing a mechanism for the implementation of the recommendations of the National Dialogue.

Volume 5 comprises the outcome documents of the National

Dialogue Conference on: governance transformation; rehabilitation of and and kick-starting South Sudan's economy; security sector reforms; and recommendations for social cohesion. The documents include the final resolutions of the national conference and a communique.

Although the National Dialogue fulfilled its stated objectives, without an implementing mechanism, the practical value of its work is still to be realized. The National Dialogue reports are therefore presented for eclectic action by the different government agencies that may wish to use them. The Reports were indeed presented by UNDP to the annual conference of the State Governors and Chief Administrators of Special Administrative Areas in December 2022 and were very well received. Otherwise, the reports are for the record and for the prospective future application by interested actors.

In any case, the reports document a unique experience in the history of the country and in that sense constitute a national treasure that will enrich the dialogue on the challenges of nation-building for generations to come.

'Clearing the Dimming Vision of the Liberation of South Sudan: Celebrating the 10th Anniversary of Independence'

By the SUDD Institute, in its Weekly Review, July 11, 2021 [96]

This review is based on the my presentation to the Roundtable convened by UNMISS in Juba on the 6-7 July 2021, to Commemorate the 10th Anniversary of South Sudan's independence. The remarks and views reflected in the review are the author's and are not to be attributed to UNMISS or the Sudd Institute.

---

96. Published by the Nation, Nairobi, Kenya, on July 8, 2021 as, *'We should clear dimming vision of the liberation of South Sudan.'*

1. The Challenge in Context

Shortly after independence, South Sudan was plunged into a civil war that has intermittently devastated the country ever since. Though essentially a struggle for power between and among individual leaders of the SPLM/SPLA, which had championed the struggle since its inception in 1983, the war soon began to be perceived as an ethnic conflict that primarily pitted the Dinka and the Nuer against each other. Since then, the people of South Sudan who had been fighting and sacrificing for the ideals of freedom, equality, dignity, and prosperity have been reduced to a nation massively displaced internally or forced into refuge in the neighboring countries, or dispersed as refugees in many countries around the world.

As President Salva Kiir Mayardit said, upon independence, in a meeting of the leadership of the ruling SPLM, South Sudanese were a proud people who held their heads high and were widely respected the world over. Now, they are no longer proud or respected. Devastated by pervasive internecine violence throughout the country with severe humanitarian consequences in areas of vital necessities, they now bend their heads low in humiliation and in desperate need of international assistance. "Why have we done this to our people?" the President asked rhetorically.

In this review, I contextualize my observations by highlighting three main issues. The first issue is that major developments in South Sudan during and after the liberation struggle have been a process of a dynamic interplay between internal and external forces. The second is that the crises the country has faced since independence have emerged as a result of a power struggle between and among the leaders and their associates at the national level, with the relative neglect of the rest of the country.

My last point is that the policy synthesis of these two factors calls for collaborative efforts with the country's international partners in responding to the underlying challenges, both at the national and local levels.

2. The Turbulent Road to Independence

In order to fully appreciate the value of independence, it is important to recall the challenges that propelled the liberation war, the difficulties that had to be overcome in the process leading to the exercise of self-determination, and the support many friends and people of goodwill from the international community rendered to help make independence possible. South Sudanese fought against discrimination, domination, marginalization, and humiliation imposed on them by an identity crisis which had two dimensions. The first dimension was that the ruling Arab-Islamic minority, though an African-Arab hybrid, misidentified itself as monolithically Arab. The second was that this distorted self-identification by an ethnic minority was imposed on a country of immense racial, ethnic, and cultural diversity, which was then defined as Arab, with implications that relegated non-Arabs, particularly Southerners, to a lower-class citizenship, with implicit gross inequalities. All attempts by the South to foster a framework of inclusivity and equality by postulating a Vision of New Sudan failed, which made the demand for self-determination with the objective of secession imperative. Nonetheless, we must recall that there was a very strong opposition to the exercise of self-determination and especially to the principle of South Sudanese independence.

Such opposition to self-determination with the prospects of secession came from many quarters inside and outside Africa. These include prominent leaders in the African Union and the United Nations. Even our friends did not like to see the Sudan divided. I was a strong supporter of self-determination not so much to divide the country, but as a pressure on the government of the Sudan to create conditions for consensual unity.

I recall a discussion I had with Former President Jimmy Carter who opposed the independence of South Sudan, saying that no one wanted the Sudan divided. My argument was that even if unity was the desired option, to say that no one wanted separation was to remove the pressure in support of unity.

I was honored to co-chair the Task Force that was set up by the Washington think tank, the Center for Strategic and International Studies, (CSIS), to develop an advisory paper on US Policy to End the War in the Sudan. I was the only Sudanese among the fifty to sixty members, with interest and expertise on the Sudan, and all of them except me were opposed to the right of self-determination and the prospects for Southern Sudan independence. They even argued that the United States had no strategic interests in the Sudan and that the only significance of the Sudan was its involvement in international terrorism, destabilization of the region, and humanitarian crisis in the country. They wanted support for the peace process in the Sudan to be left to European allies, with remote support from the United States. They also argued against any mediation that would support the prospects of separation by the South.

Playing my cards discreetly to moderate my obviously biased self-interest, I argued that contrary to what they said, Sudan was a country of great strategic importance, being a meeting point of Sub-Saharan and North Africa and of races, religions, and cultures, with potential for reconciliation or confrontation that could have ripple effects for the Middle East.

Sudan's involvement in international terrorism was due to the war in which the Arab-Muslim North reacted against Western Christian support for the South, which made them join hands with the Middle Eastern Muslim terrorists, on the principle that the enemies of my enemies are my friends. The same was true of the destabilization of the region which was again a reaction to African support for the South. And obviously, the humanitarian crisis was a direct consequence of the war.

The obvious policy implication was that by ending the war, involvement with terrorism would stop, destabilizing the region would cease, and humanitarian crisis would commensurately end. I argued that the United States, as the sole superpower, could not be disinterested in a country of such global strategic location and potentials in both positive and negative ramifications.

As for the risk of partition, I argued that the best way to safeguard the unity of the country was not to declare opposition to unity, but to stress the potential threat of partition if conditions for unity were not attractive. To avoid partitioning the country, I suggested that we had to make possible the impossible by reconciling the irreconcilable and proposing the formula of 'One Country, Two Systems,' so that the North could pursue their Arab-Islamic agenda while the South followed its African secular agenda.

As we know, the US eventually played a pivotal, mediating role in the peace process on the basis of the formula of 'One Country, Two Systems,' during the interim period. Meanwhile, the right of self-determination with the option of secession for the South had to be affirmed as a credible threat to the leadership that they must create the appropriate conditions for sustaining unity or expect the South to opt for secession.

3. Self-fulfilling Prophecy After Independence

The reason for the opposition to Southern secession was not only because it was feared that breaking up the country would set a bad example for Africa, but that an independent South Sudan would be torn apart by ethnic violence, be a failed state, collapse and be a serious security risk for the region and internationally.

My response to that argument was that we needed to know whether the sources of the crises that would result in state failure or collapse were going to be internal or externally generated so that we should prepare for appropriate responses. It turned out that some of those who raised those concerns were paradoxically working to promote the very crises they were warning about.

When I explained all this to our national leaders, the response was a categorical assertion that we would not collapse or be a failed state. In response, I advised against complacency and stressed that we must prove the prophets of doom wrong every day. Tragically, what was feared by those who opposed our independence is what has happened, and for some, it was a self-fulfilling prophecy to which they themselves contributed.

The country has since confronted a myriad of crises and failures that run counter to the ideals and aspirations for which the people of South Sudan struggled and sacrificed for decades. Our people fought for a New Sudan Vision of full equality of citizenship and shared human dignity without any discrimination on grounds of race, ethnicity, religion, culture, and gender.

Conflicts of identity do not emanate from mere differences, but from the manner in which differences are managed to generate inequality, real or perceived, to a degree unacceptable to the disadvantaged. Although our crisis of national identity with Khartoum was severe because of the sharp racial, religious, and cultural differences and the gross discrimination associated with those differences, identity is relative, and conflicts can result from differences that may not be so striking. Given as an example, Somalia, which is one of the most homogeneous countries in the world, has been torn apart by clan differences.

We in South Sudan are being torn apart by ethnic differences and discrimination or inequalities, real or perceived. In almost every country with diversities of various forms and degrees, there are often elements of inequality. National leaders are, therefore, called upon to repeatedly renew their commitment to policies and measures aimed at promoting inclusivity and equality. South Sudan is no exception. Indeed, we are experiencing elements of what we struggled against, a system in which citizens were divided and stratified on the basis of identity. This is unsustainable.

4. The Disappointment of a Betrayed Liberation

Many of us in varying ways, means, and degrees, took part in the liberation struggle and were very proud and gratified when independence was achieved, but are now deeply disappointed by the way our performance has betrayed the dreams and aspirations of the struggle. Our friends, international partners, and all men and women of goodwill from around the world, who helped us achieve that glorious goal and shared our joy of having liberated our people and country, are now also deeply disappointed by our man-made post-independence crises and failures.

Those who might have contributed to our demise probably now realize that these crises have no borders and that we are in this together. In a book I published after the partition, *Bound by Conflict: The Dilemmas of the Two Sudans,*[97] I argued that unity and separation are degrees of ongoing relations that could be weakened or strengthened, depending on the will of the people and their leaders.

I also argued in that book that though the two countries were now separate, they were still bound together by conflicts in which they each

---

97. Francis M. Deng in collaboration with Daniel J. Deng, *Bound by Conflict: Dilemmas of the Two Sudans,* Fordham University Press, 2016 – see p. 103.

supported militias and rebels from both sides. I said that they needed to cooperate with each other to end their internal wars and stop being "bound by conflicts" to being "bonded by solutions," which has been happening over the last few years.

5. Partnership in Pursuit of a Shared Goal

As we now endeavor to restore peace, security, and stability in our country through the credible implementation of the Revitalized Peace Agreement (RPA), we must be both inward and outward-oriented. Inwardly, we must urgently move beyond focusing on chapters one and two of the RPA that deals primarily with power sharing and security arrangements.

In this regard, we should recognize that the RPA and the National Dialogue are complementary processes, one internationally initiated and conducted from the top involving the elites and focusing on power sharing, and the other by definition nationally owned and involving the views of the people at all levels throughout the country and covering all substantive areas of concern. Even those opposition parties who were initially not involved in the National Dialogue ought to recognize that the issues covered were nonpartisan and were of interest to all the people of the country. The Revitalized Agreement has the leverage of regional and international support; National Dialogue has the authenticity, integrity, and legitimacy of the will of the people.

We must prioritize taking peace to the countryside to end inter-communal violence, ensure the security of the rural areas, encourage our people to return to their villages, give them essential services, tools, and basic support for them to build their homes and cultivate their food and generate self-reliant development. What I am calling for here is to revitalize, to use a now popular term, the strategic objectives of the Liberation Movement to prioritize farming and use oil to fuel economic growth through increased investment in agriculture, to take town to the villages, and to build physical infrastructure.

Looking outwards, we must engage our friends and partners in a candid, constructive dialogue, to explore a common ground and join hands in working together toward the goals we share, instead of acrimonious confrontations that only weaken our efforts and render us less effective in achieving our shared goals.

In this connection, we must remember that sovereignty can no longer be used as a barricade against international involvement in the internal affairs of a country but should rather be seen as a concept of State responsibility to protect and assist its population, to ensure their physical safety and respect for their human rights and dignity, and provide for their basic needs, with the support of international friends and partners, if necessary.

If a state manifestly fails to discharge its national responsibility with the result that its people suffer in large numbers, the world will not stand by and watch without some form of intervention. The best way to protect sovereignty is to discharge the responsibilities of sovereignty and to ask for help from international friends and partners if needed.

To our friends and partners, we say that being in need makes one vulnerable and particularly sensitive to humiliation and insult, which means that constructive and productive partnership requires a deferential attitude and avoiding offensive ways of delivering messages. Often, the problem with a tough message is not so much in what is said, but in how it is said. This is particularly important to note in the African context. More specifically, a productive engagement with South Sudanese demands candid, non-acrimonious, constructive dialogue on how to manage the situation and pave the way forward to achieve our shared goal for durable peace, security, stability, and prosperity.

6. The Promise of Strategic Optimism

Finally, pessimism and despair cannot be options in confronting crises. Well-grounded strategic optimism must be the only way forward. Such post-independence crises, as the ones now facing South Sudan, are common to most countries emerging from foreign domination and the challenge is the ability to overcome them.

Optimism is more assuring than hope. While hope entails waiting passively for the action of others, often associated with the benevolence of Divine Intervention, optimism implies tangible action with reasonably predictable outcomes. Hope is wishful thinking; optimism is promising action, done, planned, or perceived. Optimism does not rule out risks, obstacles, and even setbacks, but rests on determination, persistence, and a creative search for alternative means.

As the saying goes, the real challenge in life is not to avoid falling, for that may be nigh impossible, but the determination and the ability to get up and march on after falling. In the process of falling, getting up, and marching on, we need our friends and partners who supported our independence and have stood with us through thick and thin in managing the challenges of our post-independence crises.

'A Personal Perspective on the Ngok-Twic Conflict in Abyei'

The SUDD Institute Review, February 22, 2022

Ever since the border conflict in Abyei between groups of Twic Mayardit Dinka and the Ngok Dinka of Abyeim in the border market town of Aneetm broke out on February 10, 2022, there has been a flurry of reactions on both sides of the conflict at home and abroad. In this heated climate, in which emotions on both sides run high, truth becomes the primary victim. Under these circumstances, I wanted to refrain from making any public statement, in case what I say is misunderstood or deliberately misconstrued on both sides and risks adding fuel to the fire. In the end, I decided that silence in such a crisis is also untenable.

I have been highly moved by some of the messages to which I feel irresistibly driven to respond. The most moving was a message from a child whose age I could not tell from his appearance, but who could not have been older than ten. He spoke very powerfully in Arabic and identified himself as the son of a Twic father and a Ngok mother to make the point that the two communities are closely interconnected and are indeed one people.

The second message, by the Ngok Dinka cartoonist, Adija, presents the Ngok Dinka being pierced by the Arab with a knife and stabbed with a spear in the back by a fellow Dinka/South Sudanese. While I have had access to the accounts of the Ngok about the Twic attack building up with letters by the Twic Commissioner and Twic politicians in Juba, and culminating in the armed assault on February 10, and the defensive reaction of the Ngok to the situation, there are also reports of gruesome acts committed by the Ngok whom the Twic allege initiated the hostilities. These include allegations of beatings, the burning of Twic huts, and of course, killings, which the Ngok categorically deny.

The third message about the situation is the perspective of the Sudd Institute in its Weekly Review[98] titled *'Ngok-Twic Border Conflict: A Manifestation of Botched Socioeconomic Development in South Sudan,'* which raises the issues involved in the Ngok-Twic border conflict as more widespread in the country and embodies national dimensions of poverty, lack of services, development, and related employment opportunities.

---

98. The Sudd Institute, *Ngok-Twic Border Conflict: A Manifestation of Botched Socioeconomic Development in South Sudan,* in Weekly Review, Febuary 15, 2022.

In situations involving violent confrontation, people tend to see only the negatives. However, the Ngok Dinka and Twic Mayardit are considered one people. Together with Ruweng in Upper Nile, they were annexed to the administration of Kordofan in 1905 to ensure greater administrative protection against the Misseriya slave raiders. Kuac, a Twic section, was under the Ngok Dinka leadership of Chief Kwol Arob. The British later offered these communities the option of reverting to their respective administrations. While the Twic and Ruweng chose to return to the South, Ngok Paramount Chief Kwol Arob decided to remain in Kordofan to play a peace and reconciliation role to safeguard the interests of the people of the South Sudan in their border relations with the Arabs of the North. This position, which Paramount Chief Deng Majok, Kwol Arob's son and successor reaffirmed and reinforced, was emphatically applauded by many South Sudanese Chiefs and elders, foremost among them Chief Giir Thiik of Apuk, Chief Ayieny Aleu, Court President of Noi in Tonj, in the tape-recorded interviews I conducted in Juba in 1973 for my book, *Africans of Two Worlds: The Dinka in AfroArab Sudan,*[99] two Twic Chiefs, Benjamin Lang Juuk, Chief of Akuar (Twic), and Madut Ring, the father of Bona Malwal, Chief of Kuac (Twic), in the interviews, also tape-recorded, conducted for my book, *The Man Called Deng Majok: A Biography of Power, Polygyny and Change.*[100] In my interviews with the Ngok Dinka for that book, I was told that Ngok elders wept over the news that the Kuac Twic had been separated from the Ngok. Until he died, Chief Deng Majok unsuccessfully sought to restore the unity between Ngok and Kuac. Though separated administratively,

99. Francis Mading Deng, *Africans of Two Worlds: The Dinka in Afro-Arab Sudan,* Yale University Press, 1978 – see p. 28. Re-issued as *The Changing World of the Dinka,* Africa World Book, 2022.

100 Francis Mading Deng, *The Man Called Deng Majok: A Biography of Power, Polygyny and Change,* Yale University Press, 1986 – see p. 35.

the two communities remained closely connected and continued to see themselves as one people and stood together against attacks from the neighboring Misseriya Arabs. Therefore, the view of the ordinary people on both sides is that this current conflict does not reflect the will of the people, but the ambitions of a few political entrepreneurs.

Crises are also wake-up calls that open eyes to the deeper causes of the conflict. It must be emphasized that the contested claims in the conflict were mostly concocted by those individual political entrepreneurs, who are largely motivated by personal interests in winning popularity, and not by the chiefs and elders who not only know the facts on the ground but are also committed to peaceful coexistence among their people. Indeed, peace and reconciliation within and between neighboring communities are the core objectives of leadership in traditional society. Of course, rights and wrongs are rarely equal, but they are never one-sided. People do not go to war to kill, and risk being killed, without a compelling cause. And it is not the interest of the comfortable political leaders that should matter the most, but those of the foot soldiers or warriors whom those leaders instigate to go to kill and risk getting killed for reasons quite marginal to the pressing material needs and sense of security and dignity of the ordinary people.

The issues involved in the current Ngok-Twic border conflict should be approached from the perspective of proximate causes and the deeper underlying factors. In terms of proximate causes, the conflict focuses on the management of Aneet town and its market, specifically the decision of the Chief Administrator of Abyei to modernize urban planning by surveying the land, which implies demarcating the borders. That has implications for the ownership of the revenues accruing from taxation. These material issues should not generate violent confrontation, as they can be amicably discussed and resolved peacefully.

There are deeper issues of boundaries demarcation which, though sensitive and difficult, should also be amicably resolved. Some leaders, including among the Twic, wisely argue that discussing the sensitive issue of boundaries should be deferred until the more urgent and important issue of the final status of Abyei between Sudan and South Sudan is resolved. Although there is much to commend in this argument, I do not see the need to avoid discussing and resolving an issue on which the facts are clearly established and need not tear the communities apart and leave it to fester and explode sometime in the future in even more aggravated form. There are many sources that can be and have indeed been, consulted to guide the discussion and agreement on the borders.

In the negotiations with the North, maps from the US Library of Congress that went back to the early 1990s and in the archives of the University of Durham in the UK were effectively used by the SPLM in their negotiations with the Sudan Government to determine the historic boundaries of the Ngok Dinka. These maps were later consulted by the Abyei Boundaries Commission (ABC) which was mandated by the Abyei Protocol of the CPA to determine the boundaries of the Ngok Dinka. There are also maps of the 1956 borders between the South and the North, which also represent the borders of the Ngok Dinka with their neighbors in the former provinces of Bahr el-Ghazal and Upper Nile to the south, the east, and the west. There is the map of the ABC whose finding was supposed to be final and binding. Then there is the decisive map of the International Court of Arbitration at The Hague, which revised the northern, eastern, and western borders of Ngok Dinka territory. The Court made some changes in the borders with the northern neighbors, and the borders to the east and the west, but left the southern border of 1956 as confirmed by the ABC. Some Twic leaders claim that they were not parties to the border negotiations and agreements; nonetheless, no community should argue that they are not bound by an agreement signed by their government. Finally, there is the knowledge of the tribal chiefs and elders who know their boundaries with their neighbors very well, and who were extensively consulted by the ABC experts in determining the boundaries and attended The Hague Arbitration. One thing our people are traditionally known for is that they are deeply religious, God-fearing, and believe in telling the truth as the most assured way of gaining divine justice. Lying is one of the mortal wrongs among our people for which divine punishment is unavoidable, sooner or later.

There are even deeper causes that need to be urgently addressed to bring sustainable peace and security to the rural communities throughout the country. These include rural poverty amidst the abundant natural wealth of the country. This is the reason I find the Sudd Institute's article advocating the urgent provision of services, rural development, and employment opportunities for youth and women quite persuasive. Particularly appealing is the restatement of the objectives of the SPLM/A of taking the amenities of the towns to the rural areas, using oil revenues to fuel the engine of agricultural development, and building an extensive network of roads to connect communities and facilitate rural trade.

All this said, there is no reason the communities cannot sit and amicably discuss their differences and find mutually agreeable solutions on contested issues. Judging from the number of allegations, fabrications, exaggerations, and outright hate talk being promoted on social media by members of these two communities at home and around the world, the situation is far more serious and explosive than we may realize. I strongly believe that dialogue must be urgently undertaken in earnest at three interconnected levels: at the local level between the traditional leaders and elders of both communities; at the state level between the governors and members of their respective governments; and at the national level between the respective leaders of the two communities and the Central Government. Since the participants at these levels are implicated as interested personalities, I suggest that the President, who is the uniting Head of the Nation, and therefore above ethnic differences, should appoint a Senior Spec ial Representative, assisted by a team of mediators and technocrats to facilitate the proposed dialogue at all the three levels.

Our international friends and partners, specifically the two UN missions, the United Nations Mission in South Sudan (UNMISS) and United Nations Interim Security Force for Abyei (UNISFA), also have an important role to play in these inter-communal dialogues. Both have convening capacities as neutral mediators. With the material support of the sympathetic members of the donor community, they can also play a catalytic role in mobilizing humanitarian and development agencies, governmental and non-governmental, to assist with the delivery of social services and the generation of development and employment activities.

One important observation that the Ngok Dinka must bear in mind is that President Salva Kiir Mayardit and the Government of South Sudan acted promptly to stop the violence and take steps to investigate the situation and place responsibility for what happened on individuals who must be held accountable. The cooperation of the SSPDF (formerly the SPLA) with the UNISFA, and particularly the intervention of Division Three from Aweil to reinforce peace and security with a decisive assertion of power, is something the Ngok Dinka have never experienced in their chronic conflicts with the Missiriya Arabs and the partisan attitude of the Sudanese Government in Khartoum in favor of the Missiriya. This should be viewed by the

Ngok Dinka as decisive evidence that they have the full protection of the Government of South Sudan as fellow citizens of the country, without any discrimination, even though their final status between Sudan and South Sudan remains unresolved. This aspect of the situation alone is one that the parties must bear in mind as they negotiate the final status of the area. While the Ngok historical connection with the Sudan should be acknowledged and catered for in any negotiation and resolution of the dispute over the final status of Abyei, the fact that the Ngok Dinka can count on protection from the Government of South Sudan and so far never from the Government of the Sudan must be a crucial consideration in determining the status of Ngok Dinka between the two countries.

When the late, popular Ngok Dinka singer, Nyankol Mithiang, asked the rhetorical question "How did Abyei get left out?" she was right in alluding to the undetermined status of Abyei between the two countries, but she was wrong in that South Sudan has now abandoned the Ngok Dinka. The Ngok Dinka are South Sudanese under the Constitution of South Sudan. They now have an administration by which they are self-governing under the President of South Sudan. And all the services in the area are provided by South Sudan at par with all the other states of the country. Considering that Abyei remains a contested area, President Salva Kiir Mayardit and his Government have been remarkably decisive in catering for the interests of the Ngok Dinka. The two communities, the Ngok and the Twic must recognize that the perpetrators of this conflict do not legitimately represent them as communities. And the Ngok Dinka must recognize that whoever is involved in the crisis from Twic does not represent the South Sudanese people and the Government of South Sudan.

It is worth reiterating that in crises, there are always opportunities to be tapped and built upon. This crisis has reaffirmed the position of the Ngok Dinka as South Sudanese and Khartoum should have a serious look at the moral and political implications of this reality. It has also awakened discussion of critical issues relating to the plight of our rural masses who are afflicted with the hardship of poverty and competition over scarce resources. As I am known for saying, "What is not said is what divides." I should note that this crisis should be a wake-up call for us to discuss the issues involved openly and candidly with the determined objective of resolving the differences through talking and not through fighting.

In this process and at an opportune time, the elders of the two communities should be convened to reaffirm and publicly restate to their communities the historic ties between their respective communities, revitalize the cultural, moral, and spiritual bonds that have united their people for centuries, and disavow and condemn the divisive strategies of self-serving political entrepreneurs. Above all, we should applaud the evenhanded manner the leadership of South Sudan has managed the situation and should encourage them to sustain this uniting approach to inter-communal disputes and apply it to similar inter-communal conflicts that are destabilizing our rural areas throughout the country.

In that connection, it is worth considering the creation of a National Commission for Inter-Communal Peace and Reconciliation to pursue this overriding objective throughout the country. There has been a rise in communal conflicts in South Sudan since the signing of the Revitalized Peace Agreement (RPA). While the instances of inter-communal disputes are widespread throughout the country, recent cases include Leer, Rumbek, Bor, Akobo, Tambura, and Tonj. These are only examples in which communities have been engulfed in extreme sectarian/communal violence. The work of the proposed Commission will focus on inter-communal disputes both preventively and correctively, working closely with other institutions with related mandates in the country and with relevant international partners. Relevant also is an initiative that we recently undertook to promote inter-communal cultural dialogue toward a better understanding of our respective cultural value systems, their commonalities, their differences, and the prospects for their complementarity. The ultimate objective would be to develop a unifying national identity and value system that can guide governance, constitutionalism, and guiding principles for dialogue with our international development partners.

In addressing the current inter-communal conflicts, the mandate of the National Commission for Inter-Communal Peace and Reconciliation should be to turn this local crisis into a stimulus for addressing generic national challenges with similar causes and manifestations. The overriding strategy should be constructive engagement to explore a common ground, resolve conflicts and unify efforts for pursuing shared objectives. Again, partnership with international peacebuilding, humanitarian, and development agencies, governmental and non-governmental.

'A Joint Statement on the Recent Ngok-Twic Conflict'
By Bona Malual Madut and Francis Mading Deng, Sunday, April 3, 2022

With the outbreak of the conflict between the Ngok and the Twic, Bona Malual, a prominent national figure from Twic, and I issued a statement calling for an end to the violence and reconciliation between the communities:

> *Today we had an honest discussion at the invitation of Her Excellency, Rebecca Nyandeng de Mabior, Vice President of the Republic of South Sudan, at her residence. The lunch meeting*

presented us with the opportunity to share ideas on how to support the presidential fact-finding Committee headed by H.E. Vice President Hussein Abdelbagi Ayii, which H.E. President Salva Kiir Mayardit has commissioned.

Like the rest of the country, we were shocked to learn that the Ngok Dinka of Abyei and Twic Dinka of Warrap were involved in a brutal conflict that first broke out on February 10-12, 2022, due to the dispute over the border market town of Aneet. The conflict has resulted in the unfortunate loss of lives, including women and children, from both sides. The human impact of such conflict brings the bitter grudge of war for both of us as elders from these two neighboring and brotherly communities.

Mindful of the presidential committee mandate, our gathering today allowed us to examine our diverse opinions on how best we can complement the fact-finding Committee, given that both of us have already spoken to the Committee individually.

In our discussions, the Vice President expressed her belief that the process of reconciliation will ensure the accuracy and reaffirm the unity of the Ngok and Twic communities. She further explained that the reconciliation and frank engagements would allow both sides to address historical tensions, grievances, and misconceptions between the Ngok Dinka of Abyei and the Twic Mayardit Dinka of Warrap State. In addition, Vice President, H.E. Rebecca Nyandeng, spoke at length about the importance of reconciliation dialogue following the conclusion of the fact-finding reports.

We call on the leaders of the two Dinka communities to demonstrate leadership by stopping this senseless violent conflict. These leaders understand that war destroys more than human lives and property because it also damages social capital and ties, especially in the case of Ngok Dinka and Twic Dinka, brotherly and sisterly neighbors who took up arms during the liberation struggle against their common enemy. We encourage both communities to understand that their common enemy is still very much around and must be confronted jointly by the two communities.

In peace and unity, we call for cooperative relations between the Ngok and Twic Dinka. Both communities, mainly youth leaders, should allow the fact-finding Committee to finish its work and permit justice to take its due course. Although the damage done has transformed the physical landscape of the town of Aneet, not coming together prompts an even greater transformation of social relations, creating a full-blown culture of hate that never existed between the two communities.

In this contemporary society, we fear that violence can become normalized and woven into the fabric of our daily life, and that is not a welcome practice for the Ngok and Twic Dinka. We call on our people on both sides to immediately cease all hostilities, await with respect the findings and recommendations of the fact-finding Committee, and initiate at the earliest possible opportunity the process of reconciliation to restore their historic relations of kinship as one people. We also call on the Government of South Sudan to engage the Government of Sudan to expedite the resolution of the crisis of the final status of the area in accordance with the aspirations of the people and bring a speedy end to the long-suffering of the Ngok Dinka of Abyei, which remains a significant source of concern for the Government and people of South Sudan. Although these differences and disagreements resulted in painful memories for both communities we urged that these should not undermine hundreds of years of peaceful coexistence, inter-marriages, and shared cultural values between Ngok and Twic Dinka communities.

'National Implications of the Ngok-Twic Conflict'

An Open Letter to the Ngok Dinka Community, June 2022

On February 10-12, 2022, violent conflict broke out between the close kindred Dinka groups, the Ngok Dinka of Abyei and the Twic Mayardit of Warrap State in South Sudan. Tension had recently been mounting between the two communities over contested borders, especially the market town of Aneet claimed by both sides. The Twic were administratively transferred to the North by the British together with the Ngok Dinka in 1905 and although most of the Twic sections later reverted back to the administration of Southern Sudan, the Kuach section of Twic remained in the North under the Paramount Chieftainship of the Ngok until the early 1940s when the section was administratively returned to the South, an event which reportedly made some Ngok elders weep over the partition.

The two communities of Kuach and Ngok were considered the closest kin groups, with the same initiation marks and song and dance styles. Their Chief, Madut Ring, and my father were very close friends. Until Father died, he tried to persuade Madut Ring to have their two tribes reunite. The conflict was therefore a fratricidal surprise. But, as is generally the case with intra-communal conflicts, it has become extremely bitter. This, combined with simultaneous attacks from the North, made the Ngok feel that the attacks were coordinated with the Missiriya Arabs. The Ngok felt that their brothers from the South had stabbed them in the back in alliance with their Arab enemies, a betrayal that was more painful than the attacks by the Arabs. Because some of the elements among the attackers were members of the South Sudanese army, the Ngok felt that they were being targeted not only by the neighboring communities but by the two governments of Sudan and South Sudan. Their anger reflected alienation from South Sudan, which I thought was a strategic mistake that required correction.

That was the reason for this open letter.[101] Because the political climate was extremely volatile and the Ngok Dinka community was overwhelmingly supporting my long-standing proposal for the Ngok to be autonomously self-governing between the two countries, Sudan and South Sudan, during an interim period, after which they would then decide their final status, I was advised against making the letter public, as it would confuse the Ngok population. However, I believe that the advice I am offering is important and of strategic value to our community, which is why I have decided to include it in this volume.

I am taking the liberty to share with you some personal reflections on how I see the crisis our area and people of Abyei are in and how best to get out of the quagmire. We are all aware that our Ngok Dinka community of Abyei is going through an extremely traumatic period, with existential threats from the North, recently also emerging from our Southern border. The persistent attacks from our Northern neighbors, the Missiriya Arabs, and their allied Governments in Khartoum, constitute a systemic affliction we have come to expect as part of the identity wars that have raged in the Sudan for decades. But the recent violent clashes with our Southern neighbors, the Twic Dinka, are particularly shocking precisely because they have generated a fratricidal feud between kith and kin. We know that a feud within the family is more embittering than hostility with strangers or outsiders. Our Dinka say that the curse you inflict upon yourself is more painful than that inflicted upon you by a stranger.

Nevertheless, on both the Northern and Southern fronts, we must guard against losing our balance of judgment and strategic perspective

---

101. The letter was selectively shared with members of the community but not released to the public.

in reacting to this very challenging situation. As we agonize over how to respond to both situations, we must bear in mind two glaring realities. One is that we are undoubtedly South Sudanese in every way and must never consider cutting our bonds of blood, territory, history, and destiny. We have been actively engaged in the liberation struggle of South Sudan in all its phases, and although we the Ngok Dinka have not fully achieved the specific objectives that propelled our people to join the war of liberation, we have derived significant benefits from the struggle that we must not overlook. We should not allow our aspiration for the ideal to become the enemy of our realistic gains.

The second reality is that we occupy a turbulent strategic border with considerable security risks and challenges, but also with attendant opportunities. The security of our borders largely depends on the peaceful coexistence and cooperation with all our neighbors to the North and the South, and between their respective governments in Khartoum and Juba. For a significant part of our modern history, we indeed managed the border relations quite successfully through the wisdom and constructive engagement of our traditional leaders with their Northern counterparts. It is not with your relatives and friends that you strive to negotiate, achieve and maintain peace; it is with your adversaries, sometimes deadly dangerous enemies. But this is by no means an easy feat. Nor is it all in our hands alone. We need a helping hand from those who wield state power in both Khartoum and Juba and the watchful eye of the concerned regional and international actors.

The British colonial rulers played a moderating role between us and our Northern neighbors, as they indeed did between Northern and Southern Sudan. With independence, two devastating wars erupted between Northern and Southern Sudan, with Abyei becoming incrementally getting involved as part and parcel of the Southern liberation struggle. Indeed, Abyei has suffered severely from the consequences of those wars. In 1965, the Ngok Dinka experienced brutal clashes with the Missiriya Arabs because the Arabs had killed a Dinka man from Aweil Dinka and severed his arms which they used for beating drums, a gruesome assault that the Ngok considered a dehumanizing insult and humiliation to the dignity of the Dinka. And in 1970 the Paramount Chief of the Ngok Dinka, Abdalla Moyak Deng Kuol, was assassinated by Northern security forces in Abyei because he had opposed their seizing the cattle of innocent South Sudanese herders who were wrongly accused of involvement in the rebel movement.

The agreements that ended the wars between the North and the South did not resolve the crisis that had promoted the Ngok Dinka to join the liberation struggle in the first place. I have documented the role played by the Ngok Dinka freedom fighters in numerous books and articles over the years. I have also documented the way the Ngok Dinka have been shortchanged in the implementation of the agreements that ended those wars. Although the 1972 Addis Ababa Agreement reconciled the North and the South for ten years, Abyei was denied the exercise of the right granted them by the Agreement to decide by a plebiscite to join the South from which it was severed and annexed to the North in 1905. As a result, Abyei remained engulfed in the abyss of wartime harassment, repression, torture, and killings.

Even more, than the first war in which Ngok Dinka freedom fighters played a well-recognized heroic role, large numbers of Abyei young men and women joined the SPLM/A, fought gallantly, and rose up the ranks of leadership in large numbers. Although the 2005 CPA, and its Abyei Protocol, gave the Ngok Dinka the same right that the Addis Ababa Agreement had given them, to decide by a referendum whether to remain under Northern administration or join the South, history repeated itself as the Government of the Sudan obstructed the full implementation of the Abyei Protocol. Khartoum presented unacceptable conditions for the Abyei referendum, specifically that the nomadic Missiriya herders, who traverse the area for several months during the dry season in search of grazings and sources of water for their herds, must vote in the referendum, and that they must share the administration of the Abyei area during the interim period. The Missiriya voting in a referendum that would allow the Ngok Dinka to leave Northern administration would be like allowing the North to vote in the referendum that entitled the South to secede from the North. And on the Missiriya sharing the administration of the Ngok Dinka, nowhere in the Sudan, Africa, or elsewhere in the world does a tribe or community administer itself alone and then demand sharing the administration of its neighboring tribe or community.

With these insurmountable differences between the Parties, the Abyei referendum that was to be exercised simultaneously with that of the South was deferred by an agreement between the leaders of the South and Abyei to allow the South to vote for its independence in the belief that the Abyei issue would be subsequently resolved with the support of a stronger Government of an independent South Sudan. However, the Abyei referendum continued to be obstructed by Khartoum and the Government of the independent South Sudan carefully avoided confrontation with Sudan over the issue of Abyei. And yet, the Government of South Sudan encouraged and logistically supported the people of Abyei to organize their own referendum, which they did in a smooth, peaceful, credible, and transparent manner. The Ngok Dinka voted overwhelmingly, almost by consensus, to join the South. As expected, Khartoum opposed the referendum and of course, rejected the outcome. Neither did the international community recognize the result. And even the Government of South

Sudan paradoxically refrained from recognizing the outcome of the referendum to avoid confrontation with the Sudan.

The mediation of the African Union and the United Nations, through the African Union High-Level Panel, led by Former President Thabo Mbeki of South Africa, tried hard but failed to bridge the differences. They however presented a proposal that the AU Peace and Security Council endorsed and the UN Security Council welcomed as a sound African solution to an African problem, which was a popular normative African slogan. Khartoum however maintained its stance and the African Union and the United Nations lacked the tools for imposing the solution on the two Governments. Periodic resolutions by the Security Councils of both organizations only reiterated their calls on the two Governments to negotiate a mutually acceptable solution to the problem of Abyei.

An equally divisive issue has been the demarcation of the borders of the Ngok Dinka territory. The Abyei Boundaries Commission (ABC) mandated by the Abyei Protocol of the CPA to determine the boundaries of the Ngok Dinka and whose determination was to be final and binding came up with a report that the Government in Khartoum rejected, alleging that the Commission had exceeded its mandate. The case was eventually taken to the International Court of Arbitration at the Hague, which, in order to find a common ground for peace, revised the determination of the ABC by ceding to the North about a third of the territory allocated to the Ngok Dinka. Although the Court of Arbitration decided to be final and binding, and was initially accepted by both sides, and applauded by Khartoum as a victory for them, Sudan Government subsequently reneged on its implementation.

As a result, Abyei remained an area of intense insecurity with repeated attacks that included a massive invasion by the armed forces of the Sudan in 2009 and 2011, and a pattern of armed incursions by Missiriya militia. The violent clashes of 2011 over Abyei prompted the United Nations Security Council to establish the United Nations Interim Security Force for Abyei (UNISFA), to protect civilians. In many ways, this is the best thing that has happened to the Ngok Dinka in recent years, indeed since the 1956 independence of the Sudan. And yet, although Abyei is stipulated by the UN Security Council to be a weapons-free zone, UNISFA is unable to provide adequate protection within the whole area demarcated by the Hague Arbitration Award, popularly known as The Box. As a result, the Ngok Dinka have therefore continued to be killed by armed militants from the North, sometimes in the presence of UNISFA. This was tragically the case with the assassination of the Paramount Chief Kuol Adol Deng in May 2013 by Missiriya militants while he was on a peace mission to the Missiriya within The Box.

As a result of all this, the Ngok Dinka have remained in a status of virtual statelessness, without the protection and assistance normally expected to be provided by the state for its citizens. In order to resolve the impasse over the final status of Abyei, I made a proposal about a decade ago that aimed at a creative search for a way out of the impasse our area has been in during and after the two wars between the North and South, now Sudan and South Sudan. My objective was to develop a formula that would grant the people of Abyei self-rule as a state that would remain connected to the Two Sudans, a win-win arrangement in which there would be no winner and loser, while the Ngok Dinka would retain their identity and status as South Sudanese. This would in many ways be within the framework of the dual citizenship stipulated by the Abyei Protocol for the interim period and the Mbeki's proposal that Abyei be a border state that would continue to be a conciliatory link between the two countries. The formula also provided for fostering peaceful coexistence and cooperation between the Ngok Dinka and their neighbors, and a comprehensive development strategy that would reinforce and consolidate regional peace and security.

I first presented the proposal to the UN Security Council in 2014 when I was the Permanent Representative of South Sudan to the UN, but as a personal initiative and not an official government position. And over the years, I have reformulated and elaborated it in various documents and have tried to promote it in numerous circles among the Ngok Dinka at home and abroad. The proposal however proved controversial. Those who wanted the issue of the final status immediately addressed and resolved saw the proposal as a distraction and also as a compromise that would keep Abyei connected to the North, which they found objectionable. However, recently, the proposal has received increasing support from a wide spectrum of our people, both inside the country and with the Diaspora. Much of this support is also an expression of frustration and anger fueled by the hostilities from both sides, and particularly from the South. As a result, the supporters of the proposal are interpreting self-rule as a framework for delinking Abyei from both Sudan and South Sudan. This has motivated me to try to elaborate on what I called the two fundamental realities which I referred to earlier, our unwavering ethnic, cultural, and political identity as Southern Sudanese, and our responsibility as a border community with a strategic role to play in promoting inter-communal and inter-state regional peace, security and development cooperation.

The first reality which must be highlighted is our identity and identification as South Sudanese. Whatever our disappointment with the failure of the Government of South Sudan to fully and decisively attain the resolution of our final status, we must not lose sight of the significant benefits we have gained from our belonging to South Sudan. The liberation struggle in which our people played a widely acknowledged and appreciated patriotic role has given us the Abyei Protocol. Against obvious odds, the Interim Constitution of South Sudan recognizes the Ngok Dinka of Abyei as citizens of South Sudan. Furthermore, the Government of South Sudan, specifically President Salva Kiir, established Abyei as a Special Administrative Area, with all the state organs at par with the other Special Administrative Areas and the ten states of South Sudan. Whatever public services Abyei now receives are provided by the Government of South Sudan. And when hostilities broke out between the Ngok and the Twic, the Government of South Sudan sent in forces from the South Sudan Defense Force to stop the violence. And President Salva Kiir appointed a high-level committee under the chairmanship of one of his Vice Presidents to investigate the sources of the conflict, end the violence, and lay the foundation for lasting peace and reconciliation.

From personal discussions with the President, I know first-hand how much he cares about the situation of the Ngok Dinka of Abyei whom he sees as his people, and is keenly aware of the urgent need for a resolution of their problem. In my opinion, the issue is not a lack of political will on the part of the Government of South Sudan or the President, but the objective difficulties they are facing in finding a solution acceptable to the Government of the Sudan and the neighboring communities. The international community will never come in and impose a solution by force on the Governments. All they can do is use various diplomatic ways of persuading the parties based on recognizing that the legitimacy of their sovereignty lies in their responsibility to protect their citizens. That is why President Salva Kiir, whom I have kept informed on all my moves. has supported my efforts as a needed search for a common ground to bring relief to our people. And that is why I have repeatedly stated that if our proposed arrangement can bring peace, security, and stability to Abyei, President Kiir and indeed our well-wishing fellow citizens of South Sudan would be relieved and happy that Abyei is at long last at peace, secure and stable.

The conflict between the Ngok and the Twic is a domestic quarrel that will sooner than later be amicably resolved with the constructive mediation of the state authorities and traditional leaders and elders. After all, given the intense intermarriage between two communities, there is hardly a family that has not suffered the loss of a relative by some affinity or not mourning the tragic feud that has surprisingly disrupted the kinship ties between the two communities. Whatever short-sighted political or material interests that drove some leaders to instigate this violence will dissipate and normalcy will be restored. The Ngok Dinka territory is conterminous to the territories of their fellow Dinkas to the South and Ngok Dinka natural land resources are interdependently and inextricably shared with the herding communities to the South and North.

We should also not consider our relations with the Sudan as a lost cause. After all, our relations with the Missiriya and Khartoum have not always been adversarial. Our history with them has been marked by both adversity and cordiality. Nor should we view the whole country as monolithic in their attitude toward us. Chief Deng Majok was able to win supporters among the Arabs to the point where he was elected President of the Missiriya Rural Council which was overwhelmingly Northern Arabs and a negligible Southern minority. He was also at times able to pit the center in Khartoum against his local adversaries in support of his Ngok Dinka people. Several generations of Ngok Dinka leaders are widely acknowledged by leaders of Dinka communities in the South as having been gatekeepers who protected the land and interests of their Southern Sudanese people against infringements at a challenging and contentious border area. I have documented these historical facts in a number of my publications. I myself signed a document with General Mahdi Babo Nimir which forcefully articulated the grievances of the Ngok Dinka that must be addressed to restore the erstwhile cordial ties between our communities. And I have seen videos of Missiriya intellectuals stating fairness and justice for the Ngok Dinka as the bases for restoring peace and security in the area. The SPLM was able to gain considerable support for its New Sudan Vision from significant elements of the North. The fact is that at moments of conflict, people tend to see only what divides, the negative aspect of relations. With peace, the parties open their eyes and see what unites them with their former adversaries. We saw that after the Addis Ababa Agreement when Southerners became even more committed to unity with the North. And we are now witnessing cordial ties evolving between South Sudan and Sudan since the CPA.

So, let us not be overwhelmed and kept down by the bitterness of animosity. We must liberate our vision to rise up to the challenge of rebuilding a peaceful, conciliatory and cooperative region that serves the best interest of our border communities and by extension the Two Sudans. After all, who gains from animosity and violent confrontation, but only the political entrepreneurs and war merchants? By contrast, all stakeholders stand to gain from peace, security, stability, and prosperity. Ngok's self-governance as a border state through a credible agreement between the two countries and security guarantees by the region and the international community provides a common ground that serves the interest of all the stakeholders. Whatever our status, we are South Sudanese whose identity cannot be questioned by anyone. And our patriotic war heroes have reaffirmed that by making the ultimate sacrifice in both wars of liberation. And our peace, security, stability, and prosperity would be also gained to our kith and kin further South. Let us strive to broaden support for our cause without threatening the deeply rooted solidarity with our Southern Sudanese kith and kin.

I still believe that our area has suffered for far too long from the impasse over the implementation of the agreements on the future status of our area and that it is imperative for us to now search for practical strategies for overcoming the hurdles blocking our way toward a better future. I believe that a self-government arrangement that keeps us connected to South Sudan while fostering cordial conciliatory ties with our neighbors to the North and their Government in Khartoum is the most constructive way forward. An arrangement along these lines can immediately be agreed upon by the two governments with international guarantees for a stipulated period as providing a framework for the resolution of the issue of the final status for Abyei. Or it can be agreed upon as an interim arrangement for a specified period for confidence building to pave the way for a harmonious decision by the Ngok Dinka on their final status. I humbly present these ideas with no claim to any certainty that they represent the only path to the salvation of our people. I stand ready to welcome and applaud any other initiatives that can better deliver our people from their chronic predicaments.

I would like to conclude by reiterating my main point: We must find a way out of our quagmire from which our people have suffered enough and must be rescued. This can only be through an agreement between the parties with international guarantees. This is only possible if we can find a common ground that serves the vital interests of all the stakeholders. The anger emanating from frustration is fully understandable, but we should not allow it to prevent us from rising to the challenge of exploring the best way of ensuring peace, security, stability, and prosperity for our people in constructive partnership with our neighbors to the South and the North, South Sudan, and Sudan.

'The Search for a Common Ground'

Proposal for the Security and Stability of Abyei, August 2022

There has been considerable debate among the Ngok Dinka on my proposal for peace, security, and stability for Abyei which I first introduced about a decade ago. This was a report on the workshop that endorsed that proposal.

There a newly formed group, Abyei Voice for Security and Stability (AVSS), with another group, Keep It Confidential, (KIC), which, between them, have initiated an inclusive forum for dialogue among the Ngok Dinka at home and abroad that overwhelmingly endorsed the proposal. They organized a workshop that was engaged for over a month on ways to improve the proposal and promote it for consideration by the relevant decision-makers nationally and internationally.

As I repeatedly said to the forum, I refrained from continuing to be involved in these discussions because the proposal had moved on and I did not want to be a distraction in their constructive deliberations. Besides, over the years, I have discussed the proposal with the relevant sectors of the Ngok Community: tribal leaders, intellectuals, elders, women, youth, students, and groupings of various sizes, both inside the country and in the Diaspora. But, without being cynical, I believe there are people who may have hidden personal agendas or who, if they have not been personally involved in the discussions, hold the view that the issue has not been discussed. Needless to say, talking to everyone is an unattainable goal.

I must admit that some of these people are sincere and are making points that are worthy of serious consideration. However, the fact is that most, if not all, of those points, are either addressed in the proposal or have been repeatedly debated in the Workshop Forum and in many other discussion groups over the years. I have also elaborated on the proposal and the relevant issues in my various publications. So, either the proposal and my numerous writings on it have not been read, or the critics have deliberately disregarded them.

The mistake is that these critics were added to the workshop organized by AVSS and KIC after the issues had been thoroughly debated for over a month. They were therefore correct in asking why they were being invited to join a discussion that had already been concluded. It is fair to say that the debate will of course continue and that people have every right to voice their concerns. But there are many other venues for channelling views, rather than taking advantage of a forum to which one was invited to contribute to the constructive development and promotion of an already adopted proposal. Since this was the stated objective of the invitation, the honorable thing to do was to decline participation for the obvious reason of conflict of interests.

In any case, I want to make a few general observations on the concerns that have been presented. Let me begin by expressing my sincere appreciation for the compliments made by some of the critics about my contributions to the cause of our people and country over the years. At the risk of being self-serving, I would like to elaborate on this point for those who may not know. I have indeed been personally engaged with advocating and advancing the cause of South Sudan and of our area of Abyei throughout my adult life. I am most grateful to President Salva Kiir for publically honoring me for this contribution. This latest proposal is my attempt to find a way out of the current suffering of our people. It is now quite clear that the governments of the two countries, Sudan and South Sudan, together with the international community, have come to a dead-end in finding a solution to the Abyei crisis. They are openly admitting that fact and calling for new ideas, but how long can we wait passively and hope that a solution will eventually come? And from where will it come? We must guard against making idealism the enemy of realism.

Some of our people may know that I was the one who got the issue of Abyei included in the 1972 peace negotiations and the Addis Ababa Agreement that gave the people of Abyei the right to decide by a plebiscite whether to remain in the North or join the South. My original argument was that Abyei should be recognized as part and parcel of the South, which the Government of course rejected. The provision of the Agreement was a compromise suggested by Abel Alier at the Addis Ababa negotiations that the issue be left for the Ngok Dinka to decide. The Government of Nimeiri reneged on implementing the Abyei plebiscite. And the Regional Government of Abel Alier in Southern Sudan did not want to disturb their newly achieved peace with the North by confronting Khartoum on Abyei. As a result, while the North and the South were at peace, Abyei remained virtually at war with the North.

The persistent conflict over the Abyei issue led to the arrest of some twenty Ngok Dinka leaders, including some of our leading chiefs, among them the Paramount Chief, Kwol Deng Majok Kwol (Kwol Adol), and political leaders, led by Dr. Zachariah Bol Deng, and prominent members of the Ngok political elite. They were publicly condemned to be charged and tried for treason, which, as we all know, is punishable by death. It took me months of intensive negotiations with the authorities to secure their release.

In an effort to end the continuing suffering of our people, I took the initiative and persuaded Nimeiri to give Abyei an autonomous administration headed by Justin Deng Aguer, with a team of Ngok government officials seconded from North and South, to be directly under the Presidency. As Ambassador to the United States and then Minister for Foreign Affairs, USAID provided funding for the project and implementation assistance came from the Harvard Institute for International Development, (HIID). That brought some relief to our people and security to the area, for which, as we know, the late Minyiel Row composed very powerful and popular songs.

As is well known to some of our people and is kindly acknowledged by the leadership of our country, I also played a significant role in supporting the cause of South Sudan in Washington during the second war through a long advocacy process that dramatically reversed the negative policy of the US toward the SPLM. Our efforts eventually culminated in the creation of the CSIS Task Force on US Policy to End the War in the Sudan, which I was honored to co-chair with Stephen J. Morrison, and on which I was the only Sudanese. After months of intensive deliberations, I was able to persuade the Task Force, against considerable initial resistance, to recommend US leadership of the peace process and support for the right of Southerners to self-determination. Senator John Danforth was appointed by President George Bush as his Special Envoy to lead the mediation team. In our Task Force report, we proposed the formula of 'One Country, Two Systems' for the interim period. That formula is widely credited for guiding Senator Danforth in his mediation. Mutrif Siddig, who was a leading member of Sudan Government delegations, told me that they read the report at least four times during the negotiations.

My advocacy for Abyei was always central in all my efforts for peace in the Sudan. Again, history repeated itself in that the provisions of the Abyei Protocol of the CPA have not been implemented, and the government of South Sudan, while sincerely concerned about the plight of the people of Abyei, as was the case with the Regional Government of South Sudan under the Addis Ababa Agreement, is avoiding the risk of confrontation with the Sudan over Abyei. As a result our people are continuing to suffer, while South Sudan and Sudan are at peace and developing cordial bilateral relations.

Personally, I do not think the inaction is because the leadership of South Sudan does not care about the people of Abyei. After all, the President has decreed Abyei a Special Administrative Area within South Sudan. Unfortunately, this is a one-sided decision that has not been officially recognized by the Sudan Government or the international community. It is quite obvious that South Sudan cannot impose a solution on the Sudan and is trying to avoid conflict in Abyei. Leaders of South Sudan have indeed admitted that fact to me. The international community too cannot impose a solution on the two governments. In the end, all they can do is mediate a solution that the two governments will accept. We must help them in their search for common ground in resolving the problem of Abyei. And that is what I have been trying to do with the proposal.

In the effort to support the two governments and the international mediators in exploring a potentially agreeable solution, we are proposing self-administration as a form of self-determination that will play a linking and conciliatory role between the two countries. That is what the Abyei Protocol and Former President Thabo Mbeki envisioned when they referred to the bridging role of Abyei, to which the hard-liners object. It is indeed in that spirit that I have over the years shared the proposal with the leaders of both Sudan and South Sudan, and with our international interlocutors. On the whole, they have generally been understanding and encouraging, although they are aware of the differences of opinion within our Ngok Dinka Community. When I first presented the proposal to the Security Council in 2014, members of the Council expressed appreciation of the fact that it was an effort to accommodate the interests of all concerned. The Chinese Permanent Representative went as far as saying that it was a win-win arrangement and that he could not see how anyone would oppose it.

In the search for a common ground, I would like to stress two points. The first is that the envisioned self-administration must be for the Ngok Dinka alone and does not in any way give any room for sharing with the Missiriya. As I have always said in all languages I know, Dinka, Arabic, and English, and in spoken and written words, nowhere in the Sudan, South Sudan, Africa, or in the world, as far as I know, does a community govern itself and then share the administration of another community. The Ngok and the Missiriya should be each self-governing and agree on arrangements for managing their bilateral relations as mutually independent communities.

The second point I want to stress is that no agreement that is agreeable to our people can deny us the fact that we are South Sudanese on any identity grounds. We belong to South Sudan racially, ethnically, culturally, and geographically. What is required by a common ground is an arrangement that will reconcile our belonging to South Sudan with meeting the vital interests of the Sudan and our Missiriya neighbors. The Missiriya should be guaranteed peaceful coexistence with the Dinka and their seasonal access to water and pastures. The goal is for all stakeholders to see Abyei positively as a peaceful and conciliatory link and not a point of conflict. That is the detail the two countries are called upon to negotiate and agree upon.

Needless to say, we are not in a position to officially table a proposal ourselves. All we can do is facilitate the negotiating process with ideas. It is indeed as a resource person that I have been contributing ideas to the cause of peace for our people. The international mediators are in fact soliciting ideas from all interested parties and resource persons. We are also trying to help prepare the ground for our people to be receptive to a negotiated common ground, should our proposal get recognition in the negotiations or be considered as an element in the outcome.

I have always said that if our critics have an alternative solution that can bring an immediate end to the suffering of our people, I will be one of those who will hail their success with deep appreciation and gratitude. Perhaps the energy of the critics should be better invested in constructively engaging with the Government of South Sudan to offer constructive and practical ideas to help the government in its negotiations with the Sudan government and have their views over the final status of Abyei considered seriously and hopefully adopted.

The proposal does not in any way contradict the provisions of the Abyei Protocol but is on the contrary trying to reactivate its implementation. We have no fundamental disagreement with our critics on substantive objectives, but on how best to pursue those objectives. If they could deliver practical alternative means of achieving our shared goals, I am sure they would gain popular support from our people and my own sincere appreciation. We are all aiming at the same goal and should avoid dissipating our energies negatively through distracting and disempowering infighting.

Some people argue that we should not be advocating alternative security arrangements when we already have UN protection forces in Abyei. I should note that the UNISFA, is by definition a temporary arrangement that is periodically renewed under the threat of immanent termination if the parties do not reach an agreement on Abyei. I always tell the concerned decision makers that UNISFA cannot exit and leave a vacuum. Imagine what would happen if the UN Force were to leave a vacuum! Finding a durable solution is therefore an urgent imperative.

I would like to emphasize one important point, I think we do great injustice to our legendary traditional leaders who managed to maintain peace, security, and stability in our area under the most challenging circumstances. British administrators have written and have told me that it was indeed because of the wisdom of those Ngok leaders that Abyei became an island of peace surrounded by border communities devastated by violent conflicts. And the peace, security, and stability they established in their border area also benefited the tribes south of us. Leaders from these Dinka tribes told me in extensive interviews that it was indeed the constructive role those leaders played that ensured peace and security for their people. This point was strongly echoed by Twic, Malual, and Rek leaders alike. Chief Giir Thiik went as far as telling me that if it were not for Ngok leaders, some of the tribes in our Southern region might have disappeared.

Unfortunately, the challenges those leaders faced on our turbulent borders are still with us and we have not lived up to their level of accomplishment in reconciling and harmonizing the conflicting interests in the region. Calling them uneducated compared with our now educated generation of today is to confuse wisdom with formal education. As someone who has invested much effort in collecting the views of our traditional leaders and elders, I have great reverence for their wisdom and am indeed very proud to have documented it.

Finally, let me reiterate that no solution will bring lasting peace, security, and stability to our area that does not enjoy the endorsement and genuine commitment of all the stakeholders at all levels, from local to global. The two governments and our immediate neighbors to the North and South must all agree for peace, security, and stability to be achievable and sustainable. So, let us open up to constructive engagement in search of a common ground that ensures win-win solutions, instead of winner-loser formulations or outcomes.

Thank you for your patience in reading this long explanation of my proposal for resolving the Abyei crisis. I sincerely hope that I have not offended anyone and if I have inadvertently done so, please accept my sincere apology.

'Rising from the Ashes'

Review of *South Sudan: Beyond Ethnic and Political Inertia*

Peter Lam Both, Africa World Books, 2022

Peter Lam Both's book, *South Sudan: Beyond Ethnic and Political Inertia* is a 'must read' for anyone concerned with the violent conflict that erupted in South Sudan in December 2013, less than two years after its independence on July 9, 2011, and has devastated the country ever since. The conflict has largely been viewed as ethnic, pitting the Dinka under the leadership of President Salva Kiir Mayardit, and the Nuer, led by his First Vice President, Dr. Riek Machar. I find the book very impressive and compelling not because the subject it is addressing is new, but because of the insight, the details, the nuances, and the objectivity the author brings to the discussion of the issues involved. The book is well written with lucidity and clarity which makes it a very compelling reading.

I first got to know Peter Lam when the National Dialogue Leadership assigned me the responsibility of chairing an Ad-Hoc Committee whose objective was to bring on board all the political parties, both in the government and in the opposition, to join the National Dialogue. The opposition parties had understandably boycotted the National Dialogue which they saw as the initiative of the ruling party, specifically the President, to polish the image of the regime. After the Revitalized Peace Agreement (RPA), that was signed in Addis Ababa on September 12, 2018, it was thought opportune to invite all the parties to join the National Dialogue. But political agendas and aspirations differed, and the National Dialogue remained controversial. The task to which I was assigned was therefore very challenging. Although Peter Lam represented the ruling SPLM, he was most effective in bridging the differences through a thoughtful, objective, and constructive analysis and presentation of the case for a unified approach. He was catalytic to the success of our Ad-Hoc Committee. Peter Lam's treatment of the conflict that has bedeviled the country reflects elements that had impressed me in the role he played in the Committee.

Lam addresses, head-on, the issue of whether the conflict is driven by ethnic differences and competition or by the ambitions and rivalries of the politicians. He does so with meticulous analysis of the perspectives of the individual leaders involved, their ambitions, and the legitimate concerns of their ethnic communities - neither of which should be taken lightly. I have always been intrigued by the interplay between the role of political entrepreneurs and the legitimate grievances of the ethnic groups they purportedly represent in identity-related conflicts. Political scientists generally contend that ethnic conflicts are driven by politicians exploiting ethnicity and not by ethnicity itself. This is usually linked with the tendency to dismiss or downplay ethnic identity as a significant variable in conflict analysis and resolution, allegedly because the concept is viewed as too nebulous and intangible, difficult to define, and therefore not a meaningful subject of negotiation. This amounts to dismissing ethnicity, or the broader concept of identity, as a fictional construct that has no real existence.

It has always been my view that one cannot exploit what does not exist and that it is not only unrealistic but indeed offensive and dangerous to deny the existence of ethnicity or other forms of identity. What seems to be overlooked or underestimated is the fact that the distribution of power and material assets is often based on identity, whether racial, ethnic, cultural, or religious, or defined by any other factors. What is critical then is not the mere fact of identity differences, but how those differences are managed.

With respect to South Sudan, Peter Lam articulates the problem very succinctly when he writes: "It is tribalism that threatens national unity and stability, not the tribes per se. Tribalism, therefore, is a manipulative method used by political leaders to mobilize their ethnic groups against others in order to gain their political objectives in a given country."[102]

As he elaborates: "Though the main driver of the conflict was a power struggle between and among leaders within SPLM as to who should lead the country after the independence was achieved, certain leaders presented the problem to their people as an ethnic conflict."[103]

So, what precisely is it in tribal or ethnic identity that the politicians exploit? I believe it is the sense of collective grievance against inequality emanating from mismanagement of diversity. This is often reflected in allegations of intolerable injustice in the shaping and sharing of power, national wealth, and other values, material or intangible, and even symbolic. Injustice means that some groups enjoy the full rights of belonging to the national identity framework, while others are discriminated against, marginalized, and even excluded from fully sharing the rights of citizenship. The alleged inequality may only be perceived rather than real, but that does not prevent the entrepreneurs from exploiting it with what Peter Lam describes as a 'myopic view' of the leaders, backed by an ill-informed mass following.[104]

In South Sudan, the author maintains that: "The war was fought predominantly along ethnic lines as though ethnicity were the cause. Due to this myopic view of the conflict, it was difficult for many South Sudanese leaders to remain objective and view the conflict for what it was. Instead, they presented it to their people as war between the Nuer and Dinka, which was not true. As a consequence, many South

102. Peter Lam Both, *South Sudan: Beyond Ethnic and Political Inertia,* Africa World Books, 2022, p. 5.
103. Ibid.
104. Ibid.

Sudanese people lost their lives believing that they were fighting an ethnic war. They did not know that they were fighting for the interest of their leaders to gain power. The worst thing was that by the time some of them realized, it was too late. The genie had already left the bottle. The country had already caught up in flames."[105]

Lam asserts that the politicians in fact knew that what they were saying to mobilize their people was not true and they were misleading them, which underscores the element of exploitation as Peter Lam narrated: "South Sudanese leaders who advocated and called this war ethnic knew that it was not true. They knew that such a description was deceptive, yet they used it to discredit the South Sudanese body politic as a Dinka system in order to have the legitimacy to mobilize their ethnic bases for support to challenge the government militarily. As is well known, the Government of South Sudan has never been a Dinka government. It represents South Sudanese people across the world. This narrow characterization of war as being ethnic was influenced by opposition leaders, activist groups, authors of books and articles on the war in South Sudan, as well as reports by international human rights and humanitarian organizations which were influenced by the agenda of the opposition political parties."[106]

What I find ironic is that Lam presents the situation in a balanced way that defies the usual characterization of the war as senseless, reckless, or irrational, when in fact the principal actors have a clear opportunistic calculation of what they are doing, wrong or even immoral as it may be. If one recognizes the designs and strategies of the opposition in their ruthless drive to gain power, one must also appreciate the countermeasures of the government and its leadership to defend and retain its power. The arguments often levied against the

---

105. Ibid, p. 10.
106. Ibid, p. 6.

leadership, therefore, does not adequately consider survival defense mechanisms against the perceived existential threat posed by armed insurgencies. Lam makes the reader appreciate the point of view of every actor, whether or not you sympathize with them or vehemently disagree with their position. But, of course, rights and wrongs are never equal! Nor does Lam claim moral equivalence in the position of the adversaries. In fact, he and some Nuer colleagues took sides with the Dinka-led government and suffered the consequences.

Indeed, one of the most moving aspects of Lam's account is the predicament those who rise above factionalism to promote the cause of unity and the common good of the nation face in sharply divisive identity-related conflicts. As he put it: "Standing for the unity and interest of the country in an ethnically charged environment like South Sudan in 2013 was very challenging. On the one hand, logic and reason dictate that we are all South Sudanese, and our allegiance should be to all our people in the country regardless of their ethnicity. But, on the other hand, one also belongs to a particular ethnic group just like the other leaders who stand in support of their ethnic bases. The two loyalties should naturally complement each other as they are mutually reinforcing. But this has not been the case in South Sudan where conflict proliferated along ethnic lines. Supporting the interest of the country at the apparent expense of one's ethnic interest was uncommon, and it made others to question our mental equanimity."[107]

Peter Lam does not hide or dismiss his identity as a Nuer. Far from it, he acknowledges it and upholds it as a basis for his responsibility to work for the interest of both sides of the conflict whose members he sees as equal fellow citizens to whom he owes equal responsibility of leadership: "For us, logic and patriotism dictate that our people are the people of South Sudan as a whole, not just the Nuer. We were

---

107. Ibid.

troubled by the way our people were killing themselves in the country in various locations. We knew that the Nuer were killed and so were other South Sudanese in the Nuer areas. Our concern was to end the war quickly before it could destroy even more lives."[108]

Unfortunately, that patriotic leadership is often not appreciated by most people on both sides. It can indeed be a very painful and lonely position that only exceptional courage and determination can sustain. I witnessed this position with one of Peter's Nuer colleagues, General James Hoth Mai, who was the Chief of General Staff during the war that was seen as pitting his people against the Dinka. I was very impressed by what he was doing and indeed I often voiced my praise for him in circles that included Dinka. I was shocked to hear some people express opposite views against him, even accusing him of undermining the fighting capacity of the army. When I first met him in his office, General James Hoth told me that even before the outbreak of the violence, he had been under pressure from the Nuer who wanted to go to war with the Dinka over their grievances and that he was being criticized for remaining on the wrong side of an ethnic war. As Peter explains: "Their patriotic standpoint was the exception, not the norm. Their position became so unorthodox that its validity was questioned by many Nuer and leaders from other ethnic groups as being too utopian. For taking such a stand, we were disowned and isolated by both sides to the conflict. The Nuer community... deleted our names from the community list as in their view, we became 'Dinka' since we did not support their cause."[109]

Particularly painful was the way they were not only rejected by the Dinka but also marginalized by the government in which they were serving. I quote Lam's words in detail because I believe his message

---

108. Ibid.
109. Ibid, p. 7.

must be impressed upon the conscience of every fellow citizen as an important experience from which to draw crucial lessons to guide future conduct. Thus: "It could have made sense if the government and a majority of our Dinka colleagues in power reciprocated our patriotic resolve and standpoint. However, we had less, if not, non-existent recognition and support from the Government of South Sudan and the SPLM at that time. Even an acknowledgment of our role as stated above by the government could have made the difference. Instead, the government isolated us with the exception of newfound SPLM Nuer members who were originally from the ruling party in the Arab Islamic regime in the Sudan, the National Congress Party (NCP). Some elements in the government thought we did not leave the government because we were trapped. They assumed we were waiting for Dr. Riek Machar to take overpower so that we could join him. They totally misunderstood our resolve and commitment to this country and the SPLM. We remained here for South Sudan and not for anything else."[110]

Marginalized by their own government, and rejected by their Dinka compatriots, they were truly in an identity void: "For a majority of our Dinka brothers and sisters, we were 'Nuer' and nothing else. The fact that our presence legitimized the Government of South Sudan which they led couldn't come close to the mind of those running the government. Our state of affairs in government was in jeopardy confirming what my friend at the United Nations Office in South Sudan told me in December 2013 "that the political victims of this war would be the Nuer patriots because they belonged to nobody, but the country."[111]

And, of course, to the Nuer, they were nothing short of traitors for the ethnic cause of their people: "The Nuer in opposition fumed with

110. Ibid, p. 84.
111. Ibid, p. 7.

anger towards us for not supporting the cause of Dr. Riek Machar or joining them in the war of revenge. They could not get their heads around the reason why we refused to join them. They said that we were bought by Dinka to stay aloof from the war. Hence, they coined the term '*Nuer wew*' or as Pendle put it frankly, 'Nuer of Dinka Money' to describe us. For them, we became their enemy number one. In their social media writings and video postings where they incite the Nuer to revenge and kill the Dinka, they never missed the opportunity to take a swipe at us. 'We will get you. We will kill you first before the Dinkas."[112]

The case of South Sudan represents the dilemma of identity and diversity which is widely shared in varying degrees by many countries. I witnessed this in my two United Nations mandates, first as Representative of the Secretary-General on Internally Displaced Persons for twelve years and then as Special Advisor of the Secretary-General for the Prevention of Genocide. In my field missions around the world, I saw the crisis of national identity manifested in the conflict between aspirations for national unity and the demand for equality and even self-determination by minorities. I am often left wondering how those identity groups in conflict would ever get together to become one united nation.

The constructive way out of the conundrum of such conflicts is not to deny the existence of ethnicity or identity, but to ensure inclusivity, equality, and respect for the dignity of all groups, without discrimination on any ground. This was in essence the New Sudan ideal the people of the Sudan, led by South Sudanese, were fighting for. The vision of a 'New' dispensation of full equality is one that virtually every country in the world, not least South Sudan, desperately

---

112. Ibid, p. 8.

needs. It is by invoking gross inequality that political entrepreneurs exploit ethnicity or identity for their self-interested ambitions for power and wealth. But since perceptions do not necessarily reflect facts, remedial measures must be accompanied by mass education and political enlightenment on the facts to guard against false allegations by politicians.

In addressing the perceived grievances, we must look for guidance to our fundamental cultural values and normative principles of conflict management and resolution. Our cultures of South Sudan have been thoroughly studied by anthropologists, although we have unfortunately not made effective use of those studies. Peter Lam in fact refers to some of the major concepts that have been documented in the anthropological studies of our societies. Among these are such notions as acephalous political systems, stateless societies, tribes without rulers, the segmentary lineage system, balanced opposition, and ordered anarchy. These concepts, which our people have sometimes found objectionable as reflective of western paternalism and condescension, were central to our Nilotic societies. The Oxford anthropologists and their colleagues in related institutions championed them with implicit admiration as embodying principles of good governance, democracy, respect for human rights, and constitutionalism. If we observed and applied them, they could help shape an admirable model state that constructively balances unity with ethnic and cultural diversity. That was indeed what the colonial rulers did when they adopted the policy of indirect rule, which post-colonial administrations abandoned as part of colonial exploitation of culture as a tool of domination.

One of the aspects of the book which I find very attractive is his invocation of the ideals of the liberation struggle as a basis for optimistically charting the way forward: "The purpose for which we liberated ourselves from domination was to be free and build a united democratic and prosperous country for ourselves. We did not seek freedom for its own sake, but to use it as a catalyst to advance our country and bring ourselves to be counted among the best nations of this earth."[113]

Arguing that the development of nations is never a straight line, but a zigzag, he quotes Nelson Mandela's famous saying that "the greatest glory in the living lies not in never falling, but in rising every time we fall." According to Lam, Mandela was talking about the power to persist in life and get up every time one falls to fight over gain. He stated: "As a people, we have come a long way to stop now. We fought for nearly a century for our freedom. We cannot look back but learn from the past and move forward. I always say that the greatest strength of the people of South Sudan during the liberation struggle was always found at their weakest point. This means that when we realize our divisions cannot serve us any better, we always unite our ranks and face challenges with herculean effort. And we have always won when we turned away from perdition."[114]

I share Peter Lam's optimistic disposition which I frequently link to two normative principles that have always guided me in my personal and public life. One is that pessimism should be avoided as it leads to a dead end, while optimism, provided it is strategically grounded, stimulates creative and productive action. The other principle is that there are nearly always opportunities in crises and the challenge is to explore them and make effective use of them in seeking corrective remedies. Peter Lam cites the experiences of the post-war United States and the reconstruction of the European countries in the aftermath of World War II as lessons that "should teach us that losing one's path does not

---

113. Ibid, p. 9.
114. Ibid.

signal resignation, but the beginning of developing great nations."[115]

Foreword to 'Politics of Ethnic Discrimination in Sudan: A Justification for the Secession of South Sudan'
Dhieu Mathok Diing Wol, PhD, 2nd edition, Africa World Books, 2022

1. The Book and the People

Politics of Ethnic Discrimination in Sudan: A Justification for the Secession of South Sudan by Dr. Dhiew Mathok Diing Wol,[116] is unique in that the author writes from the vantage point of an exceptional combination of qualifications for performing the task he has set for himself. Apart from the academic credentials that qualify the manuscript for the Ph.D. degree, it has the added advantage of a participant-observer with insight from his background as a member of Malual Dinka in which his father was Paramount Chief. Dr. Dhieu Mathok is also a politician and statesman, having been a minister in the government of the Sudan, when it was one country, and is now a cabinet minister in the government of National Unity of South Sudan. With these credentials, the reader is privileged to get into the complex and intricate world of intertribal relations in the wider national context of racial, ethnic, religious, and cultural diversity. The book covers a wide range of issues with remarkable depth and insight. Although it primarily focuses on Malual-Rezeigat relations, it links them to the national levels of North-South Sudanese politics and inter-communal politics of South Sudan. Commensurately, this foreword addresses those aspects of the study that relate to the politics of identity and diversity in the context of Malual-Rezeigat relations, the extent to

---

115. Ibid.

116. First published by New Vision Publishing and Printing Company, Kampala, 2010.

which they link local and national levels through the penetration of central authorities, and their extension to the international level, largely through a concern with humanitarian and human rights issues in the country.

The book was first published in December 2010 and the author explains that in the first edition he made three predictions that came to be and which motivated him to revise the book for issuing this second edition. These predictions include the overwhelming choice of the people of South Sudan for independence; the outbreak of border conflict between South Sudan and Sudan in 2012; and the eruption of civil war in South Sudan in 2013. The author thoroughly examines the dynamics of locally-generated conflicts that grew to become nationwide and extend further to involve international actors. This was the case with both Dinka Malual-Rezeigat Arab and Dinka Ngok-Missiriya Arab situations.

Dinka Malual, like all their fellow Dinka groups, are known to be very proud and ethnocentric. Central to their cultural value system is a concept of immortality through progeny, the continuation of the identity and influence of the dead among the living, and inter-generational linkages in change and continuity. Although this is an agnatic system that favors the male line, women are very powerful and influential as mothers of the line. It is precisely because of their influence that the role of the father must be emphasized as a function of the mind, while the closer attachment to the mother is acknowledged as a function of the heart. In both cases, ancestral values require solidarity, unity, and harmony within the family, the kin group, and the wider community. Being remembered and revered also demands adhering to the principles of individual and communal dignity and integrity. The place of the individual in society is determined by conformity to these fundamental values.

It is not an exaggeration to say that in their traditionally isolated world, the Dinka saw themselves and their culture as the ideal model of God's creation. But they are not unique in their self-esteem. Exalting one's identity is the essence of being human and it is universal. Identity is inherent in every individual as a member of the family, kinship, and the wider community. Also inherent in identity is a sense of pride and dignity as a human being in a given social and cultural context. Subjectively, and especially viewed in isolation, every social and cultural group idealizes itself as a model of human dignity. It is only when the group gets in contact with other groups and issues of diversity arise that the subjective sense of superiority comes into question. Diversity almost inevitably raises the challenge of inter-group interaction, mutual influence, stratification, and potential inequality.

2. Malual-Rezeigat and Ngok-Missiriya Contexts

The author confirms that the relations between Malual and Rezeigat in the context of North and South Sudan, now two different countries of Sudan and South Sudan, are far more complex than is normally reflected in popular discourse. This complexity is most pronounced between the ethnic groups at the borders of Upper Nile and Bahr el-Ghazal, whose interaction with their Northern Sudanese neighbors are for the most part permeated by ambiguities and ambivalences. This may involve a contradictory combination of both embracing and resisting interracial cross-cultural influences and assimilation. But as Herskovits observed, they give and take in varying forms and degrees, but some mutual influence is unavoidable. Ironically, this often entails a degree of discrepancy between what is perceived and what is real. The animosity between ethnic groups sometimes leads to not seeing anything positive in the other group and not recognizing or acknowledging any shared characteristics of mutual influences. Evidence of inter-racial and cross-cultural influences between the neighboring groups across the North-South borders are often visible, but tend to be ignored or dismissed, because of hostility and animosity.

The anomalies of inter-communal relations between North and South Sudan are often associated with Abyei, probably because the Ngok Dinka represent a people who are for all intents and purposes South Sudanese, but are administered in the North in the same province with their Missiriya Arab neighbors. Dr. Dhiew Mathok in fact devotes a section of his book to the case of Abyei. But as this book reveals, the relationship between Malual and Rezeigat has many similarities as well as differences with the Ngok Dinka Missiriya situation. The differences in their situation relates largely to their separate administrative affiliation to North and South Sudan. The author presents the relationship between the Malual Dinka and the Rezeigat as involving a dynamic interaction that alternates between peaceful coexistence and cooperation through trade and violent confrontation over resources. While this is also true of the Ngok-Missiriya relations, reports of the British administrators indicate that the Malual-Missiriya relations have generally been more conflictual, perhaps because the Ngok and the Missiriya were administered in the same province and district.

For the same reason, historical memories of conflicts between the Ngok and the Missiriya tend to be more intense. It is a well-known sociological fact that conflicts within close relationships tend to be more embittering than conflicts with more distant adversaries. At moments when relations are peaceful and cooperative, people tend to see the positive as peers in their interaction, including historical memories. When conflict becomes violent, much of what people see and remember is animosity and nothing peaceful. A personal experience revealed to me the alternating views on history and the influence of peace and conflicts in their perception. I conducted two sets of interviews with Ngok Dinka chiefs and elders in the mid-1970s. I had already interviewed prominent Dinka chiefs from different tribes of South Sudan. The specific questions posed concerned the history of contact and relationship with the Arabs of Northern Sudan and the future prospects for unity and integration.

I conducted the first interview shortly after the Missiriya had attacked lorries carrying Dinka passengers going back to their home areas and massacred about a hundred people, including women and children. The perspective of those interviewed was totally negative. They said, "God created us different from the Arabs. We were created black and the Arabs were created brown. And our ways have been totally different since creation." Arab character and moral values were presented in a very negative light, while Dinka character and culture were perceived as embodying moral ideals. According to the Dinka, there was no basis for unity, far less integration; the two people must remain separate into the distant future.

I conducted the second set of interviews after a successful Ngok Dinka-Missiriya Arab peace and reconciliation conference in which I assisted Abdel Rahman Abdalla, the Minister of Public Service, who chaired the negotiations. The perspective of those interviewed was radically different from those of my first interviewees: "God created us with the Arabs as twins," they asserted. Some added the white race to make for triplets. They also acknowledged that people had mixed racially and culturally and that there were many well-known families in Ngok Dinka society with Arab blood. They even predicted that mixing would continue and that people, in the end, would all become one. [117]

A balanced view of the situation is that the Dinka have been more resistant than receptive to intermarriage and cultural assimilation with

---

117. The materials from those interviews produced two books, *Africans of Two Worlds: The Dinka in Afro-Arab Sudan,* Yale Press 1978, and *Dinka Cosmology,* Ithaca Press, 1980. Reissued as *The Changing World of the Dinka* (2022) and *Dinka Worldview: Elders Reflect on the Past, Present and Future of their People* (2023), Africa World Books.

the Arabs. In the exceptions, cases where intermarriage takes place, both the Arabs and the Dinka prefer that their men rather than women marry across the divide. This is because their patriarchal system favors integrating the progeny of mixed marriages into kinship. Ironically, because of their proximity to the North, both the Malual and the Ngok Dinka have been defensively impervious to Arab influence. The Ngok Dinka, though administered in the North, has paradoxically been even more resistant to Arab-Islamic influence. There is probably less interracial marriage between the Arabs of the Sudan and the Ngok Dinka than there is between the North and other Southern Sudanese in other border areas in Upper Nile and Bahr el-Ghazal. This is however a complex situation where what is admitted may be different from what is in fact the case. People who display hostility to all that is Arab may well be among the most influenced by Arab culture.

3. Connection to Regional and National Actors

There is reason to believe that while interaction between Malual Dinka and their Rezeigat neighbors have been broadly inter-communal, the relationship between the Ngok Dinka and the Missiriya Arabs was traditionally personal at the level of their respective leaders, going back several generations, although education has now broadened the bases of contact. Anthropologists and British administrators who served in the area have observed that the Ngok Dinka are more centralized under one leadership than the other Dinka tribes and that their political system has been significantly influenced by the association of their leaders with their Arab counterparts. It is also argued that the geographical isolation of the Ngok Dinka from the control of the central government has also strengthened their autonomous indigenous system of administration. This indicates the extent to which linkage to external sources of control and authority impacts the local power dynamics.

In contrast to the case of the Ngok-Missiriya elite-led inter-relationship, the Malual-Rezeigat contacts and conflicts appear more inter-communal. Dr. Dhiew Mathok indeed explains that the conflicts between the communities revolved around competition over a natural resource like grazing land, water, and fishing prospects, but an aggravating factor was the involvement of the central government which exploited the tribes and turned them into agents of the government in its power struggle, especially in North-South civil wars. According to the author, "Arab tribes, like Reziegat of Southern Darfur and Messiriya of Southern Kordofan, were used in order to fight their neighbors in Northern Bahr el-Ghazal and Northern Upper Nile, resulting in soured tribal relations at the South-North border, and undermining the fact that there are common interests between these tribes."[118] The situation also gave the Malual the support of the armed rebel groups in the South which created a relative balance of power that contributed to inter-communal peace and reconciliation.

Dr. Dhieu Mathok observes that when the SPLA/M leadership and the local authorities of Reziegat, Missiriya, and Dinka Malual people realized that the war had cost the people dearly and those suffering the most were innocent people living on the border, they formed Peace Markets with Reziegat and Misseriya. "This motivated them to devise means of making people-to-people grass-roots peace. They made local peace agreements without the consent of the government or the SPLA/M leadership. They maintained their contacts in the peace markets, setting up administration units of the markets between the tribes. The markets became an effective unifier for the Dinka Malual, Misseriya, and Reziegat people. The exchange of goods and materials went on smoothly. Sometimes the traders came from Khartoum and

---

118. Dhieu Mathok Diing Wol, *Politics of Ethnic Discrimination in Sudan: A Justification for the Secession of South Sudan,* Africa World Books, 2022, p. 132.

other big towns to purchase from the peace markets."[119] The protection the Malual had received from the rebel forces in the South has now been strengthened by the even more effective protection of the government of South Sudan.

The use of markets as peacebuilding institutions has also been experienced by Ngok Dinka-Missiriya Arabs relations. Despite the intensified conflicts with the Missiriya since the independence of South Sudan with which the Ngok Dinka have had internationally unrecognized de facto affiliation as citizens, the Aneet market, which is deep in Ngok Dinka territory has been playing the role of an important trade link with South Sudan. The peace committees and community police established by the two communities have been instrumental in fostering peace and reconciliation at the grassroots, albeit with obvious limitations. The market has also been an agent for promoting a broader-based trade with various areas in South Sudan, including major urban centers. Aneet market, at the border with the Twic Dinka, has also played a similar role, although it recently experienced violent border conflict between the Ngok and Twic.

The main difference between the Malual-Rezeigat situation and that of the Ngok Dinka and the Missiriya has been the support Malual have received from South Sudanese armed groups, and since independence, from the government of South Sudan. Prior to the involvement of external forces, there was a degree of parity in the military capacity of both sides of the North-South border. The Dinka had the advantage of using light spears that could be darted from a distance, as opposed to the heavy spears that the Arabs used and which required close proximity for stabbing the enemy. But the Arabs used horses that gave them a comparative advantage. These relative advantages

---

119. Ibid, p. 111.

on both sides resulted in a degree of parity in their fighting capacities that fostered peaceful coexistence. The author quotes the Assistant District Commissioner of Baggara (Missiriya) as reporting: "These Dinkas have never been subdued by the Arabs when it comes to fighting, they gave as good as they got."[120] The author also observed, "The balance of power between Reziegat, Messeriya, and Dinka Malual was more or less the same and no tribe could overweigh the other."[121] Later, however, the fact that the Arabs were the first to acquire modern weapons gave them a decisive advantage over the Dinka. Under British colonial rule, the even-handedness of the central government administration ensured a degree of parity that maintained peaceful coexistence.

After independence, during the two North-South wars, Abyei was under the administration of the North and therefore in the lion's den, so to speak. The independence of South Sudan has offered the Ngok Dinka significant support, but Abyei is still contested and remains in a relative vacuum of state responsibility between the Two Sudans. As a result, the Ngok Dinka have not had the kind of protection the Malual have received from the Southern-based armed rebel groups, and now from the government of the independent South Sudan

Since most South Sudanese ethnic groups at the borders with the North have enjoyed the relative protection of their Southern security forces, they are ironically more secure and less antagonistic toward the Arabs than the Ngok Dinka. When people are not oppressed and have the freedom of choice, they tend to be more receptive to influence from the people with whom they interact than when they feel coerced or threatened into assimilation. That was indeed the experience of South Sudanese before and after the two agreements with the North, the 1972 Addis Ababa Agreement and the 2005 CPA. Although the

120. Ibid, p. ix.
121. Ibid.

South Sudan Liberation Movement, and its military wing, Anya-Nya, fought a separatist war, once the peace agreement was concluded, Southern Sudanese became more unionist than Northern Sudanese.

Since the CPA, Muslim calls for prayers in Juba today are now being heard in a way that indicates that resistance to Arab cultural and Islamic influence is being replaced by greater receptivity to both. South Sudanese have become very much at home with the Arabic culture, much of which they had already absorbed without openly acknowledging it. Today, weddings, funerals, and cuisines in South Sudan are unmistakably Northern Sudanese in origin. One can validly say that while the Northern Sudanese political agenda in the South failed, their cultural program has been a success.

I recall occasions when I gave lectures or talks around Juba, including in the universities, and although I had assumed that I should talk English as the widely known language, I received notes requesting me to speak Arabic. Although English is the official language, and some prejudice against the Arabic language may be lingering on, this also indicates a significant moderation of the previous prejudice against Arabic as a language of oppression. This prejudice came across most vividly in my interview with Chief Makuei Bilkuei of Paanaruw, who said, "I don't speak Arabic. God has refused my speaking Arabic. I asked God, 'Why don't I speak Arabic?' And he said, 'If you now speak Arabic, you will turn into a bad man.' And I said, 'There is something good in Arabic? And he said, 'No, there is nothing good in it.' So, your father would go and talk with Babo and I would remain with the others."[122] I have had many highly educated Ngok tell me that they resisted learning Arabic or are not good at it because of their resistance to the language.

122. Francis M. Deng, *Dinka Cosmology*, Ithaca Press, 1980, reissued as *Dinka World View: Elders Reflect on the Past, Present and Future of their People,* Africa World Books, 2023, p. 69.

4. The Involvement of International Actors

One of the issues that the book discusses in depth is slavery which attracted the involvement of the international community in response to the alleged violation of human rights and humanitarian principles. The issue apparently raised some controversy, with the government arguing that what was involved was an abduction, not slavery. Whatever the label, the abduction or enslavement of women and children became one of those areas which drew the attention of international human rights and humanitarian organizations and activists. External involvement supported a program of slave redemption that allegedly became a source of large-scale corruption. Many South Sudanese and international observers found it unfathomable to pay the abductors for their crime, instead of being held criminally accountable. Worse, the practice was reported to have entailed a practice by which South Sudanese, posing as Arab abductors, presented Dinka children from the surrounding areas to play the role of abducted children.

Dr. Dhieu Mathok writes: "Local villagers are rounded up to pose as slaves when Christian groups arrive with briefcases full of money. The 'slave traders' are sometimes disguised as (sic) rebel soldiers from the SPLM."[123] The author gives a graphic description of the process: "The slave redemption made for powerful human drama. A line of children emerged from the African bush. A slave trader in front wrapped in the white robes of an Arab. Furthermore, before them, waiting with a bag of money at his feet, was a white, Christian man. The procession halted under the shade of a tree. There was discussion, then money changed hands. Suddenly, the trader gave a nod, the slaves walked free and there were cries of joy as families were reunited in freedom at last.

---

123. Dhieu Mathok Diing Wol, *Politics of Ethnic Discrimination in Sudan: A Justification for the Secession of South Sudan,* Africa World Books, 2022, p. xi.

Many newspapers focused their attention on this issue."[124] The practice was eventually brought to an end by the SPLM/A. The pressure of the international community forced the government of Sudan to cooperate in the creation of the Committee for the Eradication of Abducted Women and Children. (CEAWC). This was a government mechanism in which Arab and Dinka tribal leaders cooperated. Nevertheless, only a relatively small number of women and children were redeemed.

What I found particularly intriguing in the book, with respect to the issue of slavery, was the confirmation of the differences in the practice in African and Arab societies compared to that of the Western world. In the case of Sudan, abductees/slaves were adopted and assimilated into the family and community and indeed into the wider society. A child of an Arab slave master and his slave woman was considered free and equal to the children of free mothers. In the West, to the contrary, a child of a slave master with his slave woman is the slave of his own father, who treats him/her as such and would even sell him/her to another slave owner. It is well known that many proud so-called Arabs of Northern Sudan are descendants of slave women from the South and the West. It is indeed ironic that these individuals of partial slave background insult Southerners whose ancestors had successfully resisted or escaped slavery.

Dr. Dhiew Mathok wrote, "When a captive left the battle area and reached the enemy territory, he/she felt quite secure. For Dinkas, ladies were treated as daughters and sisters. It was prohibited to marry a girl or woman captured by your immediate family or clan. Men automatically became members of that community. They got married and were treated as part of the family. At Dar Reziegat, war victims and those captured reaching their area were considered as family members;

124. Ibid, p. 108.

nobody was allowed to assault them or even point them out, otherwise, he/she faced legal measures from the tribal leadership."[125] One of the reported ironies in the work of CEAWC was that many abductees got quickly assimilated and did not want to return to their Dinka parents or community. Some of them would even deny being Dinka and become contemptuous of their own Dinka ethnicity and culture.

Dr. Dhiew Mathok, quoting from a British Assistant District Commissioner, observed: "It might be true that cases of Dinka slaves in Arab hands and vice versa would be the most difficult to deal with. In reality, they are the easiest of all because both tribes realize that it is useless to claim the return of a relative long in Arab hands as the slave will not agree to return to his own people. It is the same with Arabs in Dinka hands. They become Arabicized and Dinkaized after a few years."[126]

Despite these divisive practices, relations between the ordinary Dinka Malual and Rezeigat were generally cooperative and conciliatory. The author wisely observes that while governments at the center come and go, neighbors remain: "The neighborhood between the Dinka tribe in the South and Baggara tribes in the North will not change because of separation or unity between South and North Sudan. So, it is important for these tribes to bear in mind that political institutions do change but neighborhoods do not unless someone decides to move to another place. Something that is not possible for tribes like the Dinka Malual or Reziegat."[127] National authorities must also realize that conflicts between their proxies at the local level can escalate and eventually affect their relations. They might even provoke civil wars.

---

125. Ibid, p. 36.
126. Ibid, p. 37.
127. Ibid, p. 134.

This has indeed been the result of using tribal militias in North-South wars in the Sudan. I addressed this issue in my two books, *Sudan at the Brink: Self-Determination and National Unity,*[128] and *Bound by Conflict: Dilemmas of the Two Sudans.*[129] *Sudan at the Brink* was published as the referendum was approaching and predicted to overwhelmingly favor secession. In the book, I argued that unity and separation were degrees of an ongoing relationship, which could be strengthened or weakened, depending on the will of the people and their leaders. The central argument of *Bound by Conflict,* which was published after the secession of the South, was that despite the partition of the country into two different states, they remained negatively bound together by conflicts. The two countries were each recruiting, arming, and deploying tribal militias to fight their conflicts by proxy. The policy implication was that if they were to achieve national unity and improve their bilateral relations, they had to turn being bound by conflict to being "bonded by solutions." This would require that they cooperate and help one another to resolve each other's internal wars. The first concrete step in that direction was the role Sudan played in brokering the Revitalized Peace Agreement (RPA) in South Sudan. South Sudan then reciprocated by mediating the resolution of Sudan's internal conflicts, a process that is still ongoing.

5. Diversity and the Crisis of National Identity

Sudan and South Sudan are both experiencing a crisis of identity which may differ in form and degree, but the essence of which calls for ensuring unity in the context of competing identities. It should

---

128. Francis Mading Deng and Kevin M. Cahill, *Sudan at the Brink: Self-determination and National Unity,* Fordham University Press, 2010 - see p. 101.

129. Francis M. Deng in collaboration with Daniel J. Deng, *Bound by Conflict: Dilemmas of the Two Sudans,* Fordham University Press, 2016 – see p. 103.

be stressed that the source of conflict is not the mere differences of identity, but how diversity is managed. In pluralistic states, identity conflicts often entail discrimination, marginalization, and exclusion. The population is often dichotomized into those who are viewed as first-class citizens and enjoy all the rights and duties of citizenship, and those who are denigrated into the status of second-class citizens and denied the full rights of citizenship. In most cases, this results in conflicts that could be violent and might escalate to genocidal levels.

The challenge then is to adopt a strategy for constructively managing diversity toward inclusivity and equality. As the author observes, "Diversity of nations has not been a problem, but if people are denied their rights and live in a situation of political exclusion then, it will turn into a problem. This may result sometimes in a rebellion or a military coup in some countries. For this reason, Sudan has been witnessing a long political struggle between the South, whose largest population is Christians and of African ethnic origin, and the North whose origins are Arab and Muslims by religion."[130]

Successive governments "failed to evolve a Sudanese identity, a Sudanese commonality, a Sudanese commonwealth that includes all Sudanese and to which all Sudanese pledge a united loyalty irrespective of their religion, race, or tribe."[131] This dichotomy proved difficult to bridge to the degree that justified the secession of the South into the independent state of South Sudan. Viewed in a wider global context, identity factors are generic and dynamic. Differences can go down to divide members of a community and even a family.

Three options seem obvious for resolving the crisis of national identity. The ideal is to create an identity framework of inclusivity and

---

130. Dhieu Mathok Diing Wol, *Politics of Ethnic Discrimination in Sudan: A Justification for the Secession of South Sudan,* Africa World Books, 2022, p. 94.

131. Ibid.

full equality as citizens. That was the New Sudan Vision which the SPLM/A, stipulated and fought for, but could not achieve militarily. The second option is one of unity in diversity, which entails respect for the differences within a unified national framework. Sudan experimented with this option through the regional autonomy for Southern Sudan under the 1972 Addis Ababa Agreement. It was also practiced under the 'One Country, Two Systems' formula for the interim period under the 2005 Comprehensive Peace Agreement.

Dr. Dhieu Mathok writes that the ruling National Congress Party and Sudan Government "required that the Sharia be the center of any agreement that must be concluded with the South... until the concept of 'One Country, Two Systems' was introduced in Naivasha as a temporary arrangement for the six-year and half interim period, 2005-2011. This led the SPLM to opt for self-determination as a fall-back position".[132] The formula of 'One Country, Two Systems,' was developed by the Task Force on U.S. Sudan Policy, which I was honored to co-chair with Stephen J. Morrison.[133] The Task Force was established by the Washington-based Center for Strategic and International Studies (CSIS) to develop a coherent policy for the role of the United States in mediating the Sudan peace process. that developed this formula.

Our objective in developing and proposing that formula was to salvage the unity of the country through a system of unity in diversity during the interim period that would enhance the prospects for making unity an attractive option. As I argued to the Task Force, since preserving the unity of the Sudan was the preferred option of the international community, we should strive to make the impossible

---

132. Ibid, p. xv.

133. Francis M. Deng and J. Stephen Morrison, *U.S. Policy to End Sudan's War*, Report of CSIS Task Force on U.S. Sudan's Policy, Febuary, 2001 – see p. 173.

possible and reconcile the irreconcilable. 'One Country, Two Systems' was our proposed solution to the riddle. While the formula was effectively applied by the mediation team led by Senator John Danforth that facilitated the negotiation of the CPA, it turned out to be a step toward the unavoidable secession of South Sudan.

Burundi and Rwanda, which have identical ethnic compositions and divisions involving three groups, Hutu by far the majority, Tutsi a third, but the most powerful group, and Twa, a small minority. Following the 1994 genocide, Rwanda decreed a policy that requires the national identification of all the citizens as Rwandese and outlaws any references to ethnicity as a divisive colonial construct. This strategy, though representing the preferred model, appears to ambiguously present what ought to be as what in fact is. It also puts the cart before the horse in that recognizing the reality of diversity should precede evolving an integrated national identity.

In a way, this is the policy that Burundi seems to have adopted by acknowledging the diversity of the country into the three ethnic groups and developing a strategy for accommodating them equitably. Although no strategy for evolving an integrated national identity is declared, this should be understood to be an implicit aspect of nation-building.

Most African countries follow the dual strategy of accommodating diversity while aspiring toward an integrated national identity. This was reflected by an African head of state, President Yoweri Museveni of Uganda, in his comment on my keynote presentation at a high-level African symposium in which I advocated constructive management of diversity for addressing the national identity crisis in Africa. He argued that while managing diversity is an applaudable strategy, the goal of nation-building in Africa must be integration.

6. A Vision for the Way Forward

Although Dr. Dhiew Mathok's book focuses on the relationship between Malual Dinka and the Rezeigat, it applies with equal poignancy to other South Sudanese bordering the Sudan generally, and the Ngok Dinka in particular. In the end, it is very much about the Two Sudans which, despite the secession of South Sudan, remain connected by internal conflicts that spill over their borders. South Sudanese fought long wars against successive governments in Khartoum, with resistance as their uniting identity framework. It was largely a negative self-identification by which Southerners largely defined themselves as non-Arab and non-Muslim.

The New Sudan Vision alled for inclusively and equality within a national framework of Sudanism. But that vision was mostly perceived as the invention of John Garang which South Sudanese accepted only as a tactical or strategic ploy for neutralizing opposition against secession, which remained the hidden objective of the overwhelming majority of South Sudanese struggle. When that goal was achieved, the prediction that South Sudan would fall apart once the uniting factor of resistance to Northern domination was gone proved to be true. In a way, that was a self-fulfilling Northern Sudanese prophecy that they endeavored to bring about.

So, where does South Sudan go from here? It seems to be that the Vision of New Sudan of inclusivity and full equality without discrimination on any ground still holds. After all, identity is a relative term and cannot be focused only on the Arab-Islamic North and the African-Secular South of the Old Sudan. As the case of Somalia demonstrates, identity differences can go down to the level of clans and even pit families and ambitious individuals against one another. South Sudanese identity groups that are now in conflict need to reverse their negative self-definition as non-Arab and non-Muslim, or negatively distinguishing themselves from each other. We need to develop a positive perspective on our national identity and related cultural values. We need to understand the cultural values of each of our multiple ethnic groups individually and comparatively, to discern their commonalities and differences, and explore the prospects for their complementarity. We need to construct a uniting national identity framework based on the potential enrichment from our pluralistic sources, one to which all South Sudanese can all share a common sense of belonging with pride and dignity.

'Culture and Constitution-Making in South Sudan'
The SUDD Institute [134]

1. Abstract

It is widely recognized that African constitutions are of foreign origins and for the most part, remain persistently eurocentric. While there are universally shared structures, parameters, and principles that generically characterize virtually all constitutions worldwide, every constitution is supposed to reflect the characteristics, values, and norms particular to the country concerned. There is therefore a demand for African countries to reform their constitutions and contextualize them, building upon their own cultural values and norms.

While there is a consensus on this vision, realizing it presents considerable challenges that can thematically be classified as conceptual and operational. The main conceptual issues related to the role of identity as determined by a variety of factors, prominent of which are ethnicity and culture, how they play out in the context of diversity in a pluralistic State, resulting in competition over power and national resources, and the

___
134. Publication pending.

ensuing threat to the peace, security, and stability of the country. The operational dimension of the challenge is how to discern the shared principles from the multiplicity of national cultures that should be constitutionally recognized and utilized, what areas of the constitutional frameworks are amenable to cultural incorporation, and how the relevant cultural values and norms can be infused in the drafting of the constitution.

How these conceptual and operational dimensions can effectively be addressed in drafting a contextualized constitutional document and application in the broader functional process of constitutionalism is the challenge facing constitutional experts and scholars and practitioners from related disciplines and professions. This paper is part of a wider project aimed at influencing the constitution-making process in South Sudan, inter-communal cultural dialogue, cross-cultural understanding toward promoting peace and reconciliation, and a broad culturally based contribution to education in South Sudan. Indigenizing constitutionalism in Africa has both a generic dimension relevant to African countries in general, and a specific focus on individual countries, in this case, South Sudan, and as a mechanism for preventing, managing, and resolving ethnic conflicts.

2. Culture and Constitutionalism in South Sudan

South Sudan became independent on July 9, 2011, after decades of armed struggle against successive governments in Khartoum dominated by an Arab-Islamic elite in Northern Sudan which had inherited power from the Anglo-Egyptian colonial administration. This system of domination was fueled by a crisis of national identity with two principal dimensions. One was that the ruling Arab-Islamic minority, which is essentially African, interfused with assimilated Arab and Islamic elements, and identified itself as purely Arab, reinforced by Islam. The second is that this distorted self-identification was imposed on a country of immense racial, ethnic, cultural, and religious diversity which was then labeled as Arab, with stratifying discriminatory implications for non-Arabs and non-Muslims. The so-called Arabs of central Sudan occupied the status of first-class citizens, the non-Arab Muslim groups of Darfur in the West, the Nuba and Fung bordering the South, and the Beja in the East became second-class citizens. And as a leading member of the Ethiopian-Eritrean refugee community in the Sudan said to me, the refugees from those countries with a complexion close to that of the Sudanese 'Arabs,' fell into the third class, while South Sudanese became fourth-class citizens in their own country. If one adds to the equation the Muslims from Nigeria and other West African countries, they in effect occupied the fourth-class status, which relegated the South Sudanese to fifth-class citizenship.

South Sudanese struggle was waged in two phases. The first phase began with a military rebellion that erupted in August 1955, four months before the Declaration of Independence on January 1, 1956, and escalated into a full-fledged civil war, spearheaded by the South Sudan Liberation Movement and its military wing Anya-Nya. That first phase of armed struggle aimed at independence for South Sudan and raged for seventeen years and was ended by the Addis Ababa Agreement of 1972 in which South Sudan accepted a compromise of regional autonomy within unity. Ten years later, that agreement was unilaterally abrogated by the government in Khartoum, which triggered the second phase of the struggle, which broke out in 1983, championed by the SPLM and the SPLA.

Unlike the first liberation struggle that aimed at the independence of South Sudan, the SPLM stipulated a New Sudan Vision that would address the stratifying crisis of identity by creating a framework of full equality without any discrimination based on race, ethnicity, religion, culture, or gender. That Vision transcended the North-South divide and inspired the marginalized groups in the North, which joined the Sudanese People's Liberation Movement/Army in large numbers. Although the Movement posed a credible threat to the Arab-Islamic agenda of the successive regimes in the North, it could not impose the Vision of New Sudan by military means, and through a peace process initiated by the sub-regional organization, the Inter-Governmental Authority for Development, supported by the African Union, the United Nations, and the Troika countries of the United States, the United Kingdom, and Norway, the SPLM/A settled for the CPA that granted the South the right of self-determination through a referendum which it exercised in favour of independence, while it gave the rebel areas of the North to vote for an administrative system of their choice, a right which remains to be fully exercised.

Less than two years after independence from the North, South Sudan fell into a devastating conflict that soon assumed an ethnic dimension that demonstrated the relativity of identity and the crisis associated with the mismanagement of diversity. South Sudan is essentially experiencing the same crisis of national identity that generated the liberation struggle in the first place, albeit with differences in form and degree. What is incontrovertible is that the liberation of South Sudan for over half a century and longer has been pursued under a negative identity framework of being non-Arab and non-Muslim, and vaguely identifying as African, without a clear sense of what they are culturally. The challenge posed by this paper is therefore twofold. First, it tries to address the generic African quest for a system of governance and constitutionalism that is grounded on African cultural values and institutions. And second, it focuses this challenge on the context of South Sudan to identify the cultural values that are representative of the people of South Sudan. Since the population of South Sudan comprises an estimated 64 ethnic groups, each with its own sense of identity and related cultural values, this challenge is further amplified by the need to know their individual value systems, the extent to which there are common values, what differences there are among them, and the extent to which they complement each other to create a synthesis.

Although South Sudan is currently torn apart by a myriad of crises, inter-communal conflicts constitute one of the major concerns. While the long wars that devastated the country for decades brought the people of South Sudan together in the liberation struggle and the ethnic communities are getting to know each other better than they did in the past when they were still isolated from one another, they are paradoxically also revealing that they do not know much about one another and their respective sub-cultures. This is at the core of the country's identity crisis that is paradoxically becoming increasingly ethnically based for a people who resisted Arab-Islamic domination based on a shared identity as South Sudanese.

The inter-communal conflicts now threatening national unity are at least in part due to the way diversities have been managed or perhaps more accurately mismanaged. This is, in significant part, due to the relative ignorance about one another and the values of inclusive mutual accommodation and respect that should provide a common ground and be among the cardinal principles of building the nation.

Several concerned South Sudanese representing different ethnic groups, (including the author of this paper), recently initiated a project of inter-communal cultural dialogue that aims at addressing this challenge but is still to be more functionally developed. The project initially targeted twenty-six representatives from a sample of twelve ethnic groups, including Azande, Bari, Dinka, Chollo (Shilluk), Kakwa, Kuku, Latuka, Luo, Madi, Moro, Nuer, and Pajulu. The objectives of the project include:

a. To know the cultural values of the various ethnic groups or communities which have been ignored or undermined by the forces of modern education and development;

b. To learn about each other's cultural values, the shared elements in the respective cultural models, and the prospects of complementarity and synergy among them;

c. To make effective use of this complementarity and synergy to develop a common ground toward a national cultural framework that is enriched by diversity;

d. To formulate a framework of good governance and constitutionalism that is oriented to indigenous cultural values and institutions; and

e. To formulate a set of principles to guide South Sudanese diplomacy in its relations and negotiations with regional and international partners and interlocutors.

The project is envisaged to be implemented through a two-prong approach. One is a survey based on specific questions that could be answered in writing or tape-recorded interviews. The second is focused group discussions around the same questions and the reports from the survey. It is planned that the result will be widely shared to inform policies internally and with international partners. The project will require immediate action in several areas:

a. Convening a meeting of experts representing ethnic groups from the ten states of South Sudan;

b. Facilitating the conduct of the surveys technically and logistically in the ten states and an expert analysis of the results;

c. Convening an enlarged meeting representing major ethnic groups to evaluate the results and formulate a consensus document; and

d. Commissioning an expert to prepare a constitutive or governance document that applies the relevant principles of the South

Sudanese value system to the major concepts or elements of established constitutionalism that lend themselves to cultural contextualization.

Although the initiative for inter-communal cultural dialogue has been widely well received, it remains a work in progress that is still to be more fully developed and operationalized. Consultations are in progress with the objective of engaging several partners representing the Ministry of Justice and Constitutional Affairs, Ministry of Peace, Ministry of Education, Ministry of Culture and National Heritage, and pertinent United Nations agencies. The goal of the project, therefore, is to contribute to the making of a culturally sensitive constitution, infuse cultural values into the curriculum of education at all levels, promote an overall appreciation of individual and collective cultural values, and through recognition and respect of diversity as a source of enrichment and strength, foster peace, unity, and harmony among the ethnic groups. This is a process that will be ongoing, but judging from the enthusiastic response to the proposal, it is hoped and expected that the visibility of the process will in itself have a positive impact on the cultural crisis in the country.

3. The Generic Quest for Indigenous Constitutionalism

Constitutions are largely concerned with access to state power, division of powers, the functioning of major state institutions, relationships between and among state organs, and respect for human rights and fundamental liberties. The process of drafting, adopting, implementing, monitoring and operationalizing, and monitoring the application of a constitution is mostly an exercise by the elite at the national level, with the help of legal experts. Generally, the political leaders and senior government officials responsible for constitution-making are often concerned with the way the constitution will serve their own political objectives, even though they claim to be serving the interest of the nation and people whose interests they purport to represent. In principle, it is the people who should determine the constitutional identity of the country. Few citizens, even in advanced countries, understand what the constitution is about; it is even less likely that the few who do appreciate the intricacies of constitutional identity. It is therefore incumbent upon the constitutional experts, scholars, and practitioners responsible for drafting the constitution to cater to the wider interest of the country and its citizens.

While there are recognized structures, parameters, and normative principles that form a constitution generically speaking, every constitution must embody the fundamental values and norms that are particular to the specific country concerned. A constitution is supposed to reflect the spirit of the people of the country. Ideally, what is involved is not only the broad participation of the people in constitution-making, crucial as that is but the embodiment of their cultural values, norms, and functional principles.

This is particularly true of a people emerging from foreign domination which typically denies the subject population the dignity of their cultural values and the normative principles of their indigenous social order. As the authors of *The Nation State: A Wrong Model for the Horn of Africa* opined, "after colonial education was not designed to grow out of the African environment... designed to give young people pride as being members of African societies, but one that sought to install deference towards all that was European and capitalist. No concession was made to the past, and no attempt was made to recognize, interact, or integrate with anything the African tradition might have to offer. This was not a process of cultural diffusion familiar in world history, but of cultural deracination."[135]

This is the case with the people of South Sudan who have not only struggled for ideals of freedom, liberty, equality, and dignity that must continue to be a source of inspiration and guidance but have been subjected not only to the domination of British colonial rule but an Arab-Islamic 'internal colonialism' within an otherwise 'independent' country. Both imposed their cultural frameworks that disregarded and denigrated the cultural values of the people that now need to be revived, respected, and applied. The constitution of South Sudan must therefore reflect both the ideals for which the people struggled for decades and make use of the fundamental norms of their cultures.

4. Foreign Roots of African Constitutionalism

It is well known that post-independence constitutions in Africa were modeled after the constitutions of the colonizing countries. It is also a historical fact that colonial rulers put in place the basic institutional structures of the constitutions of their home countries, without adhering to the ideals of fundamental rights and civil liberties embodied in those constitutions as practiced in their home countries.

Paradoxically, the constitutions which the exiting colonial powers bequeathed to their successors in the post-colonial state contained those lofty principles which they themselves never observed during their colonial rule. For the same reason, the independence constitutions did not last long. Political leaders were not familiar or comfortable with a democratic system and were indeed fearful of

---

135. John Markakis, Günther Schlee and John Young, *The Nation State: A Wrong Model for the Horn of Africa*, Max Planck Research Library for the History and Development of Knowledge Studies. 14, 2021, p. 22.

limitations on their powers, which they knew colonial authorities themselves did not observe. These foreign model constitutions were often overthrown by military coups with little or no tears shed and a trend toward developing homegrown constitutionalism began. As Yash Ghai observed, "It is indeed a brave and perhaps a foolish academic who undertakes a major study of an African Constitution, for the probability, is that its overthrow will precede the publication of the study."[136]

There is now an increasing demand and trend toward involving the people in constitution-making. The reality, however, is that constitution-making remains an elite exercise by constitutional lawyers and politicians, with expertise in generic constitutionalism. Even when the people participate in the drafting of their constitutions, the substantive content remains basically the same, with some reforms within the normative framework of the centralized power structure. And because a constitution essentially aims at regulating, controlling, and limiting the exercise of power by the national wielders of state power, the tendency is to adopt a constitution as a matter of formality, with substantive contents that favor the status quo or the major players in the constitutive process. Even when adopted, constitutions are, in practice, usually ignored, undermined, self-interestingly amended, or unconstitutionally abrogated.

It is noteworthy and laudable that post-colonial governments have embarked on different degrees of decentralizing power from the centralized colonial systems to disperse and share powers at all levels, from national to local. This is a positive and laudable development but orienting African constitutionalism cannot be achieved merely through decentralization while maintaining the normative framework

---

136. Yash Ghai, *'Constitutions and the Political Order in East Africa,'* International and Comparative Law Quarterly, 21, No 3, July 1972.

of imported constitutionalism. Nor is granting authority to traditional leaders to manage local administration sufficient for indigenizing the system of administration. Decentralization therefore only partially addresses the call for the cultural contextualization of African constitutionalism. If a nation's constitution and the attendant governance framework are to establish a viable system for constructively managing diversity, it must embody the soul of the nation by reflecting the cultural values and norms of all the peoples of the country as central elements of constitutionalism.

An appropriate African constitutional identity should be more than dressing up Eurocentric constitutional models with colorful African garbs. Ultimately, the political stability needed to promote peace, security, and development can only take place within the framework of a constitution that promotes the generic principles of constitutionalism that are universally stipulated, while taking full account of the country's ethnic, religious, cultural, and linguistic particulars. While there will continue to be tensions as countries strive to accommodate the often divergent aspirations of the different communities, this is critical to establishing a sense of self-identification and self-determination needed for a credible, shared constitutional identity to emerge.

The challenge for Africa is more than designing a culturally appropriate constitution, that applies to the African state model itself. As the authors of *The Nation State* noted, in much the same way the African cultural values were disregarded in developing constitutional models appropriate to Africa, in building the state in Africa, "colonial organizers eradicated indigenous history and culture, and quelled any beliefs and values that could obstruct the assimilation process. In Walter Rodney's words: 'to be colonized is to be removed from history, except in the most passive sense.' The assimilado was taught to disdain the past. Tradition was 'primitive,' 'savage,' 'primordial,' and 'uncivilized.' Local religions were called 'idolatry' and 'animist'; its practitioners were 'wizards,' 'sorcerers,' and 'witch doctors.' Universal creeds like Islam and Christianity that had already taken root in the continent were the exception, and became integral components of national identity in places like Ethiopia, Sudan, and Somalia."[137]

Although the *Nation State* study focuses on the Horn of Africa, the argument of the authors is relevant to the continent of Africa as a whole. As they state, "The Horn of Africa is an extreme example of a phenomenon that is not uncommon in subSaharan Africa: the imposition of a model of political organization in an entirely alien setting regardless of consequences. Fundamental to this phenomenon are the divisions opened between tradition and modernization, nation and tribe, urban and rural society, the ruling elite, and the rest of the population. Much of subSaharan Africa's political turmoil is the result of this Procrustean experiment."[138]

The responsibility for the alienation of the African elites from their own cultural values and institutions has now shifted to the African scholars and intellectuals who have internalized the Western World view. As the authors of the *Nation State* observed, "The success of the hegemonic project drove a wedge between the urban, Westernized elite—a small minority—and Africa's rural population—a vast majority—whose life still follows a traditional rhythm. The two are separated by a cultural gap that alienates the masses from their rulers; it is a disjunction that is the source of many of Africa's problems."[139]

Being Western-oriented, social sciences, even when they produce

137. John Markakis, Günther Schlee, and John Young, *The Nation State: A Wrong Model for the Horn of Africa Studies*, 14, Max Planck Research Library for the History and Development of Knowledge Studies 14, 2021, p. 22.

138. Ibid, p. 54.

139. Ibid, p. 23.

African scholars, are too ingrained in the problem to be the engineers of a solution. As the authors of *The Nation State* observed, "Founded in the West and dominated by Western scholars, the discipline thrives on modes of analysis that privilege European categories or ascribe greater rationality and agency to Western actors above all others. It is impossible to question the universal validity of the Western model within the limits of this discipline for there is no room for an alternative within its analytical spectrum. Because this methodology is part of the standard curriculum, scholars of African studies, including Africans, tend to be unprepared to challenge it. Any attempt to raise the topic elicits the stock response: what is the alternative?"[140]

The authors do not venture to offer an answer to the question, their objective being "to provoke a debate on the crisis of the nationstate that will focus on the alien model itself, not on the African setting. They aim to do this by presenting the manifold impact of the crisis on two levels of society in the Horn: national and local."[141]

5. Genesis of Constitution Making in the Sudan

Modern Sudan was a creation of the Turko-Egyptian Conquest that ruled the country from 1821 to 1885. Infamous for extreme corruption and misrule, the Turko-Egyptian administration was overthrown in 1885 by the forces of the religiously inspired revolutionary, Mohamed Ahmed, who became known as the Mahdi, the Islamic Messiah. Initially armed only with spears, the Mahdi scored victory after victory, acquiring arms from the defeated and demoralized government forces until he miraculously liberated the country from foreign rule, giving the Sudan its first glory of independence. The Mahdist killed and beheaded the Governor-General, Charles George

---

140. Ibid, p. 4.
141. Ibid.

Gordon, a British war hero popularly known as the Chinese Gordon because of his military exploits in China, who was then in the service of the Turo-Egyptian administration of the Sudan. He was killed on January 26, 1885, only two days before a force that was sent to rescue him arrived.

The Mahdi died shortly after his miraculous victory and was succeeded by Abdullahi ibn Muhammad El-Taishi from Darfur, better known as The Khalifa. Although the Mahdiyya, as the Mahdist Revolution is known, was initially popular with the people of the Sudan, including the South, as a liberation movement, Khalifa's rule turned out to be a period of gruesome suffering from a myriad of tragedies, including the intensification of slave raids in the South, pervasive famines, and mass atrocities from internal wars, all leading to the virtual collapse of the state. That reign of terror lasted until 1898 when the bitter memory of the humiliating murder of General Gordon prompted Britain to join Egypt in the reconquest of the Sudan and the establishment of the Anglo-Egyptian Condominium Administration, an unprecedented form of colonial rule that governed the country until independence on January 1st, 1956, making the Sudan the first African country to achieve independence a year before Ghana.

The British, who were the dominant partner in the Condominium, decided to rule the Sudan as two separate parts, North and South, which were racially, religiously, and culturally distinct. The British in the Sudan moderated the imposition of the Eurocentric system of governance. Mindful of the remnants of the Mahdist Movement and the threat of Islamist revivalism, they respected the Islamic orientation of the North and its related notion of Arabism as a racial and cultural concept. More by omission than by design, Southern Sudan was also saved from the colonial practice of imposing a culturally Westernized system of governance, except for basic military domination. The

South was kept separate and largely neglected under strong military administrators. Christian Missionaries were encouraged to proselytize and introduce basic education and health services aimed at making the South contrastingly Christian and African. Through the Closed Districts Ordinance, contact between the two parts of the country was severely restricted. That was the root of the separatism that would later haunt the national movement for independence and the development of a constitution of a unified country, with the North favouring a centralized Islamic state and the South demanding a federal secular state or the exercise of full independence from the North.

Sudan's tortuous path in constitution-making after independence from Anglo-Egyptian rule has been mired in intense political rivalry between various sectarian Islamist factions and the major political parties that they patronized. All of them shared the vision of an Islamic State but were divided by their competition for political power. Sectarian parties were, however, pitted against the leftist movement, championed by a strong Communist Party that was sympathetic to the cause of Southern Sudan. Although the Communists favoured a secular state, they maintained due regard for the popular Islamic sentiments of the North. And, of course, the South was vehemently opposed to any form of an Arab-Islamic constitution. It is the resistance of the South to the Arab-Islamic orientation of the political parties and the military dictatorships that alternated with them in the control of the government that accounted for the intermittent wars the country suffered since independence.

Sudan became independent under the Self-Government Statute of 1953 which operated as the Transitional Constitution, pending the adoption of a permanent national constitution. That objective was to elude the country for half a century as Sudan went through a succession of wars and military dictatorships. The first war broke out in the South in August 1955, only four months before independence. By 1958, the country had its first military coup under the leadership of General Ibrahim Abboud, primarily aimed at ending the war in the South. Abboud's failure and the Sudanese resentment of his dictatorial rule led to a popular uprising and the restoration of parliamentary democracy in 1964. The elected government tried to promote the adoption of an Islamic Constitution without success, as the South and sympathetic Northern allies opposed it.

Despite the ruthlessness with which the government intensified the war against the South, the elected government also failed to achieve a decisive victory. The army again seized power in 1969 under the leadership of Colonel Jaafar Mohamed Nimeiri, in alliance with the Communists. As the Communists sympathized with the cause of the South, the regime immediately took steps to find a solution to what was popularly viewed as the Southern Problem. The Communist allies however tried to seize power from within in 1971 to effect a more complete socialist system, and the regime was on the verge of defeat, but Nimeiri triumphantly returned even more popular. Having now alienated both the right and the left, he turned to the moderates and enlightened technocrats at the center, who favored a negotiated peace with the South. The regime was able to conclude with the Southern Sudanese Liberation Movement in 1972 the Addis Ababa Agreement, which granted Southern Sudan Regional Autonomy. The government moderated the role of religion by stipulating Sharia as a source of legislation, from which the South was exempted, a thin disguise that the South accepted as a compromise. The terms of the Agreement were incorporated into the first attempt at a permanent constitution.

The Sectarian Right continued to pose a threat to the regime and even waged an attack in 1976, which became known as the Libyan Invasion because it was staged from Libya with the support of its strong man, Colonel Muammar Gadhafi. Nimeiri, believing that the South had been decisively neutralized, concluded a reconciliation agreement with the opposition and the Religious Right. This was eventually followed by a full-scale imposition of Sharia on the whole country and the amendment of the relatively secular constitution to become more Islamic. Nimeiri had underestimated the determination of the South to resist the imposition of an Arab-Islamic agenda on the country. In 1983, Southern Sudanese staged the most formidable rebellion that culminated in the creation of the SPLM, with its military wing the SPLA. The stated objective of the SPLM/A was no longer Southern secession, but the creation of a unified New Sudan of full equality, without any discrimination on the ground of race, ethnicity, religion, culture, or gender.

The vision of the SPLM began to inspire the Sudanese across the North/South divide and attracted rebels from the marginalized non-Arab regions of the North, particularly from the Nuba Mountains, Southern Blue Nile, and Darfur to join the revolution. Nimeiri was in turn overthrown in 1985 and an elected civilian government took power. The failure of the elected government to end the war led the army to openly threaten another military takeover. The Islamists seized the opportunity to piggy-back on that threat and staged their own military coup, led by General Omar Hassan Ahmad Al-Bashir, with the objective of imposing an Islamic Constitution, even if that led to the separation of the South, now seen as a chronic threat to the Arab Islamic agenda of the North. After years of extremely difficult negotiations involving the region, with international support, the military regime of Omar Al-Bashir concluded the CPA with the SPLM. This eventually led to the SPLM conceding the New Sudan Vision for the whole country by accepting the right of self-determination for the South which eventually ended in the independence of South Sudan on 9th July 2011.

The CPA installed an interim constitution for Sudan and Southern Sudan, but in the wake of South Sudan's secession, both countries undertook appropriate constitutional review processes. On the verge of independence, South Sudan amended its interim constitution into a transitional constitution of a sovereign state. However, less than two years after independence, in December 2013, a devastating civil war broke out and raged until it was ended in 2015 by the Agreement for the Resolution for the Conflict in South Sudan, (ARCSS). The Agreement was brokered by the Sub-Regional organization, Inter-Governmental Authority for Development, (IGAD). A Joint Evaluation and Monitoring Committee, (JMEC), was established to oversee its implementation. But violence again erupted in 2016, which once more necessitated the intervention of IGAD, resulting in the revitalization of the 2015 Agreement. The Revitalized Agreement for the Resolution of the Conflict in South Sudan, (R-ARCSS), was signed on September 12, 2018, with the Revitalized Joint Monitoring and Evaluation Committee, (R-JMEC), to oversee its implementation.

Pursuant to Article 6.7 of R-ARCSS, the reconstituted R-JMEC was mandated to convene a Workshop for the Parties to the R-ARCSS to agree on the details for the Permanent Constitution-making process. Accordingly, the Workshop on the Permanent Constitution-making process was convened from 25th to 28th May 2021 in Juba. The Max Planck Foundation for International Peace and the Rule of Law, a German think tank that specialized in constitution-making, facilitated the Workshop. The resolutions of the Workshop on the Permanent Constitution-Making Process for the Republic of Southern Sudan, convened and facilitated by R-JMEC and Max Planck Foundation, 28 May 2021, Juba, South Sudan. The outcome of the Workshop was to form the basis of the legislation that would govern the process of making the Permanent Constitution for the Republic of South Sudan.

In a meeting convened in preparation for the workshop, the need for cultural orientation of constitution making was raised. The representatives of Max Planck Foundation responded that their role was to assist with the technical aspects of constitution-making and that issues related to the substantive content of the constitution were entirely for the people of South Sudan to determine. The issues on which the Workshop was designed to engage the participants, in small groups and during plenary sessions, to discuss and reach an agreement, focused on the following:

i.   To outline the process for preparing the draft constitutional text;

ii. To clarify the roles and mandates of the various institutions involved in the constitutional process, as identified under chapter VI of the R-ARCSS, and

iii. To define civic education and public participation in the Permanent Constitution-making process, to ensure meaningful participation.

Although not explicitly stated, these issues exclude the cultural consideration in constitution-making. This raises the question of whether the technical aspects of constitution-making identified can be totally separated from the substantive content of the outcome document. It becomes incumbent upon those who support the role of culture in constitution-making to be more diligent in ensuring that the fundamental cultural values of the people feature in all aspects of the constitution-making process.

The challenge for constitutionalism in South Sudan is not only to make effective use of indigenous cultures in the making of an appropriate constitution but also to implement the provisions of the constitution. It can be argued that the failure to implement the constitution may directly relate to its alien form and content. But as Yash and Jill Gahi observe in their constitutional study for the National

Dialogue, the view of the people who participated in the grassroots consultation was that the current transitional constitution is generally good, though not culturally adapted, but that the main problem is lack of implementation.

It can be reiterated with credibility that the failure to adhere to the commitments under the constitution emanate from ignorance of its provisions which can also be related to the fact that the constitution is a dead letter that does not represent or reflect the spirit of the nation and its people. Unless the constitution is embedded in the cultural values and aspirations of the people, it will remain alien to the body politic and rejected, ignored, or simply irrelevant.

6. The Challenge of Diversity in Constitutionalism

The evolution of the crisis of constitutionalism and the mismanagement of diversity that is a major constraint in nation-building in Africa goes back to the paradoxical legacy of colonialism that established a unified modern state in Africa, but also sew the seeds of ethnic tensions and conflicts by bringing together within the colonial state tribes with different cultures, lifestyles, and economies. For a considerable length of time into the colonial rule, these different tribes in their relative isolation did not know much about each other and the colonisers kept them apart, to prevent them from uniting against foreign rule. People were given unequal access to education, the language of the rulers, and employment opportunities, because of which their erstwhile differences were deepened, and inequalities emerged that eventually generated tensions and conflicts.

Under colonial rule, the independent and confederal systems that had prevailed among indigenous communities were replaced by a centralised system in which the foreign rulers monopolised power, with civil servants trained to assist them in junior positions. A significant concession was made to accommodate indigenous cultures in the rural areas, where tribal chiefs were deployed as an inexpensive mechanism for maintaining law and order and were given limited authority to apply customary law and administratively manage their communities' local affairs. This became known as the indirect rule in British colonies. Hardly any attention was given to developing a sense of nationhood to constructively manage the diversity of races, ethnicities, tribes, languages, religions, and inter-communal relations. Doing so would have contradicted the divide and rule strategy of the colonial government.

Experience around Africa demonstrates that a major threat to peace, stability, and progress on the continent is the manipulation of 'tribe' and ethnicity for political ends. The very notion of the tribe was seen as a backward concept that is at best eradicated and at worse exploited initially by the colonial powers and after independence by political entrepreneurs. As the study of *The Nation State,* in the Horn of Africa observes, "African nationalism rejected Western political and economic domination, but it did not reject cultural domination. It embraced it and reinforced it through the rapid expansion of Western education, one area of development in which African states made great progress."[142] The result was an even greater vigor in fighting tribalism which was viewed as encouraged by colonial domination as part of their strategy of divide and rule. "Nation-building required the transcendence of ethnicity, the living cell of society, and replacement with a nation that did not yet exist. Nation-building was launched with a frontal attack on African tradition and its defenders. 'Tribalism' became a social defamation and a handy weapon in political contests;

---

142. John Markakis, Günther Schlee, and John Young, *The Nation State: A Wrong Model for the Horn of Africa,* Studies 14, Max Planck Research Library for the History and Development of Knowledge Studies 14, 2021, p. 23.

in some instances, reference to one's 'tribe' was outlawed. The accusation of tribalism was successfully used to preempt claims to a share of political power by traditional authorities, who could have served as intermediaries with the masses, but were sidelined instead."[143]

In *The Nation State*, Africa is negatively compared with Asia and the Middle East in the ability to negotiate a synergy in cultural interaction, perceived as an African intellectual failure: "The internalization of the Western worldview by the African elite deprived Africa of its own organic intellectuals, born from its own womb to represent and convey the values, norms, and logic of its own history, culture, and tradition to future generations. The African elite proved unable to negotiate and mediate the process of breakneck acculturation that threatened to overwhelm their societies; in other words, they could not 'resist, appropriate, interpret, and transform' as Asian and Arab nations have done to mitigate the impact and protect their own cultures and identities. As a result, sub-Saharan Africa does not produce knowledge relevant to its own reality and remains as dependent on imported knowledge as it does for capital and technology. Africa does not produce solutions for its own problems but depends on foreign 'specialists' whose expertise does not derive from their knowledge of Africa. In the bitter words of one of their own, African intellectuals function as 'paid native informants for foreign donors.'"[144]

The interplay between the role of political entrepreneurs and the legitimate grievances of the ethnic groups they purportedly represent in identity-related conflicts has been a subject of considerable debate among scholars. Political scientists generally contend that ethnic conflicts are driven by politicians exploiting ethnicity and not by ethnicity itself. This is usually linked with the tendency to dismiss or

143. Ibid.
144. Ibid.

downplay ethnic identity as a significant variable in conflict analysis and resolution, allegedly because the concept is viewed as too nebulous and intangible, difficult to define, and therefore not a meaningful subject of negotiation. This amounts to dismissing ethnicity or the broader concept of identity as a fictional construct that is not an easy subject of analysis or conflict mediation and resolution.

This is however contested by some social scientists. Professor Catherine Kelly, a political scientist at the United States Defense University, in reaction to an earlier version of this paper, denied the allegation while conceding the difficulties of studying ethnicity, "I generally agree with the critique and approach in the paper, but I disagree that political science entirely dismisses the relevance of cultural/social identities. We are ham-handed about how we talk about it on many occasions, but there are a few good analyses that scope the conditions that make such identities more or less politically detrimental to peace and stability... The takeaway there is not that identity doesn't matter, but that it does so profoundly."[145] Professor Kelly acknowledges that "There is no question that much of the academic literature on constitutionalism is Eurocentric. So, the job of reconsidering what we know about what works for constitution-making in Africa is a formidable one, and one that is likely to be different in different contexts on the continent, with the case of South Sudan being a very particular but important one... Even if we know the elements of a particular sociocultural context that could be useful for making a legal order more resilient, elite political interests can often get in the way of us properly integrating those elements into the system. This is especially difficult because often what we need for more resilience are social and cultural mechanisms that create or reinforce a set of checks

---

145. Professor Catherine Kelly, personal correspondence.

and balances (whether from state or society) on predatory elite behavior that could spoil the peace and erode the constitutional order."[146]

This point is also stressed by the authors of *The Nation State*, "Ethnoculturalism (derided as tribalism) is invariably cited as the source of political instability that has undermined modern government in Africa. However, ethnoculturalism is a reality, a fact of life. Like the nation, it is a social construct, neither timeless nor universal. While there has always been cultural and linguistic variation in Africa, the features that define these variations often shifted gradually and formed cultural continua, rather than delineating discrete groups. In many cases, strictly defined ethnic groups were created in the colonial period, solely for administrative purposes. Nevertheless, the concept of ethnic groups has a remarkable appeal for political identification and is much more of a reality on the ground than the concept of a nation. African states comprise dozens or hundreds of ethnic groups, some of them representing millions of people and larger than many nations."[147]

Putting the blame solely on the explication of ethnicity by political entrepreneurs is setting up a straw man. Obviously, one cannot exploit what does not exist. It is not only unrealistic but indeed dangerous to deny the existence of ethnicity or other forms of identity. What seems to be overlooked or underestimated is the fact that the distribution of power and material assets, the question of who gets what and how, is often based on identity, whether racial, ethnic, cultural, religious, or defined by other factors. What is critical then is not the mere fact of identity differences, but how those differences are managed, and the consequences of such management.

---

146. Ibid.

147. John Markakis, Günther Schlee, and John Young, *The Nation State: A Wrong Model for the Horn of Africa*, Studies 14, Max Planck Research Library for the History and Development of Knowledge Studies 14, 2021, p. 13.

Peter Lam Both, a South Sudanese politician and statesman, has recently written an insightful book still to be published on the conflict that erupted in 2013 in South Sudan and has devastated the country ever since. The conflict is widely perceived as pitting the ethnic Dinka and Nuer communities against each other. Lam, himself a Nuer, succinctly refutes this perception. He writes, "It is tribalism that threatens national unity and stability, not the tribes per se. Tribalism, therefore, is a manipulative method used by political leaders to mobilize their ethnic groups against others in order to gain their political objectives in a given country." He elaborates: "Though the main driver of the conflict was power struggle between and among leaders within SPLM (Sudan People's Liberation Movement) as to who should lead the country after the independence was achieved, certain leaders presented the problem to their people as an ethnic conflict."[148]

The author concedes that the war was fought predominantly along ethnic lines as though ethnicity were the cause. "Due to this myopic view of the conflict, it was difficult for many South Sudanese leaders to remain objective and view the conflict for what it was. Instead, they considered it as a war between the Nuer and Dinka, which was not true. Consequently, many South Sudanese people lost their lives believing that they were fighting an ethnic war. They did not know that they were fighting for the interest of their leaders to gain power. The worst thing was that by the time some of them realized, it was too late. The genie had already left the bottle. The country was already in flames."[149]

So, what precisely is it in tribal or ethnic identity that the politicians exploit? The answer lies in a shared sense of collective grievance against what is seen as inequitable management of diversity. This is

---

148. Peter Both Lam, *South Sudan: Beyond Ethnic and Political Inertia,* Africa World Books, 2022, p. 5.
149. Ibid, p. 10.

often reflected in allegations of intolerable injustice in the shaping and sharing of power, national wealth, and other values, material, or intangible, or even symbolic. Injustice means that some groups enjoy the full rights of belonging to the national identity framework, while others are discriminated against, marginalized, and even excluded from fully sharing the rights of citizenship. The alleged inequality may only be perceived rather than real, but that does not prevent political entrepreneurs from exploiting it with what Peter Lam describes as the "myopic view"[150] of the leaders, backed by an ill-informed mass following.

In the South Sudanese conflict, according to Peter Lam, "South Sudanese leaders who advocated and called this war ethnic knew that it was not true."[151] So, the politicians were deliberately misleading the people, which underscores the element of exploitation. "They knew that such description was deceptive, yet they used it to discredit the South Sudanese body politic as a Dinka system to have the legitimacy to mobilize their ethnic bases for support to challenge the government militarily. As is well known, the Government of South Sudan has never been a Dinka government. It represents South Sudanese people across the world." It is particularly noteworthy that Peter Lam, a Nuer leader, an intellectual, and himself a politician, is disputing the Nuer allegation against the Dinka as an ethnic group and sees this myth as promoted by vested interests nationally, and internationally. "This narrow characterization of war as being ethnic was influenced by opposition leaders, activist groups, authors of books and articles on the war in South Sudan as well as reports by international human rights and humanitarian organizations which were influenced by the agenda of the opposition political parties."[152]

---

150. Ibid, p. 6.
151. Ibid.
152. Ibid, p. 10.

Peter Lam is not arguing that the Nuer were not killed by the Dinka in the conflict, nor is he saying that the Nuer as a people had no collective concerns or grievances. His argument that the Government is not Dinka does not refute the allegation that the government is Dinka dominated. Lam's main point is that Nuer leaders were fighting for their own ambition for power, not for the genuine cause of their people. This is of course a very thin line which may not be easily understandable to ordinary people, which is why it is relatively easy for politicians to exploit their grievances.

It must be emphasized that identity-related conflicts are not caused by differences per se, but by the way diversity is inequitably mismanaged, thereby triggering a demand for equality. Mismanagement of diversity often classifies and stratifies groups, with some occupying a privileged status that entitles them to the rights of citizenship, while others are discriminated against and denigrated into second or lower-class citizens. Reacting against such injustice, sometimes through armed resistance, risks provoking a counter-insurgency onslaught that could escalate to genocidal levels. Preventing and resolving such conflicts, therefore, requires acknowledging and respecting the identity and dignity of every group through constructive management of diversity to promote inclusivity and full equality, without discrimination. This also means that national sovereignty must be seen as entailing state responsibility to protect and assist all citizens on an equal basis and not be seen as primarily a concept of barricading the state against foreign intervention. If the state manifestly fails to provide the needed protection and assistance for its people, with the consequence that its citizens suffer and die in large numbers, it is incumbent upon the international community to step in and provide remedial protection and assistance. This is the essence of 'Sovereignty as Responsibility,' which I developed with colleagues at the Brookings Institution African

Studies Program.[153]

The concept has been restated by the Canada-sponsored International Commission on Intervention and State Sovereignty as The Responsibility to Protect (R2P or RtoP), which has been construed as prioritizing intervention and is therefore controversial among the weaker Third World countries.[154] The most effective way of safeguarding national sovereignty is discharging the associated responsibility and seek international support if needed. This is a global challenge from which hardly any country is immune.

Options for the management of diversity remain contestable. Several questions pertaining to the options need to be addressed. Should the goal be integration into one unifying national identity? If so, based on which of the contending identities? Should diversities be acknowledged and equitably accommodated? If so, can some form or degree of inequality be avoided? Is unity an overriding goal that should be preserved at all costs or should extreme cases of incompatible differences warrant partition? Is a newly invented framework of unity that is not based on any of the existing models possible? These are daunting questions for which there are no easy answers.

Several country cases offer contrasting models worthy of comparative consideration. Rwanda is decisively following the integration model which asserts that all their people must identify themselves as Rwandese and not as Hutus, Tutsis, or Twas. As Marc Lacey observed, Rwanda, a "country where ethnic tensions were whipped up into a frenzy of killing, is now trying to make ethnicity a thing of the past. There are no Hutu in the new Rwanda. There are no Tutsi either. The

---

153. Francis M. Deng, Sadikiel Kimaro, Terrence Lyons, Donald Rothchild, and I. William Zartman, *Sovereignty as Responsibility: Conflict Management in Africa*, The Brookings Institution Press, 1996 - see p. 115.

154. *The Responsibility to Protect: Report of the International Commission on Intervention and State Sovereignty*, International Development and Research Center, IDRC, Co-Chairs, Gareth Evans and Mohamed Sahnoun 2001. See also *The Responsibility to Protect: Ending Mass Atrocity Crimes Once and For All*, Garth Evans, The Brookings Institution Press, 2008.

government, dominated by the minority Tutsi, has wiped out the distinctions by decree."[155] According to Lacey, "it is not just considered bad form to discuss ethnicity in the new Rwanda. It can land one in jail. Added to the penal code is the crime of 'divisionism,' a nebulous offense that includes speaking too provocatively about ethnicity."[156]

Brett Hartley approaches the policy from the perspective of the third ethnic group, the Twa, (Batwa), whom he sees as negatively impacted by the denial of ethnicity: "Constituting less than one percent of the population, Batwa have fared poorly in Rwanda's reconstruction, which is centered on an ambitious program of reconciliation and nation-building in which the Policy of National Unity and Reconciliation acts as a lodestar for reconfiguring Rwandan society. Designed to promote unity by rejecting traditional divisions of ethnicity "creating one Rwanda for all Rwandans," the policy "officially abolish[es] ethnicity." It is premised on the argument that (Ba)Hutu, (Ba) Tutsi, and (Ba)Twa are social categories racialised by colonial rulers, and means officially 'there are no Hutu or Tutsi (or Batwa) in today's Rwanda, only Banyarwanda (people of Rwanda).[157]

Burundi, whose population comprises those very three ethnic groups of Hutu, Tutsi, and Twa, has chosen to recognize diversity as a reality that should be equitably managed. Lacey noted that "Rwanda's approach contrasts markedly with that employed in neighboring Burundi, which has the same ethnic makeup as Rwanda and the same recent history of ethnic violence. Burundi's transitional government has opted to set aside certain positions for Hutu and certain positions for Tutsi. The two ethnic groups rotate the presidency. A Tutsi held it

155. A Decade After Massacres, Rwanda Outlaws Ethnicity,' Mark Lacey, New York Times, April 9, 2004.
156. Ibid.
157. B.R. Hartley, *Rwanda's Post-Genocide Approach to Ethnicity and Its Impact on the Batwa as an Indigenous People: An International Human Rights Perspective,* QUT Law Review, Vol 15, Issue 1, pp. 51-70, 2015.

for 18 months, and now a Hutu fills the seat."[158]

Sudan was torn apart by a crisis of national identity in which the ruling minority mislabeled their mixed African-Arab mold as simplistically Arab, with Islam as an integral component, and then imposed this distorted mold as the national identity framework that then misrepresented the country as Arab Islamic. Attempts by the rebel SPLM to manage diversity constructively by stipulating a Vision of New Sudan of full equality without discrimination failed and ended in partitioning the country with the independence of South Sudan. And of course, the other model followed by most African countries is a composite management system that juggles with different forms and degrees of unity in diversity.

It can be argued that all these models are contextually plausible. The Rwandan model is largely aspirational, what ought to be. The Burundian model is a pragmatic management of the reality of diversity. The synthesis between them may well be a phasing process, to recognize and manage diversities as they exist as a first phase, but to facilitate a process of progressive interaction toward a fully integrated model that transcends the diversity of identities. Sudan experimented with this arrangement through the 1972 Addis Agreement that granted South Sudan regional autonomy and the 2005 Comprehensive Peace Agreement that was based on a model of 'One Country, Two Systems.' These two arrangements envisaged a process that would gradually evolve into a New Sudan, of an integrated Sudan of full equality. The failure of this creative experimental model based on constructive compromise of idealistic pragmatism led to the partition of the country. The hybrid model being followed by most African countries is probably a normative starting point that requires reform and

---

158. Ibid, p. 52.

improvement toward a more effective utilization of indigenous cultural values.

Reform generally means building on what exists. Every stable social order is based on fundamental values and institutional structures that determine the way it manages and resolves conflicts and mobilises and utilises its human and material resources. These cultural values and related institutions form a holistic model that should be relevant to the development of a normative framework of good governance, conflict prevention, human rights protection, socio-economic development, and nation-building, in other words culturally contextualized constitutionalism.

Toward that objective, people need to have a sound appreciation of their own local cultures to enter a constructive dialogue with other groups in the country to promote mutual understanding, accommodation, and a cross-cultural process of give and take toward equitable integration. This process of dialogue between and among cultures can then be extended to more inclusive regional and international contexts and should play a role in negotiating international human rights and humanitarian norms and instruments. This is critically important to the documentation and promotion of culture and to the cultural contextualization of constitutionalism, good governance, and nation-building. Modern education is externally oriented and transmits knowledge that deprives young people of information about their indigenous cultures, their values, their traditions, and their history. Currently, modern education essentially alienates school children and students of higher learning from their background and related cultural values.

The problem is compounded by the ethnic plurality in a state and how to realistically select the one to incorporate into the national framework of education, governance, and constitutionalism. As Catherine

Kelly asked, "Which of many delineations of cultural pluralism are most strategic for African constitutionalists to embrace? How many ethnic or linguistic groups get formal recognition in national laws and policies? What does that formal definition of such groups mean for other 'imagined communities,' that are not included there? How do the politics behind specific choices in this domain affect whether a constitution is likely to 'stick'? This is a social dilemma, but it is also a math problem of sorts. Of the groups getting formally recognized as part of a culturally contextualized constitutional process, to what extent do formal institutions provide explicit provisions for ethnic, linguistic, or religious balance in the legislature, judiciary, and executive branches." [159]

7. Identifying Appropriate African Cultural Values

One of the most operationally challenging tasks in the cultural contextualization on constitutionalism is identifying the cultural values that need to be built upon in constitution-making. As noted earlier, every cohesive society has an integrated, coherent, and established system based on fundamental values and institutional structures that determine the way it mobilises and utilises its human and material resources and allocates rights and duties. Over a long period of experience, trial and error, this eventually results in a functional framework of optimum communal acceptance by broad consensus and establishes a stable system that is stable, self-sustaining, and resistant to disruptive change. Such shocks as violent conflicts may be so severe as to shatter the existing order, necessitating the development of a new logic for determining and allocating operational roles. But change must be a process of reforming what exists, not the obliteration of what

---

159. Professor Catherine Kelly, personal correspondence.

is existing, to be replaced by something totally new or novel to the society. At the core of what exists is identity, individual and collective, around which the value system evolves.

Identity, which begins from early life in a family, community, and wider social formations, and related cultural values-systems, is essential to the integrity and dignity of the individual and the community to which he or she belongs. It is from those roots that an individual or a particular group finds the moorings of inner security in the broader context of a pluralistic nation and beyond. The diversity resulting from cross-cultural interaction causes comparative stratification that generates the demand for equality.

In his innovative study of reconciliation in South Africa and the leadership role of Nelson Mandela, Fanie du Toit highlights the relevance of indigenous cultural values in Mandela's political transition, an individualized expression of a normative reality that is more widely shared by urbanized cosmopolitan Africans: "Mandela seemed to be able to adopt ever-widening allegiances and causes, yet it is equally clear that he never renounced the traditional loyalties and deeply held beliefs that first promoted him to join the liberation struggle... By not abandoning his identity as a Xhosa and an African, and by valuing the universal dimensions reflected in his local identity, he was able to demonstrate how the universal should be anchored in and justified in terms of the local and the particular. In other words, it is possible to conclude that his embrace of the fight for the rights of all South Africans while drawing on his identity and heritage to do so, played some role in his decision to pursue reconciliation as political strategy."[160]

The author explains that it was indeed the contrast between the

---

160. Fanie du Toit, *When Political Transitions Work: Reconciliation as Interdependence,* OUP, 2018, pp. 11-12.

identity and dignity he enjoyed in his local background and the indignities of discrimination under apartheid that provoked Mandela to
rebel: "When he moved to Johannesburg as a young lawyer some years
later, Mandela discovered that his boyhood freedom had in fact been
limited to those idyllic childhood days and that the freedom to be a
professional adult simply did not exist for him as he set out to start
a career in law. That began his fight for basic individual rights... In
time, after he experienced firsthand, the recalcitrance and racism of
the regime, he joined the ANC and eventually turned freedom fighter,
beginning a new clandestine life in pursuit of rights for his people."[161]

From the studies of the cultures of South Sudan that are already
available, there are cultural concepts with well-established values
that are reflected in different terms in the local languages but share
normative principles of unity and harmony, balance the interest of
the individual with that of the community, and protect the dignity
and integrity of every individual as an integral part of the community. These normative principles are almost identical to the famous
Bantu concept of *Ubuntu,* which Nelson Mandela, Archbishop Tutu,
Thabo Mbeki, and other African leaders and scholars universalized.
Essentially, *Ubuntu* is a concept of shared humanity in which the
interests of the individual are in harmony with the community or
humanity. In the words of a white South African scholar, *Ubuntu* "is
a cultural ideal popular throughout Sub-Sahara Africa that emphasizes
social interconnectedness as the most basic reality that shapes both
individual and society."[162]

A similar concept prevails in Ethiopia, though not effectively
applied. Prime Minister Abiy Ahmed Ali, in his acceptance speech

---

161. Ibid. p. 21.

162. Ibid, p.195. (See also Francis Mading Deng, *Identity, Diversity, and Constitutionalism in Africa,*
pp. 89-100).

for the Nobel Peace Prize, invoked the Amharic concept of *medemer,* which means togetherness for synergetic unity, peace, and reconciliation. The Prime Minister saw *medemer* as a concept of a social compact of love, forgiveness, and reconciliation. According to the Prime Minister, *medemer* stipulates that you are your brother's or sister's, keeper. He called on the Ethiopians to use the best of their past to build a new culture. The Prime Minister later wrote a book on the concept.[163] In a two-part review of the book, Professor Alemayehu G. Mariam wrote in Part I, "I regard *'medemer'* not so much as a 'book' but as the 'philosophical' equivalent of an open source 'software' such as Ubuntu *for use or modification as users/practitioners or other 'developers'* see fit."[164]

Under the title, 'Why did the author write 'Medemer'? Professor Mariam identifies five reasons:

1. Ethiopians (Africans) need to develop a modern Afro-centric philosophy/system of ideas that reflects their history, culture, traditions, and challenges.

2. Ethiopians (Africans) have failed miserably in their efforts to indigenize imported ideologies they barely understood and which at best have marginal relevance to their circumstances. Wholesale imported ideologies have done considerable long-term damage to Ethiopian (African) politics, societies, and economies.

3. Ethiopians (Africans) should be eclectic and selective in adopting beliefs, ideas, and methods from the West and the East and carefully integrate only those ideas that harmonize with the African experience, traditions, practices, and realities.

---

163. Abiy Ahmed, *Medemer*, Tsehai Publishers, Amharic Version, launched on October 21, 2019.

164. Al Mariam's Commentaries, "*Medemer*" by Abiy Ahmed, Ph.D., An Interpretive Book Review, (Part I), Commentary, Ethiopian
News Agency, Reliable News Resource, October 20, 2019.

4. Ethiopians (Africans) need to take a fresh look at their deeply seated and longstanding problems, issues, and aspirations through an African lens and not through the distorted lens they have chosen or have been forced to use. Their lens should be focused squarely on contemporary African realities including poverty, disease, ignorance, one-man, one-party rule, widespread human rights violations, abuse of power and disregard for the rule of law, corruption, and so on.

5. Ethiopians (Africans) can use *Medemer* as their own homegrown forward-looking philosophy/system of ideas to overcome the burdens of the past and to find a pathway to lasting peace and prosperity in their country and in the continent.[165]

In Part II of the review, Professor Mariam observes "The author proposes Ethiopians use their commonly shared values that have been the bedrock of their common heritage to develop consensus. Ethiopians have lived in peace and harmony for much of their history. They have shed their blood together against foreign aggression time and again as one people. They share deeply rooted faith, cultural and family ties."[166] It is painfully ironic that Ethiopia subsequently experienced its worse threat to unity under a leader who has advocated the traditional values of togetherness and received international acclaim for his vision of peace, unity, and harmony.

The normative principles of 'Personhood' among the Akan people of West Africa also emphasize similar indigenous values of interpersonal and inter-communal relations that share much with the East African and Southern African just outlined. Ajume Wingo, writing on the Akan concept of personhood states, "The culture of the Akan

165. Ibid.
166. Ibid.

people of West Africa dates from before the 13th century. Like other long-established cultures the world over, the Akan have developed a rich conceptual system complete with metaphysical, moral, and epistemological aspects. Of particular interest is the Akan conception of *persons*, a conception that informs a variety of social institutions, practices, and judgments about personal identity, moral responsibility, and the proper relationship both among individuals and between individuals and community."[167]

H. M. Majeed, writing on the works of Kwame Gyeke and Kwasi Weridu noted, "The moral foundation of personhood, to a large extent, links the individual with the community. For the one described as a 'person' does not act with total disregard for the well-being of the community. After all, at the human level, morality is not something that an individual alone can bring about without other humans. In other words, social relations are critical to the question of morality. This means that, to a large extent, and in support of Gyekye, personhood is achieved based on how one relates to members of one's community."[168]

These concepts indicate that there is much in common among African traditional cultures that can be built upon in the development of culturally oriented principles of good governance, conflict prevention, and nation-building. Toward that objective, South Sudanese need to have a better appreciation of their own local cultures in order to engage in a constructive dialogue with other groups in the country to promote mutual understanding, accommodation, and cross-cultural

---

167. Ajume Wingo, 'Akan Philosophy of the Person, Stanford Encyclopedia of Philosophy, Dec 27, 2006, p. 1.

168. *The Nexus between 'Person,' Personhood, and Community in Kwame Gyekye's Philosophy*, H. M. Majeed, UJAH Journal of Arts and Humanities, Vol 18, No. 3, 2017. p. 30. For details, see Kwasi Weridu '*The Moral Foundation of an African'* in *Philosophy from Africa and Kwame Geyekye, 'Person and Community in African Thought'* in P.H. Goertzee and A.P. J.Roux, (eds), *Philosophy from Africa: A Text with Readings,* 2nd ed New York, Oxford University Press, 2002.

process of give and take toward equitable integration. This process of dialogue between and among cultures can then be extended to more inclusive regional and international contexts.[169]

What is being advocated here is relevant to what the Founding Fathers of African independence aspired to achieve. Although the current situation in Africa is largely one of disconnect between the prevailing Eurocentric governance systems and the indigenous African cultural values and institutions, the need for cultural orientation has been an unheeded call by the Founding Fathers. This was reflected in the normative visions they declared: Nkrumah's Consciencism; Nyerere's Ujamaa; Kaunda's Humanism; Kenyatta's Harambee; Senghor's Negretude; and Mobutu's Authenticite.' These concepts centered around African socialism as a concept that was distinct from Western capitalism and European socialism. African socialism aimed at sharing resources and services in a traditional African way, as opposed to the European version of the concept. Writing on the African version, William Friedland and Carl Rosenberg noted, "Many African politicians of the 1950s and 1960s professed their support for African socialism, although definitions and interpretations of this term varied considerably. As many African countries gained independence during the 1960s, some of these newly formed governments rejected the ideas of capitalism in favour of a more afrocentric economic model. Leaders of this period professed that they were practising 'African socialism.'[170] A common theme in the various approaches to African socialism was

---

169. For details on the concept, see Rosilyn M. Borland, *Gacaca Tribunals and Rwanda After Genocide: Effective Restorative Community Justice or Further Abuse of Human Rights,* http://www.american.edu/ sis/students/sword/Current-Issue/assay1.pdf. See also Francis Mading Deng, *Identity, Diversity, and Constitutionalism in Africa,* pp. 100-102.

170. Julius Nyerere of Tanzania, Modibo, Keita of Mali, Léopold Senghor of Senegal, Kwame Nkrumah of Ghana and Sékou Touré of Guinea, were the main architects of African Socialism, William H. Friedland and Carl G. Rosberg Jr., (eds), African Socialism, California, Stanford University Press, 1964, p. 3.

social development guided by building on the African identity and what it means to be African, and the avoidance of the development of social classes within society. [171]

These normative concepts, though sincere, tended to be politically motivated and aimed at legitimizing otherwise authoritarian rule. The priority objectives of fostering national unity and accelerating socio-economic development were used to justify one party system, 'African socialism,' leadership without term limits, and denial of human rights, fundamental freedoms, and civil liberties. And as the authors of the *Nation State* effectively argue, the challenge of building on African identity and cultural values goes beyond socio-economic development and relates comprehensively to state and nation-building for Africa.

8. South Sudanese Indigenous Cultures

Developing a culturally oriented system of governance and constitutionalism requires a close understanding of the indigenous cultures on which to build. This is not an easy feat, particularly where there are multiple cultures to consider. South Sudan has an estimated 64 ethnic groups, each of which demands and deserves equal consideration in building a culturally rooted nation. It must be noted that the cultures of South Sudan have been thoroughly studied by anthropologists, although we have not made effective use of those studies. In the famous Oxford University Institute of Anthropology, Evans-Pritchard on the Nuer and Godfrey Lienhardt on the Dinka were pioneers in the study of South Sudanese societies and placed them on the global map of the discipline. No student of anthropology around the world would not have heard

171. Fenner Brockway, *African Socialism*, London, The Bodley Head, 1963, p. 3.

of the Azande, or the Nuer and their fraternal conflicts with their kindred group, the Dinka.

John Gai Yoh wrote, "It is in this context that the British government sent Evans-Pritchard to study the Nuer and Azande political, economic and social ways of life. During his interaction with the Nuer, Evans-Pritchard was surprised by their openness and free interaction with different age groups within the society. He thought that they were communally cooperative. They shared everything, except their wives."[172]

"Evans-Pritchard observed that the Nuer did not have a centralized political system, rather, they were ruled through what he termed 'ordered anarchy.' This characterization of Nuer political system implies that they were organized, but not well structured...Two South Sudanese Nuer scholars tried to respond to Evans-Pritchard assertions. Dr. Michael Duany wrote his Ph.D. thesis entitled *Neither Palaces Nor Prisons: The Constitution of Order Among the Nuer*, in which he disapproved of Evans-Pritchard theory of 'Ordered Anarchy.' Duany argued that the Nuer Political system was institutionalized and governed by what he referred to as 'The Constitution of Order" and not by 'ordered anarchy,' as claimed by Evans-Pritchard."[173]

Peter Lam in his book alludes to some of the major concepts that have been documented in the anthropological studies of South Sudanese societies. Among these are the characterization of our societies as acephalous political systems, stateless societies, tribes without rulers, segmentary lineage systems, balanced opposition, and ordered anarchy. These concepts, which some of our people consider

---

172. Ibid.

173. Michael Duany, Ph.D. thesis; Neither Palaces Nor Prisons: The Constitution of Order Among the Nuer. 1992. https://paanluelwel.com/wp-content/uploads/2017/09/neither-palaces-nor-prisons-the-constitution-of-order-among-the-nuer-phd-dissertation-by-dr-wal-duany.pdf

objectionable as reflective of Western paternalism and condescension, were championed by the Oxford anthropologists and their colleagues in related institutions with implicit admiration.

One of the central issues that emerged in the grassroots and regional consultations of the South Sudan National Dialogue is the intense hostility among communities, focusing in particular on what is perceived as Dinka domination and the nationwide devastation caused by the conflict between the two major ethnic groups, the Dinka and the Nuer, who are seen as dominating the government, the army, and the security sector. The dominating role of these two Nilotic groups is often associated with cultural hegemony presented in some areas of the country as a conflict between Dinka cattle herders and Equatorian farmers. As one person from an Equatorian Consultation put it: "People who try to dominate others don't know that all the tribes in South Sudan have their own cultures, and all these cultures are not the same. If I go with my own Kakwa culture to the Bari community and want to rule over them with our Kakwa culture, it will bring a very big conflict." Another person, referring to the Dinka and the Nuer, said, "It is as though the country belongs to two big tribes." Yet another said, "The Dinka claim that they are the majority; does it mean that we the minorities have no rights?"[174]

The views of South Sudanese judges and the practicing lawyers whom I interviewed for my study for Customary Law in the Modern World, my second book after *Tradition and Modernization*,[175] underscore the strongly-felt sentiments of the people about the crisis of national identity represented by the pluralistic legal system in Sudan's

---

174. *South Sudan National Dialogue,* (Volumes 2 to 5), United Nations Development Programme (UNDP, 2021), p. 148.

175. Francis Mading Deng, *Tradition and Modernization: A Challenge for Law among the Dinka of the Sudan,* Yale University Press, 1971 —see p. 15.

war of identities.[176] Customary law emerges in the interviews as the symbol of the culture and identity the South Sudanese had fought so hard and so long to defend until they achieved their independence. While acknowledging that certain aspects of customary law, especially those that discriminated against women and children, needed radical reform, South Sudanese lawyers and judges I interviewed saw it as the normative foundation of the legal system of an independent South Sudan that should guide legislation and governance in South Sudan. How this was to be accomplished was never made clear and remains an unfulfilled aspiration. Section 5 of the Transitional Constitution of South Sudan includes the customs and traditions of the people. Section 6. (1) provides that, 'All indigenous languages of South Sudan are national languages and shall be respected, developed and promoted.'[177] As the views of minority groups demonstrate, these groups feel culturally discriminated against in the independent South Sudan.

In 2015, the Ministry of Justice, Local Government Board, and UNDP South Sudan jointly commissioned a series of studies for the Ascertainment of the Customary Laws of fourteen communities of South Sudan.[178] In the Foreword to the volume of the customary laws of a group that included the Acholi, Lokoya, and Madi communities, the Honourable Jeremiah Shaka Moses Wani, Under-Secretary of the Ministry of Justice, wrote, "Recognizing customary law is about recognizing our competence and recognizing the strength which comes from our culture, which is the core of our identity. In its day-to-day operation, the legal system takes cognizance of and applies our culture,

176. Francis Mading Deng, 'Evans-Pritchard and *The Paradox of Anthropology,* in Andre' Singer, (ed), *A Touch of Genius: The Life, Work, and Influence of Sir Edward Evans-Pritchard,* Sean Kingston Publishing and Publishing Services, Herefordshire, United Kingdom, publication forthcoming).

177. The Transitional Constitution of the Republic of South Sudan, 2011, p. 3.

178. Tumaini A. Minja, *Leveraging Customary Laws for Conflict Resolution and Building Societies,* Consultant, 2015.

our heritage, and our histories, and they are constructed in a way that is capable of providing justice for our people and communities."[179] The Undersecretary went on to say, "Customary law is largely empowering in many indigenous communities because it is a form of social organization and justice that maintains and sustains traditions that go back millennia. A community is most likely to have a healthy sense of order when control comes from agreed norms from within. Over time, there is nothing more debilitating to a community than a lack of control, and an ongoing perception of ability among the people of that community to look after themselves."[180]

An aspect of the paradox of anthropological studies among the societies of South Sudan is that they documented the cultures of the people and by doing so also spotlighted ethnic differentiations, which becomes divisive, albeit inadvertently. The representation of the people by a foreign observer risks an inevitable degree of misrepresentation or distortion. This is true even of the highly acclaimed works of Evans-Pritchard. As I was preparing the Foreword to Andre Singer's volume on E.E. Evans-Pritchard,[181] I decided to ask a few South Sudanese intellectuals from the communities which he had studied how, in their opinion, Evans-Pritchard is remembered in their communities. These included Azande, Nuer, Anuak, and Shilluk in the order in which he studied them, and by extension, the Dinka. What I received was a range of views, some quite objective, others rather critical, and most of

---

179. Customary Laws Project, Series 2, Volume 1, p. 1. A similar Foreword is used in Volume 2 of Series 2 comprising the customary laws of the Bari and Kakwa Communities, p. 9. See also, *In Search of a Working System of Justice for a New Nation: The Ascertainment of the Customary Laws of the Toposa, Lokoto (Otuho) Lange and Lopit Communities of South Sudan*, 2/15/2012 and *The Ascertainment of the Customary Laws of the Balanda Bviri, Bongo, Ndogo, and Mundari Communities of the Western Bahr el-Ghazal and Central Equatoria States of South Sudan*. 2/15/2012.

180. Ibid.

181. Francis Mading Deng, 'Evans-Pritchard and The Paradox of Anthropology, in Andre' Singer, (ed), *A Touch of Genius: The Life, Work, and Influence of Sir Edward Evans-Pritchard*, Sean Kingston Publishing and Publishing Services, Herefordshire, United Kingdom - publication forthcoming.

them positive. Even those who were critical saw his studies as having prominently placed the people of South Sudan on the world map.

Jok Madut Jok, Professor of Anthropology at Syracuse University, offered an overall appraisal of the works of Evans-Pritchard and their relevancy to contemporary challenges of State and nation-building in South Sudan: "As post-colonial societies grapple with their past and how to know it, EP (Evans-Pritchard) has rendered South Sudanese unable to say categorically whether British Social Anthropology sold them to empire or helped them record ways to remember aspects of their own past. He will always be remembered fondly, first for getting the descriptions of religion, marriage, livelihoods, and inter-ethnic relations correctly, and secondly, for his impact on the discipline in his *The Nuer: A Description of the Modes of Livelihood and Political Institutions of a Nilotic People*,[182] which remains a classic in anthropology, in the critique that this book has triggered the world over."[183]

Jok applies the dilemmas of anthropology to Africa generally; "By the same token, there are increasing voices within South Sudan, Africa or the Global South in general, that criticize anthropology as a particular way of knowing and knowledge production, that EP's work may have generated a narrative about the Azande, the Nuer and the Anyuak (Anuak) of South Sudan, a narrative that is built on a foundation that misread the social structure of these communities, masking stories about women as free agents, not cognizant of issues of sexuality, gendered power relations and simply took what men reported and which has now come to constrain these communities in a straight jacket as if time and space had not touched their ways

---

182. E.E. Evans-Pritchard, The Nuer: A Description of the Modes of Livelihood and Political Institutions of a Nilotic People Oxford, The Clarendon Press, 1940.

183. Jok Madut Jok, op cit.

of life."[184]

Although it is virtually impossible to give due consideration and individual attention to every one of them, the inability to achieve the ideal should not inhibit doing what is practical and desirable, though short of the ideal; models that are representative of cultural clusters can be discerned. It is with that in mind that the Dinka model, which not only represents the culture of the overwhelming majority of the people, estimated at 40 percent of the total South Sudan population with much in common with the other Nilotic groups, especially the Nuer, the second largest group in the country, provides a useful sample of indigenous culture. The objective is not to postulate it as a national framework but as an example of what is required to be done with other models to collect the diverse cultures of South Sudan from which to conduct comparative analysis and develop a synthesis that can be viewed as a normative framework for the country.

9. Principles for Developing a Permanent Constitution

The Workshop on 'The Constitution Making Process for the Republic of Southern Sudan,' that was convened on 25-28 May 2021, with the theme: 'Designing the Path to a Durable Constitution for South Sudan,' agreed on the following fundamental principles:

i. Reaffirm that the Permanent Constitution-Making process in the Republic of South Sudan shall be guided by the provisions of Chapter VI of the R-ARCSS (RevitalizedAgreement for the Resolution of the Conflict in Southern Sudan) and based, among others, on the eight fundamental principles as outlined in Article 6.2 of the R-ARCS, namely:

ii. Supremacy of the People of South Sudan;

---

184. Ibid.

iii. Initiating a federal and democratic system of government that reflects the character of South Sudan in its various institutions taken together, guaranteeing good governance, constitutionalism, rule of law, human rights, gender equity and affirmative action;

iv. Guaranteeing peace and stability, national unity and territorial integrity of the Republic of South Sudan;

v.   Promoting people's participation in the governance of the country through democratic, free and fair elections and the devolution of powers and resources to the states and counties;

vi. Respecting ethnic and regional diversity and communal rights, including the right of communities to preserve their history, develop their language, promote their culture, and express their identities;

vii. Ensuring the provision of the basic needs of the people through the establishment of a framework for fair and equitable economic growth and access to national resources and services;

viii. Promoting and facilitating regional and international cooperation with South Sudan; and

ix. Committing the people of South Sudan to peaceful resolution of national issues through dialogue, tolerance, accommodation, and respect of others' opinions.

These are of course broad principles that need to be elaborated and substantiated in the process of developing and drafting the constitution, which is the overriding objective of this paper. In particular, the role of culture should not be limited to the local level or to the communities but should inform national norms of good governance and constitutionalism.

The critical questions that should be addressed in conceptualizing and formulating a framework for culturally contextualizing constitutionalism would be: What are the key elements in the constitution that lend themselves to cultural orientation? These would probably include various forms of decentralization; balancing majority rule with the protection of minorities; protection of human rights and fundamental liberties; and respect for the rule of law in its varying forms. This is of course an illustrative and by no means exhaustive list; many more elements can and should be added to the list, as detailed below.

10. Parameters of Contextualized Constitutionalism

The foregoing sections of the paper have tried to address conceptual issues of identity, diversity, and the need for equitable mismanagement of diversity in the political, economic, social and cultural life of the country. Gross intolerable injustice generates conflicts that cause varying degrees of human suffering and death, escalating to mass atrocities that could become genocidal. The remaining sections of the paper focus on how these crises can be practically addressed in a culturally contextualized constitutionalism. This is indeed the most challenging part of constitution-making. The overriding goal of constitutionalism is ultimately to establish a constitutive process aimed at ensuring and sustaining peace, security, stability, and development in a country. While the requisite normative framework stipulates the exercise of power through popular democratic participation, democracy as a concept has generated a great deal of controversy not only in the African, context but worldwide, with cross-cultural nuances. The core of the problem in Africa is that constitutionalism and specifically liberal models of democracy have not been able to constructively address the challenges of unity and diversity.

Western notions of democracy have tended to focus on elections, based on the principle of one person one vote. But countries are not comprised of one persons; they are also communities and groups defined by various identity factors. This poses a serious dilemma for ethnically diverse or pluralistic societies, where the value of every individual rests in being a vital member of the community and people tend to vote on the bases of their politicized ethnic or cultural identities. The core of the dilemma is that there is an inherent contradiction in the process. On the one hand, democracy requires that the will of the majority should prevail. On the other hand, the winner-take-all outcome can become a dictatorship of numbers, where the majority imposes its will on the minority. In countries where wielding power means access to resources and vital social services, the stakes can be very high and the elections violently contentious. What is even more incongruous is that it disregards the fundamental normative principle of consensus-building in indigenous African decision-making process.

The alternative must be to marry the best of the Western system with the best of the African indigenous systems to retain those elements of the Western concept and practice of democracy that have universal validity while refashioning an African constitutive system by drawing on the indigenous values and institutions and fostering a sense of dignity and national pride based on an authentic vision of the state and nation-building.

There are also universal principles of human rights and humanitarian normative frameworks which states are obligated to protect and be internationally accountable. In South Sudan, there is also potentially the issue of citizenship as populations have been dispersed around the world by war induced forced displacement and refuge abroad. Many have acquired dual citizenship. Many were born in their countries of refuge. During the National Dialogue, controversy arose on whether dual citizens or spouses in mixed marriages should be allowed to hold constitutional posts. These factors, and other conventional considerations, raise questions about the determination of citizenship and the rights and duties of dual citizenship.

A way of resolving the conceptual and operational dilemmas of cultural contextualization of African constitutionalism, specifically bridging national and global perspectives, is to recast sovereignty as a responsibility to protect and assist citizens, and not to focus primarily on using it as a barricade against international scrutiny and involvement in internal affairs, which may be justified under certain compelling circumstances. This requires that the state shoulders the primary responsibility for its people, but seek, or at least accept, the assistance of the international community when needed. The agenda for discharging national responsibility in making the constitution and operationalizing it through the wider notion of constitutionalism should include, but not limited to, the following:

i.   Stating in the preamble the overriding importance of culture as a source of inspiration and guidance in the construction of state institutions and decision-making processes to consolidate independence, promote an endogenous state and generate a self-sustaining process of nation-building with confidence, dignity, and national pride;

ii. Enshrining various forms of consensus-building approaches in decision making, including conflict prevention, management, and resolution, based on the famous African notion of sitting under a tree and discussing until an amicable decision is reached;

iii. Upholding constructive management of diversity as a strategy aimed at inclusivity and equality of all ethnic groups in the shaping and sharing of power and national resources as a strategy for ensuring national unity, and harmony, and stability;

iv. Ensuring the democratic choice of the people for their leaders through a free, fair, and culturally-oriented system of elections, conducted by a credibly independent national agent, with appropriate international assistance, and balancing majority rule with deferential recognition and accommodation of minorities in the government to promote inclusivity, unity, and harmony;

v. Respecting the dignity of every individual and group by stipulating a Bill of Rights that respects individual human and collective people's rights, civil liberties, and fundamental freedoms, as core elements of the African values and normative principles that balance the rights and duties of the individual with those of the community, the core of the African Charter 'human and people's rights;'

vi. Stipulating the appropriate conditions for granting citizenship and recognizing the rights and responsibilities of dual citizenship, bearing in mind the unique circumstances of South Sudan and the prolonged wars that have resulted in massive displacement internally and externally;

vii. Incorporating fundamental principles of African jurisprudence in the administration of justice, which would prioritize arbitration, compensation for wrongs, and reconciliation above punitive measures that are not essential to the maintenance of the rule of law and public order;

viii. Adopting a federal system and an enhanced form of decentralization that devolves power to the local communities as a basis for ensuring self-administration as a form of internal self-determination to safeguard consensual unity in diversity;

ix. Encouraging the return of internally displaced populations and refugees to their areas of origin in the countryside and providing them with essential services, employment opportunities, and socio-economic development in fulfillment of the liberation policy of taking power to the people;

x.   Spreading the services and amenities available in the cities and towns to the rural areas to be accessible to the people to discourage urban influx and promote even development in the country through self-reliance and resilience measures that approach development as self-enhancement from within instead of dependency on external support;

xi. Ensuring effective exploration and exploitation of the natural resources and wealth of the country and diversifying the sources of production and distribution, with special emphasis on the development of agriculture and livestock, and directing oil revenue toward supporting the diversification of the economy;

xii. Recognizing and reinforcing the role of traditional authorities in the modern governance system and giving them the powers and resources to enhance their capacity to effective governance and maintain the rule of law and maintain peace and security in their areas and with neighboring communities;

xiii. Transforming the youth age-setting system in warrior societies from a means of recruiting fighters into a collective force for reconstruction and development and provide them with incentives to make their peace-building role more attractive than the lure of engaging in violence;

xiv. Promoting gender equality by upholding respect for women as wives and mothers while promoting the participation of women in economic and public life, to give them gender representation at par with men;

xv. Transforming traditional reverence for nature as a sacred aspect of creation into the modern respect for the environment and supporting international programs for the protection of the environment;

xvi. Developing self-reliance in development as a self-enhancement from within, in a process of 'transitional integration,' that links national strategies with prudently planned complementarity with the wider global economies, rather than see development as an external commodity to be imported with dependency on external actors; and

xvii. Incorporating culture in the educational system at all levels from schools to universities and other institutions of higher learning to ensure that the curriculum is endogenised by focusing it pragmatically on relevant epistemic concepts, cultural orientation, national history, normative frameworks, practical skills, and employment opportunities, the overriding goal being to make education responsive to the country's development framework and strategies, and the needs the people.

These are only examples of what is needed in the cultural contextualization of constitutionalism in South Sudan as a model example of an African continent-wide strategy. They are of course subject to appropriate reformulation, redrafting and categorization for incorporation in suitable chapters or sections of the constitution.

The overriding objective is to develop an authentic model of endogenous African constitution and the related concept of constitutionalism that is grounded in African cultural values and institutions and addresses the specific issues of the African political realities with due regard to universal structures and norms of constitutionalism. In his Foreword to *Identity, Diversity and Constitutionalism in Africa*,[185] Former President of Nigeria, General Olusegun Obasanjo advocated "the view of an Africa that builds on its time-tested cultural ideals, and institutionalized practices... I might also note that these values have much to offer not only Africa but the world. Just as Western

---

185. Francis Mading Deng, *Identity, Diversity, and Constitutionalism in Africa*, Foreword by General Olusegun Obasanjo, Former President of Nigeria, United States Institute of Peace Press, 2008 see p. 119.

democracy enshrines certain universal values, so does the African worldview."[186]

11. Conclusion

Professor Chaloka Beyani, the Zambian Constitutional lawyer who has contributed significantly to the drafting of constitution in a number of African countries and played a key role to the development of the 2009 African Union Convention for the Protection of Internally Displaced Persons in Africa (The Kampala Convention), recently wrote in a private communication, "Modern constitutions are made by the people for the people, and it is the people at grassroots level that matter and count the most as the people. In this sense, the cultural values of the people have to drive the basis of the constitution more generally as a characteristic of the sovereignty of the people, also under a chapter on national values, but if recognised and accepted by the people as an imperative, then it has to permeate the basis of the constitution in terms of its fundamental structure, governance, Bill of Rights, and dispute settlement, in addition to the traditional role of the judiciary. It is a challenge indeed, but it has to be part of the will of the sovereignty of the people in articulating their vision of constitutionalism."[187]

Analyzing the various cultural systems to identify commonalities, differences, possible complementarities, and restating a shared national framework of cultural values that should be enshrined in a national constitution. These values were favorably viewed as embodying indigenous principles of good governance, democracy, respect for human rights, and human dignity. If we observed and applied them, they could help shape an admirable model state that constructively balances

---

186. Ibid, p. xii.
187. Chaloka Beyani, Constitution Making in Southern Sudan, London, June 1, 2021.

unity with ethnic and cultural diversity. That was indeed what the colonial rulers did, albeit for their own administrative convenience, when they adopted the policy of indirect rule, which post-colonial administrations abandoned as part of colonial exploitation of culture as a tool of domination.

While our initial focus must of course be on developing an appropriate culturally contextualized constitutionalism for the country, the longer-term process of applying a similar process to the wider African context must be borne in mind. Ironically, South Sudan provides a fertile ground for this cultural experimentation as it is one of the least affected by modernizing and Westernizing transformation. South Sudan could indeed provide a model potentially adaptable to other African countries. Much is already being done by African constitutional experts in various institutions in Africa and elsewhere in the world from which the South Sudanese project could learn and benefit. With the wider African context in mind.

To recap the implications of what all this means for the appropriated guidelines in developing a culturally contextualized constitutionalism, flexibly interpreted, the required action should include:

• Devolving autonomous powers to the local level to enable communities to govern themselves on the bases of their indigenous values and institutions, using their own local resources with complementary support from the center;

• Developing principles and institutions of constitutionalism at the national level that promote constructive management of diversity based on the principles of inclusivity and equitable participation in the shaping and sharing of all material and moral values as reflected in such African normative concepts and values from comparative South Sudanese ethnic communities.

I would like to end this paper with four specific recommendations:

1. First, we need to revisit the normative principles enunciated by the Founding Fathers of our newly independent countries which turned out to be unfulfilled dreams. We need individual scholars conversant with these declared concepts to study them more thoroughly to develop the value systems they embodied.

2. Second, there is need to study more thoroughly and elaborate the normative principles enshrined in such concepts as *Ubuntu, Medemer, * Personhood, *Cieng* and similar concepts which should be postulated in preambular paragraphs of national constitutions as normative guidelines and used to develop a shared African cultural value system on which to build a regional policy framework.

3. Third, we should convene an inter-disciplinary team to discuss the documents emerging from these initiatives and consider their value in developing a culturally contextualized African system of governance and constitutionalism at both the national and regional frameworks and their potential application in international negotiations.

4. Fourth, to extract from the exercise major normative principles that offer guidance in developing an African position in international debates on the development or reforms of normative instruments and related institutional arrangements.

The conceptual and operational issues which this paper has tried to address are daunting, but so are the paradoxical stakes and opportunities of balancing localization and globalization in a world that is both unifying and fragmenting. Implicit in these paradoxes are the risks of conflicts on the one hand and the potential of mutual understanding, cooperation, and cross-cultural enrichment on the other hand. That is at least the aspiration I have tried to pursue with relentless optimistic search for opportunities in crises and determined resistance to pessimism as a dead end that should be avoided.

C. Regional Level

'Policy Orientation and the Study of African Law'
Temple Law Quarterly, Winter 1967 [188]

This paper restates elements of customary law with the review to reforming it to address issues related to discrimination of women and children and to facilitate socio-economic development.

'Development in Context'
in *Modernization in the Sudan*,
by M.W.Daly, Lilian Barber Press, 1986. [189]

The purpose of this article is to see development as an internally generated self-reliant process of enhancing the quality of life from within, building primarily on internal resources and institutional structures and cultural values, rather than be perceived as a foreign commodity that has to be imported from outside the context.

---

188. Also published in *A review of African Law, Adaptation and Development* by Leo Kuper and Hilda Kuper, (eds), University of California Press, 1966.

189. Paper delivered in 1982 at the 25th World Conference of the Society for International Development in Baltimore, Maryland.

'Crisis in African Development, A Social and Cultural Perspective'

Rockefeller Brothers Fund Annual Report, 1984

This paper is essentially a reflection of approaching development in the context of societal values and institutions as a self-enhancing process of self-enhancement from within.

'African Development Dilemmas'

Excellence and Beyond, Global Conference Summary, 1985 [190]

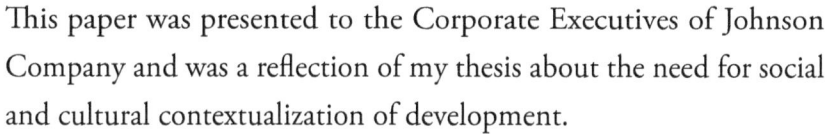

This paper was presented to the Corporate Executives of Johnson Company and was a reflection of my thesis about the need for social and cultural contextualization of development.

'Security Problems: An African Predicament'

Keynote address to the African Studies Association,

Bloomington, Indiana, 1981 [191]

This paper was presented on the occasion of the Herskovits Award for my book, *Tradition and Modernization*,[192] and was therefore a statement of the thesis of the book which was my doctoral dissertation. It advocated the strategy of transitional integration of the fundamental values and institutions and the progressive objectives of modernization.

---

190. Paper presented at the Johnson Wax Global Conference, Rio de Janeiro, Brazil, September 1521, 1984.

191. Also published in: *African Security Issues: Sovereignty, Stability and Solidarity*, by Bruce E. Arlinghaus, (ed), Boulder, Colorado: Westview, 1984.

192. Francis Mading Deng, *Tradition and Modernization: A Challenge for Law among the Dinka of the Sudan*, Yale University Press, 1971 - see p. 15.

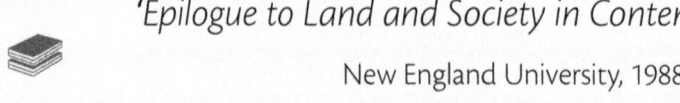

'Epilogue to Land and Society in Contemporary Africa'
New England University, 1988

Land is a fundamental element of identity that is founded on sensitive factors that are not only connected to material livelihood, but are also associated with ancestral continuity and therefore spiritual and religious values. Traditionally, land therefore belongs to the living members of the family and the community, many generations that are dead, and innumerable generations to be born into the long timeless future. That is why land in traditional tenure land cannot be sold or otherwise alienated outside the family or the community. And yet, the modern demands of development requires reforming the traditional tenure system. Ultimately, the guiding principle must be that possession and ownership of land cannot be simply one of absolute individual control and management by an individual or group, but a multi-layered system of land use including shared degrees of ownership and possession.

'Dilemmas of Nation-building: Racism, Ethnicity and Development in Africa'
Ethnic Studies Report, vol. IX, no. 2, July 1991

This paper addresses the on-going debate between the trend to ignore or even deny racial, ethnic and related inequities in development opportunities to addressing them as elements of identity as a factor in conflicts through constructive management of identity.

'Africa and the New World Dis-Order,
Rethinking Colonial Borders'

The Brookings Review, vol. 11, no. 2, Spring 1993 [193]

Africa and the World Dis-Order addresses the grey area between the old order of bi-polar confrontation between the super powers to a new multi-polar world in which the strategic interests of the super powers are withdrawn and human rights and humanitarian concerns are emerging as major bases of international relations. This poses the two-prong strategy of reassigning responsibility to the countries and sub-regions immediately concerned as recasting sovereignty as responsibility of states to protect their citizens and if necessary seek international support.

'IGAD Mediation of the Sudanese Conflict'

Concept paper for the Inter-Governmental Authority on Drought

and Development (IGAD) conference in Addis Ababa,

Ethiopia, February 24-25, 1995

This was one of the papers I prepared for the IGAD conference as a member of the Resource Persons' Group that contributed significantly to the eventual success of the process.

---

193. Also published in Global Visions, by Jeremy Brecher, John Brown Childs, and Jill Cutler, (eds), Boston, South End, 1993.

'Egypt's Dilemmas on the Sudan'
Middle East Policy, vol. IV, September 1995

Egypt's dilemma in the Sudan is essentially the result of the dual African-Arab character of the country that presents a crisis of identity that confronts Egypt and other Arab countries with ambivalence in approaching the Sudan. This ambivalence generates both exaggerated claims over the Sudan as Arab for self-serving purposes and denial of the Sudan when it takes positions that are not favorable to the Arab world. Ironically, Sudan is often welcomed as a mediator in intra-Arab conflicts precisely because of its marginality as an Arab country. Sudan's support for the Camp David Accord between Egypt and Israel, which President Nimeiri and I promoted against the advice of all pertinent pan-Arabist tendencies in the country, was a good example of Arab disaffiliation of the Sudan as an Arab country.

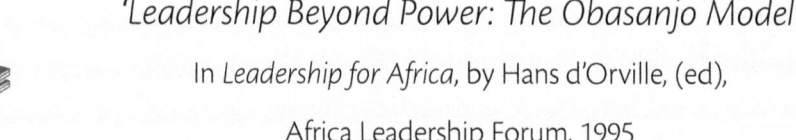

'Leadership Beyond Power: The Obasanjo Model'
In *Leadership for Africa*, by Hans d'Orville, (ed),

Africa Leadership Forum, 1995

One of the reasons why African leaders cling to power and resist retirement is the sharp difference between the spoils of power and the loss of leadership privileges once out of power. In my own experience as someone who worked closely with General Olusegun Obasanjo after he handed power to an elected President, I saw him remaining very active on the African and international scene and as a member of the Inter-Action Council of Former Heads of State and Government. This paper was written for an edited volume of essays prepared in honor of Obasanjo while he was incarcerated by the Nigerian dictator Sani Abacha.

'Identity in Africa's Internal Conflicts'
American Behavioral Scientist, vol. 40, no. 1, September 1996

This paper addresses the challenge of identity not so much because of differences but from the mismanagement of differences which must be addressed both to prevent conflicts and to find appropriate solutions.

'Ethnicity: An African Predicament'
The Brookings Review, vol. 15, no. 3, Summer 1997

This argument makes the point that ethnicity is a factor in conflicts that must be addressed. The tendency in the scholarly world has been to argue that identity by itself is not a source of conflict but a factor exploited by political entrepreneurs in their self-serving quest for power. The paper argues that politicians could not exploit a non-existing factor that ethnicity is a factor, and that it often involves grievances that need to be addressed being abused by self-serving political entrepreneurs.

'Genocide, Violence, and Civil Society'
In *Encyclopedia of Africa South of the Sahara,*
by John Middleton, Editor-in-Chief, volume 2,
New York, Charles Scriber's Sons, 1997, pp. 207-214

Genocide is one of the most heinous crimes that the international community is committed to prevent and punish when it occurs. For the same reason, it is considered so sensitive that the tendency is to deny it and even avoid or challenge the allegation of the crime. For that reason, I advocate demystifying genocide to remove it from being perceived as too sensitive to touch and bring it down to earth as an extreme degree of identity-related conflict of identities that results from mismanagement entailing gross inequities and discrimination to promote equality and non-discrimination.

'Managing Diversity in Africa: A Challenge to State Borders'
Le Temps Stratégue, May/June 1998, No. 81

This paper makes the argument that the wars of identity in many countries, including in Africa, result not from the mere differences, but from the mismanagement of the differences that leads to discrimination, marginalization, and denial of the rights of citizenship. Constructive management is essentially the strategy for correcting the elements of this mismanagement.

'Out of Africa: The Fate of the State and International System'
In The Future of War, by G. Prius and H. Tromp (eds),
Kluwer Law International, The Netherlands 2000, pp. 133-145

The argument of this paper was that most states, with a focus on Africa, are acutely divided, which often creates a protection vacuum that the international community is often needed to provide a remedial response. Without a national status which would ensure that the citizens are protected by their state, the population would be stateless with no state protection. They would therefore need the international community to step in to provided needed protection.

'Human Rights in the African Context'

In *A Companion to African Philosophy*, by Kwasi Wiredu,

Oxford, Blackwell Publishing 2004, pp. 499-508

The core of this paper was to make the point that human rights should be culturally contextualized in order to counter the challenge to the universality of human rights by alleging that they represent foreign imposition of the West against Third World countries.

Introduction to '*Kampala Convention and Its Contribution to International Law*'

By Mehari Taddele Masu,

Eleven International Publishing, Netherlands, 2014

The book for which this is an Introduction examines the African Union Convention on the Protection and Assistance of Internally Displaced Persons known as the Kampala Convention which entered into force on 6 December 2012. This makes Africa the first region to adopt a legal instrument on the issue based on the Guiding Principles on Internal Displacement which we developed under my mandate as Representative of the Secretary-General on Internally Displaced Persons and which I presented to the Commission on Human Rights in 1998.

'Preventing Mass Atrocities in Africa: The Case of the Two Sudans'

In *Peacekeeping in Africa*, by Tony Karo

and Kudrat Virk, (eds), Palgrave Macmillan, 2017

The notion of mass atrocities implies a devastating level of violence often reflected in genocide, war crimes, ethnic cleansing, and crimes against humanity. In addition to the 1948 Convention on the Prevention and Punishment of the Crime of Genocide and a wide array of other human rights instruments, international commitment to preventing such atrocities is embodied in the outcome document of the 2005 World Summit of Heads of State and Government, which is enshrined the emerging concept of the responsibility to protect (R2P). The evolution of this concept has been widely documented. It is rooted in the normative principle of "sovereignty as responsibility" – developed through the Washington-based Brookings Institution's Africa Program, which I founded and directed for 12 years (1989–2001) – as a conceptual framework for approaching post–Cold War conflicts in Africa. We framed the program around two conceptual questions. First, what were the policy priority areas of concern in Africa that the program should address? Second, to what extent had the end of the Cold War by 1990 affected the way we should approach and address these issues on the continent? The answer to the first question was almost self-evident. The Africa policy agenda had to address violent conflicts, democratic governance, human rights, sustainable development, and gender equality.

Although we carried out, or commissioned, studies in all these areas, our approach to post–Cold War conflicts in Africa entailed a key shift from viewing these conflicts as part of the proxy confrontation between the United States (US) and the Soviet Union – prevented, managed, resolved, or aggravated through the bipolar control mechanisms of the two superpowers – to seeing them in their proper national and regional contexts, with responsibilities for addressing them re-appropriated accordingly. Apart from our research agenda at the Brookings Institution, I also acquired considerable insights through my experiences as the Representative of the United Nations (UN) Secretary-General on Internally Displaced Persons (IDPs) from 1992 to 2004 and as Special Advisor of the UN Secretary-General on the Prevention of Genocide from 2007 to 2012.

In order to prevent mass violence and related atrocities in Africa, the root causes of conflicts must be identified and addressed. Drawing on my extensive engagement with issues related to the prevention of mass atrocities, in this chapter I focus on the experience of the Sudan, a country that before the independence of South Sudan in July 2011 was, in many ways, a microcosm of Africa. Located at the heart of the continent, Sudan and South Sudan are surrounded by nine neighbors – Egypt and Libya to the north; Chad, the Central African Republic (CAR), and the Democratic Republic of the Congo (DRC) to the West; Kenya and Uganda to the south; and Ethiopia and Eritrea to the east – with Saudi Arabia across the Red Sea, all of whom have contributed to their pluralistic population composition. Despite the partitioning with the independence of South Sudan, the two countries remain intrinsically interconnected by shared history, ongoing tensions, and conflicts over several unresolved issues.

D. Global Level

'Racialism at the Meeting Point'

In *Disappointed Guests*, London, 1965

This was selected as one of ten best essays in a national competition by foreign students on racialism in the British Isles. This paper was initially written as one of the papers resulting from the Scandinavian study tour. I later revised it and submitted it in a nationwide competition of essays on racialism in the United Kingdom written by foreign students. The ten best essays were selected to be included in an edited volume. But I felt strongly that the title chosen for the volume, *Disappointed Guests,* did not reflect the theme of my essay.

In my paper, I distinguished between racial consciousness and pride as elements of identity which were universally shared by all groups. My argument that all groups see their identity and related cultural values as the ideals of God's creation. Every group therefore considers itself superior to all others. This superior self-perception is innocuous in isolation. It becomes problematic in a pluralistic context when a group tries to impose its superior self-perception on others through racial discrimination and other acts of denigration and subjugation. I gave apartheid South Africa as an extreme example of that form of racism.

The policy implication of my argument was that we are all potential or passive racists to the extent that we consider ourselves a superior model of humanity. If we recognize that shared human prejudice, then we will see what is in common to all of us. We could then begin to know more about each other and respect the humanity that we all share. We can even begin to appreciate what is good in each other's identity and its value system that can be mutually enriching through a give and take in the context of inter-racial and cross-cultural interaction.

I felt that the title of the edited volume which projected the authors as disappointed and angry was contrary to my thesis. I threatened to withdraw my essay from the book. I was however persuaded that my essay was the exception and that the title reflected the subject matter of the other essays. Besides, my essay would speak for itself. K.D.D. Henderson, a former colonial governor in the Sudan with whom I became quite close, advised me not to worry about coming across as critical of the English. As he put it, the opposite would be the case, for the English wonder whether something is wrong if they are not criticized. Whether that was true or not, he certainly allayed my concern

Clearly the theme of my essay reflected my Dinka view. Nor was I right in assuming that contact and interaction at the meeting point always lead to better understanding and mutual respect. I was clearly oblivious to the generally accepted truism that 'familiarity breeds contempt.' Over the years, I would witness enough to correct my naïve original assumptions.

'The Family and the Law of Torts'

Houston Law Review, vol. 4, no. 1, Spring/Summer 1966 [194]

This paper was a revised version of a paper I wrote for a course in the L.L.M program. It was a comparative analysis in which I argued that the African and Western Law of Torts was based only on aspects of the institution of the family: property for the West and procreation for Africa, which did not see the family holistically as a multifaceted institution based on a complex combination of normative principles.

---

194. Also published in *Sudan Law Review and Reports*, 1965.

The policy implication was to develop a more comprehensive view of the family as a social unit that served many interconnected objectives.

'Extracts from the Diary of a Sudanese Student'

Hibbert Journal, nos. 25356, 1965/66 [195]

These articles resulted from a study tour in Scandinavia in 1963 at the invitation of a Swedish writer who was writing a book on the welfare system in Scandinavia and wanted an African perspective.

'Law and Disorder Around the World'

Columbia Journal of Law and Social Problems, vol. 9, no. 1, Fall 1972 [196]

The core of this paper is to see law as the outcome of a power process involving the pursuit of values through institutions. Law is not an abstract concept whose effectiveness can be taken for granted. To be effective, authoritative decision-makers must pragmatically reconcile competing interests and address the genuine grievances of disadvantaged groups if the legal system is to gain legitimacy in the eyes of all the pivotal participants in the process.

'Diversity and NationBuilding' and 'New Trends in International Law,' published in the book *Diplomacy and Development*, Ministry of Foreign Affairs, 216, 1974.[197]

The premise of this paper is that the challenge of nation-building

---

195. A four-part presentation, including: *'Religion in Sweden,'* (A different version of *'Religion in Sweden'* appeared in Vertex, no. 5, 1966, p. 16), '*The Family as a Basis of Society, Racialism at the Meeting Point, and The Paradox of Contemporary Civilization.'*

196. Proceedings of the Thirteenth Annual Columbia Law Symposium.

197. These papers were also presented at the Diplomacy & Development conference, Khartoum, January 1520, 1974.

is constructive management of diversity which later became the guiding principle in my engagement with governments pursuant to my mandates on internal displacement and genocide prevention.

Foreword to 'The Primal Mind: Vision and Reality in Indian America'

By Jamake Highwater, French Edition, New York: Harper & Rolo, 1981

In this book, the American Indian author, Jamake Highwater, explored the often misunderstood Indian worldview. He examines the cultural aspects of American Indian ritual, art, oral traditions, architecture, ceremonial dance, and native perceptions of time and space. He contrasts the ideas and intellectual aims of Western culture with the life-styles, attitudes, and world views of North American tribal peoples and other primal peoples of the world. And he emphasizes the need for Westerners to finally come to understand and value the philosophy and vision of native American cultures, to the mutual benefit of both civilized and primal man.

In the Foreword, I discuss the close similarity between Highwater's American Indian perspective and the African cultural outlook, as described by Rev. John V. Taylor in the similarily titled, *The Primal Vision*,[198] a leading publication on African Christianity in which the author suggests that the Christian mission should learn from indigenous African culture, essentially the same message Highwater advocates in *The Primal Mind* about the potential contribution of the American Indian culture to the modern, Western worldview.

---

198. Rev. John V. Taylor, *The Primal Vision, Christian Presense African Religion,* Hassell Street Press, 2021 - first published by SCM (Student Christian Movement) Press, 1963.

'Armaments and Development'

A study prepared for the International Development
Research Center, Ottawa, Canada, 1984

This report was the outcome of the first assignment I received after resigning my position in government, in 1983, after turning down the assignment as Ambassador to Ethiopia.

'Internally Displaced Persons'

Reports of the Representative of the Secretary-General,
submitted to the Commission on Human Rights annually
and to the General Assembly biennially between 1993-2004

This, and the five reports that follow, were prepared and presented to the Commission on Human Rights and General Assembly in fulfillment of my mandate on internal displacement.

1. 'Internally Displaced Persons'

A Report of the Representative of the Secretary-General. Addenda: Profiles in Displacement mission reports on the over 30 countries visited in fulfillment of the mandate of the UN RSG on IDPs 1992-2004.

2. 'Human Rights, Mass Exoduses and Displaced Persons'

A Report of the Representative of the Secretary-General. Addendum: Guiding Principles on Internal Displacement, submitted pursuant to the Commission on Human Rights resolution 1997/39, E/CN.4/1998/Add.2. February 1998.

3. 'Human Rights, Mass Exoduses and Displaced Persons'

A Report of the Representative of the Secretary-General. Addendum: Compilation and Analysis of Legal Norms, Part II: Legal Aspects Relating to the Protection against Arbitrary Displacement, submitted to the Commission on Human Rights resolution 1997/93, E/CN.4/1998/53/Add.1. February 1998.

4. 'Human Rights, Mass Exoduses and Displaced Persons'

A Report of the Representative of the Secretary-General. Addendum: Guiding Principles on Internal Displacement, submitted pursuant to the Commission on Human Rights resolution 1997/39, E/CN.4/1998/Add.2. February 1998.

5. 'Human Rights, Mass Exoduses and Displaced Persons'

A Report of the Representative of the Secretary-General. Addendum: Compilation and Analysis of Legal Norms, Part II: Legal Aspects Relating to the Protection against Arbitrary Displacement, submitted to the Commission on Human Rights resolution 1997/93, E/CN.4/1998/53/Add.1. February 1998.

'Frontiers of Sovereignty: A Framework of Protection, Assistance, and Development for the Internally Displaced'

Leiden Journal of International Law, vol. 8, no. 2, 1995

This paper also makes the case for international action when states fail to provide protection and assistance for their people.

'The International Protection of the Internally Displaced'

The International Journal of Refugee Law, vol. 7, Oxford University, 1995

The paper makes the same case as the previous paper calling for international action in response to state failure to provide the needed protection.

'Dealing with the Displaced: A Challenge to the International Community'

Global Governance, vol. 1, no. 1, Winter 1995

The same as above.

'Blood Brothers: An African Reflects on Race and Ethnicity'

The Brookings Review, vol. 13, no. 3, Summer 1995

In this paper, I began to apply the lessons from the Sudan concerning the discrepancy between the myths of racial self-perception, which often artificially exaggerated the differences, and the commonality of shared elements of identity. The case of the Sudan between the self-perception of the North as Arab, which sharply distinguished them from the African South, despite visible evidence of shared African elements is an obvious example. In Burundi and Rwanda, I was told that the margin of error in distinguishing a Tutsi from a Hutu was 30 percent. In the United States, where the African-Americans are often a mixture of black and white, but where people are categorized into black or white despite the obvious mix, is a distortion of reality. Quite apart from being a distortion, it denies the mixed race parental dualism of procreation and heredity. It turns what should be an enrichment into an impoverishment.

'State Collapse:

The Humanitarian Challenge to the United Nations'

In *Collapsed States: The Disintegration and Restoration of Legitimate Authority*, by I. William Zartman, (ed), Boulder, Colorado: Lynne Rienner Publishers, 1995.

This chapter discusses the compelling issue of the collapse of the state which results in a vacuum of protection and assistance for the needy victims of conflict generated humanitarian crisis. The complex set of issues that arise from this situation has three interrelated dimensions: understanding the root causes of the problem, designing appropriate strategies of responding to the immediate needs of the victims, and formulating longer-term measures for addressing the problem at its roots to develop and ensure sustainable solutions. Partnership in responding to the situation should also include phased actions by the state immediately concerned, subregional and regional organizations, and ultimately the United Nations and other pivotal international actors. This partnership should approach national sovereignty as a normative concept that places the primary responsibility for protecting and assisting needy citizens on the state, with international support as needed, and a more robust international intervention when a state manifestly fails to meet its national responsibility, even with international assistance.

'Reconciling Sovereignty with Responsibility: A Basis for International Humanitarian Action'

This is an earlier version of what we eventually developed in the chapter titled Sovereignty as Responsibility: A Basis for International Humanitarian Action, in *Africa in World Politics*.[199]

'Advocate for the Uprooted'

Interview, (Refugees), United Nations High
Commissioner for Refugees, no. 103, I, 1996

The interview was an opportunity to discuss my mandate on internal displacement and the approach I had adopted in engaging with governments and international humanitarian and human rights agencies on behalf of the internally displaced.

---

199. John Harbeson and Donald Rothschild, (eds), Africa in World Politics Boulder, Colorado: Westview, 1995

'Sovereignty and Humanitarian Responsibility: A Challenge for NGOs in Africa and the Sudan'

In *Vigilance and Vengeance,* by Robert I. Rotberg, (ed),

The World Peace Foundation, Brookings Institute, 1996

This paper addresses the dilemma of assuming that populations are protected by their own governments, which is often not the case, and therefore the need for international humanitarian intervention. It also argues for the limits of state sovereignty and the need for external action when states do fail to protect their populations.

'Curative Prevention: Breaking the Cycle of Displacement'

In *Preventive Diplomacy,* by Kevin M. Cahill, (ed),

New York: Basic Books, 1996

Using a medical metaphor, this paper tries to diagnose the causes of internal displacement in order to both provide preventive measures and design appropriate curative response.

'Exodus within Borders'

Co-authored with Roberta Cohen, Foreign Affairs,

Volume 77, Number 4, July/August 1998, pp. 12-16

This co-authored paper is a standard discussion of the crisis of internal displacement and the need for international protection.

'Displacement Studies and the Role of Universities'

Lecture to a Conference of German Academic Exchange

Service, University of Kassel, Germany, 2002

In this paper, my usual theme of the need for international action to fill the vacuum of national failure to provide protection for the internally displaced, put in the context of the research and educational function of universities.

'Beyond Cultural Domination: Institutionalizing in the African State,' in Beyond State Crisis: Postcolonial Africa and Post-Soviet Eurasia in Comparative Perspective

By Mark R. Beissinger and Crawford Young, Washington, D.C.

Woodrow Wilson Center Press, 2002, pp. 359-384

My paper focused on the generic issue of identity in the context of the wars in the Sudan and the quest for a New Sudan normative framework.

'Internal Displacement: A Challenge of Peace, Security and Emergency Relief Operations in Nation-building,'

In Emergency Relief Operations, By Kevin M. Cahill

A joint publication of Fordham University Press

and The Center for International Health and Cooperation,

New York, N.Y, 2003

This again is a replica to the central theme of my approach to the global crisis of national displacement.

'The Plight of Internally Displaced Persons: A Challenge to the International Community'

UN High Level Panel on Threats, Challenges and Changes, March, 2004 [200]

The theme of this paper is identical to that embodied in the numerous writings on the subject. It covers basic information on numbers, areas of displacement around the world, causes of displacement and the needs of the displaced.

'Trapped Within Borders: The Plight of Internally Displaced Persons'

In *Human Security for All: A Tribute to Sergio Vieira de Mello,*

By Kevin M. Cahill, (ed), Fordham University Press 2004

This book was the outcome of a conference in honor of Sergio Vieira de Mello, who was brutally killed in Baghdad, where he was Special Representative of the US Secretary-General, assisting in the reconstruction of the war shattered state. I had known Sergio when he was Deputy High Commissioner for Refugees, then as High Commissioner for Human Rights, and in his new position in East Timor, where he was establishing the foundations of a post conflict independent state. Although my article was on the plight of the internally displaced, I opened with a personal reflection in tribute to Sergio.

In my opening paragraphs, I wrote: "Since the conference from which this conference emanated was a tribute to Sergio Vieira de Mello, I would like to begin with the news from Baghdad on 19

200. Published on the Brookings website in April, 2004: https://www.brookings.edu/articles/the-plight-of-the-internally-displaced-a-challenge-to-the-international-community/

August 2004. Once the tragedy was announced, and, especially when Sergio's name was mentioned by CNN, I remained glued to the television, following the developments by the minute. The world waited with a mix of anxiety and hope, but then the tragedy hit–he was gone. Although we know that sooner or later we will all follow the same destiny, when death comes so prematurely and at a time when one is so desperately needed in this world, such news is simply devastating." I then proceeded to give my personal tribute of the person I knew:

> "It is extremely rare to find an individual who achieved the level of excellence in virtually all aspects of his work as Sergio did. He was outstanding intellectually, charismatic, witty, charming, diplomatic but forthright, courageous, and firm. His service to humanity through the United Nations, which took him to troubled spots around the world - Sudan, Cyprus, Mozambique, Peru, Lebanon, Cambodia, Bosnia, Rwanda, Congo, Kosovo, East Timor, and tragically Iraq - attest to his dedication to the ideals of this world organization, the UN's search for peace, security, and the dignity of the human family."

I concluded my remarks with these personal words:

> "I got to know Sergio in connection with our mutual interest in the UN's work on behalf of the internally displaced of the world, the topic on which I now want to focus."

'The Challenge of State Failure and Internal Displacement'
The Center for Conflict Resolution,
Cape Town University, South Africa, 2006[201]

Internal displacement represents the real challenge to national sovereignty. It is internal which means that it falls under national sovereignty. But internal displacement typically reflects a crisis of identity which acutely divides the country with the internally displaced falling in the category of the enemy and far from being protected are often persecuted. The challenge of my mandate as Representative of the Secretary General was to develop normative and institutional arrangements for protecting and assisting the internally displaced population through cooperation between the U.N. and the governments concerned.

'Divided Nations: The Paradox of National Protection'
Presented at 2006 Syracuse University Conference on
"Legal Evolution: Toward a World Rule of Law"[202]

This is a statement of the thesis I pursued in my numerous writings on the crisis of national identity and the vacuum of responsibility that necessitates international action. This calls for engaging the governments on the assertion of sovereignty as a barricade which I believe is best done by stipulating sovereignty as responsibility.

---

201. Policy brief for a paper presented to a meeting organized by the African Center for Conflict Resolution.

202. Published by The Annals of the American Academy of Political Science, 2006.

'Divided Nations, The Paradox of National Responsibility'

In *The United Nations Organisation: What Future?*

Volume 19, Macalester International, Summer, 2007

Macalester was one of the Universities that awarded me an honorary doctorate. This paper was a contribution to their study of the United Nations. The central theme of the book was that the United Nations was an essential organization that needs reform, but is indispensable. My paper made the argument that the United Nations is paradoxically an organization of most divided nations in which the dispossessed need international involvement to provide remedial protection and assistance. But states are generally predisposed to resist such involvement as a violation of national sovereignty. This is why recasting sovereignty as responsibility for the state is required to protect its population and if necessary call for assistance from the international community. But if a state fails to provide the needed protection or refrains from requesting international support, the responsibility to intervene must then fall on the international community under the rubric of the United Nation.

Foreword to *'Compilation of Risk Factors*

and Legal Norms for the Prevention of Genocide'

The Jacob Blaustein Institute, 2011

Genocide is one of the most heinous crimes known to humankind. Although humanity is expected to unite to prevent, stop, and punish it, allegations of genocide evoke emotionalism and denial from both the alleged perpetrators and those who would be called upon to intervene to stop it. This is why genocide is generally recognized after the fact, when the perpetrators are gone or defeated and the determination of the crime becomes a judgment of the victor over the vanquished. Early prevention, before the crisis escalates to genocidal levels and denial sets in, becomes the most constructive way to go.

The Jacob Blaustein Institute for the Advancement of Human Rights, by preparing the *Compilation of Risk Factors and Legal Norms for the Prevention of Genocide*,[203] has provided us with a guiding tool for engaging governments in fulfilling their international obligations to prevent and punish the crime of genocide. The risk factors, clustered under systematic discrimination and life integrity violations, combined with a list of special circumstances that can encourage genocidal behavior, identify essential elements for constructively managing diversity. In many respects, they complement the Framework of Analysis which my office has developed for assessing the risk of genocide in a given situation. What is critically important to bear in mind is that every state, whether acting alone or with the support of the international community, is obligated to endeavor to prevent the commission of genocide. While this is a formidable challenge, states can respond effectively to the threat of genocide by taking timely preventive action and, if necessary, calling on the international community to assist. Situations leading to genocide are often predictable and can even take years to develop, which provides sufficient opportunity for preventive measures.

In order to facilitate constructive dialogue with governments and other key stakeholders, my office is striving to demystify genocide from being viewed as too sensitive an issue for comfortable discussion, to one that can be prevented or halted by being better understood as an extreme form of identity-related conflicts. These conflicts do not

---

203. *Compilation of Risk Factors and Legal Norms for the Prevention of Genocide,* The Jacob Blaustein Institute for the Advancement of Human Rights, in cooperation with the Office of the Special Advisor on the Prevention of Genocide, United Nations, 2011.

emanate from mere differences, but from gross inequalities generally reflected in egregious human rights violations: discrimination, marginalization, exclusion, dehumanization, denial of fundamental rights, and persecution.

In virtually all genocidal situations, society is acutely divided on the bases of such factors as those identified in the 1948 Convention on the Prevention and Punishment of the Crime of Genocide—nationality, race, ethnicity, and religion. The dichotomy is between in-groups, who enjoy the rights and dignity of citizenship, and out-groups, who are excluded from enjoying fundamental rights and freedoms. When these out-groups seek international protection, a narrow, negative concept of sovereignty is invoked as a barricade against international involvement. The ultimate outcome may be a nation in violent confrontation with itself. It is often the out-group's desperate reaction to gross inequalities and the counter-reaction by the dominant group, that may provoke insurgencies and genocidal counter-insurgencies. Structural prevention therefore requires constructive management of diversity to promote equitable distribution of power and resources and to ensure respect for all human rights. Prevention also calls for stipulating sovereignty as a positive concept of state responsibility, with international accountability.

Identity conflicts need not entail violent confrontation between opposing groups. Genocide can occur in times of war or in situations of relative peace. Even without a violent reaction to conditions of gross inequality and indignity, a particular group can be labeled as posing an imagined existential threat of one kind or another and be targeted for genocidal persecution or otherwise subjugated. That was indeed the case with the Jews in Germany, the Armenians in Turkey, minorities in Cambodia, the Muslims in Bosnia, and the Tutsis in Rwanda.

Since problems of diversity and disparity are global, the potential for genocidal conflicts is equally global, although some regions are more vulnerable than others. Furthermore, not all countries perform equally well in their management of diversity; some manage well, others not so well, while others fail dismally. This is why it is important to conduct case studies to identify best practices that can be emulated and worst practices to be avoided.

Where there is cause for concern, my office conducts an in-depth assessment of the situation, using a Framework of Analysis, focusing attention on eight factors that cumulatively increase the risk of genocidal violence. These are:

i.   Intergroup relations and record of discrimination;
ii. Circumstances that affect the capacity to prevent genocide;
iii. Presence of illegal arms and armed elements;
iv. Motivation and acts that encourage divisions between groups;
v.   Circumstances that facilitate the perpetration of genocide;
vi. Acts that could be elements of genocide;
vii. Evidence of "intent to destroy in whole or in part";
viii.Triggering factors.

The Framework is envisaged as a tool by which states can look at themselves in the mirror, assess their own performance, identify areas in which they are doing well, where they need to improve their performance, and what preventive measures are needed.

The Genocide Convention clearly establishes the obligation incumbent on States parties "to prevent" genocide; however, while the treaty stipulates this obligation, it does not elaborate further on its scope. This ambiguity has given rise to one of the most significant challenges my office faces in fulfilling its mandate—identifying a universally acceptable threshold for the existence of the risk of genocide.

In 2008, I urged the Jacob Blaustein Institute (JBI) to create this compilation, drawing on normative sources, including the 1948 Convention on Genocide, international human rights and humanitarian law, the Statute of the International Criminal Court, and the jurisprudence of international courts, tribunals, and bodies. I then participated in meetings with experts, scholars, and specialists who advised and consulted with JBI on the text of the compilation. It was my view that the JBI compilation, once completed, would "encourage States to fulfill their genocide prevention obligations." The compilation is an invaluable contribution to my office's efforts to address the legal ambiguities in the Genocide Convention. It undertakes the first effort to identify "risk factors" and "areas of concern" that may lead to genocide based on normative legal sources. The compilation demonstrates that there are a host of legal norms, such as those establishing protected rights and the principle of non-discrimination, dispersed throughout different instruments—national, regional, and international—that are relevant to the prevention of genocide.

JBI's compilation complements and reinforces our Analysis Framework. It aims to promote consistency in the approach to genocide prevention adopted by my office, the international community, states, and other stakeholders, while, at the same time, reflecting the diverse manifestations of genocidal situations. The JBI compilation and my office's Analysis Framework together, should serve as complementary tools to better enable stakeholders to identify problem areas needing attention and to take the remedial measures to prevent the escalation of situations to genocidal levels. The normative base provided by the compilation can provide a foundation to the development of monitoring and genocide prevention efforts by states and the special adviser and of advocacy initiatives by nongovernmental organizations. The norms identified in the compilation make it clear that circumstances giving rise to a risk of genocide—and thus to a need for genocide prevention efforts—can occur, like genocide itself, in times of relative peace as well as in times of conflict. Throughout history, genocide has occurred in societies in which different national, racial, ethnic or religious groups became involved in conflicts related to their identities. However, those genocidal conflicts were often preceded by serious systematic discriminatory practices and other human rights violations against targeted groups. It is these practices and violations, among others, that the compilation identifies in such copious detail.

The compilation does not suggest that every human rights abuse per se should be interpreted as giving rise to a risk of genocide; on the contrary, the compilation clearly states that the "risk factors" it identifies are triggered by severe and systematic abuses of human rights, rather than being isolated incidents of abuse. It thereby incorporates the high threshold inherent in the definition of the crime of genocide—which the International Court of Justice has found must be established by proof "at a high level of certainty appropriate to the seriousness of the allegation"—into the process of identifying situations in which a risk of genocide is present. Nevertheless, prevention requires protecting all human rights for all groups at all times without discrimination on any grounds.

The choices members of the international community make regarding how and when to respond to prevent genocide should be based on a strong commitment to upholding fundamental values and to protecting human lives and groups; these choices also will determine whether we uphold the promises of "never again" that we have repeatedly made to victims of past genocides.

I give my wholehearted endorsement to the JBI's compilation and look forward to my office and other stakeholders continuing efforts to develop and expand upon strategies for the prevention of genocide.

Foreword to '*Genocidal Nightmares:*

Narratives of Insecurity and the Logic of Mass Atrocities'

By Abdelwahab El-Affendi, (ed), Bloomsbury, 2015

From a wide variety of interdisciplinary perspectives, this book addresses one of the most daunting challenges for humanity — genocide and mass atrocities. The book poses dilemmas that rotate around the philosophical narratives about hate and evil, and their manifestations in genocidal violence and mass atrocities. These are more than 'nightmares,' for people wake up from nightmares with a sigh of relief, while the calamitous consequences of responding to exaggerated and sometimes misconceived nightmarish fears are tragically real.

The normative and moral dilemmas which the book successfully exposes center on the role of the individual culprit, the communal violence that propels killings to the level of mass atrocities, the contextual dynamics that trigger the frenzy of mass murder, and the luring culture that nurture a deeper propensity toward the elimination of 'them' that presumptively threaten 'us.' These dynamics are enormously complex and do not lend themselves to easy summation in the limited space of a Foreword. Whether emphasis is placed on 'evil' personalities, their 'evil' deeds, mass obedience to the dictates of deranged authoritarian leaders, or the devastating incitement of hostile environments, the moral dilemma in the perception of the perpetrators categorically dichotomized between their risk of being eliminated by a perceived enemy and waging a pre-emotive attack aimed at eliminating that supposedly threatening enemy. From the perspective of the victims, to try to explain the source of the threat to address the root causes would be tantamount to condoning the atrocity or dulling the moral outrage, even implying that 'all of us are potential perpetrators of evil' under similar circumstances. On the other hand, countering the perceived threat in kind logically means that "responding to genocide must then be genocide,"[204] as El-Affendi graphically puts it.

The book highlights another dilemma in the choice between the threat of punishment as deterrence and pre-emotively removing the source of fear that provokes the resort to genocide. This, of course, echoes the unresolvable question of whether capital punishment is a deterrence to murder. I would, however, tend to agree with El-Affendi that it is unlikely for those set on a course of committing mass murder to stop and reflect on any punishment they might incur for their criminal acts. On the other hand, if expectation can be credibly be established that individual leaders who plan, incite and direct genocide and other atrocity crimes will sooner or later be held accountable, that could conceivably deter prospective culprits from committing those crimes. Nevertheless, I would contend that the indictment of incumbent leaders in conflict situations who are still needed to play a role in resolving atrocious conflicts poses a genuine moral dilemma.

Notwithstanding this moral dilemma, the book makes a plausible case for prioritizing upstream prevention. This in turn requires a proper diagnosis of the problem and developing appropriate strategies for addressing the root causes of genocide and mass atrocities. While I agree with the authors that 'fear' is a central factor in the root causes, my own focus is on the implications of identity conflicts that degenerate into genocidal violence, with fear, of course, as a major contributing factor. The core of identity conflicts does not emanate from mere differences, but from the manner in which those differences are mismanaged to stratify people into the in-groups who enjoy the

---

204. Abdelwahab El-Affendi, (ed), *Genocidal Nightmares: Narratives of Insecurity and the Logic of Mass Atrocities,* Bloomsbury, 2015, p.xi.

rights of belonging into the dominant group, and the out-groups who are marginalized, discriminated, denigrated and denied the dignity of equality. When they react against these gross inequalities, sometimes through violent protest, the dominant group reacts with a vengeance that could become genocidal. The obvious remedy is constructive management of identity to create an identity framework of inclusivity, equality, and shared dignity of belonging on equal footing.

Review of 'When Political Transitions Work: Reconciliation as Interdependence'

By Fanie du Toit, Oxford University Press, 2018

When Political Transitions Work: Reconciliation as Interdependence, by Dr Fanie du Toit,[205] is an innovative, stimulating, and provocative study which provides much material for thought and imagination. As the argument goes, the first step in reconciliation is for the parties to recognise that peaceful coexistence, mutual recognition and respect, and pragmatic nonviolent cooperation in a process aimed an incrementally reforming the future is the way out of the quagmire. The ideal of solving all the major problems dividing them should be pursued as a promise that cannot be given a time frame for accomplishment. Arguably, "reconciliation cannot wait for the day when all differences have been resolved before it can begin or indeed progress. Reconciliation is a process that is based on the commitment of former enemies to work together nonviolently, despite historic differences and the unfinished business of the past on the understanding that issues

---

205. Fanie du Toit, *When Political Transitions Work: Reconciliation as Interdependence,* Oxford University Press, 2018.

will be resolved over time."[206]

The process rests on recognising intrinsic interconnectedness and interdependence. Whereas apartheid, in the words of Archbishop Desmond Tutu, aimed at what he called "unscrambling the racial omelette,"[207] the racial entanglement that cannot be undone, "reconciliation represented a political agenda that, as its point of departure, admitted to the fundamental (unchangeable) and comprehensive (political, economic, social and moral) interdependence of all citizens. Interdependence was acknowledged, not only as a given fact, but as a possible norm for how society ought to organize itself in future, as a promise of justice to come."[208]

De Klerk reaffirmed this framework when he reportedly said, "There is but one way to peace, to justice for all: that is the way of reconciliation, of together seeking mutually acceptable solutions, of together discussing what the future South Africa should look like, of constitutional negotiation with a view to permanent understanding."[209] Paradoxically, it is usually after an intensive, costly and painfully exhausting violence, what has been described as "mutually hurting stalemate, that the warring parties can open up to more constructive compromises."[210]

As du Toit explains, "Arguing that reconciliation is morally or strategically desirable is one thing, but to convince a divided nation that it is actually possible and practically workable – that a new future is around the corner – is quite another." Post-apartheid government and leaders "set out to put reconciliation into practice in a country that

---

206. Ibid, p. 138.
207. Ibid, p. 42.
208. Ibid, p. 33.
209. Ibid.
210. Ibid.

had never before experienced black and white citizens in intentionally reciprocal and mutually beneficial ways."As pressing as building trust was being seen to "directly address the wrongdoings of the past and the lingering resentments these have created. Otherwise, peace is likely to be temporary."[211]

As du Toit convincingly argues, "If a transition is meant to deliver, within a matter of years, the complete erasure and closure of an evil past, then clearly South Africa's transition did not work." He argues, on the other hand, that South Africa's transition did indeed work in that "political violence was replaced by largely nonviolent political contest action; the apartheid state was replaced by a constitutional democracy with institutions that since 1994 have acted at least partially effectively in curving executive impunity…and a vast array of policies and measures have been undertaken to improve the lives of poor South Africans, which has led to the gradual but steady increase in the life expectancy of all South Africans." Although this does not make the case of South Africa simply "a good story to tell," the record "goes a long way to dispel the Afro-pessimism so typical of many 'critical' studies of South Africa."[212]

The reconciliation that ended apartheid now seems to be obviously the right thing to have done, but for decades talking to the apartheid regime was strongly resisted by both Africans and the international, anti-apartheid community. In the early 1970s, as Ambassador to the Scandinavian countries, which were in the forefront of the international, anti-apartheid movement, and later as Minister of State for Foreign Affairs, I persistently spoke out in international fora in favor of talking with the regime, to probe into the rationale for their racist attitude. If the objective of the African National Conference (ANC) was

---

211. Ibid, p. 8.
212. Ibid, p. 9.

to create a non-racial South Africa, how could that be achieved without talking to apartheid leaders? The reaction against my position was nearly always unanimous. My views, stated in an African-American Conference we hosted in Khartoum in 1978, were reported by a South African newspaper, which prompted our Ambassador in Tanzania, which was the leader of the frontline countries, to write a report to the Ministry, on what he defensively described as a "very sensitive development."[213]

I cannot argue that I was right and those against me were wrong. As du Toit explains, perhaps what was needed was the amount of pressure exerted by a combination of internal liberation struggle, international support for the struggle, and sustained international sanctions that crippled the South African economy for the conflict to be 'ripe for resolution.' As du Toit acknowledges: "The fall of the Berlin wall in 1989 marking the end of the Cold War in its peculiar radicalized manifestation in Southern Africa, certainly contributed, as did increasing international isolation and condemnation of the regime, as well as sustained waves of domestic protest, pressure, and sabotage from a mix of civil society and other interest groups as well as underground resistance movements."[214]

Du Toit however argues that a major factor was that South African "leaders of certain ilk" seized that historic opportunity to lead the country to the desired outcomes, noting "the inception of reconciliation depended critically on political leadership of a particular kind that came, for better and worse, …exemplified by Nelson Mandela, and to some degree as well, Frederick Willem de Klerk."[215] According

---

213. Author's own records - internal diplomatic message.

214. Fanie du Toit, *When Political Transitions Work: Reconciliation as Interdependence,* Oxford University Press, 2018, p. 18.

215. Ibid.

to du Toit, "Mandela…was no naïve political push over. It was his keen appreciation for concrete opportunities to further the struggle for justice, alongside his hard-fought convictions, which led him to reconciliation."[216]

Mandela was well aware of the price that had already been paid in lives lost and the ongoing cost of the stalemate in armed struggle. In his own words, "We had the right on our side, but not yet the might. It was clear to me that a military victory was a distant if not impossible dream. It simply did not make sense for both sides to lose thousands if not millions of lives in a conflict that was unnecessary. They must have known this as well. It was time to talk."[217] Du Toit notes that, "Both Mandela and De Klerk recognized the possibility of combining realpolitik with deeply held conviction, and, crucially, they acted on it. Each extended an olive branch to his enemy and won the chance of a better life for the majority of South Africans."[218]

I visited South Africa for the first time when Mandela was still in prison, but intense international efforts to have him released were underway and the momentum for talks was building. Former President of Nigeria, General Olusegun Obasanjo, invited me as a resource person of the Inter-Action Council of Former Heads of State and Government, to accompany him and former Prime Minister of the United Kingdom, Edward Heath. The visit to South Africa was a follow up to the 1986 Mission of the Commonwealth Eminent Persons. I remember Obasanjo telling me, after our meeting with De Klerk and his Cabinet, "They must release Mandela. Only he can save this country."[219] I was impressed by the emphatic tone of

216. Ibid, p. 38.
217. Ibid, p. 22.
218. Ibid, p. 38.
219. Authors' recollection.

Obasanjo's statement. But it has always been my view that putting an almost exclusive faith and hope in Mandela, as the international community was doing, risked an inevitable fall into an abyss, once he was gone. While that has not happened, I believe my concern was realised to a degree.

I was glad to see du Toit 'humanize' Mandela, and 'save' him from being idolized and turned into a mythical character. He portrays him instead as a towering leader of his people, but one who closely collaborated with others to do what he did. I was particularly moved by the passage in which du Toit wrote about the idealization of Mandela: "I am unsure which Mandela is being referred to…the real historical figure, flaws and strengths included, or an idealized, even fictional, figure. Mandela was undoubtedly a giant of his time, but his reputation posthumously seems to have grown even larger, perhaps too much so. He now seems to enjoy a kind of secular beautification that makes it virtually impossible for any contemporary leader to emulate him, far less to improve on his ideas. I believe this would have horrified the real Mandela."[220]

I particularly appreciated the way du Toit argues for a degree of parity between Mandela and De Klerk, although he also makes clear that there was no question of moral equivalence between their respective political agendas. Although their relationship was and continued to be understandably agonising, "a growing sense of their interdependence - the indispensable role of their adversary in realizing the aspirations of their respective struggles - provided a firm platform for cooperation. They were 'in this together.'"[221]

Du Toit concludes, "Apartheid was an egregious crime against

---

220. Fanie du Toit, *When Political Transitions Work: Reconciliation as Interdependence,* Oxford University Press, 2018, p. 7.

221. Ibid, p. 32.

humanity and the struggle against it a justified defensive war for basic human rights. But, it is my position that, although De Klerk remains controversial and in some ways the 'lesser partner' in the reconciliation story, even his staunchest critics today must admit that he too played a key role. Without De Klerk, it is difficult to imagine a nonviolent end to apartheid."[222]

The pursuit of reconciliation by Mandela and De Klerk was by no means a feat of lofty idealism but the exercise of "visionary leadership...It is possible, indeed probable, that reconciliation arose not out of any notion of personal forgiveness but from a pragmatic acknowledgment of the intractability of a military stalemate, and of the power of reconciliation to change things fundamentally."[223] As Mandela reportedly stated, "there are times when a leader must move out ahead of the flock and go off in a new direction, confident that he is leading his people in the right way."[224]

I witnessed, under rather fortuitous circumstances a reflection of Mandela's personal attributes that may help explain the shrewd yet humanistic qualities of leadership he displayed in negotiating with the apartheid regime. It was at an intimate dinner in Cape Town, attended, among others by his wife-to-be, Graca Machel, as well as Lisbeth Palme, the widow of the Swedish Prime Minister, Olof Palme, and the Nigerian Nobel Laureate, Wole Soyinka. People were very critical of African leaders generally, and Mandela argued that he had come to know many good African leaders and that lumping African leaders together as bad was grossly unwarranted. His position was dismissed as a reflection of his well-known goodness and forgiving attitude. I noticed that Mandela was visibly getting restless and impatient. Looking at his

---

222. Ibid, p. 19.
223. Ibid, p. 38.
224. Ibid, p. 22.

watch, indicating that he was about to leave, he made his concluding comment: "Every human being, however bad, by virtue of being a human being, there is some goodness in him. If you want to cooperate with him, look for that goodness and build on it. That is how you can make the best of the situation."[225] With those words, he got up and left. I was in full agreement with him in the discussion, but it was after he left that I strongly spoke out in support of his position.

Laudable as the South African reconciliation is, considering the economic and social disparity that racially divided South Africans, finding a common ground was a nigh impossible undertaking. When I visited South Africa with Obasanjo and Health, I was struck by the differences between Cape Town, one of the most beautiful cities I have seen, and Crossroads, just outside the city, one of the worst slumps I have ever seen anywhere in the world. In sharp contrast to my chronic optimism, I concluded that reconciliation could not be possible. No amount of investment to lift up black South Africans would be enough to bridge the gap with the whites. Furthermore, any amount of resources taken from the whites to uplift the blacks would be too much for them to accept. I am glad that my pessimistic prediction was wrong and that reconciliation was achieved.

I was impressed by du Toit's account of Mandela's background, born and raised as he was in a cohesive society, regulated by the principles of *Ubuntu*, a concept which embodies the social norms of unity, harmony and respect for human dignity. *Ubuntu* stipulates a framework of shared humanity in which the interest of the individual are in harmony with those of the community. According to du Toit, *Ubuntu* "is a cultural ideal which affirms that people become fully human only through their interactions with other with other people."[226] According

---

225. Authors' recollection.

226. Fanie du Toit, *When Political Transitions Work: Reconciliation as Interdependence,* Oxford University Press, 2018, p. 53.

to the norms of *Ubuntu,* "disregarding the human dignity of others fatally wounds one's own humanity." Archbishop Desmond Tutu calls *Ubuntu* the "the very essence of being human" and "Africa's gift to the world."[227] *Ubuntu* has been credited as the African moral foundation of reconciliation based on interdependence that led to the eradication of the apartheid system in South Africa.

Viewed from a different vantage point, it was arguably the denial of the values and the dignity associated with *Ubuntu* that propelled Mandela from a free happy childhood in the countryside to an angry and eventually determined freedom fighter. According to du Toit, "Mandela attributed his driving force towards the horizon – his quest to be free – to his experiences as a Xhosa child growing up in the deeply rural, peaceful hills of Eastern Cape of South Africa. As a boy there, herding cattle across the rolling fields of Transkei, he wrote of feeling free in every way – free to swim in the streams that criss-crossed the local village, to roast mealies (corn) under the stars, and to ride the oxen he guided along the narrow footpaths."[228]

As du Toit observed, "Mandela seemed to be able to adopt ever-widening allegiances and causes, yet it is equally clear that he never renounced the traditional loyalties and deeply held beliefs that first promoted him to join the liberation struggle…By not abandoning his identity as a Xhosa and an African, and by valuing the universal dimensions reflected in his local identity, he was able to demonstrate how the universal should be anchored in, and justified in terms of, the local and the particular. In other words, it is possible to conclude that his embrace of the fight for the rights of all South Africans while drawing on his particular identity and heritage to do so, played some

---

227. Ibid, p. 195.
228. Ibid, pp. 20-21.

role in his decision to pursue reconciliation as political strategy."[229]

Du Toit goes on to explain that it was indeed the contrast between the identity and dignity Mandela enjoyed in his local background and the indignities of discrimination under apartheid that provoked him to rebel: "When he moved to Johannesburg as a young lawyer some years later, Mandela discovered that his boyhood freedom had in fact been limited to those idyllic childhood days, and that the freedom to be a professional adult simply did not exist for him as he set out to start a career in law. That began his fight for basic individual rights… In time, after he experienced first-hand, the incalcitrance and racism of the regime, he joined the ANC and eventually turned freedom fighter, beginning a new clandestine life in pursuit of rights for his people."[230]

Did the peace and reconciliation Mandela negotiated achieve for his people what he had struggled for on their behalf? The obvious answer is 'Yes, but.' Since the end of apartheid, I have been to South Africa on numerous occasions and have witnessed conflicting perspectives on what has been achieved. Chatting with taxi drivers, as I generally tend to do, I got two contrasting views that reflected both dissatisfaction with the reconciliation for not having adequately addressed the grievances of black South Africans and acceptance of the incremental approach to peace and its incremental benefits. One driver posed a rhetorical question to me: "Is this what we have been struggling for, only to have some black faces in the government, while we remain in poverty and the whites still control the wealth of our country?"Another taxi driver presented an opposite view: "We know the whites still control the economy, but we also know that it will eventually accrue to us. We will wait patiently; we do not want to rock the boat."[231]

---

229. Ibid, pp. 11-12.

230. Ibid, p. 21.

231. Personal recollections.

Accommodating conflicting positions that are seemingly irreconcilable, but can and must be made compatible and reconcilable, without being oblivious to their inherent incompatibility, reminds me of my differences with a colleague who is a leading figure in conflict resolution. He argued that conflict is inherent in human relations and that it is futile to try to prevent or resolve it; the most that can be done is to manage it. My position was that the normal state of human interaction, if the moral code of conduct stipulated by the social order is observed, is one of peaceful and cooperative relationship. Conflict, especially if violent, is a breakdown of the normal state of affairs; the aim of conflict resolution is therefore to restore the normal state of peaceful and harmonious relations.

I agree with the social restorationist paradigm as described by du Toit that "Human society is not... an arena of danger and violent competition, but rather... a delicate web of cooperation, through which sufficient levels of trust exist, or can be generated."[232] According to this framework, "war is... what happens when things go fundamentally wrong in the community of human relations. Unlike liberalism, where violence is often seen as an inevitable, violence is understood as a disastrous denial of how the world does and should work."[233] Peace and reconciliation should aim at restoring of the disturbed order.

Two eminent Africans, Wole Soyinka, and Professor Mahmoud Mamdani have criticized South Africa's reconciliation for falling far short of addressing the economic and social injustices of the apartheid regime. Soyinka, referring to the Truth and Reconciliation Commission, asked the question, of whether the "truth shall set you free" and offered an answer, "maybe... but first, the truth must be set

232. Fanie du Toit, *When Political Transitions Work: Reconciliation as Interdependence,* Oxford University Press, 2018, p. 134.
233. Ibid, p. 135.

free." According to him, and quoted by du Toit, "Where there has been inequity, especially of a singularly brutalizing kind... that robs one side of its most fundamental attribute - it's humanity - it seems only appropriate that some form of atonement be made, in order to exorcise that past...reparations, we repeat, serve as a cogent critique of history and thus a potent restraint on it repetition."[234] He went on to pose a rhetorical question, "What really would be preposterous or ethically inadmissible in imposing a general levy on South Africa's white population?"[235]

Du Toit seems to concur: "There can be little disagreement that reparations as a whole have fallen well short of expectations. Importantly though, this failure cannot fully be laid at TRC door in terms of either the design or implementation of its mandate. Arguably, it is more about a lack of political will and institutional capacity, as well as about competing priorities in government, than about the work of TRC as such."[236] Reportedly, the recommendations of the TRC included proposals for wide-ranging institutional reforms, especially with respect to the role of big business that had supported and benefitted from apartheid. These included a call for the establishment of a Business Reconciliation Fund and the imposition of a wealth tax, "a once-off levy on corporate and private income, a once-off donation of 1 per cent the market capitalization of each company listed on the Johannesburg Stock Exchange, as well as a retrospective surcharge of corporate benefits and of all golden handshakes given to senior public servants since 1990." Such funds "could provide non-repayable grants, loans, and/or guarantees to business-related funding for black small entrepreneurs in need of either ...skills or capital for the

234. Ibid, p. 91.
235. Ibid, p. 91
236. Ibid, pp. 104-105.

launching of a business." The rationale was that business had at least a "moral obligation to assist in the reconstruction and development of post-apartheid South Africa through active reparative measures."[237]

Mahmoud Mamdani characterized the South African peace accord as "reconciliation without justice." While acknowledging South Africa's reconciliation as commendable, he argues, and quoted by du Toit, that "the transition failed to transform power relations between white and black citizens beyond the limits of the political elites...Victims and perpetrators continue to live together in a context in which perpetrators still wield considerable power...This makes the transformation of historical power relations even more important."[238]

Accountability for the crimes committed under apartheid is an issue which du Toit addresses in depth but remains seemingly unresolved because the government allegedly did not implement the recommendations of the Truth and Reconciliation Commission. It is the subject of ongoing debate between the advocates of peace and those for justice. This has often been perceived as a conflict between the African approach, which is more oriented toward forgiveness and reconciliation, and the European approach, which leans more toward punitive justice.

I have always argued that South Africa aimed at bridging the two positions. According to du Toit, "The TRC Act eventually settled on a form of amnesty that depended on the condition that applicants made full disclosure, established political motive, and demonstrated proportionality of the crime to the stated political objective. The conditionality of the South African amnesty provisions meant that no blanket amnesties were granted."[239]

---

237. Ibid, p. 105
238. Ibid, p. 92.
239. Ibid, p. 69.

Du Toit's thorough analysis of the different theoretical schools of thought on the central themes of reconciliation portrays the complexities of each school focusing on a piece of the puzzle. Clearly each piece alone cannot stand the scrutiny of the cross-cultural world in which we live. As du Toit argues, "It is therefore important, even as differences and contestations are acknowledged, not to give up on pursuing theoretical clarity that at least attempt (sic) to account for what can be expected, offered, and hoped for when societies seek to reconcile."[240]

I would like to end this review with the dilemmas with which I began. The dilemma presents two options. One is to end the violent manifestations of conflict and agree to reconcile, coexist and cooperate in a process that provides some remedies, without full redress of the causes of the conflict. The other is to continue the violent struggle for change until the major grievances generating the conflict are address. In the case of South Africa, the conflict had already gone on for so long and the damage done was so great that the choice was arguably not as difficult as it might sound. While the case of apartheid was admittedly extreme, what happened therefore is what eventually happens in protected conflict situations.

Perhaps the real question is whether this policy framework for managing conflicts can be applied to early phases of conflicts to save lives and end the suffering of masses of the population. Although the objective of full redress is the normal demand of liberation struggles, most violent conflicts eventually get resolved on the bases of principles that were quite apparent from the start. This means that the suffering and the loss of lives are really unnecessary and morally unwarranted. Nearly always, these conflicts end with compromises that are not far

---

240. Ibid, p. 124.

from the framework analysed by this book. What might be required is aiming at the best compromises that can gain optimum acceptance and support from both sides. How such an equation can be developed and how the parties who at early stages of the conflict can be persuaded to mutually agree to this more constructive, though not perfect, alternative, is the daunting challenge. Given the element of pride and the need for face-saving in such situations, third party mediation is critically needed to break the deadlock. This book is a must-read and the innovative strategic approach it implicitly proposes must be taken seriously.

Foreword to *'Collaboration with I. William Zartman: A Partnership of Ideas'*

In *I. William Zartman: Pioneer in Conflict*
Management and Area Studies, Springer, 2019

This Foreword discusses the elements of William Zartman's vast volume of scholarly and professional work, and our close collaborations in establishing the African Studies Program at The Brookings Institution and the co-authorship of several publications in the program, as well as my contributing chapters to his edited volumes.

Part Three:
Anatomy of the Context

---◆---

Conceptual Framework

The classification of my works under the four participational levels: local, national, regional and global implies the significance of family and cultural background. The normative principles that inspired and guided me in my research and professional work are closely connected to that foundation. In reviewing my writings about subjects contextualized under levels: local, national, regional and global, a number of key concepts and their substantive connotations kept recurring to my attention. They include identity, dignity, diversity and equality. These are essential elements of culture and related values. Identity is inherent in the very being of an individual. Dignity is a function of self-worth and moral standing in society. Diversity is the outcome of interaction with others outside one's original groups. Equality is a function of respect for the identity and dignity of all human beings as individuals and communities through constructive management of diversity.

The significance of these concepts varied according to the context and the level of my engagement. Identity and an innate sense of dignity became factors of my consciousness at an early age and rooted in culture as an aspect of that consciousness. And although not always made explicit, values were inherent in the culture. Early in childhood, some members of my family and I began to move away from home up the educational ladder. Diversity emerged in connecting with members of other communities within South Sudan. And with expanding diversity arose perceptions of inequality, discrimination and the need for constructive management of diversity to promote inclusivity and equality in tune with respect for the interactive identities and related sense of dignity.

The expansion of context and the multiplicity of identities generating diversity within a shared space continued to rise with the educational ladder to Northern Sudanese institutions of learning up to the university level that opened doors to regional and global perspectives. Post graduate studies abroad ironically sharpened greater awareness of my local, national and African regional dimension and brought the global perspective in full view. Throughout this transition, I remained simultaneously connected to all levels academically, intellectually and professionally. And every phase sharpened my awareness of my identity with its flexible and yet continuous dimensions, the sense of dignity associated with that changing and yet continuous identity, and the demand for recognition, respect and equality in the context of ever expanding diversity.

A Legacy of Leadership and Responsibility

The context into which I was born, a border area between the African South and the Arab North of what was then the Republic of the

Sudan, provided a unique background that would be the pivot of my life. My people, the Ngok Dinka of Abyei, occupy an anomalous position as Southerners who, for security reasons, were annexed to the North in 1905 to be administered in Kordofan Province. The area, being ideally suited for both agriculture and cattle herding, was, and remains, a seasonal meeting-point between the pastoral tribes of both the North and the South, who converge in search of pastures and water. Abyei became, and continues to be, a racial and cultural cross-roads and a microcosm of the Afro-Arab Sudan. Generations of traditional leaders in this strategic area have been pivotal in shaping and sustaining this bridging role.

I was born and raised in a family of a long line of Paramount Chiefs on my father's side and a mother's kin group that was renowned for spiritual leadership and wisdom. I was made aware of the significance of being the son of the Chief and the attributes considered inherent in that position. I was also close to maternal relatives whose leadership virtues were also widely acknowledged. What was envisaged in leadership was not so much the honor of the status, but service to the people.

My sentiments about leadership had a personal aspect that went back to the marriage of my parents, the goals associated with Mother's conception with me, and the preordained meaning of my life as a continuation of a long line of leaders on both my paternal and maternal lineages. The Paramount Chieftainship of my paternal line which, according to mythology, went back to the time of creation, had been passed down from father to the first born son of the first wife, in line with the rules of primogeniture. My maternal lineage had also provided leaders for another section of our tribe, who were widely recognized for spiritual powers. My mother's grandfather had been forced to migrate into our paternal section to escape a blood feud and ensure the protection of the Paramount Chief. Successive generations from both lineages had become allies and close leadership associates. The marriage of my parents was intended to affirm these leadership ties and alliances.

The aspirations and dreams of my maternal grandfather and the elders of his family were reflected in their invoking and sacrificing a bull of the color Mading, and praying to God and the Ancestors that my mother beget a son for her first borne to be named Mading after the color of the bull, and to grow up, not only to be a link between the two lineages, but also to provide access to the Paramount Leadership of the Ngok Dinka tribe, even though my mother was fourth in the line of marital seniority. I was supposedly born in answer to those prayers and although this was not made very explicit to me in my early childhood, there is no doubt that I grew up in an environment in which I was made aware of the significance of my life to my family and the tribe at large. This cultivated in me a sense of purpose and a drive toward what I recognized as a destiny that I must endeavor to fulfill. In my desire to live up to what was expected of me, I consciously strove to model myself after my father, whom I recognized from the beginning to be a leader of exceptional qualities.

I grew up very proud of both my paternal and maternal lineages. But ours being a patriarchal society, I was naturally more closely associated with my father's line, specifically my grandfather and my father as models of ideal leadership. From what I heard of my grandfather from childhood days, Kwol was a Chief of great virtues and extraordinary charisma. Most of the views cited here were obtained in tape-recorded interviews for the biography of my father, *The Man Called Deng Majok: A Biography of Power, Polygyny and Change.*[241]

---

241. Francis Mading Deng, *The Man Called Deng Majok: A Biography of Power, Polygyny and Change,* Yale University Press, 1986 – see p. 35.

"Kwol's charisma was due to the word of God behind his leadership," said Monylwak Row, a Ngok Dinka elder.*" He had the authority of God behind him. He was a man created with a cool heart; a man of gentle personality. Kwol was a chief by the authority of God. He succeeded to the Chieftainship which had descended down the lineage of Arob Biong."*

According to the elder Chol Piok,

"Kwol's charisma was such that if he were seen approaching and singing his hymns, even if it were a battle that had lined itself up and ready to rage, it will pull apart and people would leave. The battle would end."

"The way Kwol Arob performed made the whole area happy with him," said Chief Lang Juk of the Twich Dinka. *"He was a good person in every respect. He was a God-fearing man, and he was very generous. He helped any needy person. He loved everybody. He loved the Twich, the Rek, the Ruweng, the Nuer and all the other tribes, even the far away Agar. He was a great leader, heard of all over; he was a great leader."*

K.D.D. Henderson, who, between 1930 and 1936, had served as District Commissioner of Western Kordofan under which Abyei fell at the time, was unequivocal in his admiration of grandfather, Kwol Arob. In a letter dated February 24, 1932, during his first visit to Abyei to inaugurate the opening of the first 'road' to Abyei, he wrote, "The Chief, Kwol Arob, is a most impressive figure, though a bare six-foot six inches and so shorter than most of his people." Some days later, in a letter dated March 3, he added, "There can be no doubt that Kwol is an extraordinarily fine Chief and settles all disputes justly and finally." In his response to the questionnaire for Father's biography, Henderson's admiration of Kwol Arob continued undiminished by the passage of time. He wrote, "I regarded Kwol as a most outstanding ruler."

Much has also been said about my father as a great leader. Ibrahim Mohamed Zein, an Arabized educationalist who knew Father well, invoking the example of the Prophet Mohammed, stated: "God always gives a leader something special and unique to him … And so it was with Deng Majok. God gave him special qualities so that he could fill his unique position. Among his greatest assets for leadership was that he was a man of unusual intellect and wide comprehension of issues... He always achieved whatever objectives he had set for himself. No situation ever confronted him that he was not in full command of. His broad outlook and unique capability placed him in a natural leadership position. He was always able to make delicate and precise calculations in any decision-making situation in time of peace or of war. He always gave great attention to showing hospitality to visitors; gifts must go to visiting dignitaries … He treated problems with wisdom, with full understanding, and he went after anything he wanted to achieve, clarifying his position quite clearly and pursuing it with diligence. These are rare leadership qualities."[242]

In another context, Ibrahim Mohamed Zein said, "For a very long time, I have wondered why social scientists or scholars who write books do not write about the personality of Deng Majok. I think he offered a tremendous opportunity for study. For a man to be able to marry hundreds of wives and be capable of producing hundreds of children, a number of which, if you multiply on the average of even a few children per wife, could approximate a thousand boys and girls — that is extraordinary. And then you add to that the children of his

242. Personal interview.

children. For a man to provide livelihood for such large number of wives, to administer them so efficiently, and to have children who, wherever you find them, are among the best in their conduct, in their dress, and in their general appearance, both boys and girls, never giving any indication that numbers had any negative effect on quality—for a man to do all that was a rare strength. I personally think that Deng Majok was a most extraordinary character."[243]

In an interview in 1980 for the biography of my father, Mohamed Abbas El Faghiri, former governor of Kordofan Province, had this to say: "I came to know the late Deng Majok in 1966 when I was transferred from Upper Nile to Kordafan as Provincial Commissioner (Governor). I had already heard of the pacifying role he had played following the Arab-Dinka conflict, which had resulted from the rumors following the Sunday incidents in Khartoum during the October Government in 1964. As a person, Nazir (Chief) Deng was kind to his people; he had a great sense of humor, patience, and imagination. He was always compromising, but for the better. As a leader, he enjoyed a strong personality, was just, fair, and firm. He could get what he wanted by diplomacy and tact. If he had had education, I am sure he would have emerged as a high-ranking African leader."[244]

Later in the interview, El Faghiri went on to say: "I knew many of the tribal chiefs of the South. With some exceptions, they tended to be instrumental, waiting to carry out instructions, rather than being suggestive. Deng Majok was a man of ideas. He was so paramount that you could hardly apply to him the North-South distinction of measurement. Chief Deng Majok could compete favorably, both in performance as a chief and in his strength of character and dignity, with the best chief in Kordofan or anywhere elsewhere in the Sudan.

---

243. Op cit.
244. Op cit.

In his clean white *jibba* and turban, he looked like a pyramid."[245]

In a private letter to me, a former British administrator, who had served in Kordofan Province wrote, "Few countries can have had such leaders as Ibrahim Moneim Mansour, Babo Nimir, Ahmed Omar, and your father."[246]

Both Grandfather Kwol Arob and Father Deng Majok reflected a remarkable combination of being culturally Arabized in some respects while proudly retaining their Dinka and essential cultural traits. They spoke Arabic, dressed in Arabian robes of white *jallabiya* and turban with *mulfah* across the shoulders and showed lavish entertainment and hospitality in the Northern Sudanese fashion. They were indistinguishable from their Arab counterparts, except for their erect outstanding height and proud Dinka profile. Perhaps because a Dinka Chief is also a spiritual leader, neither Grandfather nor Father converted to Islam, even though they observed certain Islamic norms, such as slaughtering animals according to the Islamic religious requirement, which Father explained was to assure the guests that the meat was *halal* (kosher).

The British offered my Grandfather, and later Father to choose between returning to the South their area of Abyei. This was annexed to the North in 1905 for security reasons to provide the Dinka with more effective protection against Arab slave raiders who were still active in the South. Both chose to remain in Kordofan to play the bridging role between the North and the South which the area had historically played. There is no doubt that the privileged position they enjoyed in the North was also a factor in their decision.

Those are the leaders who in the Dinka world of values, we, their children, are supposed to represent and immortalize in accordance with the Dinka principles of genetic and social continuity, a central pillar in the Dinka value system which I present in the next section.

---

245. Op cit.

246. Personal correspondence.

Part Four:
Framework of Transition and Integration

———————◆———————

The importance of my family background and the value system associated with it is that it provided a normative and behavioral framework that guided my life throughout the various stages of my journey through cultures and at all the levels covered in my writings. In a world in which races, religions, and cultures meet, co-exist, and interact, it is important to understand what each one brings into the process of mutual influence. The saying goes among the Dinka that a nobleman of one tribe is not known by a gentleman of another tribe. And yet, it is my belief that as one moves into a new social context, one strives to gain recognition for a status comparable to that of one's original status.

Since we cannot expect everything from our background to be understood, appreciated, and accepted by people with whom we come in contact, this inevitably requires strategic selectivity that combines adaptability to the new context while retaining the virtues of the original context. Continuous adherence to the principles of the original context in the new context requires both demonstrating the merits of those principles by behaving accordingly and clarifying to others by appropriate means what we consider to be of vital importance, not only to our own sense of identity and dignity but also to our contribution to the new pluralistic context. It is this which justifies the demand for recognition and respect for our identity and culturally oriented behavior from those with whom we relate across the racial and cultural divides.

The process need not be consciously calculated or articulated; it is almost inherent and deeply ingrained in our upbringing, although the degree of realization will differ from one individual to another. Whether consciously or spontaneously, inside the pluralistic context of my country or abroad, the means by which I remain connected to my background wherever I have gone and lived, and the dynamic process through which I have related to both ends of the transition, is what I have called the 'invisible bridge' (as mentioned in Part One).

In his introduction to my book, *Tradition and Modernization*,[247] published in 1971, Professor Harold Lasswell, a psychiatry-legal scholar at Yale University, highlighted the potential 'punishment' by 'an internal policeman' that might result from disregarding the moral code of one's upbringing: "Dr. Deng has brought to the task of examining his own culture an impressive objectivity of outlook that testifies to his success in acquiring the essential characteristic of a scientific frame of reference. The magnitude of this achievement is brought home to us when we consider the fact that the basic norms of a society are rather fully incorporated into the emerging personality system at an early age, and that they are subsequently defended by internal mechanisms and external sanctions. The internal mechanism levy a

---

247. Francis Mading Deng, *Tradition and Modernization: A Challenge for Law among the Dinka of the Sudan,* Yale University Press, 1971 – see p. 15.

punitive toll on the individual at the first flutter of a norm-defying image or feeling. The automatic toll is in the form of acute discomfort (anxiety) or a negative self-sentiment, such as guilt, shame, ineptness, incomprehension, powerlessness, impoverishment, or neglect. The inner policeman continues to operate after the individual has moved from his original social setting and is exposed to novel norms and sanction."[248]

Depending on the intensity and the duration of the journey between cultures, many may not survive unscathed; perhaps only a few do. Even then, the form and quality of their survival may vary from one person to another and only as a matter of degree. Many get bruised, mutilated, and reduced to a level of indignity sharply contrasting with their initial self-perception and social status in the land of their origin. Only a relative few can justifiably claim a net gain from this hazardous journey.

A concept somewhat analogous to that of the 'invisible bridge' is that of the tree. As I have often said in my speeches to my country men and women in foreign lands, a human being is like a tree; a tree with deep roots can sway with the wind, but withstand even a hurricane, while a tree with shallow roots can be uprooted and knocked down even by a light wind. A person's background and cultural values constitute the roots that keep him or her grounded and resilient against the turbulent winds of social change.

If the notion of the 'invisible bridge' which I have presented here sounds too passive, a physical structure on which to tread, then I have failed in describing what I intend to portray. What I have in mind is a dynamic concept, a means, and an end, a linkage comprising form and substance, language and content. The bridge is in effect a process of

---

248. Op cit, p. xi.

fruitful interaction, communication, and mutual influence that is both personal and universal, and, above all, profoundly humanistic.

When I was serving as my country's ambassador in Canada, a Canadian politician with apparent concern about the state of the world, in particular the relations between rich and poor countries, asked me what I thought about the impact of Western civilization on the fragile and feeble cultures and peoples of the Third World. The question was directed toward my personal experience with Western influences and how I felt about it. The implicit intention of the question, discreetly and politely stated, was how much I felt hurt by the process of Westernization, which I had undergone. My interrogator was clearly driven by a combination of admiration, sympathy, and curiosity. Although there was an element of condescension behind his question, I did not feel offended by his attitude, nor did I consider his question too personal. Instead, I appreciated the underlying concern behind his question, and I also felt a degree of empathy for his lack of political correctness, which I realized might have been based on underestimating the depth of my cross-cultural consciousness.

My answer to him was genuinely positive and optimistic. This was not because I felt so positive about the state of the world, or about inter-racial or cross-cultural relations between the West and the Third World; it was because of my own personal experience with change and the extent to which I believed I had applied, with relative success, my own constructive concept of the 'invisible bridge.'

The fact that I feel positive about it should not mislead the reader into thinking that I am underestimating the challenges involved. Nor do I claim that I have gone through it with ease and unscathed. The full truth undoubtedly lies somewhere in between, although my vision of my experience is relatively clear and to a significant degree positive. Nevertheless, at different phases of my life, I was confronted with challenges that threatened the realization of the goals I had set for myself and took me to the brink. Fortunately, with the support of key individuals and a predisposition to seek opportunities in crises, I was able to overcome the obstacles and resiliently pursued the fundamental objectives of my life amidst the complexities and uncertainties of the inter-racial and cross-cultural worlds in which I moved. Indeed, wherever I have moved and lived, I have found that there is as much that unites us in common humanity as there are elements that divide us, and that efforts to bridge the differences, though most challenging, can be very productive and the results gratifyingly rewarding. I believe there is truth in the saying, 'Smile and the world will smile back.'

I have been told by those who know me well, and told so often that I have come to believe it; that I am one of those blessed with a notable tendency to bridge cross-cultural differences. I am also told what I know to be true that despite my adaptability to new situations, I have a strong sense of pride in the dignity of my background and cultural identity, reflected in my continuing commitment to the fundamental values of my indigenous culture. And indeed, as I believe my writings reflect, I am profoundly aware of the deep roots of my origin that keep me grounded and resilient against the hurricanes of cross-cultural transformation.

Ironically, the same values and moral principles that bind me to my roots also inspire me to seek fulfillment and dignity by the standards of the new situations in which I find myself. My traditional premises and associated cultural values give me both a sense of security and a motivation to reach out for greater heights toward a more idealized and universalizing social order. To me, globalization as we now know it must also entail localization if it is to promote truly inclusive principles of universal human dignity. In my intellectual and professional life, I have consistently continued to engage at the local level, even as I was involved in national, regional and international affairs. This prompted one colleague in the central government to wonder, jokingly, whether I was Minister of State for Foreign Affairs or for Tribal Affairs. I felt flattered to be both.

Part Five:
Level of Transition and Integration

———————◆———————

Although I saw the challenges of my life in terms of striving to live up to the ancestral ideals of leadership and modeling myself after my father, it was through education that I saw an avenue and a means for fulfilling the goals that had already been set in the traditional context. In this too, I was motivated by a conscious desire to please my father, my family, and my tribal community. Indeed, in sending us away from our traditional home at Noong Village to Abyei, the administrative Center of the Ngok Dinka, where the first elementary school in our area was established, Father had challenged us to see our leaving our mothers behind and going away from home to school as an expression of love and devotion for him. From the day I went to school and throughout my education, winning the approval of Father and family was a consistent driving force in my desire to succeed and my fear of failure.

We joined Abyei Elementary School in 1943 at the early age of five. After four years in that school, one brother, Bol, and I went to

Tonj Primary School in Southern Sudan that was established by the British for sons of Chiefs and Government officials and was modeled after the English Public School system. Tonj was far away from home and throughout the school year we did not see a single person from our Ngok community. In Southern Sudan, we came in contact with people from other Dinka and non-Dinka ethnic groups, some of whom we had been made to fear as cannibals. In fact, a major factor in our going to the South was that we began to broaden our identity as Dinka. We had grown thinking of our Ngok people as *The Dinka;* other Dinka groups were designated by their sub-tribal names and otherwise collectively designated as *Thai,* implying 'All the Others.' We also began to have a vague sense of a wider national identity as Southern Sudanese. Some of the children were sons of prominent chiefs whose names were well known throughout Dinkaland. But while we felt the disadvantage of being far from home, we saw no equal to our father.

Interestingly enough, it was quite obvious that the factors which gave our father a distinctive profile over his Southern Sudanese counterparts had much to do with the cross-cultural influences from the Arab Islamic North. Father was in fact dissatisfied with our attending schools in the South instead of the North. Although the British Inspector of Education in the South had persuaded him that it was to his advantage to have children educated in both the North and the South, Father kept suggesting that we should shift to the North.

When Northern Sudanese teachers went to the South, specifically from Kordofan, we felt an affinity with them. And in the rising political consciousness in the South, we stood for decollimation and unity between North and the South in an independent Sudan. When the British gave our father the choice they had given our grandfather, whether to remain in the North or join the South, and gave him the opportunity to visit the South before making up his mind, Father, like his father before him, decided to remain in the North. He clearly saw the position of his people in the North and his own position as more advantaged in the North. Although my brother Bol does not remember, Father sought our opinion and we agreed with his position.

Our area and the schools we went to in the South were within the Christian Missionary sphere of influence as designated by the British. We therefore converted to Catholicism. Bol acquired the Christian name of Frederick, which he later changed to Zackariah, and I chose the name Francis. After Grade Six, we proceeded to Rumbek Junior Secondary School, which was then an adjunct to Rumbek Senior Secondary School, but was later relocated in Tonj as an Intermediate School.

After completing our intermediate education in the South, and eventually succumbing to Father's pressure, we went to Khor Taqqat Secondary School, then one of the three leading schools in the North, where we were the only Southern Sudanese and non-Muslims. In the North we experienced for the first time a dual process of striving to enhance ourselves cross-culturally while retaining our pride in our identity as Dinka. We recognized that Arab-Islamic identity in the Sudan was considered superior to the African identity of the South. Learning Arabic and conforming to certain Arab cultural symbols, such as dress, represented 'progress.' But we remained proud of our Dinka identity and our father remained a superior leader by any standards, even among Arab chiefs. By the way we carried ourselves and socialized, we asserted full equality to everyone and felt no inferiority to anyone. And of course, since Christian Missionaries had projected Christianity as the religion for spiritual salvation, we did not feel any need to adopt Islam.

Khartoum Taqqat also introduced us to national consciousness although that meant being more aware of the dichotomy and inequality between the North and the South. So, becoming aware of Sudanese nationhood also made us become aware of Southern nationalism that was demanding national recognition and equality. Khor Taqqat enriched us with elements of Arab culture and greater political awareness without in any way compromising our pride in our Dinka identity and the dignity associated with our family and culture.

Four years of turbulent adjustment to what was for us an alien but enriching environment ended with our admission to the University of Khartoum, where I enrolled in the Faculty of Law and Bol in Economics. Bol soon received a scholarship to study medicine in East Germany, from which he transferred to continue in Italy.

In Khartoum University, we came in contact with an even wider convergence of races and cultures, both students and Faculty members. The university and the urban life of Khartoum, Khartoum North and Omdurman - that constituted the Capital City - clearly offered the challenge of adjusting to a higher level in the process of modernization.

It was while in Khartoum University that I first got the opportunity to visit Europe in a summer program of exchange with German universities. Europe was a new and exciting world the glimpses of which I had seen only in the movies. It was extraordinary that I felt motivated to adjust to the new context while remaining equally proud of my origins.

Ironically, my colleagues from the University of Khartoum always introduced me as 'Son of Chief' which indicated that I had consciously or unintentionally made that aspect known in my Khartoum University circles. Later, at a tea party that I organized to introduce my visiting father to my Khartoum circle, and to which my German friends on a return visit to our country were invited, one German student was later to describe my father as regal and kingly, and flatteringly that he fitted the image she had created in her mind about what my father would look like.

The visit to Germany exposed me to international contacts and later led me to a wide range of further experiences in other European countries. Another major move was when I was sent to the United Kingdom for post-graduate studies, following my graduation and appointment to the teaching staff of the Faculty of Law at Khartoum University. While in the United Kingdom, I continued my cross-cultural experiences with a study tour of Scandinavia, to which I was invited by a Swedish writer to contribute an African perspective to a book he was writing about his country's welfare system. My Swedish host organized an ambitious program of meetings with prominent personalities and institutions, always covered by the media, with me often described as 'Prince' and son of a leading Chief in the Sudan. While I found it embarrassing, it fitted my aspiration of adjusting to new situations in self-enhancement while maintaining, with pride, essential elements of my original identity and culture that I considered worth retaining and projecting.

In the United Kingdom I was confronted with two challenges. One was an acute case of glaucoma for which an earlier operation in Germany proved a failure and which then threatened me with blindness. The other was a case of political persecution emanating from the North-South civil war that was raging in the Sudan and which forced me into exile and a separation from my people. The agony of these two crises led to my redefining my goals in a race against blindness and refocusing my energies toward achievable objectives before losing my sight. Critical in this respect was the urgent need I felt for completing my post-graduate studies to equip myself to be of some value even with blindness. I also focused my studies on subjects that clearly kept me connected to my background and culture, such as customary law and studying Dinka culture through the translation and analysis of songs I had collected, ultimately resulting in the book, *The Dinka and their Songs.*[249]

It was at this particular juncture that my Khartoum University Lecturer, William Twining, came to my aid and established contacts that eventually led to my going to Yale Law School in 1964, where I obtained a Master's degree and a Doctorate within three years. My focus of Dinka Studies led to my doctoral dissertation which became my book, *Tradition and Modernization: A Challenge for Law Among the Dinka of the Sudan.*[250]

More books on various aspects of Dinka society and culture followed over the years. The essence of these studies was to document of Dinka culture, identify and analyzed essential elements that are worth building on in the process of change, and making a case for their potential for synthesis with other cultures in the process of universalizing cross-fertilization. I found it most gratifying that elements of Dinka value-system, such as the concept of *cieng* that reflected the ideals of unity and harmony in human relation within and between cultures, and the concept of *dheeng,* which embodied principles of human dignity being widely recognized as having universal validity and application.

After completing my studies at Yale, I joined the Division of Human Rights in the United Nations Secretariat in New York, where I served for five years until the first civil war in the Sudan came to an end in 1972, the year I was recruited into the diplomatic service of the country. I chose human rights precisely because I felt that this was

---

249. Francis Mading Deng, *The Dinka And Their Songs, Oxford at The Clarendon Press,* 1973 – see p. 27. Reissued by Africa World Books, 2023.

250. Francis Mading Deng, *Tradition and Modernization: A Challenge for Law among the Dinka of the Sudan,* Yale University Press, 1971 -see p. 15.

an area of concern to our beleaguered people in the Sudan, but also because I wanted to see the connection between Dinka cultural values and international human rights norms. In this, I was disappointed because the approach of the United Nations and the exclusive focus on Eurocentric international human rights instruments, as the sole principles for the promotion of human rights, did not lend itself to intellectual or scholarly debate on the cross-cultural dimensions. I would later write articles and contribute chapters on this theme.

However, before the end of the war and my joining the diplomatic service, the call to return home came unexpectedly in 1969 with the tragic news that my father was critically ill, perhaps dying. With my brother, Zackariah Bol, who was then practicing medicine in the United Kingdom, we rushed back home amidst political turmoil. Colonel Jaafar Mohamed Nimeiri had just led a successful coup and seized political power in alliance with the Communist Party. Tribal Chiefs were among their targeted adversaries. Chieftainship had been abolished in the North, although it was allowed to continue in the South, where the civil war was still raging, even as the new regime was making overtures for peace. We took our father to Cairo in a vain effort to save his life from an advanced terminal cancer. [251]

Only about a week later, he died. With the cooperation of the Government, we fulfilled our father's last wish by flying his body back to the village in a military plane under the near-impossible conditions of the rainy season.

At home, we found ourselves amidst the civil war in which our people were being terrorized and constantly threatened with arrest, torture and death. After a month of trying to reconcile the unbridge-able positions of the various adversaries; the local rebel leaders, the

---

251. Mentioned previously on pages 40 & 50.

security forces, the tribal leaders, and the ordinary people, we managed to achieve a fragile arrangement that we feared would probably not hold. After reporting to the Government and making recommendations for alleviating the situation, Bol joined me on my return to the United States, leaving behind a younger brother who had succeeded our father as the Paramount Chief.

Back in the United States, we spent long hours in my New York apartment reminiscing about home, listening to the Dinka songs I had recorded, reflecting on the tragedy that had befallen our people, and pondering on what we could do to assist our brother to meet the challenges of leadership that had descended upon us, despite our distance from home.

In Khartoum, before we took Father to Cairo, a colleague and friend from Khartoum University accompanied me to visit him in the hospital. My friend had pursued his Master's Degree in Law at Howard University in the United States, and served briefly at the Legal Department in the United Nations, from which he returned to his judicial position in the Sudan. Having learned of my friend's story, Father later cited his example to me and questioned why I was not coming back to the service of my country. When I explained to him the political circumstances that had led to my going to the United States and the disconcerting manner in which I had been treated by the national authorities, my father showed full understanding. He told me that according to the ways of our Dinka, when a man is mistreated and forced to leave his tribe, it is incumbent upon his people to call on him and ask him to return with respect and dignity. "So, you wait; the country will call on you."

My father's prophesy was fulfilled only a year later when peace gradually returned to the Sudan and the Government began to approach me for an appointment. It was only after peace was fully restored in

1972 that I accepted one of several offers, that of Ambassador to the Scandinavian countries. That was to be my first assignment in a series of positions in the service of my country. The Scandinavian appointment was followed by a posting as Ambassador to United States and Minister of State for Foreign Affairs. And when I wanted to leave the government on the advice of my ophthalmologist to attend to the acute glaucoma that continued to threaten me with blindness, the President persuaded me to go to Canada as Ambassador with my ministerial status.

My vision for the post-war foreign policy of our country was premised on the principle that foreign policy is an extension of domestic policy and that diplomacy is not a matter of cleverness or speaking well, important as those are, but rather of having a positive domestic commodity to sell regionally and internationally. This entails a two prong approach: to contribute to the formulation of sellable domestic policy and to promote that positive domestic policy to gain international support. It also implies a two way communication and advocacy, transmitting the national message to the outside world, and bringing back home perspectives and critiques of the domestic policy agenda by external partners.

As I saw it, the Addis Ababa Agreement that ended the seventeen year war, (1955-1972), created a positive domestic policy framework that merited support from the international community. By granting the South regional autonomy, the Agreement created a framework of unity in diversity that allowed a short-term accommodation of religious and cultural diversity while fostering a process of interaction that would move the country toward a more unified national identity based on the equality of citizenship without discrimination on the grounds of race, ethnicity, religion, and culture.

That was the vision I stipulated in the book *Dynamics of Identification:*

A Basis for National Integration in the Sudan.[252] I also developed it as official policy in the book I wrote for the Ministry of Foreign Affairs, *Peace and Unity in the Sudan: An African Achievement,*[253] which the President presented to the Heads of State and Government of the Organization of African Unity. The vision I presented in the two books represented a precursor of the Vision of New Sudan that the SPLM/A would eventually stipulate for the country. For me, the core of that Vision was unity within a framework of full equality of race, ethnicity, religion and culture. That vision was an inspiration in my representing my country as Ambassador and Minister with pride and conviction. I believe that made me convincing to my international interlocutors.

The Addis Ababa Agreement however only provided a nebulous basis for resolving the crisis situation in my home area which had been affiliated to the administration of Kordofan in the North in 1905. The areas leaders had played a bridging role between the North and the South, but mistreatment by the Arab dominated central government had forced them to demand a return to the administration to the South. And that mistreatment also made them identify with the Southern rebels during the war which subjected them to even greater repression and aggression from the Central Government. I played a role in having the Abyei situation discussed in the Addis negotiations which resulted in a provision in the Agreement granting the Ngok Dinka the right to decide by plebiscite whether to remain in the North or join the South. That provision was not implemented.

I eventually proposed an alternative arrangement that would grant the people of Abyei a mini autonomy to run their own affairs under the

252. F. Deng, *Dynamics of Identification: A Basis for National Integration,* Khartoum University Press, 1973 – see p. 62.

253. Francis Mading Deng, *Peace and Unity in the Sudan: An African Achievement,* Co-author, Khartoum University Press, 1973 – see p. 64.

presidency and be granted services and socio-economic development which would motivate them to play the historical role the area had played as a North South bridge. The proposal was accepted by the central government and I was able to secure funding of the USAID and we invited the Harvard Institute for International Development to assist with the implementation of the project and to implement the strategy of transitional integration expounded in my book, *Tradition and Modernization.*[254] The project however proved controversial, opposed by extremists among the Ngok Dinka as compromising the objective of returning to the South, resisted by the Missiriya as favoring the Dinka over the Arabs, and rejected by the Provincial Government as interference by the Central Government in the Affairs of the Province. The situation in Abyei continued to escalate until it erupted in a local rebellion that contributed to the resumption of full scale hostilities between the North and the South.

The return to a full-fledged war in 1983 however resulted from the fact that the Vision stipulated in the Addis Ababa Agreement and which I had written about in *Dynamics of Identification,*[255] and *Peace and Unity in the Sudan: An African Achievement*[256] was challenged, undermined and reversed by the sectarian political parties and fundamental Islamists who took the country back to the old divisive and discriminatory Arab-Islamic national identity framework which ignited the war in 1983 that would rage until it was eventually ended by the CPA in 2005.

With the outbreak of the war, the President reversed his decision

254. Francis Mading Deng, *Tradition and Modernization: A Challenge for Law among the Dinka of the Sudan,* Yale University Press, 1971 - see p. 15.

255. F. Deng, *Dynamics of Identification: A Basis for National Integration,* Khartoum University Press, 1973 – see p. 62.

256. Francis Mading Deng, *Peace and Unity in the Sudan: An African Achievement,* Khartoum Universtity Press, 1973 – see p. 64.

to have me go to the UN as Permanent Representative to the United Nations and asked me to go to Addis Ababa as Ambassador to Ethiopia and the Organization of African Unity. That would have meant confronting fellow Southern Sudanese who had just rebelled against the Government. That was when I decided to resign and refused to seek any other assignment from the Government.

I asked myself what I could do to continue to work on the national issues with which I was concerned. That's when I embarked on writing novels on the theme of identity to address the hearts and minds of the Sudanese people to explode the myths of identity that divided the country and explore a common ground of unity within a framework of full quality, in other words the Vision of New Sudan. I immediately began to write *Seed of Redemption,*[257] followed shortly after by *Cry of the Owl.*[258]

When I returned to the United States where my American wife and I had established a home, I was soon offered positions in leading institutions, initially as a Visiting Scholar at the Woodrow Wilson International Center for Scholars, where I completed work on my father's biography, *The Man Called Deng Majok: A Biography of Power, Polygyny and Change,*[259] then as the First Distinguished Fellow of the Rockefeller Brothers' Fund, after which I returned to the Wilson Center as a Senior Research Associate. At the Wilson Center, I helped organize an all-party conference on the Sudan, whose deliberations resulted in the book, *The Search for Peace and Unity in the Sudan,*[260] which I co-edited with the Director of the Center, Prosser Gifford. I

257. Francis Mading Deng, *Seed of Redemption: A Political Novel,* Lilian Barber Press, 1986 - see p. 75.

258. Francis Mading Deng, *Cry of the Owl: A Novel,* Lilian Barber Press, 1989 - see p. 81.

259. Francis Mading Deng, *The Man Called Deng Majok, A Biography of Power, Polgyny and Change,* Yale University Press, 1986 - see p. 35.

260. Francis Mading Deng and Prosser Gifford, *The Search for Peace and Unity in the Sudan,* Wilson Center Press, 1987 - see p. 79.

finally settled as a Senior Fellow at the Brookings Institution, where I established the Africa Program, which I directed for twelve years, and produced numerous publications.

The conceptual framework I used in developing the Africa Program with the support of leading scholars in the field was to address several key questions for our research agenda. The first was to identify the critical issues of concern in Africa that required in-depth study with policy implications to guide decision makers. The second was to assess the impact of the end of the Cold War on the manner in which African issues were approached and addressed. On the basis of these fundamental premises, we would then undertake in-depth research on generic and contextually specific African issues.

The answer to the first question was straightforward. The obvious African priority areas included ending the rampant violent conflicts on the continent, promoting participatory democratic governance, protecting universal human rights, and generating economic growth and equitable distribution. The main focus of the program became conflict prevention, management and resolution.

We began the program with a research conference on conflict analysis that involved leading scholars in the field to clarify the pertinent conceptual issues that should be considered by the program. The outcome was a volume: *Conflict Resolution in Africa.*[261]

A series of regional and country specific studies that included East Africa, West Africa, Southern Africa, and the Sudan were conducted by experts in the field and produced books published by Brookings.

We invited scholars of African studies, both Africans and non-Africans, to each spend a year with us to conduct research and write on topics of their choice, in the areas of conflict management, human

---

261. Francis M. Deng and I. William Zartman, *Conflict Resolution in Africa,* Introduction by Former President of Nigeria, General Olusegun Obasanjo. The Brookings Institution Press, 1991 - see p. 112.

rights, socio-economic development, and the role of regional and international organizations. These studies resulted in published works. The Africa Program at Brookings soon established a credible reputation for producing and publishing books which attracted substantial support that in turn gave the Program a solid foundation within The Brookings Institution. Among the numerous publications that came out of the Project was *Conflict Management in Africa: Sovereignty as Responsibility;*[262] *African Reckoning, A Quest for Good Governance;*[263] *Strategic Vision for Africa: The Kampala Movement;*[264] *Human Rights in Africa: A Cross-Cultural Perspective;*[265] and *The Challenges of Famine Relief: Emergency Operations in Sudan.*[266]

Perhaps guided by the situation in the Sudan, I saw identity factors and the challenge of dealing with identity conflicts as a cross-cutting theme that permeated all the issues in the program. In this respect, my perspective differed from those of my academic colleagues who saw issues of identity and culture as too vague and nebulous to be a subject of analysis and conflict resolution. It would take years of persistent efforts for us to bridge our differences.

As reflected in several of my writings, including *War of Visions: Conflict of Identities in the Sudan,*[267] *New Sudan in the Making,*[268] and

262. Francis M. Deng, Sadikiel Kimaro, Terrence Lyons, Donald Rothschild, and I. William Zartman, *Sovereignty as Responsibility: Conflict Management in Africa,* The Brookings Institution Press, 1996 - see p. 115.

263. Francis M. Deng and Terrence Lyons, *African Reckoning: A Quest for Good Governance,* The Brookings Institution Press, 1998 - see p. 116.

264. Francis M. Deng and I. Willian Zartman, *A Strategic Vision for Africa: The Kampala Movement,* The Brookings Institution Press, 2002 - see p. 118.

265. Abdullahi Ahmed An-naim and Francis M. Deng, *Human Rights in Africa: A Cross-Cultural Perspective,* The Brookings Institution Press, 1990 - see p. 111.

266. Francis Mading Deng and co-authored with Larry Minear, *The Challenges of Famine Relief: Emergency Operations in Sudan,* The Brookings Institution Press, 1992 - see p. 83.

267. Francis M. Deng, *War of Visions: Conflict of Identities in the Sudan,* The Brookings Institution Press, 1995 - see p. 84.

268. Francis Mading Deng, *New Sudan in the Making?* Editor, Red Sea Press, 2010 - see p. 99.

Sudan at the Brink,[269] I continued my commitment to the quest for a New Sudan until close to the referendum of 2011 that led to Southern independence. Even then, as reflected in the book *Bound by Conflict: The Dilemma of Two Sudans,*[270] I saw the two countries still negatively connected by conflicts that overflow across their national borders and advocated turning the relationship from being bound by conflict to being bonded by cooperation to resolve their respective conflicts and restore a form association that would be a degree of reunification. That aspiration continues unabated in my perspective.

On the resolution of the situation in Abyei, history unfortunately repeated itself. The Abyei Protocol of the CPA granted the Ngok Dinka the same right the Abyei Protocol of the Addis Ababa Agreement in 1972 which had granted them, to decide by a referendum, whether to remain in the North or revert to the South. Unfortunately, Khartoum resisted the implementation of the Abyei Protocol. Again I came up with a proposal for the stabilization of Abyei, not as an alternative to the Abyei Protocol, but as an interim arrangement. The proposal aimed at providing security comprehensively over the territory of the Ngok Dinka, facilitating the return of the internally displaced and refugees to their areas of origin in safety and dignity, and providing them with social services and development. It also promoted peaceful coexistence and reconciliation with their neighbors to the North and South, and enable the area to restore its historic bridging role between North and South Sudan, now the Two Sudans. Three books document the history and challenges of the crisis situation in Abyei: *Frontiers of Unity: An Experiment of African-Arab Cooperation in Abyei,*[271] *Blood of*

269. Francis Mading Deng and Kevin M. Cahill, *Sudan at the Brink: Self-determination and National Unity,* Fordham University Press, 2010 - see p. 101.

270. Francis M. Deng in collaboration with Daniel J. Deng, *Bound by Conflict: Dilemmas of the Two Sudans,* Fordham University Press, 2016 - see p. 103.

271. Francis Deng, *Frontiers of Unity: An Experiment in Afro-Arab Cooperation,* Routledge, 2010 - see p. 42.

Two Streams: Gender Balance in Parental Legacy,[272] and *Abyei Between the Two Sudans.*[273]

My UN service began back in 1967 in the position of Human Rights Officer, after my graduate studies at Yale. I later returned to the UN service after leaving the Government. My positions included that of Representative of the Secretary-General on Internally Displaced Persons which was a voluntary service while I was at Brookings, at the functional level of Assistant Secretary-General, and that of Special Advisor of the Secretary-General on the Prevention of Genocide, on a full-time basis at the level of Under-Secretary-General.

I saw the conflicts that generate internal displacement and escalate to genocidal levels as essentially extreme forms of identity conflicts that result not so much from mere differences as from mismanagement of diversity leading to gross inequalities between those who enjoy the rights of citizenship and those discriminated, marginalized, excluded and denied the dignity associated with rights of citizenship. International involvement to provide international protection and assistance to the victims of these internal conflicts are usually blocked by the governments in the name of sovereignty.

To support the work on my mandate, my colleague Roberta Cohen and I established the Brookings Project on Internal Displacement, which we co-directed. We engaged a team of international lawyers who helped with the development of *The Guiding Principles on Internal Displacement,*[274] which I submitted to the Commission on Human Rights in 1998. The principles provided a basis of engaging govern-

---

272. Francis Mading Deng, *Blood of Two Streams: Gender Balance in Parental Legacy,* IIHS-Fordham University Press, 2021 - see p. 45.

273. Francis Mading Deng, Luka B. Deng Kuol and Daniel J. Deng, *Abyei between the Two Sudans,* Red Sea Press, 2020 - see p. 44.

274. Francis M. Deng, with Roberta Cohen, Walter Kaelin, Robert Goldman and Manfred Novak, *Guiding Principles on Internal Displacement,* UN Office for Humanitarian Affairs, 1998 - see p. 129.

ments building on the concept of Sovereignty as Responsibility by which the primary responsibility falls on the state with international support as needed. The concept however implies that when governments fail to provide the needed protection and assistance, or to invite international support while masses suffer and die, the international community will find one way or another to intervene. Abiding by the principles of sovereignty as responsibility is therefore the best way to safeguard national sovereignty. Although that approach was considered too soft on governments by some among human rights advocates and non-governmental humanitarian organizations, it was constructive and quite successful. Over the years, the Brookings Project on Internal Displacement produced a series of publications which include *Protecting the Dispossessed*,[275] a revised version of my first report to the Commission on Human Rights, *Masses in Flight*,[276] which Roberta and I co-authored, and *Forsaken People*,[277] which we co-edited.

Following my service in the United Nations, I was again called upon to serve my country in the position of the first Permanent Representative to the United Nations in New York. This was a tough assignment. I had worked very hard against those who argued against the independence of South Sudan both in Africa and in the international community, not only among some key countries, such as the Troika of Norway, United Kingdom, and the United States, but also in the United Nations. The fear shared by many was that an independent South Sudan would descend into inter-tribal warfare that would lead to state failure and create a crisis that would threaten the peace and

275. Francis M. Deng, *Protecting the Dispossessed: A Challenge for the International Community*, The Brookings Institution Press, 1993 - see p. 149.

276. Roberta Cohen and Francis M. Deng, *Masses in Flight: The Global Crisis of Internal Displacement*, The Brookings Institution Press, 1998 - see p. 151.

277. Roberta Cohen and Francis M. Deng, *Forsaken Peoples: Case Studies on Internal Displacement*, The Brookings Institution Press, 1998 - see p. 154.

security of the region and beyond. I even had heated discussions with the Secretary-General of the United Nations and the Chairman of the Commission of the African Union and other prominent African leaders on the issue.

Less than two years after the July 9, 2011 declaration of independence, war broke out on December 15, 2013. Initially this was as a result of a power struggle between the leaders of the ruling party, but soon escalated into an ethnic conflict between the two largest ethnic groups, the Dinka and the Nuer. The conflict was halted in 2015 by the mediation of IGAD, supported by the AU, the UN and the Troika countries. A year later, violence erupted again and escalated into yet another devastating conflict. A revitalization of the 2015 Revitalized Peace Agreement (RPA) was signed in September, 2018, but the implementation of the Agreement has proved quite elusive.

At about the time the initiative for the Revitalized Agreement was undertaken, President Salva Kiir Mayardit initiated the National Dialogue process and appointed a Steering Committee of over a hundred members, a Leadership of nine members, and a Secretariat representing research and academic institutions. The Leadership comprised two Co-Chairs, a Deputy Co-Chair, a Rapporteur, two Deputy Rapporteurs, and three representatives for women.

I was appointed one of the two Deputy Rapporteurs. The Steering Committee created 15 sub-committees, ten based on the old ten states, with Abyei and Boma special administrative areas, and three thematic Sub-Committees on Security, the Capital and Refugees and International Outlook, to conduct grassroots consultations throughout the country. The process was to be guided by the principles of inclusivity, credibility, transparency and integrity. These principles were strictly observed. Although the process was almost entirely funded by the Government; it was granted full freedom and throughout the years of the National Dialogue, no one was harassed or intimidated, or arrested. The reports of the sub-committees were only edited for language without interfering with the substance in any way. Inclusivity was more fully accomplished after the Revitalized Peace Agreement (RPA) through an Ad Hoc Committee which I chaired and which included all the political parties. After the grassroots consultations, three regional conferences in the three Greater Regions of Bahr el-Ghazal, Upper Nile and Equatoria, all of which were equally free. The process is planned to conclude with the National Conference.

I was also actively involved in the Revitalized Peace Process from the start and became formally appointed as one of the Stakeholders in the category of so-called Eminent Persons of whom there were two of us, with a former Vice President of the Sudan. After the Agreement, which we signed among the Stakeholders, we became members of the Revitalized Joint Monitoring and Evaluation Committee (R-JMEC).

Throughout the process, I engaged in the formidable task of trying to bridge several conflicting positions. While I advocated the complementarity of the two processes, there was strong resistance from both sides because of deep suspicions about each other's motives and objectives. I also worked hard to improve relations with the international community which were characterized by mutual suspicions and mistrust about respective positions.

As the RPA is confronted with serious implementation challenges, attitudes appear to be shifting toward the National Dialogue as the hope for the country, but I remain committed to the principle of complementarity between the two processes. My perceptions and efforts in the National Dialogue have been documented in my book, *Reflections on South Sudan National Dialogue.*[278]

---

278. Francis Mading Deng, *Reflections on South Sudan's National Dialogue*, United Nations Development Programme (UNDP), 2018 - see p. 105.

Part Six:
Linking the Level
of Transition and Integration

———————◆———————

The significance of listing my works under levels is to emphasize the element of continuity and interconnectedness in change reflected at the various phases or levels of my journey through cultures. The local level is where I was born and raised. The national level comprises early education and later government service. The regional level covers my African continental perspective and engagement. And the global level includes graduate studies abroad and later research in think tanks and finally United Nations service from which I transitioned again to serve my new country of South Sudan as the first Permanent Representative to the United Nations.

Local levels. The importance of the local level is that it represents the family and the leadership and cultural context that shaped my erstwhile worldview and acculturated me into the Dinka value system. This became a deeply rooted normative framework that continued to guide me throughout the various phases of my life. It is in this context that my sense of identity and pride in my family and society were nurtured and consolidated.

National levels. The transition into the national level began with institutions of early education. That extended my sense of identity and national consciousness to the wider fellow Dinka and South Sudanese ethnic groups. It later extended to Northern Sudanese institutions of secondary and higher learning, which maximized my national perspective. While my South Sudanese experience broadened my outlook within the same ethnic and cultural framework, experiences in the North challenged me with adjustment to a different Arab-Islamic racial, cultural, and religious context. This provided me with the opportunity for enrichment through selective cross-cultural adoption and assimilation, while retaining the essential elements of my background and pride in my family and ethnic identity. The national dimension that emerged with my service as Ambassador and Minister of State for Foreign Affairs consisted mainly of advocating and promoting a framework of equitable accommodation of diversities toward a longer-term vision of mutually enriching interaction toward a uniting national identity framework.

Regional levels. Ironically, awareness of the regional framework of my identity as an African developed in my studies and research abroad, and matured in my diplomatic service as Ambassador and State Minister. The intellectual and scholarly work at this level mostly focused on greater awareness of the African value systems and their potential contribution to a contextualized culturally oriented framework of governance, constitutionalism, nation-building and development.

Global levels. My global perspective was closely associated with my post-graduate studies and continued work in research institutions, social and institutional relationships, and later diplomatic representation and international service. From a substantive perspective, the farther away I went from the starting point of my journey through cultures, and particularly to the international context, the more I appreciated the potential values of cross-cultural mutual enrichment that were either unknown or dismissed by the outside world. In a way, it was both a defensive process of preserving our threatened identity and value system, and a genuine conviction that my culture had something of value to contribute to the global human family. This was the core of continuity in change.

The Last Word. If I were to summarize in a sentence the principles that guided me in my works and actions, linking the various levels of my journey, I would include: a deeply rooted sense of identity, dignity and self-worth; a demand for recognition, respect, and equality with others; the search for a common ground of shared humanity, mutual accommodation of diversity; and a framework of equality and mutual enrichment through cross-fertilization of interactive identities.

Part Seven:
Identity and Globalization

———————◆———————

Toward the end of November, 2019, I was surprised by a telephone call from Ali Shommo informing me that the Board of El-Tayeb Saleh Prize for Excellence in Writing had unanimously chosen me as the Guest of Honor for this year's celebrations. Ali was a colleague in the Government of President Jaafar Nimeiri in which he was State Minister and then Cabinet Minister of Culture and Information while I was Minister for Foreign Affairs. He was now Professor in the University of the Sudan. His call and message were a total surprise.

I was then in my second month of slow recovery from a vertebral compression from a fall on a wet floor on my hotel room in Juba. I conveyed to Ali Shommo my sincere appreciation and gratitude for the invitation but explained the constraints of my medical condition. Since the celebrations were to be in February, we both hoped that I would be well enough to travel.

A month before the event, I was getting better, but I was still not well enough to travel. The surgeon authorized me to commit myself to attending in principle, but to see him before making the final decision. A week before my travel, he agreed that I could travel, but that I should have someone accompanying me and should avoid lifting bags. I said that I would use a wheelchair at the airport, the airline staff would take care of me during the flight and that I would be taken care of once I landed.

In Khartoum, I was very warmly received by a high-level delegation as I exited from the plane. At the reception line were Ali Shommo, Omar Gamareldin Ismail, State Minister for Foreign Affairs, Vice Chancellor of Khartoum University, a member of the Prize Board, the Secretary General of the El-Tayeb Salih Prize, and the General Manager of Zain Company, the sponsor of the prize, and support staff. A group of photographers were intensely engaged in taking pictures. I was accommodated in the fanciest hotel in Khartoum, the Corinthia, (Gadhaffi's investment). The Ministry made a luxury car available for me during the entire period of my stay. A member of the Zain staff was assigned to escort and assist me throughout my stay, a function he carried out with great efficiency, always at hand when needed, and very discreet in his presence.

Apart from activities directly related to the El-Tayeb Salih Prize, lectures, seminars, and discussion groups offered opportunities for a constructive exchange of views on issues related to developments in the Sudan and the future prospects for bilateral relations with South Sudan.

The prize activities were conducted at the Friendship Hall where the arrangements, decoration, and the setting were truly spectacular. The opening event was marked by speeches by the leadership of Zain Company, the Prize Board, Personality of the Year, some of the recipients of prizes for several literary contributions and myself as the Guest of Honor. El-Tayeb Salih could not have been better remembered.

The second day entailed a pleasant boat ride on the Nile during which a number of authors were recognized and received medals. The final event the evening of the second day, which was as glamorous as the opening day, was for handing out monetary prizes to this year's winners. These public events were very well attended and featured musical interludes which presented various songs of the cultures of ethnic groups from around the country.

For me personally, what was most gratifying was the interest shown throughout in my books and ideas. From my first remarks at the opening session, to the various lectures, seminars and discussion groups, to the media coverage, there was remarkable interest in my books and ideas. My presentation was in the spirit of this year's theme of '*Identity in the Context of Globalization.*'

The following is an extract from the remarks I made at the opening session for the prize's award ceremony:

Some years ago, when we were still one Sudan and I was working abroad, I was asked by a journalist what it would take to persuade me to return to my country. My answer was that I had never left the country and I meant it because absence does not necessarily mean disconnection. I say the same about my connection to the Sudan today.

It is a great pleasure to be back in Khartoum and the Sudan which, despite having been torn apart by an unresolved crisis of national identity, remains our historic country.

I need not repeat how honored I am to have received the El-Tayeb Salih Prize which, both figuratively and substantively, is a reaffirmation of my sense of continued identification with the country and its culture and remains a source of pride for me.

The theme I have been asked to address in my talk, '*Identity in the Context of Globalization,*' underscores the value I attach to the enduring contributions of El-Tayeb Salih and my own modest efforts in addressing the issues involved.

I have always argued that globalization implies localization, if it is to be truly inclusive. For me personally, my life and my service have in a wide variety of ways entailed linking levels of thought and action from local, though national and regional, to global. In fact, I have recently been organizing my writings into those four-level categories.

Several key concepts are central to my worldview and linkage of thought and experience, and they should be seen as interconnected guiding principles in my journey across cultures. These concepts are identity, dignity, diversity and equality. The fact that they all end with 'ty' is coincidental, but also supportive of their interconnection.

Identity is the core of our humanity and is inherent in our subjective sense of dignity. The values associated with these are deeply rooted in the cultural context in which we are born and bred. These values however get challenged once we move into a context of diversity, where our subjective sense of identity and dignity begins to compete with the self-perceptions of others in shaping the shared space. Too often, inequality ensues and with it a counteraction of demand for equality. Let me now put these theoretical issues into the real world with which we are familiar.

As some of you know, I was born into a family that provided generations of leaders in a bridging, border area between North and South Sudan. That is of course the Ngok Dinka area of Abyei which borders the Missiriya Arabs to the North and several Dinka tribes to the South. Even before the advent of the state-centered colonial administration, these leaders established close ties with their Arab counterparts to the North. Amidst the pervasive upheavals and devastations of the nineteenth century, their diplomatic moves resulted in a semblance of peaceful coexistence between their respective communities that was a rare commodity at the time. During the most violent periods of interracial and inter-religious confrontation, their area became a constructive model whose benefits expanded to their kindred communities on both sides of the North-South divide.

Two metaphors summarize the values of this bridging role. One is associated with my father, Nazir Deng Majok, who, as the latest in the long line of Paramount Chiefs, befriended the Arab Chief, Nazir Babo Nimir, with whom they entered into a bond of brotherhood that effectively bridged racial and religious division between their respective border communities and by extension between North and South Sudan. My father used to describe himself as the thread and needle that stitched the North and the South into one *toub,* symbolizing the unity of the nation. A second metaphor comes from Father's brother and Deputy Paramount Chief, Uncle Deng Abot, who compared Abyei to the eye which is very small organ but sees a great deal.

This background must then be placed in the wider Dinka context which is part of the even broader context of the Nilotic peoples who have been well studied and documented by anthropologists. Their sense of identity, pride, and dignity are well known. And indeed their culture and related values confirm these elements of positive self-perception.

Fundamental to our Dinka value system is the concept known as *kooc e nhom,* 'standing the head (of a dead person) upright,' which embodies the quest for immortality through procreational continuity and leads to ancestral veneration that is central to our indigenous religious belief system. This is a widely shared value among most peoples, but they have a very prominent position among the Nilotic peoples.

Another central value is *cieng baai.* The word *cieng* means living together deferentially in unity and harmony, while *baai* is a collective identity that applies to family, home, village, community, tribe, and country. *Cieng* is a concept of idealized human relations that comprises a complex interconnected set of values decency, courtesy, nobility, generosity, and overall dignity. *Cieng* is culture, custom, way of life, law, conduct, and attitude. It is both aspirational, what ought to be, and experiential, what in fact is. *Cieng* has much in common with the well-known concept of *ubuntu* and the equivalent Ethiopian concept of *medemer* which Prime Minister Ahmed Abiy Ali recently invoked in his Nobel Prize acceptance speech. Like those concepts, *cieng* embraces the local community and the global family of humankind. Yet another important Dinka concept of significance is *dheeng* which embodies the values of aesthetic physical and behavioral dignity with related notions of respect, *atheek*. A person's appearance and mannerisms, how he or she dresses, walks, talks, eats, and behaves towards others are all elements of *dheeng*. These indicators are normatively linked to *cieng*. While *cieng* sets the standards, *dheeng* classifies one on the basis of adherence to those standards.

There are also prescriptive concepts that relate to leadership and the exercise of power. These include *dom baai*, control over the land and the people, *guier baai*, reform or improvement of what is controlled, and *muk baai*, maintaining or stabilizing the situation under control. These concepts require adherence to the normative principles of *kooc e nhom*, *cieng* and *dheeng*, which makes them all interconnected and mutually reinforcing.

This value system is regarded as sacred, ordained and sanctioned by God and the ancestors who are closely watching over us to reward compliance and punish violation. Heaven and Hell are not deferred to the life hereafter; they are here and now on earth. The Dinka are extremely fearful of the awesome power of the spiritual world. God and the Ancestors are constantly invoked to ensure divine justice. Indeed, the religious belief systems of our Nilotic people have been thoroughly studied and our people have been widely recognized as exceedingly religious.

I have given these details of this indigenous culture because there has been a tendency among the external actors with authority and control over our people to assume that there is a cultural, social, spiritual and moral vacuum to be filled by foreign value systems. This condescending view generally applies to Black African cultures. Quite contrary, there is an integrated, coherent, cohesive, and sanctified social order, whose virtues are time tested and validated.

This is the cultural context and normative framework into which I was born and raised. They provided me with the principles that guided me in my contact and interaction with the world beyond, how I treated people and how I expected to be treated.

The next level in my transition from local to global is national. And by national, I am of course thinking of both the South and North of our historic Sudan. My initial transition was through education which I received in both parts of the country. In the South, the challenge was to discover the extent to which we were part of a broader identity as Dinka and South Sudanese who shared the same cultural values. I discovered that people we had looked down upon and even feared as cannibals were indeed fellow Dinka and South Sudanese. It was a matter of recognizing and embracing the similarities I had not experienced or known.

The North presented a different challenge. My brother, Zachariah Bol, and I were the only Southerners in Khor Taqqat Secondary School. At that time, we saw all the other students, who hailed from all corners of the North, including Nubians, Darfurians, and Nubas, as Arabs and Muslims. That presented us with a major challenge. On the one hand we came with a very proud sense of identity and dignity which did not accept being second rate to anyone. On the other hand, the Arab Islamic culture was widely accepted not only as the dominant framework of the national identity, but as a necessary step up the ladder of sophistication and civilization. It was one to be emulated. We did both, retained our pride and continued commitment to our original identity, while also adopting and assimilating Northern cultural traits in a process of self-enhancement. We pursued this on the basis of an uncompromising demand for equality in diversity.

The same challenges and eclectic approach persisted in the University of Khartoum. Law was a subject of my own choosing and that proved to be a very good choice. But it was also a subject I had observed applied at home in my father's court, which was probably a motivating factor in my joining the Faculty of Law. Yet, while European Law, Islamic Law, and even the far-off Roman Law were being taught in Khartoum University, Customary Law was not. And yet, Customary Law in some form or another was in fact being applied in the overwhelming parts of the country, South and North. With the guidance and support of my expatriate lecturers, I initiated a program of investigating and recording Customary Law among the Ngok Dinka that became accepted and applied throughout the country. It is quite ironic that it was in the United Kingdom and the United States of America that I found African Customary Law recognized and taught as a respectable academic discipline.

The demand for equality in the framework of diversity which became the core of the New Sudan Vision proposed and expounded by the SPLM, in particular its leader, Dr. John Garang, was for me an extension and expansion of a goal I had pursued since our engagement with diversity from our time in Khor Taqqat. I recognized the expanded sense of identity and unity as positive developments, but only in a normative framework of equality. And while this became more concretely reflected in my study of Customary Law, it began to widen in scope.

The expansion of self-identification and related cultural values began to reach out to the regional African level. It is ironic that it was the broadened interaction with other cultures, primarily the West, that the African regional dimension became increasingly pronounced. And this became reflected in all aspects of the interdisciplinary scope of my post-graduate studies and later in my professional life.

African studies abroad became a core factor of the demand for recognition and equality in the context of diversity. And the process involved a two-way cross-cutting interaction between influencing international perspectives on Africa and contributing to shaping policy direction nationally and internationally. I pursued this most vigorously through my role in diplomacy and international service as a senior U.N. official and in universities and think tanks abroad. And indeed, this provided the conceptual framework for my writings, including books, articles, and fiction.

When I was a student in England in the early 1960s. I entered into a competition of essay writing on the theme of race relations in the United Kingdom which was open to all foreign students in the country. My essay, 'Racialism at the Meeting Point,' was one of the top ten selected to be included in a book for which the chosen title was *Disappointed Guests.*[279] I was disappointed by the title because it did not represent the theme of my essay. I threatened to withdraw it, but I was persuaded to leave it in the book since it would speak for itself.

The core of my essay was that racial consciousness was an aspect of awareness and pride in one's identity which all groups, in their splendid isolation, share. It is only when groups interact with others and superior self-perceptions get challenged that conflict ensues. The implication of my thesis was that at the meeting point, if we realize that we all share that proud self-perception, that should provide a

---

279. Francis Mading Deng, *'Racialism at the Meeting Point,'* in *Disappointed Guests,* London, 1965 - see p. 342.

common ground and a basis for mutual recognition and respect for one another. My line of reasoning was, if we all feel superior, then we are all equal.

Needless to say, as the current trends toward xenophobia in the world indicates, my thesis was unduly optimistic. There is validity in the popular saying that familiarity breeds contempt. The Dinka also say that a nobleman of one tribe is not known to a nobleman of another tribe.

I do not believe that my thesis is entirely wrong. Recognition and respect for each other's identity is not automatic. It requires informing and educating one another about the cultural attributes and values involved in the interacting diversities. This is what I believe El-Tayeb Salih did in his literary works, and this is what I have tried to do in my own writings and cross-cultural engagement and dialogue abroad.

I will now try to put all this in the Sudanese context. Let me begin by reiterating what those who know me must know. Whether it is a function of my background in the border area of Abyei, the bridging role my family has played in that area, or my own personal disposition, I have always aspired to maintaining and consolidating the unity of the country, but on the basis of full equality. In all my writings, foremost of which is *War of Visions: Conflict of Identities in the Sudan*,[280] I always presented three options: unity in full equality; coexistence with respect for diversity; or unavoidable partition. The first, which represented the Vision of New Sudan, was always my preferred option.

My first book on identity, *Dynamics of Identification: A Basis for National Integration in the Sudan*,[281] optimistically analyzed the flexible

280. Francis M. Deng, *War of Visions: Conflict of Identities in the Sudan*, The Brookings Institution Press, 1995 - see p. 84.

281. F. Deng, *Dynamics of Identification: A Basis for National Integration*, Khartoum University Press, 1973 - see p. 62.

historical evolution of the conflicting identities in the Sudan and the current move toward respect for diversity as steps toward developing a national identity framework that would progressively ensure equitable unity and eventual integration.

The post Addis Ababa Agreement book, *Peace and Unity in the Sudan: An African Achievement,*[282] which I prepared for the Ministry of Foreign Affairs, and which President Jaafar Nimeiri presented to the Heads of State and Government of the Organization of African Unity as a gesture of our appreciation for the African mediating role in the peace process, presented the same vision.

I continued to promote that vision for the nation in my two novels: *Seed of Redemption*[283] and *Cry of the Owl*.[284] Political developments were to prove me wrong as the divisive identity factors surged with a vigor that tore the country apart.

The Task Force that was formed by the Washington Center for Strategic and International Studies, (CSIS), to formulate and propose ideas for US policy to end the war in the Sudan, which I co-chaired, confronted me with a challenge. As mentioned earlier, all the 50 to 60 members of the Task Force, all Americans, argued that Sudan was not vital to US interests. In their view, the only importance of the Sudan for the United States was its involvement in international terrorism, destabilization of the friendly countries of the region, and the humanitarian crisis resulting from the war. Europe should take the lead in dealing with the situation and the US could assist behind scene.

I discreetly asserted an opposing point of view without abusing my position as a co-chairman and the only outsider. I argued that

---

282. Francis Mading Deng, *Peace and Unity in the Sudan: An African Achievement,* Khartoum University Press, 1973 - see p. 64.

283. Francis Mading Deng, *Seed of Redemption: A Political Novel,* Lilian Barber Press, 1986 - see p. 75.

284. Francis Mading Deng, *Cry of the Owl: A Novel,* Lilian Barber Press, 1989 - see p. 81.

the importance of the Sudan rested in its strategic location as a meeting ground of races, ethnicities, religions and cultures representing Sub-Saharan Africa and North Africa, extending into the Middle East. Sudan could be a point of peaceful contact and reconciliation or of violent confrontation with devastating global repercussions. Sudan's involvement in international terrorism was the result of the war and the sympathy and support of the Christian West for the cause of the South. This made the North align itself with the anti-West radical terrorist elements in the Middle East. The same was true of the alleged destabilization of the Black African neighbors accused of supporting the South. And the humanitarian crisis was the consequence of the war. I argued that ending the war would eliminate involvement in terrorism, stop the destabilization of the neighbors, and bring an end to the humanitarian crisis. As the sole global super power, the United States could not afford to be indifferent to a strategic situation in which the stakes are so high.

As the Task Force favored preserving the unity of the Sudan, I argued that the most constructive way of ensuring national unity was to impress upon the Sudanese authorities that their country was threatened with partition if they did not create appropriate conditions for unity. I concluded that to ensure unity, we must make possible the impossible, and reconcile the irreconcilable. That required a framework for accommodating the contrasting Arab-Islamic orientation of the North and the African-Secular vision of the South. The July 2011 report of the Task Force, *U.S. Policy to End Sudan's War*,[285] eventually proposed the 'One Country, Two Systems' formula which guided the United States in mediating negotiations that led the CPA. While the agreement gave the people of the South the right to decide by a referendum whether to

---

285. Francis M. Deng and J. Stephen Morrison, *U.S. Policy to End Sudan's War*, Report of CSIS Task Force on U.S. Sudan's Policy, Febuary, 2001 - see p. 173.

secede or remain in a united Sudan, efforts were to be exerted during the six-year interim period to make the unity option attractive.

As the Referendum of the South stipulated by the CPA was approaching, and secession seemed certain, the UN organized a Symposium in Khartoum in the slight hope that the unity option might still be made attractive. I was reluctant to give the keynote address because I thought it was too late to salvage unity, but I was persuaded to share my thoughts. In my address, I argued quite candidly that while I thought it was too late to save the unity of the country, if there was a strong political will to salvage national unity, then perhaps that might be possible by expanding the framework of 'One Country, Two Systems,' to 'One Country, Multiple Systems,' to give all the regions, East, West, North and Center, the self-governance system accorded the South, with an equitable sharing of power in the National Unity Government. I included this in the book, *Sudan at the Brink: Self-determination and National Unity*,[286] published just before the Referendum. That too proved to be unduly optimistic. The country broke apart. In *Sudan at the Brink,* I anticipated the partition of the country, but I argued that unity and separation were degrees of ongoing relations that could be strengthened or weakened, depending on the people and their leaders.

I became increasingly appreciative of the Islamic revivalist agenda as an aspect of post-colonial cultural liberation, a challenge that was facing African countries generally. Africa is still trying to free itself from the colonial yoke that imposed on the continent Eurocentric systems of governance and constitutionalism. I began to appreciate the Arab-Islamic policies in the North as an aspect of this post-colonial cultural liberation struggle. This however posed the dilemma of

---

286. Francis Mading Deng, *Sudan at the Brink: Self-determination and National Unity,* Fordham University Press, 2010 - see p. 101.

creating a unity framework with conflicting and seemingly irreconcilable diversities. How does this new liberation agenda address the challenges of unity in diversity? This is the question I unsuccessfully tried to answer in the formula of 'One Country, Two Systems.'

I must confess that when I attended the independence celebrations in Juba, I felt profoundly conflicted and ambivalent. Of course, I shared the jubilation of the Southerners celebrating in the blazing sun our hard-won freedom, but I also felt that we had shortchanged ourselves by ceding only a portion of a country which was ours together as Sudanese and whose beautiful map made it geographically the largest country in Africa that we had viewed with pride.

In the book I published after the independence of the South, *Bound by Conflict: Dilemmas of the Two Sudans*,[287] I argued that despite the independence of the South the two countries were still linked by conflicts that spill over the borders and keep them entangled in proxy wars. The implication was to turn being bound by conflict to being bonded by the search for solutions. If the two counties cooperated in resolving their internal conflicts successfully and in creating appropriate conditions, then even if they might not return to full unity, they might create a framework of close cooperation that would be a form of reunification. This is the gist of *From Bound by Conflict to Bonded by Solutions*.[288] With the recent revolution in the Sudan and the current efforts to reform the national identity framework to ensure inclusivity and the equality of citizenship, perhaps conditions are evolving toward the close cooperation I had envisaged.

All this shows that although I was never a member of the SPLM, I independently developed the Vision of the New Sudan which was

---

287. Francis M. Deng in collaboration with Daniel J. Deng, *Bound by Conflict: Dilemmas of the Two Sudans*, Fordham University Press, 2016 - see p. 103.

288. Publication pending.

more that of Dr. John Garang and of the Liberation Movement he led. I have substantiated this in my newly published book, *Visitations: Conversations with the Ghost of the Chairman,*[289] a fictionalized narrative of my intellectual and political association with John Garang. Although achieving unity in a country characterized by acute crisis of national identity and diversity has so far eluded us, it remains a lofty vision which applies to many countries in the world. The vision of Dr. John Garang remains valid not only for our Two Sudans, but indeed regionally and globally, for there is hardly any country in the world that can claim to be homogeneous, free from the challenges of constructively managing diversity.

As some of you know, I have served the international community in several UN positions. I first joined the United Nations Secretariat in 1967 as a Human Rights Officer after completing my doctoral studies at Yale Law School and served for five years before joining the diplomatic service of my country as Ambassador.

My second position was as Representative of the UN Secretary-General on Internally Displaced Persons at the level of Assistant Secretary-General. This was at the time when the Secretary-General was Boutros–Ghali. He and I had served as State Ministers of Foreign Affairs of our respective countries, Egypt and Sudan, and had worked very closely together. Boutros[290] surprised me one day with a phone call to inform me that my name had been proposed for the position which he was glad to offer me. I thanked him and told him how honored I was. But as I knew nothing about the subject, I asked him to have his people provide me with details of the position before I could give my final response. Boutros said in response, "Francis, I know you

---

289. Francis Mading Deng, *Visitations: Conversations with the Ghost of the Chairman,* Red Sea Press, 2020 - see p. 107.

290. This story is mentioned earlier in this volume - see pages xiv and 125.

well and I know how much you are concerned about these issues. Internal displacement is not only a global crisis; it is one that affects our continent of Africa the most; and in Africa, it is your country of the Sudan that is the most affected; and in the Sudan, it is your people of South Sudan that are the worst hit. I cannot see how you can turn down the offer. I will tell them that you have accepted. If you still have reservations, we can have more discussion later." Of course, I had no choice but to accept.

The third position was that of Special Advisor of the Secretary-General on the Prevention of Genocide at the level of Under-Secretary-General. The Secretary-General was Ban ki-Moon. Again, I was informed that the Secretary-General was about to appoint a person to that position and my name had been proposed. He wanted to know whether I would accept if offered the position. I responded by saying that the issue was a surprise to me, but that if offered the job, I would take it as an honor and a service to humanity which I could not take lightly. I was appointed and served in that position for five years, after which I was honored to be the first Permanent Representative of the newly independent South Sudan to the United Nations.

The two mandates on internal displacement and genocide prevention were considered very sensitive as they touched on the sacrosanct concept of national sovereignty. How to manage them therefore posed a serious challenge for me. Fortunately, in the African Studies Program at the leading Washington think tank, the Brookings Institution, which I established and directed for twelve years, we had developed the concept of 'Sovereignty as Responsibility,' one of the titles of our books in the program series. That was the concept I used in engaging with governments in discharging my two mandates.

The gist of my strategy was to approach the conflicts that generated internal displacement and genocidal wars as identity related.

What generates the conflicts is not the mere differences of identities, whether based on race, ethnicity, religion or culture, but the manner in which these identities are managed or, more correctly, mismanaged. In such acutely divided nations, of which there are far too many in the world, identity groups are stratified into those who enjoy the privileged status, with all the rights of citizenship, and those who are discriminated against, marginalized, denigrated, excluded, and denied the full rights of citizenship. Preventing and resolving such conflicts require constructive management of diversity through inclusivity, non-discrimination, respect for diversity, and full equality of citizenship.

That was the normative bases of my dialogue with governments. The first five minutes with a head of state or the minister in charge were crucial in initiating constructive dialogue. I would acknowledge that the problem was essentially internal and fell within the domain of national sovereignty, that I respected national sovereignty, but that I did not see sovereignty negatively as a barricade against the outside; rather, I saw it as a positive responsibility of the state to protect and assist its needy populations, if need be, with complementary support from the international community. I would however add, politely but affirmatively, that if a country was experiencing a crisis that the state was unwilling or unable to manage, with the result that people were massively suffering and perhaps dying, the world would not stand by and watch without some form of intervention. The best way to protect sovereignty was therefore to discharge the responsibility of sovereignty and request international support if, and when, needed. This approach proved quite successful as no self-respecting leader who claimed legitimacy could question that logic.

Sovereignty as responsibility has been widely acknowledged as the foundation of the new concept of the 'Responsibility to Protect,' more popularly known by the acronym R2P. But, although the two concepts have much in common, Sovereignty as Responsibility places the onus of responsibility on the state while the Responsibility to Protect is being interpreted as laying emphasis on international responsibility, implying the threat of intervention. It is therefore facing more resistance than Sovereignty as Responsibility

As my UN mandate has covered the last of my four levels, I would like to conclude where I began. My journey through cultures has been guided by the overriding principles that are subsumed in four interrelated concepts: identity, dignity, diversity and equality. These are reflected at four levels of my journey through cultures: local, national, regional and global. It is a well-established sociological principle that when people of different cultural backgrounds meet and interact, they influence each other in various ways and to varying degrees, depending on the intensity and longevity of the relationship among other factors. The process can be harmonious and mutually enriching or contentious and conflictual, depending on the extent to which they are mutually respectful and accommodating or condescending and intolerant of each other. The choice should be obvious, although its realization remains formidable and challenging.

Finally, I would like to reiterate that El-Tayeb Salih's works inspire and challenge us to relate to the globalizing trends of our contemporary world which bring humanity together from local to global. Sudan, including its kindred country of South Sudan, is strategically located at the confluence of races, ethnicities, religions and cultures that are as challenging to manage as they are potentially enriching. We must turn away from being torn apart by differences that are often more reflective of myths than reality and constructively move toward building on both our diversities and commonalities as sources of local and national enrichment as well as our regional and global outreach.

Afterword

When I reflect on my time in Khartoum during the celebrations of the prize I consider one of the highlights of my visit was the fulfillment of what I had come to regard as a sacred obligation. In 1989, three months after the military coup of the Revolution for National Salvation, led by Omar Hassan Al-Bashir, I met with all the leaders of the Revolutionary Command Council and requested from President al-Bashir to authorize my visiting the Former Prime Minister, Sadig Al-Mahdi, and other political leaders, who were under detention in the infamous Kober Prison. After some hesitation, surprised that I would ask to visit political prisoners, he approved and instructed Colonel Bakri Hassan Salih, the member of the Council responsible for security, to escort me to Kober. On the way, Bakri said to me, "Doctor, this is an investment into the future when our time comes." Of course, he meant that I should visit them, should the tables turn against them, and they get detained. I don't remember a response other than a courteous laughter.

Thirty years later, their time came. With their overthrow and detention, I decided, and was determined, that I must honor that request which had become almost a sacred obligation. The issue was the precise timing and how to arrange it practically. Both the time and practical arrangements came when I was invited to attend the annual celebrations of El-Tayeb Salih International Prize for Excellence in Writing as the Guest of Honor. In accepting, I requested that efforts be made to arrange for me to meet the Former President and his First Vice President. Once in Khartoum it was only when I met the leader of the revolution, General Burhan, that my request for the visit to the prison was approved and organized.

The meeting was a most moving experience. I was warmly received by the prison authorities and taken to the Office of the Prison Director General. It was a modest room with a desk and dark leathered sofas surrounding a long table at the center. I was seated with my escorts and were offered tea which I declined with thanks. I expected to be taken to the rooms of the detained leaders, as happened when I visited detained leaders in 1989. After waiting for a while, Former President al-Bashir was escorted into the room.

Al-Bashir was elegantly dressed in his white *jallabiya* and *imma* and looked relaxed, with his characteristic smile and warm embrace. "Wad el Sultan, Son of Chief, Deng Majok," he greeted me, and repeatedly calling me Zeim - Chief. We embraced very warmly and then sat on the sofas.

The prison officers also sat down. I wanted to have a private talk with the Former President, and I was not sure whether the rules would allow that. I implicitly requested by asking whether their presence in the meeting was required. They apologized and left us alone. I had decided that I would give the meeting more substance than mere courtesy. I wanted to ask him what motivated him to seize power, and to what extent he had achieved what he had set out to do.

I began by telling him the 1989 joking request by Bakri for me to visit them when their time came. I said I would have wanted to visit them anyway, but that Bakri's request had become almost sacred and that I felt morally bound to meet that request. Al-Bashir laughed as people always did whenever I told the story. I then said that I also wanted to make the meeting an opportunity to ask a substantive question. I said that the decision to seize power, with all the risks involved, and assume the challenging responsibility of running the country, is a monumental task that can only be explained by the vital importance of the objective. What drove him and what did he accomplish?

Al-Bashir was visibly moved by the question, and he answered in earnest. He began by thanking me profusely for the visit. He said that even people who had been close to them had disappeared. He stressed that he would never forget my visiting him for as long as he lived.

Al-Bashir then explained the circumstances that made him take power. He was the commanding officer in the Nuer area of South Sudan during the war. The army was in a desperate situation. They had no arms to fight the war. There was not even food for the soldiers. The situation in the country was as a whole, so desperate that a prominent leader in parliament publicly declared that even if dogs took the country away no one would stop them.

He said that the leadership of the military then gave the Prime Minister an ultimatum that unless the government acted immediately 'today' and not 'tomorrow' they would take over. There was consensus in the army that it was time for action

Once he assumed control, he said that his top priority was to end the war. If that meant allowing the South to secede in order to have peace, he would allow the South to go. Immediately after he took over, he made a statement to that effect. He also told me of some of the decisions he took in connection with the arrest of Sadig Al-Mahdi and Mohamed Osman Mirghani in which he displayed considerable flexibility in ensuring that they were treated with due deference.

My escort entered to tell us that we had a few minutes left. I commented with a few words on what the Former President had said. I deliberately avoided any reference to the International Criminal Court and his indictment for several international crimes, but I made some remarks that might have some relevance. I said that although I was not a practicing lawyer and my knowledge of the law was dated, a central principle in criminal liability is the state of mind, that is intention behind committing criminal act. I said that the manner with which he spoke indicated the extent of his conviction that he was acting in the interest of the country as he saw it and that he seemed to have a clear conscience. In the end, God would be the ultimate judge. He agreed with obvious appreciation and satisfaction.

Again, my escort peeped in to announce that the time was over. We embraced warmly and parted.

A gap in time followed before Bakri was led in. He too was neatly dressed in a white *jallabiya* and turban. Bakri too laughed when I recalled the conversation he and I had thirty years ago in which he requested me to visit them in prison when their time came. He thanked me for remembering that. He said that the question I posed about the motivation behind their seizing power required more time than was available, but he nevertheless gave an answer.

Bakri's explanation of the circumstances leading to their seizure of power were the same. He spoke of some of the things they did or tried to do, first to end the war, and then to improve the economy and alleviate the suffering of the people. But he said they had many forces working against them, particularly from the international community. He said that achievements are part of an ongoing process in which those in power do what they can and pass the challenge on to the next government. He said that the first military coup of President Abboud had its own accomplishment that included building roads and railways. Nimeiri's accomplishments included the Friendship Hall which remains a major national asset. He ended by stating that they did not know what would become of them and whether they would be freed or— and he made a gesture of his hand cutting his throat.

He then ended by saying something along the lines, "As you know, I am *aajami,* not a literary person; I am not good with words, and I have no words for adequately thanking you for this visit. I will just use the simple words 'thank you.' We receive visits from family members, but your visit is very special to me." We were told that it was time to end the meeting.

I am not exaggerating when I say that visiting those former leaders in fulfillment of a casual request made jokingly thirty years earlier is one of the actions about which I feel great satisfaction. I had been told by a lawyer friend that they were not being allowed visits and that I was going to be a unique exception. While I doubted that this was the case, my circumstances were unique. And the fact that that President Burhan made that possible is indicative of the humane cultural values of the Sudanese and what I observed as his own personal attributes, for which I am profoundly grateful.

An aspect that deeply touched me was to see the drastic change in the lives of these two military leaders. Only a short time before, they were at the zenith of power, with all the glamor that goes with being at the top. Now, they were meeting me in a very modest setting, a room of meagre furniture, being controlled and directed by modest officers who seemed to be from the marginalized regions of the country. And yet, equally remarkable, was the extent to which they carried themselves with serenity and dignified modesty. I am still pondering what to make of all that.

A possible response to the riddle came in my meeting with the former Foreign Minister, Dirdeiry Mohamed Ahmed, who had played an important role in the South Sudan negotiations. He and I had also cooperated on the issue of Abyei. Although one of the leaders of the Islamist agenda, he was not under detention. I visited him in his house. He told me that he felt that things began to go wrong with al-Bashir from 2005 and certainly in 2010. Those were high points in his leadership. He had ended the devastating war that had lasted for over two decades. And he had supported the choice of the South to secede. He thought that those were the right moments for him to step down and leave a positive legacy of leadership. The people around him for their own vested interest however impressed upon him that he was indispensable. He got caught in that trap, eventually leading to his downfall.

Dirdeiry's observation brought to mind the reaction of the UN leadership to al-Bashir's management of South Sudan's decision to secede. In a meeting of the leadership of the UN convened by the Secretary-General, which I attended, so much praise was poured on al-Bashir that I injected a joking comment in the discussion in which I said that a man who was indicted by the International Criminal Court may well be a nominee for the Nobel Peace Prize.

Dirdeiry's analytical comment on the case of al-Bashir reminds me of an experience I had with President Jaafar Nimeiri. I was then Sudan's Ambassador in the United States. Nimeiri was on a visit to Washington. As we drove to Blair House, the Presidential Guest House, I told him of a visit I took to MIT at Harvard to give a talk at the Center for International Studies. The Director of the Center, a young man in his early forties, was about to step down after four years. I asked him why he was doing that when he was still quite young. He said that four years was enough time for implementing his ideas. He wanted to give another person to apply his own ideas. I then commented, "That is the American way. They believe in change and renewal." Nimeiri responded, "That is what I said to our people, that there is a limit to what a person can do, both mentally and physically, and that the President should serve either one term of six years or two terms of four years." It suddenly dawned on me that I was talking to the wrong person. So, I immediately reacted: "But your case is different because you are establishing the revolution and that takes time." He then said, "That's what I realized in the end."

Back in Khartoum in a meeting of the Central Committee of the Ruling Socialist Union, Nimeiri surprised me by saying exactly what he had said to me in Washington and added that he would not seek another six-year term. The assembled crowd got up repeatedly, chanting, "No! No! No! Mr. President." He then gestured to the crowd to be seated. As I left the meeting with some colleagues, I told them what Nimeiri had said to me in Washington and added: It is we who make dictators!" One of them reacted, "Did you really believe him? He simply wanted to know who was for him and who was against him."

I am not sure where the truth was. What I have observed of many African revolutionary leaders is that they are very popular at the beginning as agents of change, and they modestly seek and heed the advice. As their time in power grows, they incrementally grow confidence and begin to feel that they know best. They become isolated, surrounded by people who sing the song of their being the most knowledgeable on issues. They begin to believe that they are indeed indispensable. Although I was a young Minister of State, Nimeiri began to talk disparaging to me about his senior ministers, including a Vice President, even saying about his Minister in the Presidency on whom he was known to depend heavily on, "He knows nothing." Their popularity begins to wane, and they go progressively downhill until they hit the bottom, often overthrown.

One thing I am certain about is that visiting Former President al-Bashir and his First Vice President was a most gratifying experience, clearly one of the highlights of my Khartoum return visit, and a landmark in my life. When I discussed the visit with the Prime Minister, with a smile on his face he responded, "I can see another book coming."

I would like to conclude with two observations related to the four normative principles which I outlined at the outset (in the Introduction of this volume): identity, dignity, diversity and equality. My first observation is that we need to know and appreciate our own cultures and those of our compatriots on which our identity and dignity are grounded. My second observation is that we should heed the wisdom of the cliché that those that come by sword will perish by the sword, which can be rephrased by pairing the sword with the gun. These two observations lead to the conclusion that democracy and not dictatorship must be the foundation of building a pluralistic nation. But democracy comes in varying forms that should differentiate between the fundamental norms underlining the concept and the operational means for practicing it.

Overemphasis on elections, which is the Western way, tends to be a dictatorship of numbers, which often generates its own wars by other means. Consensus by a variety of means, which is the traditional African way, is a more sustainable way of ensuring unity and harmony. Ultimately, some way of integrating these different approaches to democracy should be sought to bridge between local and global perspectives. A moral principle of magnanimity, where the winner in elections reaches out to accommodate the loser, which is akin to the Western respect for the loyal opposition, might be one way of bridging. Other formulas can be sought. The overriding objective should be to promote peace and unity, through respect for differences, and the pursuit of a common vision for the nation.

Conclusion

This volume was initially conceived as an annotated compilation of my writings, including books, articles, book chapters, and discussion papers. I focused on several principles and ideas that I considered central to the themes of my various works. These include identity, dignity, diversity and equality. To connect those ideas with experience, I decided to classify them into levels: local, national, regional and global. When I was later invited to be the Guest of Honor in the celebrations of El-Tayeb Salih Prize for Excellence in Writing, I decided to make the four principles, classified under the four levels, as the themes of my remarks at the opening ceremony and the various lectures, symposia, seminars, and discussion groups over the ten days I spent in Khartoum in connection with the celebrations.

The approach I adopted turned out to be very much in line with El-Tayeb Salih's writings and professional experience. Hailing from a small village in Nubia in the far Northern region of the Sudan, El-Tayeb Salih moved academically and professionally up the ladder to the international level and became a world-renowned journalist at the BBC and a distinguished author of fiction, including novels, short stories, and commentaries. In the process, he carried with him his primordial identity, related cultural values, and a strong sense of personal and collective dignity. He injected these into the contexts of his cross-level transition, characterized by interracial and cross-cultural diversity, in which he demanded recognition, mutual respect, understanding, and equality.

These required documentation of what he carried with him and disseminating it across the contexts and levels of his transition, contacts, interaction, and mutual influence. What is particularly striking is that this is a process that requires self-knowledge and appreciation and cross-level transmission. The educational process and mutual understanding is therefore needed at all levels. Very often, people take for granted what they are in terms of identity and related cultural values. In that condition, they may not be well equipped to transmit to their interlocutors in the cross-cultural context what they carry with them and contribute to the process of cross-cultural diffusion and enrichment. They need to read about themselves as much as others need to read about them.

This is the normative framework in which this compilation of my writings must be understood. I was born and raised in the context of the Dinka, one of the Nilotic peoples of the Sudan, who have been well studied and documented by anthropologists as exceedingly proud and conservatively resistant to cross-cultural assimilation. They view themselves as the ideal model of what God envisaged humanity and related cultural values to be. Their entry into the diversities of the real world in which they are now in contact with other peoples and their cultures, with similar ethnocentric self-perceptions begins to challenge this primordial chauvinism. In fact, in many respects, they have come to realize the fallacies of their self-esteem and that there is indeed much to be gained from other cultures and value systems.

But the resulting compromise must be demand equality in a mutually enriching process of give and take. This requires knowing each other, which in turn requires documentation and dissemination.

This itself poses delicate risks involved in positively projecting one's value system while avoiding accusations of tribalism and chauvinism. This is unavoidable where the old prejudices against 'others' persist. The dual challenge is therefore to both persuade the target audience to open their minds to the value of learning about one another and to then learn about the cultures of other groups as a potential source of cross-fertilization and mutual enrichment. This is a challenge that is reflected at all levels of diversity.

This is not only a challenge for an individual in cross-cultural transition; it is a collective challenge for education at all the four levels, beginning with the internal local, and national levels. Recently, I was interviewed by UN officials in Juba, South Sudan, in a project aimed at documenting what they called the wisdom of elders in the country. I decided to structure my contribution along the theme of 'paradoxes.' I identified four interconnected paradoxes contrasting the situation in traditional society with the changes resulting from the process of modernization.

The first paradox relates to the changing patterns of education among age groups and their implications to the normative concept of wisdom. Traditionally, wisdom accrued with age and experience with the resulting accumulation of knowledge and the process of acculturation through which the cultural and moral values were informally transmitted. 'Knowing the words,' the Dinka conceptualization of knowledge, was inherently normative and value-oriented, with a well-established moral code of conduct. In the modern context, knowledge is being acquired through formal education which, at least at the initial phases, has reversed the age order in favor of youth, who have begun to be viewed as the custodians of appropriate knowledge and related wisdom.

The second paradox is that modern knowledge, which is primarily Eurocentric, is externalized and separates the young recipients from their social and cultural background and value system. Knowledge is also becoming viewed as a value-free accumulation of information, contrary to the morally oriented transmission of knowledge as a source of wisdom.

The third paradox relates to the division of age-related functional roles in the management of society. Traditionally, the Chiefs and elders were the peacemakers, and the youth were organized into warrior age-sets to defend society against external threats; but in the modern context, elders are now the military leaders, commanders, and generals who recruit and lead the youth into war.

The fourth paradox is that the close bond between communalism and individualism is being increasingly transformed in favor of individualism. I have always made a contrasting comparison between the Western and African approaches to the balance between the interests of the individual and those of the community. In the Western context, the individual is free and enjoys maximum privacy, but with relative insignificance to the community. In Africa, the individual is more connected to the community, less free, with hardly any privacy, but has strong social bonds and significance. Which one is a more appealing model is a matter of personal preference. For me personally, and I believe for most of our people in South Sudan and Africa, the value of the individual is largely determined by family and kinship bonds and service to the community and the society.

The implication of conceptualizing the situation in terms of paradoxes is that there is a need to bridge the gulfs involved. The age issue is resolving itself in that the modern educated youth are aging and becoming elders. But the supposed source of knowledge and assumed wisdom remains modern education, which is externally oriented and culturally disconnected from tradition. This can only be remedied by reorienting the curriculum to be more relevant to the traditional cultural value system. The traditional division of functional roles between the elders as peacemakers and the youth as warriors also requires adjustment to integrate the roles behind a unified normative order that prioritizes peace, unity, harmony, and cooperation, with the use of force as a last resort pursued through a professional army that is regulated by appropriate laws and norms of war.

In the end, the ability to bridge the gulf reflected in these paradoxes is ultimately individual within the community. But even within one family and among siblings, there can be significant differences determined by a variety of factors, including variations in personal upbringing and influences. While these paradoxes and the needed remedies pose a pervasive challenge in most traditional societies, especially in Africa, they need to be contextualized into particular cultural situations to give the material a human face, both collectively and individually.

I have personally devoted much of my academic and professional life to this challenge. While documenting this personal experience may run the risk of chauvinism and parochialism, given the prevalence of diverse ethnic identities and correlative cultural pluralism, to assume that there is homogeneity that warrants an inclusive and undifferentiated approach would not only obscure useful specificities but would also be presumptuous. This would indeed be detrimental to the wealth and integrity of diversity.

That is why I have been unabashedly committed to focusing on the culture of my people, the Dinka, in the Southern part of what was the Republic of the Sudan, now divided into Sudan and South

Sudan. Abyei, my home area, was, and remains, poised between what was then the North and the South of the then Sudan, now the two countries of Sudan and South Sudan. Addressing and resolving the crises of the area in this strategic and sensitive border location remains one of the major challenges of decision-making in which the dichotomy of traditional wisdom and the politics of modern leadership are also dramatically manifested. But for me, it was the first phase on my journey through cultures, involving the four normative principles and the four levels from local to global.

The reforms needed in the educational system transcends the local and national levels and apply to cross-cultural regional and international levels. Until recently, the substance of education at all levels was urocentric, with indigenous non-Western knowledge being dismissed as insignificant. More recently, other sources of knowledge have become more recognized and respected as having a contribution to make. Even this positive change has been slow and incremental. When Black Studies and African American Studies were introduced in the United States, they were viewed with skepticism and relative condescension. But they eventually became accepted as a significant contribution to shared global knowledge.

Going beyond the world of scholarship, international policy discourse must also reflect substantive knowledge of the wealth of cultures and values that interplay in setting norms, principles, and operational patterns. This applies to virtually every area of the global policy agenda, including the promotion of peace and security, respect for human rights and humanitarian principles, prevention of genocide and atrocity crimes, and provision of social services and development opportunities.

This is of course a tall order. And so are the paradoxical stakes and opportunities of balancing localization and globalization in a world that is both unifying and fragmenting. Implicit in these paradoxes are the risks of conflicts and the potential for mutual understanding, cooperation, and cross-cultural enrichment. That is at least the aspiration I have tried to pursue; a relentless optimistic search for opportunities in crises and determined resistance to the dead end of pessimism.

Appendix:
Titles by Subject

Abyei: A Disputed Territory

An African Perspective

Biography and Memoir

---

291. A four-part presentation,including: *'Religion in Sweden,* (A different version of *'Religion in Sweden'* appeared in Vertex, no. 5, 1966, p.16), *The Family as a Basis of Society, Racialism at the Meeting Point,* and *The Paradox of Contemporary Civilization.'*

292. Reissued in 2018 by the Babo Nimir family, with an Introduction by Former Prime Minister, Sadig Al-Mahdi and a Foreword by Babo Nimir's son, Sadig Babo Nimir.

293. Reissued by The Red Sea Press, 2009.

Christian Missionaries in Sudan

'Human Rights in Africa: A Cross-Cultural Perspective'   111
Co-editor with Abdullahi Ahmed An-Na'im
The Brookings Institution Press, 1990

'Conflict Resolution in Africa'   112
co-authored with I. William Zartman, Introduction
by Former President of Nigeria, General Olusegun Obasanjo
The Brookings Institution, Press, 1991

'Sudanese Conflict In Perspective: An Action Memorandum'   165
A report prepared for the Carter Center Consultation of the
International Negotiation Network
Atlanta, Georgia, January 15-17, 1992

'Africa and the New World Dis-Order, Rethinking Colonial   335
Borders' [294]
The Brookings Review, vol. 11, no. 2, Spring 1993

'*We Must End the War*'   166
Symposium sponsored by the US Institute of Peace and the
Subcommittee on Africa of the House of Representatives
Committee on Foreign Affairs, Washington, DC, October
20-21, 1993

---

294. Also published in Global Visions, by Jeremy Brecher, John Brown Childs, and Jill
Cutler, (eds), Boston, South End, 1993.

---

295. A policy brief for a paper presented to a meeting organized by the African Center for Conflict Resolution.

Customary Law & Traditional Authority

---

296. Published by the Nation, Nairobi, Kenya, on July 8, 2021 as, 'We should clear dimming vision of the liberation of South Sudan.'

297. Publication pending.

298. This article was first published in Sudan Law Review and Reports, 1965.

---

299. Also published in: African Law, Adaptation and Development, by Leo Kuper and Hilda
Kuper, (eds), University of California Press, 1966.

300. Also published in: Sudan Law Review and Reports, 1965. A comparative value-oriented
study of an integrative view of law.

301. Proceedings of the Thirteenth Annual Columbia Law Symposium.

302. Published again as 'Dynamics of Identification,' Africa Today, 20, no. 3, Summer 1973,
p. 19.

---

303. Published in African Security Issues: Sovereignty, Stability and Solidarity, by Bruce E. Arlinghaus, (ed), Boulder, Colorado: Westview, 1984.

304. Paper presented at the Johnson Wax Global Conference, Rio de Janeiro, Brazil, September 1521, 1984.

305. Paper delivered in 1982 at the 25th World Conference of the Society for International Development in Baltimore, Maryland.

Identity Conflicts & Governance

---

306. As per the Memorandum of *"Understanding between UNDP Sudan and the John Hopkins University SAIS Center for Displacement Studies,"* January 2006.

307. Papers presented at the Diplomacy & Development conference, Khartoum, January 1520, 1974.

308. Paper presented to the symposium on AfroArab Liberation and Development.

---

309. Reissued as *The Changing World of the Dinka*, by Africa World Books, 2022.

310. Published again as: *'The Identity Factor in the Sudanese Conflict,'* in Conflict and Peacemaking in Multi-Ethnic Societies, by Joseph V. Montville, (ed), Washington: Heath and Company, 1991.

---

311. Reissued by the United States Institute of Peace Press, 2008

'*Genocide, Violence, and Civil Society*'   337
in Encyclopedia of Africa South of the Sahara, Volume 2,
by John Middleton, Editor-in-Chief,
New York, Charles Scriber's Sons, 1997, pp. 207-214

'*Sudan: The Challenge of Nationhood*'   170
in A Sourcebook on Self-Determination and Self-Administration,
by Wolfgang Danspeckgruber and Arthur Watts, (eds),
Boulder: Lynne Rienner Publishers, 1997

'*Managing Diversity in Africa: A Challenge to State Borders*'   338
Le Temps Stratégue, May/June 1998, No. 81

'*African Reckoning: A Quest for Good Governance*'   116
Co-edited with Terrence Lyons, The Brookings Institution, 1998

'*Africa's Dilemma in the Sudan*'   172
The World Today, March, Volume 54, Number 3, 1998

'*War and Genocide: Disappearing Christians of the Middle East*' 173
Middle East Quarterly, winter, 2001, pp. 12-21

'*A Strategic Vision for Africa: The Kampala Movement*'   118
co-authored with I. William Zartman,
The Brookings Institution Press, 2002

'*Green is the Color of the Masters: The Legacy of Slavery and the* 174
Crisis of Identity in the Sudan'
Academia. edu, 2004

---

312. Published by The Annals of the American Academy of Political Science, 2006

Internal Displacement

---

313. First published by New Vision Publishing and Printing Company, Kampala, 2010.

"Guiding Principles on Internal Displacement"   129
Developed in collaboration with Roberta Cohen, Walter
Kaelin, Robert Goldman and Manfred Novak, UN Office for
Humanitarian Affairs, 1998

"Exodus within Borders"   351
co-authored with Roberta Cohen,
Foreign Affairs, Volume 77, Number 4, July/August 1998, pp.
12-16

'Displacement Studies and the Role of Universities'   352
Lecture to a Conference of German Academic Exchange
Service, University of Kassel, Germany, 2002

'Internal Displacement: A Challenge of Peace, Security and   352
Emergency Relief Operations in Nation-building,'
in Emergency Relief Operations, by Kevin M. Cahill
A joint publication of Fordham University Press and The Center
for International Health and Cooperation, New York, N.Y, 2003

'Trapped Within Borders: The Plight of Internally Displaced   353
Persons,'
in Human Security for All: A Tribute to Sergio Vieira de Mello,
by Kevin M. Cahill, (ed), Fordham University Press 2004

'The Plight of Internally Displaced Persons: A Challenge to the   353
International Community,'
UN High-Level Panel on Threats, Challenges and Changes,
March 2004 [314]

---

314. Published on the Brookings website in April 2004: https://www.brookings.edu/articles/

Traditional Culture & Values Systems

the-plight-of-the-internally-displaced-a-challenge-to-the-international-community/

315. Reissued by Waveland Press, 1984, updated and reissued in 1986. Updated and reissued as *The Dinka, A Nilotic Lifecycle,* by Africa World Books, 2023.

316. Reissued by Africa World Books, 2022.

317. Reissued by Africa World Books, 2022.

318. Reissued as *Dinka Worldview: Elders Refelct on the Past Present and Future of their People,* Africa World Books, 2023.

War and Peace in the Sudan

---

319. First published in parts by the Nation in Nairobi, Kenya, July, 2021, as '*Education is key to unlocking the potential of South Sudan.*' Reproduced in full by the Sudd Institute in its Weekly Review, 2021.

320. Task Force co-chaired with J. Stephen Morrison, February 2001.

---

321. Publication forthcoming.

Index

Ingram Content Group UK Ltd.
Milton Keynes UK
UKHW012011280623
424203UK00001B/4